Stockholm Arbitration Yearbook 2023

Stockholm Arbitration Yearbook

VOLUME 5

Editors

Christer Danielsson is an independent arbitrator based in Stockholm. After fifteen years of mainly transactional work with a leading Swedish firm, he has focused on dispute resolution in the last fifteen years as counsel and now as a full-time arbitrator. He is the previous President of the Swedish Bar Association and the Swedish Arbitration Association and is designated to the ICSID Panel of Arbitrators (Sweden).

Patrik Schöldström is a Judge of Appeal of the Svea Court of Appeal. He is also an Associate Professor of the Faculty of Law of Stockholm University. He has a doctorate in arbitration law and is a former member of the Swedish Bar. He regularly writes articles and case notes. He has extensive experience as an arbitrator – chairman, sole arbitrator, co-arbitrator and emergency arbitrator – in international and domestic disputes, ad hoc and institutional.

Introduction

The Yearbook is published under the auspices of the Stockholm Centre for Commercial Law, a part of the Stockholm University Faculty of Law. It is designed to meet the information needs of arbitration practitioners and parties from all over the world. The first volume was published in 2019.

Objective

The Yearbook is designed to meet the information needs of arbitration practitioners and parties from all over the world. It provides authoritative articles, some of them with a Swedish angle, that address current matters of global concern in arbitration. Each volume includes one or more chapters accounting for developments in Swedish case law and legislation since the previous volume.

Frequency

The publication is annual.

The titles published in this series are listed at the end of this volume.

Stockholm Arbitration Yearbook 2023

Edited by
Christer Danielsson
Patrik Schöldström

Assistant Editor
Bruno Gustafsson

Editorial Committee
James Hope
Kristin Campbell-Wilson
Niklas Berntorp
Eva Storskrubb
Åsa Waller

Stockholm Centre for Commercial Law
Faculty of Law

Stockholm
University

Wolters Kluwer

Published by:
Kluwer Law International B.V.
PO Box 316
2400 AH Alphen aan den Rijn
The Netherlands
E-mail: lrs-sales@wolterskluwer.com
Website: www.wolterskluwer.com/en/solutions/kluwerlawinternational

Sold and distributed by:
Wolters Kluwer Legal & Regulatory U.S.
920 Links Avenue
Landisville, PA 17538
United States of America
E-mail: customer.service@wolterskluwer.com

ISBN 978-94-035-0358-5

e-Book: ISBN 978-94-035-0368-4
web-PDF: ISBN 978-94-035-0378-3

Editors

Christer Danielsson is an independent arbitrator based in Stockholm. After fifteen years of mainly transactional work with a leading Swedish firm, he has focused on dispute resolution in the last fifteen years as counsel and now as a full-time arbitrator. He is the previous President of the Swedish Bar Association and the Swedish Arbitration Association and is designated to the ICSID Panel of Arbitrators (Sweden).

Patrik Schöldström is a Judge of Appeal of the Svea Court of Appeal and an Associate Professor of the Faculty of Law of Stockholm University. He has a doctorate in arbitration law and is a former member of the Swedish Bar. He regularly writes articles and case notes. He also sits as an arbitrator and has participated in a number of domestic and international arbitrations (ad hoc and institutional) as chair of arbitral tribunal, sole arbitrator, emergency arbitrator, wing arbitrator, and counsel.

Contributors

Mads Bryde Andersen, professor of private law at the University of Copenhagen since 1991. Before that he practiced law at a medium-sized Copenhagen law firm. He is the author of a large number of books and articles within various legal disciplines such as contract law, the law of obligations, advocacy law, pension law and IT law. Alongside his academic career he has held a number of positions, e.g. as chair of the Danish Arbitration Institute, the Danish Financial Supervisory Authority, the IT Security Council, and the Danish Radio and TV Board.

Kristin Campbell-Wilson, former Deputy Secretary General and Secretary General of the SCC Arbitration 2012-2023.

Aleksandrs Fillers, Associate Professor at the Riga Graduate School of Law, where he teaches private international law, contract law and property law and coaches the Willem C. Vis International Commercial Arbitration Moot. He also serves as a visiting lecturer at the University of Latvia and the Riga Stradins University. Aleksandrs holds a Doctorate in Law from the Antwerp University and an LL.M. degree in International Commercial Arbitration from the Stockholm University. He is an author of numerous publications in Latvian and international journals on arbitration, EU private international law and private law.

Fabricio Fortese, Director of Mooting Activities at the Department of Law, Stockholm University, specializing in international dispute resolution. In recent years, he has held prestigious positions as a Visiting Scholar at Columbia Law and a Fellow Visiting Researcher at the National University of Singapore. A Fellow of the Chartered Institute of Arbitrators (FCIArb) and former Board Member of the Nordic-Baltic Chapter of the Spanish Arbitration Club, he possesses extensive experience in cross-border dispute resolution. Notable publications as author, editor, and co-editor include *Arbitration in Argentina* (2020) and *Finances in International Arbitration, Liber Amicorum for Patricia Shaughnessy* (2019).

Fanny Gleiss Wilborg, independent arbitrator serving as sole, presiding and party-nominated arbitrator in Swedish and international commercial disputes and with vast experience in arbitrating numerous cases across different business sectors. She handles both ad hoc and institutional arbitrations under different arbitral rules (SCC, ICC, FAI, DIS). Before re-entering the Swedish Bar Association and founding the law firm Lundberg & Gleiss, she was a senior judge and Head of Division at a District Court.

Harsh Hari Haran, Senior Associate in Ashurst's international arbitration practice, and is qualified in both India and England & Wales.

Daniel Hochstrasser, LLM, attorney-at-law, has more than thirty years of experience in litigation and arbitration. Until the end of 2022, he was a partner of Bär & Karrer in Zurich, and since January 2023, he has been a sole practitioner. He is also a Vice President of the ICC Court of Arbitration and a member of the Board of the Finland Arbitration Institute.

Katja Hoppu, Associate in the Dispute Resolution team of Roschier, Attorneys Ltd.

Emma Johnson, Partner in Ashurst's international arbitration practice and a member of the ICC's UK Arbitration & ADR Committee.

Inga Kačevska, Partner of Law Office of Inga Kačevska. She regularly acts as arbitrator, counsel and expert in international and domestic arbitrations. Dr Kačevska is acknowledged as the best arbitration practitioner in Latvia by Who'sWhoLegal from 2010 to 2023. In 2014, the Government of Latvia appointed Dr Kačevska to the Panel of Arbitrators at ICSID. She was elected to the Special Committee attached to the 1961 European Convention on International Commercial Arbitration. She is an associate professor at the University of Latvia and coached the Vis team for the past twenty years.

Knud Jacob Knudsen, Partner at Simonsen Vogt Wiig in Oslo and head of the firm's international arbitration practice. He is particularly experienced in construction disputes, both offshore and onshore, and has in-depth knowledge of international standard construction contracts, fabrication contracts and shipbuilding contracts. In addition, he also handles company law disputes, post-M&A disputes, as well as other commercial contract disputes. He has acted as counsel and arbitrator in several national and international arbitration cases and argued cases under both ICC and SCC rules. He has also argued a large number of court cases and is admitted to the Supreme Court of Norway.

Sven Lange, Partner at Busse Disputes Rechtsanwaltsgesellschaft mbH and admitted as Rechtsanwalt in Germany.

Nika Larkimo, Senior Associate in the Dispute Resolution team of Roschier, Attorneys Ltd.

Hanna Larsson, doctoral candidate in procedural law at Stockholm University. Previously advokat and owner of Advokatfirman Sture Larsson AB, Stockholm.

Helen Lehto, Partner in the dispute resolution practice at Dittmar & Indrenius Attorneys Ltd in Helsinki, Finland

Emilia Lundberg, independent arbitrator serving as sole, presiding and party-nominated arbitrator in Swedish and international commercial disputes and with vast experience in arbitrating numerous cases across different business sectors. She handles both ad hoc and institutional arbitrations under different arbitral rules (SCC, ICC, FAI, DIS). Before re-entering the Swedish Bar Association and founding the law firm Lundberg & Gleiss, she was a District Court Judge.

Olof Olsson, Associate in Westerberg & Partners' dispute resolution group, where he focuses on commercial litigation and arbitration. His work often relates to cross-border sale of goods, energy disputes and the automotive industry.

Laura Parkkisenniemi, Senior Associate in the dispute resolution practice at Dittmar & Indrenius Attorneys Ltd in Helsinki, Finland.

Carl Persson, Carl Persson, Partner at Roschier Attorneys Ltd., specialising in domestic and international commercial arbitration, as well as litigation. He acts as counsel in disputes relating mainly to M&A transactions, securities and finance, director and auditor liability and white-collar crime proceedings. He is behind several publications on procedural issues in arbitration and litigation, including a book on third party funding.

Natalia Petrik, Deputy Secretary General and Head of Business Development at the SCC Arbitration Institute.

Matthew Saunders, Partner and the head of Ashurst's global international arbitration practice. He focuses on international arbitration relating to international projects in the energy and resources sectors, with a particular focus on investment treaty arbitration.

Monica Seifert, Doctor of Laws, senior legal counsel at Kungl. Tekniska högskolan. In 2022, she defended her doctoral thesis with the title 'Arbitral Jurisdiction in Multi-Contract Relations – A Comparative Study of Swedish, Swiss and English Law' published by Jure Förlag AB at Stockholm University. Monica Seifert has a Master of Laws degree from Stockholm University and from Albert-Ludwigs-Universität Freiburg, Germany. She has previously worked at law firms in Sweden and Switzerland.

Cameron Sim, BA, LLB (Hons) (Melb); BCL (Dist) (Oxon); Attorney and Counsellor at Law in the State of New York; Solicitor of the Senior Courts of England & Wales; Solicitor and Barrister of the High Court of Australia; Solicitor of the High Court of the Hong Kong Special Administrative Region; International Counsel, Debevoise & Plimpton, Hong Kong. Mr Sim specializes in international arbitration and complex cross-border disputes, with a focus on Asia-related matters. He has represented corporates and sovereigns in arbitrations under all leading arbitration rules, frequently with parallel proceedings in domestic courts. He is the author of Emergency Arbitration (Oxford University Press 2021).

Johan Skog, Partner at Kapatens, a Nordic legal finance investment firm. He is a Swedish lawyer and admitted to practice in New York. Prior to his current position, he was a dispute resolution attorney at Mannheimer Swartling. He has written several articles and a book on third-party funding and lectures at the ICAL program at the Stockholm University.

Christer Söderlund, Senior Counsel at Morssing & Nycander. He joined the firm in January 2017 after four decades at Vinge as Partner and Senior Counsel. He was a member of the Board of Directors of the SCC Arbitration Institute (2007-2009) and was appointed by the Swedish Government to the ICSID Panel of Arbitrators in the period 2006 - 2018. He has served as arbitrator under different arbitral regimes, such as SCC, ICC, LCIA, HKIAC and ICSID and has conducted arbitrations in English, German, Spanish, Russian (and Swedish).

Felipe Volio Soley, Foreign Associate at Busse Disputes Rechtsanwaltsgesellschaft mbH and admitted as a lawyer (Abogado) in Costa Rica.

Carita Wallgren-Lindholm, Finnish national who serves as an arbitrator in commercial and investment disputes. Prior to founding her boutique in 2008, she was a corporate and dispute resolution partner in a full-service Helsinki law firm, having commenced her practice in Paris. Over the years, she has spent much working time in Stockholm. Between 2018 and 2021, Carita was the Chair of the ICC Commission on Arbitration and ADR (Paris). In 2019, she was designated by the Government of Finland to the ICSID Panel of Arbitrators.

Summary of Contents

Table of Contents

Preface

Welcome to the fifth edition of the Stockholm Arbitration Yearbook!

You will find chapters on arbitration law in general and Swedish arbitration law in particular. Some contributions are by senior and well-known authors, others by more junior ones.

We are happy to receive - at any time of the year - proposals for future contributions in the form of a short abstract.

Christer Danielsson
Patrik Schöldström

CHAPTER 1

Swedish Arbitration-Related Case Law 2022-2023

Christer Danielsson

§1.01 INTRODUCTION

This chapter will account for court cases relevant to arbitration law from the Swedish Supreme Court and Swedish appellate courts for the period 1 May 2022-30 April 2023. It does not purport to be exhaustive; the aim is to highlight cases that can be assumed to be of interest to a non-Swedish reader.

§1.02 BACKGROUND

The Swedish Arbitration Act of 1999[1] (the 'Act') applies to all arbitration proceedings seated in Sweden, whether the parties have any connection to Sweden or not.[2] The Act also sets out the requirements for foreign arbitral awards to be recognized and enforced in Sweden.[3]

Sweden has a three-tier court system: district courts, six regional appellate courts and the Supreme Court. However, district courts are only rarely involved in arbitration cases since the appellate courts are Court of First Instance for invalidity and set aside cases as well as for enforcement cases.

A Swedish arbitral award can be declared invalid if it determines an issue which under Swedish law cannot be decided by arbitrators or if the award, or the manner in

1. Lagen (1999:116) om skiljeförfarande, as amended 1 March 2019.
2. The Act, s. 46.
3. The Act, ss 52 et seq.

which it came about, is clearly incompatible with the basic principles of the Swedish legal system, i.e., ordre public.[4]

An arbitral award can be set aside (wholly or partially) at the request of a party, *inter alia*, when the arbitrators have exceeded their mandate and when, without fault of the party, an irregularity has occurred in the course of the proceedings which probably influenced the outcome of the case.[5]

An action to invalidate or set aside an arbitration award shall be considered by the Court of Appeal within whose district the arbitral proceedings were seated.[6] The Court of Appeal's permission is required in order to appeal its judgment.[7] Such leave to appeal is denied in the large majority of cases. For the case to be tried by the Supreme Court, leave is also required from that Court.[8]

Historically, invalidity and set aside actions have very rarely been successful. A statistical survey for the period 1 January 2004-31 May 2014 shows that seven arbitral awards were set aside pursuant to section 34 of the Act, while one award was declared invalid pursuant to section 33 of the Act, equal to only 6% of all decided cases.[9]

However, in the period covered by this chapter, three awards were declared invalid (of which two were in the same case), one award was set aside in its entirety and one partially.

§1.03 *REPUBLIC OF POLAND V. PL HOLDINGS S.A.R.L.*

[A] Introduction

As reported in the 2019, 2020, 2021 and 2022 Stockholm Arbitration Yearbook,[10] the Svea Court of Appeal in February 2019 rendered a judgment in a case similar to *Achmea*,[11] the *Republic of Poland v. PL Holdings S.a.r.l.* ('PL Holdings').[12] The Court of Appeal's judgment was appealed to the Supreme Court which granted leave and requested a preliminary ruling from the Court of Justice of the European Union (CJEU).

4. The Act, s. 33. In addition, under this provision an award is invalid if it does not fulfil the Act's requirements with regard to written form and signature.
5. The Act, s. 34(1), items 3 and 7. Section 34 provides for five other grounds for setting aside an arbitral award, but the two mentioned are those most frequently invoked in set aside proceedings.
6. The Act, s. 43(1). The large majority of invalidity and set aside proceedings are brought before the Svea Court of Appeal. The reason for this is that most Swedish arbitrations are seated in Stockholm.
7. The Act, s. 43(2), which provides that leave to appeal shall be granted 'where it is of importance, as a matter of precedent, that the appeal be considered by the Supreme Court'.
8. The Act, s. 43(2). Such requirement was introduced in an amendment to the Act which entered into force on 1 March 2019.
9. Översyn av lagen om skiljeförfarande ('Review of the arbitration act'), SOU 2015:37, p. 79.
10. At pp. 9 et seq. in the 2019 edition, pp. 2 et seq. in the 2020 edition, pp. 2 et seq. in the 2021 edition and pp. 2 et seq. in the 2022 edition.
11. Judgment by the European Court of Justice on 6 March 2018, *Slovak Republic v. Achmea BV*, Case No. C-284/16.
12. Judgment by the Svea Court of Appeal on 22 February 2019 in Case Nos T-8538-17 and T-12033-7.

On 26 October 2021, the Grand Chamber of the CJEU handed down its award. On 14 December 2022, the Supreme Court rendered its award.[13]

[B] Facts

In 1987, Poland, on the one hand, and Luxembourg and Belgium, on the other hand, entered into an investment treaty (the 'Investment Treaty') with a dispute resolution clause (section 9) pursuant to which investors in any of the states being party to the treaty have the right to initiate arbitration proceedings in accordance with three different options, one of which is the Arbitration Rules of the Stockholm Chamber of Commerce (the SCC Rules). Thus, the Investment Treaty is an intra-EU (European Union) Bilateral Investment Treaty (BIT for short).

PL Holdings, a company registered in Luxemburg, initiated arbitration proceedings against Poland in accordance with the SCC Rules, with Stockholm as the seat of arbitration. This was prior to the CJEU's judgment in *Achmea*. PL Holdings submitted that Poland had violated its obligations under the Investment Treaty by expropriating assets of PL Holdings in Poland. PL Holdings claimed damages from Poland.

In June 2017, the arbitral tribunal rendered a partial arbitral award in which it found that Poland had violated its obligations under the Investment Treaty by expropriating PL Holdings' shareholding in a bank and that PL Holdings was entitled to damages. In the final award in September 2017, the arbitral tribunal ordered Poland to pay substantial damages (approx. EUR 150 million).

[C] The Judgment by the Court of Appeal

Poland filed actions with the Svea Court of Appeal with regard to both the partial award and the final award. Poland requested that the awards be declared invalid (section 33 of the Act) or be set aside (section 34 of the Act) in light of *Achmea*. With regard to the set aside claim, Poland submitted that the awards should be set aside since they were not based on a valid arbitration agreement.

The Court of Appeal made the following statement with regard to its understanding of *Achmea*:

> The conclusion from the *Achmea* ruling is therefore that Articles 267 and 344 TFEU[14] would not as such preclude Poland and PL Holdings from entering into an arbitration agreement and participating in arbitral proceedings regarding an investment-related dispute. What the TFEU precludes is that Member States conclude agreements with each other, meaning that one Member State is obligated to accept subsequent arbitral proceeding with an investor and that the Member States thereby establish a system where they have excluded disputes from the possibility of requesting a preliminary ruling, even though the disputes may involve interpretation and application of EU law. Since the TFEU thus does not

13. Judgment by the Supreme Court dated 14 December 2022 in Case No. T 1569-19 (NJA 2022 p. 965).
14. The Treaty on the Functioning of the European Union (TFEU).

> preclude arbitration agreements between a Member State and an investor in a particular case, a Member State is, based on party autonomy, free – even though the Member State is not bound by a standing offer as such as that in Article 8 of the *Achmea* case or Article 9 in this case – to enter into an arbitration agreement with an investor regarding the same dispute at a later stage, e.g., when the investor has initiated arbitral proceedings. An arbitration agreement and arbitral proceedings between, on the one hand, an investor from a Member State and, on the other hand, a Member State is therefore as such not in violation of the TFEU.[15]

The Court of Appeal found that the awards should not be declared invalid pursuant to section 33 of the Act.

With regard to setting aside the awards pursuant to section 34 of the Act, PL Holdings, *inter alia*, argued that Poland was precluded from invoking that the arbitral awards were not covered by a valid arbitration agreement since Poland had participated in the arbitral proceedings without raising this objection. Under the applicable rules for the proceedings, PL Holdings argued that Poland was obligated to raise an objection concerning the alleged invalidity of the arbitration agreement no later than in its statement of defence, which Poland had not done.

The Court of Appeal found that pursuant to the applicable SCC Rules, the objection should have been made no later than in the statement of defence. Since it was not made until in the statement of rejoinder, the Court concluded, with reference to section 34(2) of the Act, that Poland must be considered to have waived its right to raise the objection.

[D] The Supreme Court's Request for Preliminary Ruling

The judgment was appealed to the Supreme Court which, as noted, requested a preliminary ruling from the CJEU.[16]

The Supreme Court formulated the question to the CJEU as follows:

> Do Articles 267 and 344 TFEU, as interpreted in [the judgment of 6 March 2018, *Achmea* (C-284/16, EU:C:2018:158)], mean that an arbitration agreement is invalid if it has been concluded between a Member State and an investor – where an investment agreement contains an arbitration clause that is invalid as a result of the fact that the contract was concluded between two Member States – by virtue of the fact that the Member State, after arbitration proceedings were commenced by the investor, refrains, by the free will of the State, from raising objections as to jurisdiction?

[E] Judgment by the CJEU[17]

The CJEU answered the questions posed by the Supreme Court as follows:

---

15. Unofficial translation.
16. Decision by the Supreme Court 21 February 2020 in Case No. 1568-19 (unofficial translation).
17. Judgment by the CJEU on 26 October 2022, Case No. C-109/20.

> Articles 267 and 344 TFEU must be interpreted as precluding national legislation which allows a Member State to conclude an ad hoc arbitration agreement with an investor from another Member State that makes it possible to continue arbitration proceedings initiated on the basis of an arbitration clause whose content is identical to that agreement, where that clause is contained in an international agreement concluded between those two Member States and is invalid on the ground that it is contrary to those articles.

Thus, the CJEU firmly shut the door to the reasoning advocated by PL Holdings and accepted by the Svea Court of Appeal.

[F] Judgment by the Supreme Court

In light of the CJEU judgment, it was clear that the arbitral awards would not stand. The primary issue before the Supreme Court was whether the awards should be declared invalid pursuant to section 33 of the Act or set aside pursuant to section 34.

The Supreme Court applied section 33 and declared the awards invalid based on the following reasoning. An arbitral award issued with reference to a clause like the one in the Investment Treaty must be deemed to have come about in an unlawful way (Sw. 'rättsstridigt sätt') since the award is incompatible with fundamental provisions and principles in the European Union and therefore also in Sweden. To uphold the awards would be clearly incompatible with the basic principles of the Swedish legal system. Accordingly, the awards shall be declared invalid pursuant to section 33 paragraph 1 point 2.

§1.04 *ICA SVERIGE AB V. BERGSALA SDA AB*

In a case brought before the Svea Court of Appeal,[18] the party having lost the underlying arbitration, ICA Sverige AB, requested that the arbitration award be set aside, *inter alia*, on the basis that the arbitral tribunal during the pandemic ordered a virtual hearing to be held against the objection of ICA. ICA took the position that the Act gives parties the right to an in-person physical hearing and that it was denied this right by the decision of the tribunal to proceed virtually.

Prior to the Svea Court issuing its judgment, this issue was the subject of intense discussion within the Swedish arbitration community. The large majority of Swedish arbitration practitioners took the view that a virtual hearing could be organized despite objections by one of the parties. The opposite view was, however, held by former Chief Justice of the Supreme Court Stefan Lindskog, the author of the leading commentary on the Act.

In its judgment,[19] the Svea Court found as follows. If the parties do not agree otherwise, it must be within the mandate of the arbitration tribunal to decide that participants can attend remotely, by voice or picture transmission. The fact that one

18. Svea Court of Appeal Case No. T 7158-20.
19. Judgment by the Svea Court of Appeal on 30 June 2022 in Case No. T 7158-20.

party opposes attendance in such a form does not alter this. However, the tribunal must always assess whether remote participation is adequate.[20]

In the present case, the Court found that the requirements for a virtual hearing were fulfilled, and the award was upheld.

The Court granted ICA the right to appeal to the Supreme Court, but ICA did not appeal.

§1.05 *PUBLIC JOINT STOCK COMPANY CHELYABINSK METALLURGICAL PLANT V. MINMETALS INTERNATIONAL ENGINEERING CO. LTD.*

The Russian company Public Joint Stock Company Chelyabinsk Metallurgical Plant (CMP) and the Chinese company Minmetals International Engineering Co. Ltd. (Minmetals) entered into a construction agreement in 2008. The contract was terminated by CMP in 2014. At that time, the major part of the work had been performed by Minmetals and had been paid for by CMP.

Minmetals initiated arbitration against CMP. The applicable substantive law was Russian law. In its award rendered in November 2017, the arbitral tribunal (consisting of three Russian lawyers) found that the contract had been rightfully terminated and ordered CMP to pay USD 16,691,176.95 to Minmetals. CMP was also ordered to assist Minmetals in taking down a temporary production unit, including assisting with obtaining necessary permissions for Minmetals' employees.

In 2018, CMP requested that parts of the award be set aside.[21] Eight different grounds were invoked by CMP.

The Svea Court of Appeal found that the tribunal had exceeded their mandate (section 34(1) item 2)[22] by having given a judgment: (i) over something other than requested, (ii) based on circumstances not invoked, and (iii) based on the arbitrators' private knowledge about margins in the construction business. According to the Svea Court, it could not be ruled out that these errors had impacted the outcome of the main monetary part of the award.

With regard to (i), the Court reasoned as follows. The arbitral tribunal has merely ordered CMP to pay a specific amount to Minmetals. Therefore, it is not immediately apparent that the arbitral tribunal's order differs from what was requested. However, the arbitral tribunal's reasons for the award show that the amount CMP was ordered to pay was compensation for Minmetals' costs and not partial and final payment under the contract which was what Minmetals had requested.

As regards (ii), the Court noted that neither party had discussed Minmetals' costs. It was the arbitral tribunal that had introduced the issue of costs and based its award on those costs.

20. The Göta Court of Appeal came to the same conclusion in its judgment mentioned below in § 1.09 (13 March 2023 in Case No. 2556-22).
21. Svea Court of Appeal Case No. T 1356-18.
22. After the amendments in 2019 this is item 3.

Furthermore, the Court found that the arbitral tribunal had not addressed CMP's argument that limitation was applicable to part of Minmetals' claim in the arbitration proceedings. This was qualified as an excess of mandate by the Svea Court. Here, too, it could not be ruled out that the error had impacted the outcome of the relevant part of the case.

Finally, the Court set aside the award with regard to the allocation of the arbitration costs and compensation for party costs.

The Court granted the right to appeal to the Supreme Court. The Supreme Court did not grant leave.

§1.06 *KINGDOM OF SPAIN V. NOVENERGIA II – ENERGY & ENVIRONMENT (SCA), SICAR, B 124550*

The Energy Charter Treaty (ECT) is an international agreement that establishes a multilateral framework for cross-border cooperation in the energy industry. It is an investment protection agreement.

Section 26 of the ECT contains a dispute resolution clause which, *inter alia*, refers to arbitration pursuant to the SCC Rules.

The Spanish energy market was deregulated in the later part of the 1990s.

In 2007, Novenergia invested in the market by acquiring eight solar cell parks.

During the years 2010 to 2014, Spain adopted regulations that reduced subventions of energy from renewable sources that had been in force since 2007.

Spain is bound by the treaty, as is Luxemburg.

Novenergia II - Energy & Environment (SCA), SICAR, B 124550 (Novenergia) is a finance company seated in Luxemburg.

In 2015, Novenergia requested arbitration against Spain pursuant to the SCC Rules. Novenergia claimed that Spain had breached Article 10.1 (Requiring a fair and equitable treatment) and Article 13 (expropriation) of the ECT.

In the subsequent arbitral award, rendered in 2018, the tribunal found that Spain had breached Article 10.1, and Spain was ordered to pay damages in the amount of EUR 53.3 million.

The same year, Spain initiated proceedings before the Svea Court of Appeal, requesting that the award be set aside or declared invalid.[23]

One of Spain's grounds for invalidity was that the dispute could not be settled by arbitration. Spain referred to the CJEU's judgments in *Achema*, *Komstroy*[24] and *PL Holdings*.

The Svea Court found,[25] primarily with reference to Komstroy (which also concerned Article 26 of the ECT), that Spain and Novenergia could not agree that the issues in dispute be settled by arbitration.

23. Svea Court of Appeal Case No. T 4658-18.
24. Judgment by the CJEU on 2 September 2021, Case No. C-741/19.
25. Judgment by the Svea Court of Appeal on 13 December 2022 in Case No. T 4658-18.

The Court summed up its findings as follows. By the CJEU's case law, it is made clear that disputes relating to the ECT must not be excluded from the jurisdiction of national courts and that, therefore, Article 26.2 c) does not apply to disputes between a Member State and an investor from another Member State regarding an investment made in the Member State.

Pursuant to section 33 (1) item 1 of the Act, a Swedish arbitral award can be declared invalid if it determines an issue which under Swedish law cannot be decided by arbitrators. The Court held that the CJEU's case law must be deemed equal thereto.

Accordingly, the Court declared the 2018 award invalid.

The Court granted the right to appeal to the Supreme Court. The Supreme Court did not grant leave.

§1.07 *OLEG DERIPASKA V. MONTENEGRO*

Russian oligarch Oleg Deripaska initiated arbitration proceedings against the State of Montenegro under a BIT entered into in 1995 between the Government of the Russian Federation and the Government of the Federal Republic of Yugoslavia. The arbitral tribunal dismissed the case on the basis that it lacked jurisdiction since the BIT referred to by Oleg Deripaska was not binding between the Russian Federation and Montenegro.

Pursuant to section 36 of the Act, an award whereby the arbitrators concluded the proceedings without ruling on the issues submitted to them for resolution may be amended, in whole or in part, upon the application of a party.

Oleg Deripaska requested that the Svea Court of Appeal should vacate the award.

The first issue confronted by the Svea Court was how in-depth its examination of the jurisdictional issue should be.

Montenegro referred to the following findings by the Supreme Court in the 2019 *Belgor* case:[26]

> When a court in set aside proceedings shall assess the arbitration tribunal's conclusion with regard to jurisdiction, it shall take into consideration that typically the tribunal is best suited to determine its jurisdiction. Therefore, the starting point for the court should be that the arbitration tribunal's interpretation and assessment of evidence is correct. In the challenge procedure it shall be assessed if the claimant has demonstrated that the tribunal incorrectly determined the reach of the arbitration agreement.

Montenegro argued that the Court in proceedings under section 36 of the Act should also make such a limited examination of the case where the starting point should be that the tribunal's interpretation and assessment of evidence is correct. Oleg Deripaska took the position that the Court under section 36 should make a full assessment of the facts and evidence invoked with regard to the jurisdictional issue.

Referring to the legal literature (primarily former Supreme Court Chief Justice Stefan Lindskog), the Svea Court found that the Supreme Court's findings in Belgor

26. Judgment by the Supreme Court on 20 March 2019 in Case No. T 5437; *see* SAY 2019 pp. 2 et seq.

should be limited to the context of that case. Belgor shall not, stated the Svea Court, be interpreted to mean that the starting point when examining a tribunal's jurisdiction should always be that the tribunal's interpretation and assessment of evidence is correct.

On the basis of this reasoning, the Court concluded that it must make a new and complete assessment of the jurisdictional issue.

The Court added that it should make no difference if the jurisdictional issue arose in set aside proceedings, proceedings under section 2 of the Act, or proceedings under section 36.

The key issue to be addressed by the Court was whether the BIT invoked by Oleg Deripaska is binding between the Russian Federation and Montenegro. After an in-depth examination of the law on state succession and treaty succession, the Court found that Oleg Deripaska had not demonstrated that the arbitration tribunal had jurisdiction over the dispute brought by him.

The Court granted the right to appeal to the Supreme Court. The Supreme Court did not grant leave.[27]

§1.08 *KB LANDBYSKA VERKET 11 V. THE GRAND GROUP AKTIEBOLAG*

In 2018, KB Landbyska Verket 11 (Landbyska Verket) entered into a rental agreement with The Grand Group Aktiebolag (Grand Group) for premises in a building owned by Landbyska Verket. The Grand Group was to conduct hotel business on the premises. The Grand Group had the right to transfer the agreement to another company in the same group without Landbyska Verket's prior written consent if the Grand Group provided acceptable security for the whole rental period for the tenant's obligations under the agreement.

The Grand Group's subsidiary, The Sparrow Hotel AB (Sparrow), conducted the hotel business. A dispute arose between Landbyska Verket and the Grand Group. The issues in dispute were whether the rental agreement had been transferred from the Grand Group to Sparrow and, if so, if Grand Group had provided acceptable security.

Landbyska Verket initiated arbitration with regard to disputed issues. Landbyska Verket's first hand claim was that no valid transfer of the agreement had occurred. Its second hand claim was that the Grand Group should be ordered to provide security for the tenant's obligations under the agreement for the whole rental period. Such security was to be unlimited or limited to an amount of at least SEK 556,400,894 or an amount determined by the arbitral tribunal found to be sufficient to cover the obligations for the full rental period.

In its award, the arbitral tribunal rejected Landbyska Verket's first hand claim. With regard to the second-hand claim, the arbitral tribunal ordered the Grand Group to issue a guarantee for Sparrow's obligations under the agreement valid for the whole rental period 'and corresponding to in total 36 month's guarantee rent'.

27. Judgment by the Svea Court of Appeal on 10 November 2022 in Case No. T 731-20.

Landbyska Verket initiated set aside proceedings in the Svea Court of Appeal.[28] The claimant's first ground for setting aside the award was that the arbitrators had exceeded their mandate by formulating its award differently from what had been claimed by Landbyska Verket.

The Svea Court found that Landbyska Verket's claim must be understood to mean that the security requested was for a specific amount and that it was already clear from the arbitral award that the arbitral tribunal had deviated from the claim. Nor could a specific amount be derived from the reference to thirty-six months guarantee rent.

The Court's conclusion was that the arbitral tribunal had distanced itself too far from what had been claimed by Landbyska Verket by not specifying an amount for the security to be provided. Accordingly, the arbitral tribunal had exceeded their mandate, and the award was set aside.

One of the judges dissented.

The Court granted the right to appeal to the Supreme Court.[29] On 26 June 2023, the Supreme Court decided that it will take the case.

§1.09 *NET AT ONCE SWEDEN AB V. TRESVE FIBER IDEELL FÖRENING*

In a minor domestic case, the Göta Court of Appeal set aside an award rendered by a sole arbitrator on the basis that the claimant in the arbitration proceedings was considered to lack legal capacity and, therefore, could not be a party to the arbitration agreement on which its claim was based.[30] The Court allowed appeal to the Supreme Court, and the Supreme Court granted leave and came to the opposite conclusion, i.e., that claimant had legal capacity. Since the defendant had other objections to the arbitral award, which had not been addressed by the Court of Appeal, the case was sent back there.[31] The Court of Appeal subsequently found against the claimant, resulting in the arbitral award standing.[32]

28. Svea Court of Appeal Case No. T 3623-21.
29. Judgment by the Svea Court of Appeal on 24 November 2022 in Case No. T 3623-21.
30. Judgment by the Göta Court of Appeal on 2 November 2021 in Case No. T 2236-20.
31. Judgment by the Supreme Court on 30 June 2022 in Case No. T 7416-21 (NJA 2022 p. 592).
32. Judgment by the Göta Court of Appeal on 13 March 2023 in Case No. 2556-22.

CHAPTER 2

Paving the Way for Justice: Arbitration and EU Sanctions Against Russia

Kristin Campbell-Wilson & Natalia Petrik

§2.01 INTRODUCTION

Prior to 2022, the European Union's sanctions against Russia targeted a limited number of individuals and entities, and had limited effect on the day-to-day administration of arbitrations for most arbitrators and European arbitral institutions. However, the legal landscape in Europe experienced a seismic shift soon after the Russian invasion of Ukraine in February 2022. Instant termination of direct investments and international trade with Russia, coupled with the rapid expansion of the list of individuals and entities subject to sanctions, created a new legal reality with profound implications for international arbitration.

Sanctions pose a critical dilemma for the regulator of effectively reconciling the core principles of access to justice, the right to efficient remedy, and the right to legal advice with the overarching objectives of sanctions. Arbitration, the sole effective legal remedy within the realm of international trade, currently finds itself in a precarious position. On the one hand, judicial proceedings and the arbitral process are exempted from sanctions. On the other hand, as demonstrated below, the arbitral process is not entirely treated equal to judicial proceedings.

This chapter has two objectives. First, it offers a concise and practical analysis of how EU sanctions against Russia impact arbitral institutions and arbitrators located within the EU. At the time of writing, in early summer 2023, sanctions continue to expand, with the EU currently preparing its eleventh sanction package. Consequently, new effects may emerge in the near future. Nevertheless, we assess the existing regulations and each relevant provision in order to aid arbitral institutions, arbitrators, and parties in navigating the complexities of the EU sanction regime.

Second, the recommendations for necessary improvements outlined in this chapter may serve as industry feedback to the EU regulator. We hope that by providing an understanding of the actions required, we can ensure that sanctions neither hinder the administration of justice by arbitrators and arbitral institutions nor undermine the rule of law.

§2.02 THE SCOPE OF THE EU SANCTIONS

The EU sanctions against Russia were implemented in 2014 in response to Russia's destabilizing of the situation in Ukraine and annexation of Crimea. These sanctions were primarily established through two key EU Council Regulations. The first, Council Regulation (EU) No. 269/2014 dated 17 March 2014, outlined a list of individuals and entities subject to financial sanctions, including measures such as asset freeze and restrictions on financial transactions with them. The second, Council Regulation (EU) No. 833/2014 dated 31 July 2014, introduced sectoral sanctions that imposed limitations on the export of goods and technologies in the defence and oil sectors. Additionally, it restricted certain Russian financial institutions' access to the EU capital market.

The two regulations apply (a) within the territory of the Union; (b) on board any aircraft or any vessel under the jurisdiction of a Member State; (c) to any person inside or outside the territory of the Union who is a national of a Member State; (d) to any legal person, entity or body, inside or outside the territory of the Union, which is incorporated or constituted under the law of a Member State; (e) to any legal person, entity or body in respect of any business done in whole or in part within the Union.[1]

In broad terms, EU sanctions are primarily intended to be enforced within the territory of the EU and are applicable to EU nationals. However, it is important to note that EU citizens are personally obligated to adhere to these sanctions, even if they reside or work outside the EU.[2]

Therefore, the EU sanctions regime may come into play in arbitral proceedings through several different avenues, depending on the actors and the circumstances in the arbitration:

- Legal counsels and arbitrators who are nationals of a Member State must comply with the EU sanction regime when providing legal services.
- EU-based arbitral institutions must adhere to the sanction regulations, including screening the parties against sanction lists when processing advances on costs.
- Parties incorporated or domiciled in the EU must comply with the sanctions regulations when conducting business, including resolving their disputes, with Russian parties.
- EU sanctions also apply if the disputed contract is governed by the law of a Member State or has an EU nexus, i.e., concerns 'business done in whole or in part within the Union'.

1. Article 17 of Council Regulation (EU) No. 2014/269 of 17 March 2014 https://eur-lex.europa.eu/legal-content/EN/TXT/PDF/?uri=CELEX:32014R0833 and Article 13 of Council Regulation (EU) No. 2014/833 of 31 July 2014 (accessed June 2023).
2. Consolidated FAQs on the implementation of Council Regulation No. 833/2014 and Council Regulation No. 269/2014, Question 35 (accessed June 2023).

- Arbitrations *seated* in the EU must also be conducted with due regard to EU sanctions regulations for the arbitral award to be valid under the *lex arbitri*.

The EU sanctions regulations provide for certain exceptions. These exceptions come in the form of *derogations* or *exemptions*. Derogations allow for seeking the authorization of a national competent authority for making particular actions or transactions under those conditions deemed appropriate by the authority.[3] Decisions on derogations are subject to the administrative procedures of each respective country, have a limited duration, and can be challenged in national administrative courts.

Exemptions, on the other hand, carve out specific transactions and services from the general prohibitions imposed by the sanction regulations. However, it is important to note that although certain services and transactions are exempt from sanctions, it does not automatically follow that *payment* for those services can be made without prior authorization from the competent authority, for instance, if payment is due from a listed person or entity.

Due to its particular nature, legal services are dealt with specifically in the framework and are allowed under certain conditions. Technically, this is achieved through the use of exemptions and derogations incorporated in regulations 269/2014 and 833/2014.

§2.03 THE LEGAL AND PRACTICAL EFFECTS OF COUNCIL REGULATION (EU) NO. 269/2014 ON ARBITRATION

The provisions of 269/2014 that are particularly relevant for arbitration include:

- Article 2 (freeze of assets);
- Article 4.1.(b) (derogation related to legal services);
- Article 5.1 (derogation related to claims arising out of arbitral and judicial decisions);
- Article 7 (payments due under arbitral decisions for the benefit of the listed parties);
- Article 8 (reporting obligation); and
- Article 11 ('no claims' provision).

[A] Article 2: The Freeze of Assets

Article 2 states:

> 1. All funds and economic resources belonging to, owned, held or controlled by any natural or legal persons, entities or bodies, or natural or legal persons, entities or bodies associated with them, as listed in Annex I, shall be frozen.

3. The list of national competent authorities is provided in Annex II to the Regulation 2014/269 and in Annex I to the Regulation 2014/833.

2. No funds or economic resources shall be made available, directly or indirectly, to or for the benefit of natural or legal persons, entities or bodies, or natural or legal persons, entities or bodies associated with them, as listed in Annex I.

Article 2 imposes an obligation on the recipient of funds to conduct thorough checks on the paying party in order to establish whether the party is subject to sanctions. The scope of the obligation is broad and involves conducting extensive sanctions controls of the majority shareholders/owners, beneficial owners, and controlling entities or individuals. In arbitral proceedings, institutions and ad hoc tribunals typically handle deposits provided by parties in advance or during the proceedings. In cases where the party receives funding, the same level of scrutiny should be applied also to the funder.

In practice, the aforementioned provisions necessitate that arbitral institutions establish due diligence procedures concerning sanctions control, regardless of whether they handle cases involving Russian parties or not. As there is no rule book dictating how to design the framework for compliance with the sanctions regulations, it is up to each institution to design one. An obvious first step is to screen parties against the sanctions lists. Circumstances which may merit further investigation include situations where a party is incorporated in a country targeted by the EU sanction programmes, such as Russia and Belarus. Additionally, parties registered in offshore jurisdictions or in jurisdictions deemed high-risk or subject to increased monitoring by the Financial Action Task Force (FATF)[4] indicate an elevated risk for sanctions-related implications. Compliance with the sanctions framework therefore may require further investigation of the parties involved, such as requesting the parties to disclose their ownership structure and beneficial owners. It is helpful if the arbitration rules of the institution empower it to compel the parties to provide such information.

Further guidance is provided by the European Commission in its official frequently asked questions (FAQ) document.[5] It recommends for instance screening beneficiaries of funds against sanctions lists and conducting investigations into adverse media reports. The European Commission further suggests conducting internet searches to determine whether the party, even if not officially designated, may be under the control of a listed person or entity. The criteria for evaluating whether a legal entity is controlled by another person or entity can be found in the EU Best Practices for the effective implementation of restrictive measures.[6] These criteria include:

(a) having the right or exercising the power to appoint or remove a majority of the members of the administrative, management or supervisory body of such legal person or entity;

4. FATF's lists are found here: https://www.fatf-gafi.org/en/the-fatf/what-we-do.html.
5. Commission consolidated FAQs on the implementation of Council Regulation No. 833/2014 and Council Regulation No. 269/2014, Chapter 2 'Circumvention and Due Diligence' https://finance.ec.europa.eu/system/files/2023-05/faqs-sanctions-russia-consolidated_en_0.pdf (accessed June 2023).
6. EU Best Practices for the effective implementation of restrictive measures, §62 https://data.consilium.europa.eu/doc/document/ST-10572-2022-INIT/en/pdf (accessed June 2023).

(b) having appointed solely as a result of the exercise of one's voting rights a majority of the members of the administrative, management or supervisory bodies of a legal person or entity who have held office during the present and previous financial year;
(c) controlling alone, pursuant to an agreement with other shareholders in or members of a legal person or entity, a majority of shareholders' or members' voting rights in that legal person or entity;
(d) having the right to exercise a dominant influence over a legal person or entity, pursuant to an agreement entered into with that legal person or entity or to a provision in its Memorandum or Articles of Association, where the law governing that legal person or entity permits it being subject to such agreement or provision;
(e) having the power to exercise the right to exercise a dominant influence referred to in point (d), without being the holder of that right;
(f) having the right to use all or part of the assets of a legal person or entity;
(g) managing the business of a legal person or entity on a unified basis while publishing consolidated accounts;
(h) sharing jointly and severally the financial liabilities of a legal person or entity or guaranteeing them.[7]

Screening should ideally be conducted at the outset of the proceedings, prior to any payment of advances on costs and, if possible, registration fees. However, there may be instances where a party becomes designated after the advances have already been paid, triggering the sanctions-related obligations of the actors involved during the course of the proceedings. In such situations, the institution should promptly notify its bank and will need to seek a derogation from the national competent authority in accordance with the relevant provision for any payments to be made during the proceedings or following the termination of the arbitration.

Ownership enquiries and information obtained from the parties and the results of the institution's own due diligence should be properly documented as proof of compliance with the sanctions regulation.[8] Arbitration rests on the foundation of trust between the parties involved, as well as their trust in the administering institution and the tribunal. Consequently, it is wise for institutions to provide clear explanations of the enquiry process and offer procedural guidance on subsequent steps as part of their

7. EU Best Practices for the effective implementation of restrictive measures, 22 July 2022, https://data.consilium.europa.eu/doc/document/ST-10572-2022-INIT/en/pdf (accessed June 2023).
8. The implications of the screening procedure in relation to GDPR are touched upon in the following publication. 'Caught between data protection and economic sanctions?' By Yuliya Miadzvetskaya, 7 May 2019, https://www.law.kuleuven.be/citip/blog/caught-between-data-protection-and-trade-sanctions/ (accessed June 2023).

service. Any inquiries into corporate and ownership structures should be transparent regarding their legal basis, purpose, and scope for screening.

It is important to note that institutional due diligence does not relieve the tribunal of its own responsibility to conduct sanctions checks. During the course of the proceedings, facts may emerge that reveal a party's exposure to sanctions, which the institution may not have discovered prior to referring the case to the tribunal. In practice, however, institutional due diligence considerably facilitates compliance with the sanctions for the tribunal and for the parties. In ad hoc arbitration, the tribunal will be responsible for conducting the due diligence process and for monitoring the changes in the sanction regulations throughout the proceedings.

[B] Article 4.1.(b): Derogation Related to Payment for Legal Services

Already, when the sanctions were introduced, a derogation related to legal services was established in Article 4.1.(b) of Regulation 269/2014. The article reads as follows:

> By way of derogation from Article 2, the competent authorities of the Member States may authorise the release of certain frozen funds or economic resources, or the making available of certain funds or economic resources, under such conditions as they deem appropriate, after having determined that the funds or economic resources concerned are: [...]
>
> b) intended exclusively for payment of reasonable professional fees or reimbursement of incurred expenses associated with the provision of legal services.

The purpose of this provision is to facilitate access to legal services, in accordance with Article 47 of the Charter of Fundamental Rights of the European Union (the Charter), as clarified by CJEU in case *Užsieniom reikalų ministerija, Finansinių nusikaltimų tyrimo tarnyba v. Peftiev.* In the case, CJEU considered an identical provision in EU Regulation 765/2006 regarding sanctions against Belarus, finding that in exercising its discretion to decide on applications for the release of frozen funds, the national competent authorities must consider Article 47 of the Charter:

> The second sentence of the second paragraph of Article 47 of the Charter, concerning the right to an effective judicial remedy, provides that everyone has the possibility of being advised, defended and represented. [...] Thus, Article 3(1)(b) of Regulation No 765/2006 must be interpreted in accordance with Article 47 of the Charter, to the effect that a freeze of funds cannot have the effect of depriving the persons whose funds have been frozen from effective access to justice.[9]

Thus, CJEU confirmed that 'legal services' are an integral part of the right to an effective remedy under the Charter.

9. Case C-314/13, ECLI:EU:C:2014:1645, §§ 25, 26 https://curia.europa.eu/juris/document/document.jsf;jsessionid=A233BE4F631E12585804B536083DADF5?text=&docid=153579&pageIndex=0&doclang=en&mode=lst&dir=&occ=first&part=1&cid=1700136 (accessed June 2023).

In the context of arbitration, the derogation in Article 4.1.(b) may come into play, e.g., in an ongoing arbitration where the advance on costs is to be paid by a listed party. Article 4.1.(b) does not explicitly specify whether it is the listed party or the recipient of the payment who should apply for the authorization. Based on the provision, however, an arbitral institution or arbitrator involved in the case as recipients of fees should, in principle, be eligible to seek authorization from the competent authority to release frozen funds. Considering the broad discretionary powers granted to the national authorities to decide on these matters, some procedural variations in each Member State are to be expected.

When submitting an application for authorization based on a derogation, the applicant needs to include certain details of the case, e.g., the name of the listed party, the purpose of the future payment, and information on bank accounts used, including the remitting, correspondent, and receiving banks involved. Additionally, evidence demonstrating the reasonableness of the preliminary fees and costs should be provided. This could involve referencing the applicable table of costs and providing the decision on the advance on costs to be paid. The specific evidence required may vary depending on the cost system employed by the administering institution, whether it be based on ad valorem or hourly fees.

Although the provision leaves the authorities discretion to decide on the conditions for the payments, the national competent authority is likely to take a cautious approach. It is the experience of the authors that one should not expect that a decision of the national competent authority will cover several consecutive payments but rather that authorization is needed for each individual transaction. All authorizations by the national competent authorities are to be reported to the European Commission. One may also expect that upon granting a derogation, the national authority will impose a deadline for the execution of the transaction and require the applicant to provide a report within a specified period of time.

In international arbitrations, legal services are provided across multiple jurisdictions, members of the tribunal may not be based in the same country as the arbitral institution overseeing the case, and one single transaction may cross multiple jurisdictions. As there are no provisions to the effect that the decision of the competent authority in one Member State should be valid or adhered to in another Member State, this implies that decisions on authorizations are valid only within the territory of the Member State where they were issued. For this reason, applications may need to be submitted in multiple jurisdictions, notwithstanding that the applications concern the same transaction. One would expect, however, that the decision of one competent authority adds value to the application process undertaken by another competent authority.

It is important to note that authorization covers the receipt of funds from a listed entity or person and does not automatically grant permission to return any unused funds. Arbitrators and institutions are advised to take this into consideration when requesting the advance on costs. Many institutions request advances to be paid in instalments throughout the proceedings. This approach may allow for a more accurate calculation of the advance on costs vis-à-vis the final costs of the arbitration. It also means, however, that each payment is likely to require a separate application for authorization.

Any unused funds from a listed entity or person should be treated as frozen and reported to the national competent authority in accordance with Article 8, *see* below.

An additional consideration is that the application process is subject to the principle of publicity in most EU countries, including Sweden (*Sw.* offentlighetsprincipen), and thus entails the disclosure of details of the arbitration to third parties. Consequently, it is to be expected that some EU-based institutions will update their rules to include provisions on compliance, specifically addressing the disclosure obligations imposed by the sanction legislation.

[C] Article 5.1: Claims Arising out of Arbitral and Judicial Decisions

Article 5.1 provides for a derogation from the freeze of assets for the purpose of enforcing judicial decisions and arbitral awards:

> 1. By way of derogation from Article 2, the competent authorities of the Member States may authorise the release of certain frozen funds or economic resources, if the following conditions are met:
>   (a) the funds or economic resources are subject to an arbitral decision rendered prior to the date on which the natural or legal person, entity or body referred to in Article 2 was included in Annex I, or of a judicial or administrative decision rendered in the Union, or a judicial decision enforceable in the Member State concerned, prior to or after that date;
>   (b) the funds or economic resources will be used exclusively to satisfy claims secured by such a decision or recognised as valid in such a decision, within the limits set by applicable laws and regulations governing the rights of persons having such claims;
>   (c) the decision is not for the benefit of a natural or legal person, entity or body listed in Annex I; and
>   (d) recognition of the decision is not contrary to public policy in the Member State concerned.
> 2. The Member State concerned shall inform the other Member States and the Commission of any authorisation granted under paragraph 1.

Article 5.1 allows for the release of frozen funds within the EU for the purpose of enforcing arbitral awards, judicial, and administrative decisions against a sanctioned party. Importantly, the article makes a distinction between arbitral awards on the one hand and judicial and administrative decisions on the other. The derogation in Article 5.1 only applies to arbitral awards rendered *before* the sanctioned party was listed, while it applies to judicial and administrative decisions rendered within the EU both before and after the listing of the party.

This requirement raises concerns regarding its coherence with the principles of effective remedy and objectives of the regulations. The aim of the economic sanctions is to hinder Russia's capacity to sustain the war against Ukraine.[10] Article 5.1 implies

10. https://www.consilium.europa.eu/en/policies/sanctions/restrictive-measures-against-russia-over-ukraine/sanctions-against-russia-explained/ (accessed June 2023).

that the enforcement of awards rendered post-designation is indefinitely halted, whereas enforcement of court judgments is permitted. The reason for the distinction between arbitral awards and decisions made by public courts is not clear.

In the views of the authors, there should be no distinction made between a court decision or judgment and an arbitral award. Both are enforceable titles as a consequence of legal proceedings in accordance with relevant laws and regulations. Courts, arbitral institutions and arbitral tribunals are providers of justice, and their decisions carry equal weight. The limitation included in Article 5.1, restricting the derogation to awards made prior to the listing, denies EU parties an enforceable remedy against sanctioned parties to the benefit of the latter. This is perhaps the most significant consequence of the article, as it contradicts the objectives of the sanction regulation, and it should be remedied by the regulator.

Furthermore, the limitation is incoherent with Article 7, which provides for the enforcement of arbitral awards in favour of sanctioned parties regardless of the time of rendering, as long as the funds credited remain frozen.

[D] Article 7: Payments due to Listed Parties under Arbitral Decisions

This article specifically addresses payments owed to the listed parties. It allows banks to accept funds transferred by third parties into the account of a listed individual or entity on the condition that any amounts deposited into those accounts are also frozen. The article is formulated as follows:

> 1. Article 2(2) shall not prevent the crediting of the frozen accounts by financial or credit institutions that receive funds transferred by third parties onto the account of a listed natural or legal person, entity or body, provided that any additions to such accounts will also be frozen. The financial or credit institution shall inform the relevant competent authority about any such transaction without delay.
> 2. Article 2(2) shall not apply to the addition to frozen accounts of:
>   (a) interest or other earnings on those accounts;
>   (b) payments due under contracts, agreements or obligations that were concluded or arose before the date on which the natural or legal person, entity or body referred to in Article 2 has been included in Annex I; or
>   (c) payments due under judicial, administrative or arbitral decisions rendered in a Member State or enforceable in the Member State concerned;
>
>   provided that any such interest, other earnings and payments are frozen in accordance with Article 2(1).

Article 7.2(c) states that the award should either be rendered or be enforceable in the Member States and, unlike Article 5.1, it treats judgments and arbitral awards equally; i.e., it does not require arbitral awards to be rendered prior to the designation of an entity or individual.

Article 7 was subject to judicial consideration by the High Court of Justice in England in the recent case of *PJSC National Bank Trust v. Mints*.[11] The case examined the impact of sanctions on civil litigation and answered the question of whether substantive judgments and arbitral awards can be rendered in favour of a designated entity after its designation, and if so, under what circumstances. The court also emphasized that the EU regulation in question applies equally to judgments and arbitral awards.[12]

The case was initiated in 2019. During the course of the proceedings, the UK Government imposed asset freeze restrictions on one of the claimants and two individuals who owned or controlled the other claimant. After the designation of the claimants, the respondents raised an objection, contending that any judgment entered in favour of the claimants would be unlawful due to the applicable sanction regime.[13]

In its judgment, the court examined both the UK and the EU sanctions, analysing the effects of Articles 7 of Regulation 269/2014 on judicial proceedings. The court observed that this provision encompasses both judgments and arbitral awards and concluded that the EU sanction regulations were not designed to differentiate between judgments and arbitral awards.[14]

The court rejected the argument that entering a judgment would violate the freeze of funds provision outlined in Article 2(1) of Regulation 269/2014:

> In order to get to this argument one has to recharacterise the entry of the judgment as a dealing in the underlying cause of action, which is not a characterisation which is apt to the EU Regulation. Nor indeed does it reflect the actual wording of Article 2 which does not mention dealing (in either part). Article 2(1) stipulates 'all funds and resources ... shall be frozen'. Even if a judgment creates a fund, entering a judgment has nothing to do with frozen assets. Article 2(2) says that 'no funds or economic resources shall be made available'.[15]

Therefore, the court concluded that 'the EU Regulation does not preclude – and logically contemplates – the entry of judgments against (and by necessary implication for) a designated person after the imposition against them of sanctions'.[16]

While a judgment from the High Court of Justice in England does not serve as an authoritative interpretation of EU law, it carries weight as it relies on an analysis of the EU regulations that were incorporated into UK law until 2018. The judgment also involves thorough research into fundamental legal principles, including legality and access to courts, based on UK, EU, and international law. The analysis made by the court demonstrates that these principles are not restricted by the sanctions legislation.[17]

11. [2023] EWHC 118 (Comm) in §2 https://www.oeclaw.co.uk/images/uploads/judgments/PJSC_v_Mints_final_for_approval_and_hand_down.pdf (accessed June 2023).
12. *Ibid.*, §28.
13. *Ibid.*, §6.
14. *Ibid.*, in §§28 and 148.
15. *Ibid.*, in §33.
16. *Ibid.*, in §36.
17. *Ibid.*, in §66.

It is important to emphasize that in the *PJSC National Bank Trust v. Mints* case, the High Court of Justice addressed claims that were unrelated to sanctions and which arose prior to the designations. Based on this judgment, and in the absence of provisions to the contrary, one could also infer that arbitral awards which concern claims which arose prior to the designation of the party and that are unrelated to sanctions may be rendered in favour of the sanctioned party. However, the situation is different when it comes to claims that fall under the 'no claims' provisions in Article 11 of Regulation Nos 269/2014 and 833/2014, which will be discussed below.

[E] Article 11: 'No Claims' Provisions

Article 11 shields EU parties from having to satisfy claims caused by the restrictive measures.[18] The article reads as follows.

> 1. No claims in connection with any contract or transaction the performance of which has been affected, directly or indirectly, in whole or in part, by the measures imposed under this Regulation, including claims for indemnity or any other claim of this type, such as a claim for compensation or a claim under a guarantee, particularly a claim for extension or payment of a bond, guarantee or indemnity, particularly a financial guarantee or financial indemnity, of whatever form, shall be satisfied, if they are made by:
>   (a) designated natural or legal persons, entities or bodies listed in Annex I;
>   (b) any natural or legal person, entity or body acting through or on behalf of one of the persons, entities or bodies referred to in point (a).
> 2. In any proceedings for the enforcement of a claim, the onus of proving that satisfying the claim is not prohibited by paragraph 1 shall be on the natural or legal person, entity or body seeking the enforcement of that claim.
> 3. This Article is without prejudice to the right of natural or legal persons, entities or bodies referred to in paragraph 1 to judicial review of the legality of the non-performance of contractual obligations in accordance with this Regulation.

The article bears a resemblance to its counterpart in Regulation 833/2014, with nearly identical wording. According to the wording of Article 11, it applies when a claim arises from a breach caused by the measures introduced by Regulation 269/2014 and when the claim is brought by a sanctioned entity or person or a party controlled by a sanctioned entity or person. Both criteria must be met for the provision to apply. In Regulation 833/2014, Article 11 applies to any claim brought by a Russian state-owned or controlled entity or to any Russian person, entity or body.[19]

Similar to Article 7, Article 11 follows the same logic in that it does not outright prohibit the adjudication of claims. This is supported by Article 11(2), which places the burden of proof on the sanctioned person or entity to demonstrate that satisfying the claim is not prohibited by Article 11.

18. Commission's consolidated FAQs on the implementation of Council Regulation Nos 833/2014 and 269/2014, Question 8, p. 18.
19. *See* Art. 11.1 a) and b).

Article 11 gives reason to question whether it permanently relieves non-sanctioned parties from satisfying claims arising out of the non-performance caused by sanctions. To answer this question, it is necessary to examine the history of 'no claims' provisions, which can be traced back to the UN sanctions programme against Iraq and the corresponding Council Regulation (EEC) No. 3541/92 of 7 December 1992 adopted in 1992.[20] The regulation prohibited the satisfaction of Iraqi claims related to contracts and transactions affected by United Nations Security Council Resolution 661 (1990) and subsequent resolutions.

The regulation established a 'no claims' regime that was materially similar to the one concerning claims by Iraq arising from the UN trade embargo. During the drafting process of the regulation, an explanatory memorandum was prepared. A portion of this memorandum is referenced in the case of *H Shanning International Ltd v. Lloyds TSB Bank plc; Lloyds TSB Bank plc v. Rasheed Bank* (28 June 2001):[21]

> The measures proposed herewith in order to implement paragraph 29 of UNSC Resolution 687 (1991) are based on the following specific considerations:
>
> (1) Non-enforceability of claims or prohibition to pay
>
> Paragraph 29 can be interpreted either as making claims by Iraq non-enforceable, or as establishing a prohibition to honour such claims. The practical consequences of each interpretation are different. A system of NON-ENFORCEABILITY would protect banks and exporters against claims mentioned in paragraph 29 of UNSC Resolution 687, by making it impossible for any Iraqi party to obtain a judgment in its favour unless it could prove that the contract or transaction was not affected by the embargo.
>
> However, such a system would allow claims being settled by agreement between the parties concerned. This would considerably weaken the protection granted, as it would expose non-Iraqi operators, in particular contractors, to pressure which might be exerted by the Iraqi side. It would also create uncertainty as to whether the contracts concerned would still have to be treated as valid obligations. Finally, this system would not permit the achievement of the other objective of paragraph 29, i.e., the prevention of retroactive compensation in favour of Iraq.
>
> Therefore, the Commission proposes a system of PROHIBITION TO HONOUR CLAIMS, which would allow to meet both the objective of preventing such retroactive compensation as well as the objective of an effective protection of non-Iraqi parties, and would establish clarity as regards the treatment of the contractual obligations concerned.

The case involved a claim based on a series of cross-bank guarantees relating to the delivery of operating theatres and medical equipment to Iraq. The UN sanctions against Iraq were imposed during the performance of the contract, which raised the question of whether the payment could be released under the bank guarantee. In the

20. Council Regulation (EEC) No. 3541/92 of 7 December 1992 https://eur-lex.europa.eu/legal-content/EN/TXT/?uri=CELEX%3A31992R3541 (accessed June 2023).
21. *United Nations Juridical Yearbook* Extract from: Chapter VIII: Decisions of National Tribunals 2001 Part Three. Judicial decisions on questions relating the United Nations and related intergovernmental organizations, Decision of House of Lords in *H Shanning International Ltd v. Lloyds TSB Bank plc; Lloyds TSB Bank plc v. Rasheed Bank* (28 June 2001), p. 491.

court proceedings, Lloyds, the bank issuing a counter-guarantee, sought declarations that it was 'permanently prohibited from satisfying any and all claims' by Rasheed Bank for payment under the Lloyds counter-guarantee. Eventually, the court determined that Regulation (EEC) No. 3541/92 indeed permanently prohibited the satisfaction of any and all claims made or to be made by the Iraqi parties, even if the sanctions were to be lifted.

Based on the aforementioned case law, it could be inferred that Article 11 is intended to provide permanent protection to EU parties from claims arising out of their non-performance due to the sanctions.

Apart from its implications on the merits of the dispute, the 'no claims' provision sparked discussions regarding the arbitrability of such cases.[22] In recent decades, however, jurisprudence has adopted a liberal approach towards tribunals' authority to arbitrate disputes that involve elements of public law, including sanctions. Such disputes are considered arbitrable by the legal doctrine,[23] and there is also extensive case law in support of this conclusion.[24] For instance, in the *Air France v. Libyan Arab Airline* case, the Quebec Court of Appeal rejected Air France's argument that the UN embargo against Libya rendered the dispute non-arbitrable.[25] The court asserted that 'contrary to Air France's contention, the UN Resolutions do not prohibit Air France from appointing an arbitrator. It would be illogical to assume that the regulation pertaining to the embargo prevents the parties from initiating the arbitration process, if only for the purpose of allowing the arbitral tribunal to rule on the applicability of the measures in question'.[26]

This being said, one may not rule out that courts in less arbitration-friendly jurisdictions might adopt a different approach.

[F] Article 8.1: Reporting Obligation

Article 8.1 reads as follows.

> 1. Notwithstanding the applicable rules concerning reporting, confidentiality and professional secrecy, natural and legal persons, entities and bodies shall:
>   (a) supply immediately any information which would facilitate compliance with this Regulation, such as information on accounts and amounts

22. *See, e.g.*, 'Sanctions and arbitrability' by Roberto Oliva, https://www.arbitratoinitalia.it/en/2022/11/11/sanctions-arbitrability/ (accessed June 2023).
23. 'Part II, Chapter 4: Authority of Domestic Courts and Arbitral Tribunals to Give Effect to Trade Sanctions', in Mercedeh Azeredo Da Silveira, Trade Sanctions and International Sales: An Inquiry into International Arbitration and Commercial Litigation (© Kluwer Law International; Kluwer Law International 2014) pp. 65-126.
24. *See, e.g.*, 'Arbitrability of Disputes' by Y. Fortier, 'Global Reflections on International Law, Commerce and Dispute Resolution', Liber Amicorum in Honor of Robert Briner. *See also* the article by Salomé Garnier Navacelle, Stephane de Navacelle and Julie Zorrilla 'When Arbitration and Compliance Meet Up: Analysis of Their First Interplay' https://docs.google.com/document/d/1Wo-uIY-m0QH1_YRZ1jkV9nLLDAqUtvF_/edit# (accessed June 2023).
25. Court of Appeal Canada, Province of Quebec, Registry of Montreal, No.: 500-09-009391-004 (500-05-043881-984), dated 31 March 2003.
26. *Ibid.*, section 47.

frozen in accordance with Article 2 or information held about funds and economic resources within Union territory belonging to, owned, held or controlled by natural or legal persons, entities or bodies listed in Annex I and which have not been treated as frozen by the natural and legal persons, entities and bodies obliged to do so, to the competent authority of the Member State where they are resident or located, and shall transmit such information, directly or through the Member State, to the Commission; and

(b) cooperate with the competent authority in any verification of such information.

[...]

In July 2022, as a part of the seventh sanction package, the EU strengthened the reporting obligations of its subjects by imposing the duty to report, notwithstanding any obligations of confidentiality or professional secrecy which may also apply.[27] Although the EU Commission clarified that the provision 'should not cover information received as part of legal representation in court proceedings',[28] the sanction regulations do not provide any formal exemptions from the reporting obligation for legal professionals.

At the moment of writing, the Council of Europe considers a Proposal for a Directive on the definition of criminal offences and penalties for the violation of EU's restrictive measures ('the Proposal'). The Proposal clarifies that the obligation to report information shall not apply to the information that legal professionals receive from, or obtain on, one of their clients, in the course of ascertaining the legal position of their client or performing the task of defending or representing that client in, or concerning, judicial proceedings, including providing advice on instituting or avoiding such proceedings.[29]

If the aforementioned text is adopted by the Council, it will function as an exemption to the reporting obligation concerning judicial proceedings. However, the mentioned provision does not explicitly address legal services rendered in arbitral proceedings, raising concerns about its potential implications for arbitrators and party representatives involved in such cases. The obligation to report a client or a party under the threat of prosecution presents a challenge when it comes to upholding the principles of justice as well as safeguarding the independence of lawyers.

If the proposed text does not grant an exemption to legal professionals from the reporting obligation in arbitral proceedings, and if the suggested penalty for non-compliance is implemented, there is a substantial risk that it will negatively impact the willingness of EU counsel and arbitrators to accept appointments in cases involving

27. Council Regulation (EU) 2022/1273 of 21 July 2022, §5 in the recitals. https://eur-lex.europa.eu/legal-content/EN/TXT/?uri=celex%3A32022R1273 (accessed June 2023).
28. Commission's consolidated FAQs on the implementation of Council Regulation No. 833/2014 and Council Regulation No. 269/2014, p. 31, Question 30.
29. Proposal for a Directive of the European Parliament and of the Council on the definition of criminal offences and penalties for the violation of Union restrictive measures, Doc. 9312/23, https://data.consilium.europa.eu/doc/document/ST-9312-2023-INIT/en/pdf (accessed June 2023).

sanctioned parties, depriving all parties of the sole effective legal remedy in the domain of international trade.

§2.04 THE LEGAL AND PRACTICAL EFFECTS OF REGULATION 833/2014 ON ARBITRATION

While Regulation 269/2014 outlines a list of individuals and entities subject to financial sanctions, Regulation 833/2014 deals with sectoral sanctions that impose limitations on the export of goods and technologies in the defence and oil sectors. The provisions of Regulation 833/2014 that are particularly relevant for arbitration include:

- Article 5b 1. (ban on acceptance of deposits exceeding EUR 100,000);
- Article 5c 1(b) (derogation related to 5b 1);
- Article 5aa (exemption for services related to access to justice);
- Article 5n (exemption on the provision of legal advisory services in arbitration); and
- Article 11 ('no claims' provision).

[A] Articles 5b 1 and 5c 1(b): Deposits Exceeding EUR 100,000

This prohibition was introduced in February 2022 as part of the second sanction package against Russia. Initially, it concerned the transactions of funds in excess of EUR 100,000 made by Russian nationals and entities from Russia. In July 2022, the prohibition was extended to include transactions made by entities *controlled* by Russian nationals or natural persons residing in Russia. The article currently reads as follows:

> [...] It shall be prohibited to accept any deposits from Russian nationals or natural persons residing in Russia, legal persons, entities or bodies established in Russia or a legal person, entity or body established outside the Union and whose proprietary rights are directly or indirectly owned for more than 50 % by Russian nationals or natural persons residing in Russia, if the total value of deposits of that natural or legal person, entity or body per credit institution exceeds EUR 100 000.

The acceptance of amounts exceeding EUR 100,000 is subject to a derogation mechanism similar to the one applied to the provision of legal services to designated individuals and entities. Under Article 5c 1(b):

> By way of derogation from Articles 5b(1) and (2), the competent authorities may authorise the acceptance of such a deposit or the provision of wallet, account or custody service, under such conditions as they deem appropriate, after having determined that the acceptance of such a deposit or the provision of wallet, account or custody service is:
>
> [...]

(b) intended exclusively for the payment of reasonable professional fees or the reimbursement of incurred expenses associated with the provision of legal services.

While the process for seeking authorization for accepting funds may mirror the one outlined in §2.03[B] above, it is important to note that authorization is necessary for any transfer of amounts in excess of EUR 100,000 originating from Russian parties or parties under Russian control, irrespective of whether they are subject to sanctions or not.

[B] Article 5aa: Exemption for Services to Ensure Access to Justice

In March 2022, by issuing Council Regulation (EU) No. 428/2022, the European Union introduced a fourth package of sanctions against Russia, which included, *inter alia*, a general prohibition to directly or indirectly engage in any transaction with publicly controlled Russian entities.[30] Since the prohibition did not include any exemptions for arbitration-related services, it created a great deal of uncertainty for arbitrators, counsel and arbitral institutions involved in arbitrations with Russian state-owned or controlled companies.

Following the joint efforts of several EU-based arbitral institutions, including the SCC Arbitration Institute, VIAC, FAI, DIS, CAM and Swiss Arbitration Centre,[31] in addressing the implications of the fourth sanctions package on international arbitration and the rule of law, Article 5aa of Regulation 833/2014 was amended through the seventh sanctions package in July 2022 to include an exemption in Article 5aa 3(g), as follows:

1. It shall be prohibited to directly or indirectly engage in any transaction with:
   (a) a legal person, entity or body established in Russia, which is publicly controlled or with over 50 % public ownership or in which Russia, its Government or Central Bank has the right to participate in profits or with which Russia, its Government or Central Bank has other substantial economic relationship, as listed in Annex XIX;
   (b) a legal person, entity or body established outside the Union whose proprietary rights are directly or indirectly owned for more than 50 % by an entity listed in Annex XIX; or
   (c) a legal person, entity or body acting on behalf or at the direction of an entity referred to in point (a) or (b) of this paragraph.
   [...]
3. The prohibition in paragraph 1 shall not apply to:

   [...]

30. §5aa of Council Regulation (EU) 428/2022 of 15 March 2022 amending Regulation (EU) No. 833/2014 concerning restrictive measures in view of Russia's actions destabilizing the situation in Ukraine https://eur-lex.europa.eu/legal-content/EN/TXT/?uri=celex%3A32022R0428 (accessed June 2023).
31. *See* Joint statement of SCC, VIAC, FAI, DIS, CAM and Swiss Arbitration Centre regarding the EU's 7th sanctions package https://sccarbitrationinstitute.se/en/news/joint-statement-eu-provides-exemption-arbitration-proceedings (accessed June 2023).

> (g) transactions which are strictly necessary to ensure access to judicial, administrative or arbitral proceedings in a Member State, as well as for the recognition or enforcement of a judgment or an arbitration award rendered in a Member State and if such transactions are consistent with the objectives of this Regulation and Regulation (EU) No 269/2014.

The provision establishes a few important rules to comply with when administering cases with Russian state-owned entities. First, it provides for an exemption for arbitration, meaning that the services performed by arbitral institutions and arbitrators are neither prohibited nor require authorization. It does, however, not cover the receipt of *payments* from the Russian state-owned entities, which are subject to the asset freeze regime under Regulation 269/2014. As explained in §2.03[B] above, authorization is still required for such entities.

Second, it imposes the requirement that the transaction is 'strictly necessary' to ensure access to arbitral proceedings. As known, international arbitration involves multiple services of a legal and administrative character, most of which are indispensable for the organization of the proceedings and, hence, ensuring access to justice: in addition to the adjudication itself, arbitration involves administration services by arbitral institutions, financial services by banks, translation and court-reporting services by language providers, facility lease services by hearing centres, etc.

The requirement that the transaction is 'strictly necessary' mirrors the terminology used in relation to legal services further discussed in §2.04[C] below. The regulator, however, does not provide clear guidance on its scope. The lack of clarity regarding which services are considered permitted and which are considered prohibited in the eyes of the EU regulator may discourage service providers from accepting assignments involving sanctioned parties and consequently compromise access to justice for all parties involved, sanctioned and non-sanctioned.

Furthermore, it is unclear why Article 5aa 3(g) is limited to the awards *rendered* in a Member State and does not include awards *enforceable* in a Member State. The current wording implies that any transactions related to enforcement proceedings of an award rendered, for example, in Switzerland or in England, would not qualify for the exemption. In the eyes of the authors, there is no reason to exclude arbitral awards rendered outside the EU from enforcement in the EU, and, as in the case of Article 5.1 of Regulation 269/2014, we call upon the EU regulator to clarify its intention and/or amend the provision as appropriate.

Finally, the article harmonizes the exemption with the objectives outlined in Regulation (EU) No. 269/2014, aiming to ensure adherence to the asset freeze provisions established by the same regulation.

[C] Article 5n: Exemption for Legal Services in Contentious Matters

This article was included in the eighth sanction package in October 2022, introducing, *inter alia,* a general prohibition on rendering legal services to legal persons, entities or bodies established in Russia. It also includes a couple of exemptions for legal services necessary to ensure access to justice and the right to an effective legal remedy.[32] The article reads as follows.

> 1. [...]
> 2. It shall be prohibited to provide, directly or indirectly, architectural and engineering services, legal advisory services and IT consultancy services to:
>   (a) the Government of Russia; or
>   (b) legal persons, entities or bodies established in Russia.
>   [...]
> 5. Paragraphs 1 and 2 shall not apply to the provision of services that are strictly necessary for the exercise of the right of defence in judicial proceedings and the right to an effective legal remedy.
> 6. Paragraphs 1 and 2 shall not apply to the provision of services which are strictly necessary to ensure access to judicial, administrative or arbitral proceedings in a Member State, or for the recognition or enforcement of a judgment or an arbitration award rendered in a Member State, provided that such provision of services is consistent with the objectives of this Regulation and of Council Regulation (EU) No 269/2014 (16).

The exemption imposes a requirement for the legal services to be 'strictly necessary'. The scope of this criterion is commented on in the Commission's Consolidated FAQs as follows: 'As explained in Recital 19 of Council Regulation (EU) 2022/1904, the prohibition of legal services does not apply to representation, advice, preparation of documents or verification of documents in the context of legal representation services.'[33] The Commission continues: 'These exceptions are to be interpreted restrictively. The term "strictly" means that there is no other way to terminate contracts or to exercise the right of defense other than to rely on the provision of these otherwise prohibited services.'[34]

Legal representation services in arbitral proceedings are typically voluntary, granting parties the freedom to advocate for themselves. Consequently, there are concerns within the arbitration community that legal services in arbitration may not meet the criteria of being 'strictly necessary' and thus lie outside the purview of exemption. Nevertheless, the principle of equality of arms in an adversarial process implies that the parties have the same procedural rights. A scenario where one of the parties is denied access to legal advice in a foreign jurisdiction, while its counterparty retains full right to engage legal counsel and other services related to the arbitral proceedings, does not conform with this fundamental principle. Hence, the comments of the Commission raise concerns in relation to the principles of due process and the

---

32. Council Regulation (EU) 2022/1904 of 6 October 2022 amending Regulation (EU) No. 833/2014 concerning restrictive measures in view of Russia's actions destabilizing the situation in Ukraine.
33. Question 26 in Consolidated FAQs on the implementation of Council Regulation No. 833/2014 and Council Regulation No. 269/2014 https://finance.ec.europa.eu/system/files/2023-05/faqs-sanctions-russia-consolidated_en.pdf (accessed June 2023).
34. Provision of services related provision: Art. 5n of Council Regulation 833/2014 Frequently Asked Questions as of 21 December 2022, Question 3 https://finance.ec.europa.eu/system/files/2022-12/faqs-sanctions-russia-services-provision_en_0.pdf (accessed June 2023).

fundamental rights enshrined in the Charter. Therefore, it should provide further clarifications on the scope of this provision.

Similar to Article 5aa 3(g), this exemption is also limited to services related to enforcement proceedings of arbitration awards rendered within the EU. Considering that enforcement proceedings take place within the jurisdiction of national courts, engaging the services of a local legal counsel becomes a vital component. The wording regrettably seems to prohibit the rendering of legal services in relation to arbitral awards rendered in non-EU arbitration jurisdictions, such as Switzerland and the UK. As mentioned above, the derogations related to the enforcement of arbitral awards under Regulation 269/2014 do not include any such limitations.

The ban on legal services under Article 5n has emerged as, arguably, the most contentious component of the sanction legislation. Presently, there are two actions against the Council of Europe pending,[35] seeking to annul the ban. The applicants claim that it constitutes an infringement of the fundamental rights to protection of privacy and access to justice, interference with the right of every litigant to seek legal advice from his or her lawyer, with the principle of professional secrecy and the principle of the independence of the lawyer.

[D] Article 11: 'No Claims' Provisions

Article 11 applies to any claim brought by a Russian state-owned or controlled entity or to any Russian person, entity or body, but otherwise resembles the no-claims provisions in Article 11 of Regulation 269/2014. The implications of Article 11 are accounted for above in §2.03[E].

§2.05 CONCLUSIONS

The EU sanctions regime targeting Russia raises concerns regarding the compromise of the parties' access to justice and right to an effective remedy. While the sanctions are designed to achieve specific policy objectives, they may inadvertently hinder access to justice. The EU should assess the potential unintended consequences of proposed measures and ensure that the restrictions imposed are clear and proportionate. Engaging in a thorough impact assessment and consulting relevant stakeholders can help strike a balance between achieving the policy objectives and safeguarding the fundamental rights of the parties in judicial or arbitral proceedings.

To address the concerns raised in this chapter, the EU should revisit and amend those provisions which make a distinction between judicial and arbitral proceedings, and update the comprehensive official commentary for clear and transparent guidance

35. Case T-797/22, *Ordre néerlandais des avocats du barreau de Bruxelles and Others v. Council* (2023/C 63/79) https://eur-lex.europa.eu/legal-content/EN/TXT/PDF/?uri=CELEX:62022TN0797 and Case T-798/22, *Ordre des avocats à la cour de Paris and Couturier v. Council* (2023/C 63/80) https://eur-lex.europa.eu/legal-content/EN/TXT/PDF/?uri=CELEX:62022TN0798&from=EN (accessed June 2023).

where needed. By incorporating mechanisms for consultation and clarification, the EU can mitigate potential challenges to access to justice while achieving its policy objectives, without undermining the rule of law.

CHAPTER 3

The Ins and Outs of Arbitrator Selection

Daniel Hochstrasser

§3.01 INTRODUCTION

When preparing for the filing of a request for arbitration (or the answer thereto), the representatives of the party and outside counsel are focused on collecting facts, developing legal arguments, and considering potential witness and expert evidence they will be able to use in the arbitration. During that already busy period, the selection of the party-appointed arbitrator or the process for selecting a sole arbitrator or presiding arbitrator is also underway. As with all the other preparatory work, the arbitrator selection is geared at winning the case or, to put it more objectively, to secure an optimal outcome of the case under the given circumstances. The following remarks might sound trivial for a lawyer who is already involved in arbitration proceedings for a long time; to those colleagues, I apologize. However, many in-house counsel and/or lawyers who are not regularly involved in arbitral proceedings might find these comments and suggestions helpful.

It is by now a standard feature of all major arbitration rules that parties have an almost unrestricted freedom to not only appoint one of the members of the arbitral tribunal (the so-called party-appointed arbitrator), and can jointly nominate a sole arbitrator as the case may be; also, they are empowered to nominate or select, if they can agree with the opposing party, the president of the tribunal. This is in contrast to older solutions in several institutions, where there was a closed list of arbitrators or where the institution insisted on making appointments themselves. Such situations, to the extent that they still exist, are not of interest for this chapter, and will thus no longer be discussed here.

For the purposes of this chapter, I will only refer to two sets of rules as examples, namely the Arbitration Rules of the Stockholm Chamber of Commerce ("SCC Rules")[1] and the Arbitration Rules of the International Chamber of Commerce ("ICC Rules," jointly referred to as "the Rules").[2] The regulations found in those rules are quite similar; for the appointment of a sole arbitrator, they say the following:

> Where the Arbitral Tribunal is to consist of a sole arbitrator, the parties shall be given ten days to jointly appoint the arbitrator. If the parties fail to appoint the arbitrator within this time, the Board shall make the appointment:[3]
>
> Where the parties have agreed that the dispute shall be resolved by a sole arbitrator, they may, by agreement, nominate the sole arbitrator for confirmation. If the parties fail to nominate a sole arbitrator within 30 days from the date when the claimant's Request for Arbitration has been received by the other party or parties, or within such additional time as may be allowed by the Secretariat, the sole arbitrator shall be appointed by the Court.[4]

For arbitral tribunals consisting of more than one arbitrator (typically three, but at least theoretically also another uneven number), the Rules state the following:

> Where the Arbitral Tribunal is to consist of more than one arbitrator, each party shall appoint an equal number of arbitrators and the Board shall appoint the chairperson. Where a party fails to appoint any arbitrator within the stipulated time period, the Board shall make the appointment.[5]
>
> Where the parties have agreed that the dispute shall be resolved by three arbitrators, each party shall nominate in the Request and the Answer, respectively, one arbitrator for confirmation. If a party fails to nominate an arbitrator, the appointment shall be made by the Court.[6]

In addition, for the president of the arbitral tribunal, the ICC Rules contain the following provision:

> Where the dispute is to be referred to three arbitrators, the third arbitrator, who will act as president of the arbitral tribunal, shall be appointed by the Court, unless the parties have agreed upon another procedure for such appointment, in which case the nomination will be subject to confirmation pursuant to Article 13. Should such procedure not result in a nomination within 30 days from the confirmation or appointment of the co-arbitrators or any other time limit agreed by the parties or fixed by the Court, the third arbitrator shall be appointed by the Court.[7]

When an arbitration starts, each party therefore has to make an early and far-reaching decision, namely who it appoints to be a member of the tribunal and (in case of a sole arbitrator and/or a president) how it wants to influence the selection of

1. SCC Arbitration Rules 2023 (sccarbitrationinstitute.se).
2. ICC Arbitration Rules 2021 (iccwbo.org).
3. SCC Rules Art. 17(3).
4. ICC Rules Art. 12(3).
5. SCC Rules Art. 17(4).
6. ICC Rules Art. 12(4).
7. ICC Rules Art. 12(5).

that person. As this chapter shows, this in fact entails a multitude of decisions on a variety of qualities of the selected person.

As a side remark, I would like to mention here that there is a rather well-established practice where the two co-arbitrators are asked to nominate the president of the tribunal, and the arbitrators are consulting with counsel of the party who appointed them. Normally, and in order to avoid difficulties and frustration, such a procedure will be agreed upon by the two co-arbitrators so that both sides have a level playing field. In such discussions, the co-arbitrator in question and appointing counsel try to define the profile of the desired chairperson, and quite often also discuss specific names that would be considered acceptable or not. Once the arbitrator and counsel have agreed on a profile and/or specific names, such information is exchanged with the other side. The arbitrators then, based on the feedback they have received, create a list of names, which the parties are allowed to rank and/or to strike in case there are conflicts or other situations that render a candidate unacceptable.

The following is a discussion of the many parameters to be taken into account when selecting an arbitrator. Not all of them will be relevant in every case, but some will always be important and should not be neglected when taking a decision. Obviously, these are subjective comments based on my experience and might not be in line with the experience other arbitration specialists have made; in that sense, they are not intended to be guidelines to be followed strictly, but rather suggestions and ideas on how to tackle an important task.

§3.02 OBJECTIVE CRITERIA

The following is the first of two lists dealing with what I would call "objective criteria," although one can, in some instances, argue whether they are truly objective, or do not also have a subjective side. The two first are independence and impartiality, which are required explicitly or implicitly by all arbitration rules from an arbitrator. No longer relevant is the old principle according to which only the president of a tribunal would be truly independent and impartial (at the time, sometimes referred to as the "umpire" or "neutral"), whereas the party-appointed arbitrators had more the role of representatives of the appointing party in the tribunal.

According to the SCC Rules, the following applies:

> Every arbitrator must be impartial and independent.[8]
>
> Before being appointed, a prospective arbitrator shall disclose any circumstances that may give rise to justifiable doubts as to the prospective arbitrator's impartiality or independence.[9]

While independence and impartiality are always mentioned as a pair, they are different and thus will be treated separately.

8. SCC Rules Art. 18(1).
9. SCC Rules Art. 18(2).

[A] Independence

Independence is defined to mean "that there are no current or past relationships between the parties and the arbitrators which may compromise or may seem to compromise the arbitrator's freedom to rule on the matter in dispute. Independence is amenable to an objective test in that it does not involve an arbitrator's state of mind."[10]

The IBA Guidelines on Conflicts of Interest in International Arbitration[11] list in their "non-waivable red list"[12] situations which clearly are not reconcilable with an independent arbitrator: The arbitrator is either a legal representative, member of the board, shareholder, or otherwise financially interested in one of the parties, or regularly advises the party or an affiliate of the appointing party, or, the arbitrator or his/her firm derive a significant financial income therefrom. Equally problematic are the circumstances described in the "waivable red list,"[13] namely shareholding of the arbitrator in a party, representation of a party, prior involvement in the case, or regular advising of a party.

Institutions will not confirm an arbitrator who does not fulfill the independence requirement, and if circumstances that question the arbitrator's independence are discovered at a later stage, this can lead to a challenge and disqualification of the arbitrator.

For the appointment process, it is very important that any circumstances that are known to counsel which are a violation of the independence requirement are taken seriously and investigated thoroughly. If it should indeed turn out that the independence of the arbitrator, for whatever reason, is questionable, one should refrain from appointing such a candidate. It will not benefit the party choosing such an arbitrator in the long run if that arbitrator becomes an active member of the tribunal for many reasons. The first is that if the circumstances are discovered later, the arbitrator would be disqualified, and if it should even be revealed that the appointing party actually knew about the lack of independence, this will reflect badly on the party (and counsel), and might well have a negative impact on the outcome of the case. Second, even if that does not happen, the other arbitrators might become aware of the problem, which might well lead to that arbitrator being isolated or not taken seriously by his fellow arbitrators, which also might have a rather negative effect on the outcome of the case for the party who has appointed that person.

[B] Impartiality

Impartiality has to be distinguished from independence because it not so much focuses on a particular factual situation but rather on the attitude or mindset of the arbitrator. It is usually defined, in a general manner, "that an arbitrator does not favor one party over the other and is unbiased with respect to the matter in dispute. It is a subjective

10. Girsberger/Voser, International Arbitration, 3rd Edition, para. 654, with further references.
11. https://www.ibanet.org/MediaHandler?id=e2fe5e72-eb14-4bba-b10d-d33dafee8918.
12. Lists 1.1 to 1.4.
13. Lists 2.2.1 to 2.7.

concept in that it primarily involves the arbitrator's state of mind. Accordingly, impartiality is much harder to prove than independence."[14]

While the appointment of a non-independent arbitrator might easily be recognized and excluded, impartiality is more tricky because it is not readily recognizable. In any case, a potential arbitrator has to make disclosures which allow the parties to make a determination as to whether the arbitrator fulfills the impartiality obligation:

> Before being appointed, a prospective arbitrator shall disclose any circumstances that may give rise to justifiable doubts as to the prospective arbitrator's impartiality or independence.[15]

The formulation "any circumstances that may give rise to justifiable doubts" is of course rather vague. In particular, it does not define any threshold as to what could potentially trigger such doubts and results in a slippery slope, which can easily cause arbitrators to stumble. The recent practice of arbitral institutions, particularly the ICC Court, leads to the recommendation that the disclosure obligation be exercised in a broad manner. Arbitrators are well advised to disclose everything that could potentially be seen as problematic, even if, from a purely objective point of view, it could be considered unproblematic. The risk of not doing so is that not only the undisclosed fact may lead to a disqualification of the arbitrator, but the fact of the non-disclosure as such could also be seen as problematic.

[C] Nationality

Commercial arbitration is often international, i.e., the parties are from different countries, and so are other players involved. Frequently, counsel are chosen by the parties not from their own home country but rather from the country of the seat of the tribunal, or the country of the applicable law. Quite often, one also sees a combination of counsel from various jurisdictions in the team representing a party. Similarly, arbitral tribunals are in many (if not most) cases composed of people of different nationality. Historically, parties tended to appoint an arbitrator from their own home country. This continues to be seen and is, as a matter of principle, considered absolutely unproblematic.

Where it gets more interesting is either with the president of the tribunal or a sole arbitrator. There, most arbitration rules have a clear view:

> If the parties are of different nationalities, the sole arbitrator or the chairperson of the Arbitral Tribunal shall be of a different nationality than the parties, unless the parties have agreed otherwise, or the Board otherwise deems it appropriate.[16]
>
> Where the Court is to appoint the sole arbitrator or the president of the arbitral tribunal, such sole arbitrator or president of the arbitral tribunal shall be of a nationality other than those of the parties. However, in suitable circumstances and provided that none of the parties objects within the time limit fixed by the

14. GIRSBERGER/VOSER, International Arbitration, 3rd Edition, para. 653, with further references.
15. SCC Rules Art. 18(2).
16. SCC Rules Art. 17(6).

> Secretariat, the sole arbitrator or the president of the arbitral tribunal may be chosen from a country of which any of the parties is a national.[17]

As regards the party appointment, one can question whether it really is helpful or has any relevance if one chooses an arbitrator from the same country as the party. This might have the effect that the appointing party has more comfort in the ability of the tribunal to understand its position because it trusts that an arbitrator from its own country will be sensitive to that party's situation. However, this could be counterproductive if the two other arbitrators, who might be from neutral countries, would view their colleague critically because he would be considered not entirely impartial because of his nationality. More important is, however, and this will be a recurring theme of this chapter, that the person nominated is somebody who has the necessary skills to act in the matter, regardless of what country he or she is from.

It is a clear advantage and to be preferred if the sole arbitrator or president of the tribunal is from a neutral country. While exceptions might be made (and are admissible according to the quoted provisions of the SCC and ICC Rules), one should be reluctant to make such exceptions. Depending on how the arbitration develops, this issue might pop up, and then it might be too late to fix it. Thus, the objective criteria of the neutral nationality of the sole arbitrator and the president of the tribunal should generally not be violated.

[D] Qualifications

From time to time, parties who decide to—instead of relying on the model clause of the arbitration institution they choose—draft their own clause, establish requirements to be fulfilled by the prospective arbitrators. For example, they state that an arbitrator needs to have technical expertise (instead of being a lawyer), or experience as a business person in a particular field, such as pharmaceutical business. The author considers such clauses to be unfortunate. When concluding a contract, it is difficult or almost impossible to predict what a potential future dispute will be about. It could revolve around technical issues, legal issues, quantum questions, or others. Thus, the criteria established for the perspective arbitrators might not be a good match at all, and one would then wish to be able to appoint somebody with different qualifications or qualities.

However, if the clause has been concluded that way, to the extent it is at all possible, the criteria in the clause should be respected if possible (there have been examples where impossible conditions were set, for example, that the arbitrator be fluent in the Bulgarian language, but could not be a citizen of that country—to find such a person with the necessary arbitration and legal experience turned out to be impossible). Not adhering to conditions will create discussions and difficulties at the outset of the case, which will delay the adjudication of the matter. In any case, it is of considerable importance that at least one of the arbitrators, ideally the chair, has a legal

17. ICC Rules Art. 13(5).

background and experience in conducting arbitration. Otherwise, the proceedings could turn into a nightmare.

[E] Language

An arbitration proceeding will be conducted in one (or in rare instances in two) language, which is determined as follows:

> Unless agreed upon by the parties, the Arbitral Tribunal shall determine the language(s) of the arbitration. In so determining, the Arbitral Tribunal shall have due regard to all relevant circumstances and shall give the parties an opportunity to submit comments.[18]
>
> In the absence of an agreement by the parties, the arbitral tribunal shall determine the language or languages of the arbitration, due regard being given to all relevant circumstances, including the language of the contract.[19]

The definition of the language of the proceedings should be one of the essential elements of any arbitration agreement. Even if that has not been done, the Rules quoted above provide for a mechanism to determine it. The most obvious is the language of the contract, which often also coincides with the language in which the parties communicated prior to concluding the contract (and thereafter). In rare instances, a bilingual contract is concluded (often this is found in contracts involving Russian or Chinese parties), with the typical layout that the contractual document is split in the middle, with the Russian/Chinese version on the right and the English version on the left, or vice versa. Quite rarely, one then actually sees proceedings where the parties submit their submissions in two languages—certainly not ideal from any perspective.

For the topic of this chapter, the language in which the arbitration will be conducted is very important for the selection of an arbitrator. It is absolutely crucial that the arbitrator is sufficiently fluent, in writing and orally, to deal with the proceedings in that particular language. An arbitrator who is limited in that regard will suffer severe disadvantages both for the arbitrator himself and for the party who nominated him. First and foremost, his understanding of the arguments might be hampered, and even more importantly, his influence on the decision-making will be limited due to his partial or total inability to communicate and discuss with his fellow tribunal members.

[F] Specific Requirements in Arbitration Clause

As already mentioned briefly, there are basically two primary ways an arbitral tribunal can be constituted: Either by the parties themselves selecting a co-arbitrator each, and those two then (with or without consulting with the party) agreeing on a president. The other one is that this is largely done by the institution itself, either *ab initio* or if one

18. SCC Rules Art. 26(1).
19. ICC Rules Art. 20.

party fails to nominate an arbitrator or if the co-arbitrators are unable to agree on a president. In those instances, the institution fills the gap and makes sure that an arbitral tribunal can be confirmed.

There are, however, cases where the parties themselves in their arbitration clause agree on a more elaborate mechanism to end up with an arbitral tribunal. This is permissible, which is explicitly stated in the SCC Rules:

> The parties may agree on a procedure for appointment of the Arbitral Tribunal.[20]

I can present here an example of a very detailed agreement on the appointment process I encountered recently:

1. The two co-arbitrators will appoint the president of the tribunal on the following terms:
2. The president of the tribunal shall not be a national of country A, B, or C.
3. Each co-arbitrator shall propose the names of three candidates after having consulted his/her appointing party, within 14 calendar days from the last of the co-arbitrators' acknowledgment of this appointment process.
4. Once the list of six candidates is established, the candidates will be immediately contacted by the co-arbitrators (without disclosing which party proposed their names) to check their availability and absence of conflict of interest. If a candidate(s) is unable to proceed due to availability or conflict, the proposing co-arbitrator shall, after having consulted his/her appointing party and carrying out an availability and conflict check, put forward an alternative candidate(s). The list will then be amended accordingly, if needed. This step 4 shall take place within 14 calendar days from step 3.
5. The co-arbitrators will consolidate the list of six candidates, which will be issued to the Parties, within 3 calendar days from step 4.
6. Each of both Parties shall remove one name from the list of 6, leaving a list of four candidates, within 4 calendar days from step 5.
7. Each co-arbitrator shall, after carrying out an availability and conflict check and after having consulted his or her appointing Party, then include one candidate of his/her preference into the list of four candidates, thereby bringing the list to six candidates. The co-arbitrators shall circulate the list of six candidates to the Parties. This step 7 shall take place within 5 calendar days from step 6.
8. Each Party can vote for the candidates by order of preference (1 to 6, 1 being the most preferred to whom 6 preferential votes are assigned) and shall communicate its order of preference to its appointed co-arbitrator. To that end, Parties may consult with its appointed arbitrator. This step 8 shall take place within 7 calendar days from step 7.
9. Taking together the Parties' voting preferences, the co-arbitrators will circulate the results of the Parties' votes and appoint the most preferred candidate, within 3 calendar days from step 8.
10. In the event of deadlock (i.e., an equal number of preferential votes), the co-arbitrators will consult with counsel to seek to find consensus and agreement, within 7 calendar days from the circulation of the results of the Parties' votes in step 9.

20. SCC Rules Art. 17(1).

11. If no consensus/agreement can be reached within the aforesaid 7 calendar days, the Parties will request the ICC to make an appointment under Article 12.5 of the Rules.

If such a procedure has been contractually agreed, it amounts to an objective criterion, and I would strongly advise against not respecting it. Otherwise, again, the risk might arise that a later award can be subject to criticism and even invalidation.

[G] Importance of Objective Criteria

The above criteria for selecting an arbitrator, which I describe as objective, are of a nature which makes them mandatory to be observed and respected. It is simply not advisable to violate any of those criteria when picking an arbitrator because this will almost inevitably lead to problems one later wishes would have been avoided.

§3.03 SUBJECTIVE CRITERIA

[A] Nationality

In addition to mandatory rules governing the nationality of arbitrators (*see* above, **§3.02[C]**, there are, of course, other considerations that must be taken into account when selecting an arbitrator. Traditionally, parties had a tendency to nominate as their arbitrator a national of their own country. This attitude was more prevalent in non-western countries, where the choice of a compatriot was considered to be a safeguard that there would be somebody on the tribunal taking the position of that party fairly into account and making sure that the arguments of that party were not overlooked in the tribunal. Sometimes, this went even further; there are anecdotal examples of arbitrators who were far too close to the nominating party, which was outwardly reflected in joint traveling to hearings, staying at the same hotel, providing hints on how to plead the case, and sometimes even providing information out of the deliberations of the arbitral tribunal. All of this was of course not permitted, but it did happen. Such behavior has become increasingly rare in recent years, and arbitrators are much more aware and respectful of their impartiality and independence obligations than they were in the past.

In my view, the qualities of an arbitrator in terms of experience, knowledge of the applicable law, language skills and personality are far more important than nationality. The bigger the case, the more important it is to have an arbitrator who possesses the necessary qualities to be a non-negligible factor within the arbitral tribunal.

Sometimes, specific constellations might prompt the selection of somebody from a specific country. For example, if counsel consider intimate familiarity with the applicable substantive law to be important for the case, it certainly makes sense to choose an arbitrator of the nationality of that legal system. At the same time, if one would rather stay away from black-letter law (and focus more on the contract or oral agreements made by the parties), the opposite might apply. For the respondent, sometimes it might, as the case may be, be better to have a national from the same or from a different country than the co-arbitrator nominated by the claimant.

As far as sole arbitrators or presidents of the tribunal are concerned, neutrality requirements have already been mentioned. In addition, it often makes sense to have somebody who is familiar with the governing legal system in the narrow sense (national law) or a wider sense (common law/civil law) in order to guarantee a proper adjudication. Finally, a certain familiarity with the local law governing the procedure at the seat of the tribunal can be an advantage. Parties sometimes invoke local rules and argue that those rules are mandatory in order to influence procedural decisions to be taken by the tribunal. It is certainly helpful if at least one member of the arbitral tribunal is able to express an informed view on the merits of such an argument.

[B] Knowledge of Applicable Law

The advantage of arbitrators who know the applicable law has already been mentioned; this is inevitably a factor when taking decisions. However, as mentioned above, sometimes one considers the case to be quite independent of the applicable law, for example, in cases where a sophisticated contract has been concluded, and any reference to a possible applicable statutory provision might be undesired, or where the case is totally fact driven, and the law will not play a role at all.

[C] Expert in Specific Area of Law

More relevant than the national law might be the area of law. There are quite a lot of cases where experience with the practices of a specific sort of transaction is key—examples are post-M&A disputes, cases involving competition law, licensing agreements, IP disputes, complex construction cases, or gas price disputes.

Particularly, if there is an imbalance of the knowledge in the particular field between the arbitrators, it is conceivable that the arbitrator who has more specific knowledge will play a dominating role. The party who has appointed an arbitrator who cannot discuss on the same level as one or both co-arbitrators will be at a disadvantage.

Many arbitration practitioners have published articles or even books on arbitration or other legal topics, which reflect their views on specific issues. Parties are well advised to review such publications before they consider a candidate for an appointment. Particularly if debates on procedural questions are foreseeable, prudence dictates to make sure that the potential arbitrator has not formulated opinions on those issues which run counter to the interests of the party in question. Sometimes, interviews with an arbitrator (*see* below, **§3.04[D]**) are used to get an understanding of the candidates' views on legal issues. Such discussions are, in my view, already borderline, even if they remain at the surface of the legal issue because they might be perceived as an attempt to predetermine the arbitrator's view on legal questions that will become relevant in the framework of the arbitral decision.

For the sake of completeness, one should also mention that an arbitrator who has publicly advocated a specific position regarding the case that is being arbitrated, whether in a public paper or speech or otherwise, might also be subject to challenge, according to the IBA Guidelines.[21] This has to be distinguished from the publication of a general opinion (such as in a Law Review article or public lecture) concerning an issue which also arises in the arbitration if this opinion is not focused on the specific case, according to the IBA Guidelines.[22]

[D] Experience in Specific Types of Cases or Fields of Business

An example of cases where specific experience is helpful are, for example, gas-price or similar cases, complex construction disputes, M&A disputes, license and patent disputes and others.

The best evidence for such specific experience is if one has direct information about the candidate's involvement in arbitrations in the specific field, either from clients or trusted colleagues in one's own or a different law firm. Sometimes, however, such direct information is not available regarding a possible appointee who fulfills the other criteria discussed in this chapter.

Here is the place where one should mention tools that have appeared more recently on the market, namely the selection of data on arbitrators. One of the well known is Arbitrator Intelligence, a platform which describes its purpose as "enabling parties and counsel to share information and feedback about arbitrators."[23] The purpose of that organization's reports is to make arbitrator appointments more predictable and, thus, the arbitral process more effective by offering insights about arbitrators who might otherwise not be known, thus adding diversity, certainty and wisdom to the process of selection of arbitrators.[24] The database is still in the process of being built up, but it certainly has the potential to be an important and valuable tool when taking the decision on an arbitrator. For the time being, the information found in the database seems incomplete, and its use is rather expensive. The publishing house Kluwer also offers similar tools, such as "Profile Navigator and Relationship Indicator Tools," which provide access to profiles of arbitrators, expert witnesses and counsel.[25]

Moreover, there is a concern that some of the information provided might not always be fully reliable. There is a tendency to overstate one's experience in marketing materials, which is, for example, reflected in the description of a lawyer's background on his or her website. Therefore, such resources must be used with a grain of salt and should, in any case, be verified independently, for example, by counterchecking with colleagues who have worked with the particular individual, or by conducting an interview with the candidate (*see* below, E.4).

---

21. List 3.5.2.
22. List 4.1.1.
23. https://arbitratorintelligence.com.
24. As described by Gary Born, Chiann Bao and Mohamed S. Abdel Wahab in quotes on the above website of Arbitrator Intelligence.
25. https://www.wolterskluwer.com/en/solutions/kluwerarbitration/practical-tools.

[E] Reputation and Standing in the Arbitration Community

Arbitration is a field where there is a growing (but still rather limited) group of specialists who enjoy a good or excellent reputation as arbitrators. Ranking organizations such as Chambers, Legal500 and WWL add to the notoriety of leading specialists. While those well-known arbitrators used to be domiciled mainly at the places known as arbitration hubs, the geographical reach has expanded exponentially in recent years. The number of those people is still larger in places with a lively arbitration scene, such as London, Paris, Switzerland, Sweden, Singapore and others, and rather small in countries where arbitration is less prevalent. If one wants to have an arbitrator who plays a strong role within the tribunal, the choice of somebody with a strong reputation might be a risk-free decision.

[F] Age and Gender

Arbitration used to be the playing field for highly experienced, white-haired gentlemen. These times are definitely over, and gender diversity is probably greater than in most other fields of the law. Many highly reputed arbitrators are in their forties or early fifties, while, of course, there is still the occasional septuagenarian or even octogenarian who enjoys a lively practice. And certainly, age per se is no advantage or disadvantage, one way or the other. In any case, one might take into account that complex cases often go on for three or more years, and the biological clock is ticking. The practice of arbitration institutions shows that there is a non-negligible number of elderly arbitrators who, in the course of a case, have to be replaced for health reasons or even death. Therefore, it is prudent to at least mention to the client at the appointment stage that age might be something to consider.

Diversity is an important target for arbitral institutions, and the ratio of female arbitrators is regularly published by such institutions. Institutions are under pressure to contribute to diversity by taking into account not only gender but also geographical elements when making appointments. Whether and to what extent parties and counsel also have an obligation in that regard is open for debate. At the end of the day, what really counts for counsel is to find the best arbitrator for the case, whether male or female.

[G] Availability and Interest

Not only at the beginning of the case, but also during the document production phase, the time of the hearing, and when the award needs to be drafted, an arbitrator needs to devote considerable amounts of time to the case. Only an arbitrator who has the time necessary to fulfill these tasks will actually have an influence on the outcome of the case. As with all lawyers (and humans in general), there sometimes is the tendency for people to shoulder more than they can actually carry. From time to time, one hears about arbitrators who are in terrible delay with delivering awards and fulfilling their tasks, sometimes leading to sanctions and (as one hears) blacklisting of arbitrators by specific institutions. While such instances are rare, availability is definitely a factor to be considered. Thus, choosing the busiest arbitrator is not always the wisest decision. Particularly if the amount in dispute in a matter is not huge, there might be a danger that an arbitrator neglects the case and devotes his time to more lucrative work. This must be avoided. For smaller cases, it is thus recommendable to focus on younger arbitrators, who will make sure that they do a good job when they have an opportunity to prove themselves in one of their earlier appointments.

Positive are examples of arbitrators who decline appointments when they see that their calendar is already full and anticipate that they will not be able to devote sufficient time to a matter. While, as an immediate reaction, a party proposing somebody who then refuses the appointment for lack of time might be disappointed, this attitude is actually commendable.

Generally, the more interest an arbitrator has in a case, the better for the parties.

[H] Efficiency

Surveys among users of arbitration regularly show that one of the most important expectations is that a decision be rendered swiftly and without undue delay. Institutions therefore put particular focus on the requirement of efficiency. It is an important goal that cases are dealt with quickly, and thus, the Rules make this very clear:

> In all cases, the Arbitral Tribunal shall conduct the arbitration in an impartial, efficient, and expeditious manner, giving each party an equal and reasonable opportunity to present its case.[26]
>
> The final award shall be made no later than six months from the date the case was referred to the Arbitral Tribunal pursuant to Article 22. The Board may extend this time limit upon a reasoned request from the Arbitral Tribunal or if otherwise deemed necessary.[27]
>
> The arbitral tribunal and the parties shall make every effort to conduct the arbitration in an expeditious and cost-effective manner, having regard to the complexity and value of the dispute.[28]
>
> The time limit within which the arbitral tribunal must render its final award is six months. ... The Court may extend the time limit pursuant to a reasoned request from the arbitral tribunal or on its own initiative if it decides it is necessary to do so.[29]

One of the most important requirements for an arbitrator is that he or she actually has time to deal with the case. This is of particular importance for the chair or sole arbitrator because they are in charge of the most time-consuming tasks, namely the drafting of procedural orders and, ultimately, the final award. There is nothing more frustrating for parties who have conducted a case diligently than to wait for six or nine months, or even a year until they obtain a decision from the tribunal. Quite rightly,

26. SCC Rules Art. 23(2).
27. SCC Rules Art. 43.
28. ICC Rules Art. 22(1).
29. ICC Rules Art 31(1).

institutions are concerned about such situations. The ICC, for example, has developed a practice according to which fees of the tribunal are reduced by at least 5% or 10% if the deadline of three months to submit an award to the ICC Court for scrutiny is not respected. The reduction is adjusted depending on the amount of delay, taking into account not only the delay but also possible special circumstances.[30]

[I] Prior Experience

The best basis to appoint a particular arbitrator is of course if one has prior experience with the colleague in an earlier case, be it as counsel before the arbitrator or sitting together on a panel. To see an arbitrator dealing with a case will provide you with a firsthand impression of how that person works and handles a case and is a very reliable basis to make a recommendation to the client.

If one does not have direct experience with somebody, professional colleagues might be a valid source for descriptions of firsthand experiences. Colleagues are usually more than willing to share experiences, certainly, if they were particularly good or particularly bad. "Blind" appointments of somebody one has never heard about, but is recommended by the client or somebody else whose judgment one does not trust, is rather dangerous and normally not to be recommended.

§3.04 SOLE ARBITRATOR AND PRESIDENT OF THE ARBITRAL TRIBUNAL

[A] Specific Profile

Sole arbitrators and presidents of the arbitral tribunal require specific qualities. They are the ones leading the arbitration; in the case of a sole arbitrator, he or she will be the sole decider of the matter, and in the case of the president, the swing vote creates a majority.

To illustrate the multiple tasks of the presiding arbitrator or sole arbitrator, reference can be made to a recent LinkedIn post of Finnish arbitrator Gisela Knuts after a hearing, describing the tasks she had to tackle during that hearing: Instruct the witness on the procedure during the examination; follow the examination and take notes of potential questions; examine the exhibits shown to the witness and take notes of points made; rule on objections raised by counsel; follow live notes on the screen in front of you; manage potential questions from the co-arbitrators; keep track of the time; and doing all of this while the witness might be speaking in a language you do not understand with the simultaneous translation in your other ear.[31]

30. For details, *see* https://iccwbo.org/news-publications/news/icc-court-announces-new-policies-to-foster-transparency-and-ensure-greater-efficiency/#:~:text=for%20draft%20awards%20submitted%20for,reduced%20by%205%20to%2010%25.
31. https://www.linkedin.com/feed/update/urn:li:activity:7057755665452171265?updateEntityUrn=urn%3Ali%3Afs_feedUpdate%3A%28V2%2Curn%3Ali%3Aactivity%3A7057755665452171265%29.

In order to end up with a chair or sole arbitrator who is up for the job, the following are a few points to be considered.

[B] Heightened Expectation of Neutrality

It has already been mentioned that, as a matter of principle, the neutrality requirement is the same for all arbitrators—independence and impartiality are expected, and there is no tolerance in that regard for the party-appointed arbitrator.

However, strict neutrality is of course even more important for the arbitrator who might turn out to be the decider, not only when it comes to taking a decision but also in procedural matters. The sole arbitrator or president is expected to have no tendency towards one or the other party whatsoever.

[C] Experience

The sole arbitrator and president of the tribunal will be the ones drafting the decision. An arbitral award has to fulfill certain expectations:

> The Arbitral Tribunal shall make its award in writing, and, unless otherwise agreed by the parties, shall state the reasons upon which the award is based.[32]
>
> The award shall state the reasons upon which it is based.[33]

Drafting of arbitral awards is a difficult task and requires some experience. Since the quality of the award might be the factor determining whether it withstands scrutiny (of the arbitral institution, of courts to which one can appeal, or at the enforcement stage), both in terms of language, structure, and stringency of the reasoning. Only arbitrators whom one can expect will be able to discharge that task are good choices for sole arbitrators or presidents.

[D] Case Management Abilities

To run an arbitration can be as easy as a walk in the park—if the counsel are constructive and experienced, parties sincerely interested in a speedy resolution of the case, the co-arbitrators interested, diligent and easy to get along with, and the case neither factually nor legally overly complex. Those cases are the exception. Proceedings get more and more complex, parties and counsel create difficulties where there should not be any, production of documents, challenges, counsel changes, COVID-19 pandemic, remote hearings, sanctions—all of these factors contribute to an impression that there are no easy cases anymore.

In order to deal with those difficulties, something that you might simply summarize as experience is crucial. Some arbitrators have a natural ability to deal with

32. SCC Rules Art. 42(1).
33. ICC Rules Art. 32(2).

the procedural intricacies of a case, and others have it less. Clearly, the sole arbitrator or president is the person who has to manage the case and bring it forward and do everything to lead it to an efficient end.

If the parties have an influence, they should do everything to make sure that whoever ends up in the driver's seat knows what he or she is doing. This is one of the many reasons why it is sometimes risky to leave the choice of arbitrator to an institution instead of trying hard to agree with the other side on somebody both sides trust.

[E] Personality and Social Competence and Leadership Qualities

Everybody who has to lead a group of people, in every walk of life, is better at doing so if he or she has leadership skills and an impressive personality to establish him or herself as a natural leader. Social competence will help in dealing with difficult situations in the proceedings, of which there are usually quite a few, not only during case management conferences and hearings, but also within the arbitral tribunal, where the struggle to come to a decision can result in a burden on the relationships of the arbitrators.

[F] Infrastructure and Resources

There are two elements here that need to be considered. The first one is the technical infrastructure and the second are resources to deal with a case. An arbitrator who can use a secretary or assistant to the tribunal will be able to react quicker than somebody who types procedural orders himself. To have an office where one can hold case management conferences (or even hearings) is also helpful. This is not so important for the party-appointed arbitrator, but might be a factor when choosing a chair or sole arbitrator. In the old days, sometimes university professors were notoriously underequipped in that regard. Nowadays, this seems to be less of an issue.

§3.05 ETHICAL ISSUES

[A] Arbitrator from Country of a Party

It has already been mentioned that there are instances where the identity of the origin of a party and the arbitrator has turned out to be problematic. Far be it for the author to generalize here.

[B] Relationships with Arbitrator

One of the most frequent bases for a (successful) challenge is that an arbitrator had a too close relationship with counsel or the appointing party. Therefore, it might not be advisable to appoint the best friend or a former attorney of a party, even if one considers that not to be a problematic relationship. A challenge where more comes to light than what was anticipated is unpleasant and might derail the whole proceedings.

[C] Multiple Appointments

The same applies to multiple appointments. Rules are quite restrictive; for example, the already mentioned IBA Guidelines consider problematic if the arbitrator has, within the past three years, been appointed as arbitrator on two or more occasions by one of the parties or an affiliate of one of the parties;[34] the arbitrator currently serves, or has served within the past three years, as arbitrator in another arbitration on a related issue involving one of the parties,[35] and the arbitrator has within the past three years received more than three appointments by the same counsel or the same law firm.[36] It is shocking that sometimes arbitrators are quite reluctant to be transparent as regards multiple appointments and provide incomplete information; this is unacceptable and has, in recent times, led to the disqualification of arbitrators who were overly restrictive in disclosing circumstances of this kind.

[D] Interviews with Potential Arbitrator?

In some cases, parties wish to conduct an interview with a potential arbitrator. This is an area where one should tread carefully. While a 30- to 60-minute conversation about the experience of the potential arbitrator is acceptable, any direct discussion of the case is not. The Chartered Institute of Arbitrators has developed an enlightening guideline entitled "Interviews for Prospective Arbitrators."[37] It emphasizes that while "Interviews with prospective arbitrators prior to appointments allow parties to obtain a more complete picture of candidates," an interview also "carries risks that may be perceived as undermining the arbitrators' impartiality and independence."[38]

Matters that can be discussed, according to the Guideline, are past experience and attitudes to the conduct of arbitral proceedings; expertise in the subject matter of the dispute; availability; and (in cases of ad hoc arbitrations) the prospective arbitrator's fees and other terms of appointment.[39] What should not be discussed, however, are specific facts or circumstances of the dispute; positions or arguments of the parties; the merits of the case; and/or the prospective arbitrator's views on the merits, arguments and claims.[40] The Guideline also makes clear that interviews with

34. List 3.1.3.
35. List 3.1.5.
36. List 3.3.7.
37. https://www.ciarb.org/media/4185/guideline-1-interviews-for-prospective-arbitrators-2015.pdf, with interesting commentaries.
38. Guideline, p. 14.
39. Guideline, Art. 2.
40. Guideline, Art. 3.

prospective sole or presiding arbitrators are subject to specific restrictions, in particular, that they should be interviewed by parties jointly.[41]

[E] Chemistry Between Arbitrators

A good tribunal is one where an open and constructive discussion is possible. Arbitrators who like and respect each other are more likely to come up with a wise and balanced decision than a fractioned tribunal that is barely on speaking terms. Therefore, it is quite appropriate to inquire with a potential arbitrator about his or her experience with colleagues who are already on the tribunal. At the same time, the president of a tribunal will certainly take into account, when considering whether to accept an appointment, if he can imagine working with the two co-arbitrators based on prior experience.

[F] High Profile Arbitrators

Clients sometimes want the best-known and famous arbitrator for their case because they consider that this will be helpful for their position. For reasons already briefly mentioned earlier, this might not always be the best approach. An arbitrator who is sufficiently experienced for a specific case and has enough time and interest to devote to the matter is better than a high-profile arbitrator who does not devote sufficient time. Therefore, one should always look at the case and determine what level of experience and reputation of the arbitrator is really required and appropriate.

[G] Institutional Support for Diversity and Youth

The ICC states the following:

> Increasing diversity and inclusion has been a key priority for ICC Court President Claudia Salomon since she took over the leadership position in 2021, Ms Salomon said 'Arbitrator diversity in all forms is essential to the legitimacy of international arbitration by ensuring that the arbitrators represented in cases reflect the diversity—and values—of the global business community.' [...] 'In house counsel, outside counsel and co-arbitrators all have a crucial role to play if we are able to see a sizable increase in the diversity of arbitrators,' Ms Salomon said.[42]

There is not much to add here; the goal of broadening the diversity base for arbitrators goes in the right direction, and the already successful attempt to open up arbitrator positions for younger practitioners is positive.

Whether and under what circumstances counsel follow the guidance given by the ICC is a decision to be taken on a case-by-case basis. Ultimately, it is the decision of the client who is chosen as party-appointed arbitrator, taking into account all the

41. Guideline, Art. 4.
42. https://iccwbo.org/news-publications/news/icc-acts-to-encourage-diversity-in-selection-of-arbitrators/.

parameters discussed in this chapter. I would certainly support that when discussing potential candidates, counsel who advise clients present a broad range of potential arbitrators, ranging from diverse backgrounds and do not focus on a narrow group of people from the outset.

[H] UK-Specific: Arbitrators from the Same Chambers

While it is hardly conceivable that parties would choose or an institution would confirm a tribunal where two of the arbitrators are from the same law firm (at least, I have never seen something like that in practice), it is not unusual that arbitrators from one of the London chambers act in cases where other barristers from the same chambers act as counsel, for example. Interestingly, such a situation is accepted based on the argument that chambers are not law firms, and members of the same chambers do not share income. This view raises certain questions, to say the least. In particular, the historical setup of chambers, where indeed the various barristers operating from the same building shared nothing but paid for their room and the work of the clerk but were otherwise totally independent, is hardly reflective of the actual situation. Nowadays, leading chambers have a homepage where all the barristers are listed and where they praise their collective experience, very similar to law firms. Thus, at least in my view, one can hardly maintain the fiction of total independence. Whether and to what extent the choice of an arbitrator from the same chambers as counsel is advisable or not is open for debate. One could at least imagine that, in the enforcement stage, such a setting would raise some serious eyebrows.

§3.06 SUMMARY AND RECOMMENDATION

As this chapter has tried to demonstrate, there is a multitude of parameters that can and should be taken into account when exercising a party's right to appoint an arbitrator or to participate in the discussion regarding a president or sole arbitrator. This task must be taken seriously, and tackled without delay once a case starts, because deadlines are running, and inquiries with potential candidates may take time to conduct conflict checks and examine the candidates in detail.

I would suggest the following procedure to find a party-appointed arbitrator:

- Starting point is a careful analysis of the case regarding the parameters discussed in this contribution (subject matter of the actual dispute, amount in dispute, applicable law, venue, nationality of the parties, arbitrator appointed by the other party).
- Preliminary definition of a profile of the candidates.
- Discussion and alignment with the client on the profile.
- Establish a long list of candidates fitting the profile (at least ten).
- Conduct research on the candidates from publicly available sources.
- Narrow down the list of candidates to five, always in consultation with the client.

- Contact the candidates with a view to their availability for the case.
- Further research on the candidates on the short list, contacting colleagues to get feedback, and possibly conduct interviews.
- Decision on candidate and appointment.

If a sole arbitrator or president needs to be found, it is crucial to start the process with a discussion between counsel (for a sole arbitrator) or the two co-arbitrators. The aim is to agree on a fair and transparent process, which allows both sides to end up being comfortable with the arbitrator ultimately chosen. As mentioned above, it is always preferable to agree on an acceptable sole arbitrator or chair than to insist on a particular type of candidate, not to come to an agreement and then to delegate the decision to the institution. This does not mean, however, that one should simply accept a candidate proposed by the other side if that proposal is unreasonable and unacceptable.

CHAPTER 4

Straddling the Divide Between Lawful and Unlawful Expropriation in International Law

Christer Söderlund

§4.01 INTRODUCTION

A basic tenet of customary international law is that the taking of privately-held property is a legitimate exercise of state power, provided specific criteria as to public purpose, non-discrimination, due process and compensation are met. In other words, an act of expropriation which fulfils these criteria is lawful, and, as a consequence, does not engage the state's responsibility for what is termed as an internationally wrongful act. However, if one or more of these criteria is lacking, the taking will be unlawful. This will bring into cause the responsibility of the state which follows from the commission of an internationally wrongful act.

At the heart of actual adjudication of investment disputes based on allegations of unlawful expropriation is, without exception, the matter of absent compensation. At first glance, it may seem that the principles dealing with compensation to the investor who has suffered deprivation of its property are not affected by whether the expropriatory act is qualified as lawful or unlawful. However, in actual fact, there are significant distinctions both as regards the legal qualification to be undertaken and the methodology to be applied. These distinctions may bring about widely differing economic outcomes in a particular case (while they also – despite the application of quite distinct methodologies – may result in much the same economic outcome).

§4.02 EXPROPRIATORY ACTION BY SOVEREIGNS: A BRIEF BACKGROUND

The taking of private property of 'aliens' by sovereigns has taken on different guises throughout recent history. A hundred years ago, foreign investors experienced a total and irreparable deprivation in across-the-board nationalizations in the wake of revolutionary societal transformations (Russia, Mexico). Later on - in the period of decolonization post-WWII - such state measures usually consisted in the taking of foreign stakeholders' investments in the extraction of hydrocarbon and other mineral resources.[1]

Since late 1950, a considerable part of the expropriation debate was conducted within the UN in the context of 'permanent sovereignty over natural resources'. This led to some controversy starting in the second half of the sixties, leading to, *inter alia*, the 1973 UN General Assembly Resolution 71 and Article 2(2) of the 1974 Charter of Economic Rights and Duties of States (also a UN General Assembly Resolution). Essentially, these resolutions affirmed the right of states to determine the matter of compensation and the right of their national judiciaries to deal with these issues (and, *a fortiori*, strongly condemned the so-called gun-boat diplomacy of earlier times).

Even if these United Nations resolutions do not have force of law, they certainly created uncertainty as to the continued applicability of the legality requirements, in particular as regards the level of compensation. This, in turn, brought about the need (experienced by developed, capital-exporting countries) to explicitly deal with the legal requirements to be satisfied in order for an expropriation to be lawful in investment treaties. However, as a general proposition, it is fair to say that the language of BITs only articulate a codification of customary international law.

In recent decades, expropriatory action has taken on more insidious forms where, in essence, formal title to assets is retained by the investor but where - though legislative and regulatory action - the value of the investment is rendered nugatory (i.e., by the withdrawal of a manufacturing licence well before its expiry date). Such action is usually referred to as 'indirect expropriation' or as 'creeping' expropriation, where a series of successive legislative or regulatory acts, or gradual measures of physical dispossession, title to the invested assets eventually becomes economically meaningless.[2]

Generally speaking, outright expropriation rarely occurs nowadays. Cases in recent decades regularly involve what the investor sees as indirect expropriations but where the state party considers that the measures constitute the legitimate exercise of

1. *BP Exploration Co. (Libya) Ltd. v. Libyan Arab Rep.*, 53 ILR 297, 337-340 (1973); *Texas Overseas Petroleum Co. (TOPCO) v. Libyan Arab Rep.*, 17 ILM 1 (1977); *The Libyan American Oil Company v. Libya* (1977) and *Kuwait v. American Independent Oil Company* (1982); *Libyan American Oil Co. (Liamco) v. Libya*, 20 ILM 1, 59, 61 (1981); *State of Kuwait v. American Independent Oil Co.*, 21 ILM 976, 1024 (1982).
2. Such composite state conduct is foreseen in Art. 15 of the ILC Articles: '15. Breach consisting of a composite act 1. The breach of an international obligation by a State through a series of actions or omissions defined in aggregate as wrongful occurs when the action or omission occurs which, taken with the other actions or omissions, is sufficient to constitute the wrongful act.'

legislative or regulatory authority. As a consequence, no compensation has been offered to the investor, resulting in a large number of investment disputes. Therefore, many investment disputes will unfold in the twilight zone between the state's legitimate regulatory action and unlawful takings.

However, recently and exceptionally, there has been a string of cases dealing, again, with old-style, full-scale expropriations following Russia's unlawful annexation of the Crimean peninsula in 2014. As a consequence, certain Ukrainian entities with establishments (also) in this territory have raised investment claims under the Ukraine-Russia BIT for the loss of assets in Crimea. Russia has chosen not to take part in these proceedings but has resisted jurisdiction on the basis that the relevant BIT covers only investments after 2014 (when the investments attained a 'cross-border' character). As far as I know, in all cases,[3] the tribunals have found in favour of jurisdiction and setting aside actions (in Geneva and Paris) have so far been unsuccessful.

These cases offer certain points of interest as they call for the application of the investment treaty in circumstances which were certainly not anticipated by the drafters and for which it was not designed: The investments were domestic (Ukrainian) investments when made but under Russian de facto control by force of a land grab in breach of international law[4] and not susceptible of recognition by the international community.

§4.03 COMPENSATION UNDER CUSTOMARY INTERNATIONAL LAW

One may not say that the situation under customary international law is altogether settled and precise as to the criteria that render an expropriation lawful. While requirements as to public purpose, non-discrimination, due process and compensation are hardly controversial, different views have been expressed as to the standard of compensation and modalities of payment. While the leading *Factory at Chorzow* case (which concerned an unlawful expropriation) expressed, in passing, that compensation in cases of lawful expropriation should be limited to 'the value of the company at the time of dispossession, plus interest to the date of payment', voices have been heard in favour of a lower standard of compensation,[5] or even, in the context of large scale nationalizations, no compensation at all (invoking the national treatment standard).

There is no reason to believe that the situation under customary international law will be much clarified in the future. This is for the reason that the adjudication of standards and methodologies for determining compensation and other criteria will not

3. *Aeroport Belbek LLC and Mr. Igor Valerievich Kolomoisky v. Russia*; *PJSC CB PrivatBank and Finance Company Finilon LLC v. Russia*; *PJSC Ukrnafta v. Russia*; *Stabil LLC et al. v. Russia*; *Everest Estate LLC et al. v. Russia*; *Lugzor LLC et al. v. Russia*; *PJSC Oschadbank v. Russia*; *NJSC Naftogaz of Ukraine et al. v. Russia*; *PJSC DTEK Krymenergo v. Russia*.
4. A peremptory norm of international law, codified in Art. 2(4) of the UN Charter: 'All Members shall refrain in their international relations from the threat or use of force against the territorial integrity or political independence of any state [...].'
5. *See*, for instance, M. Sornarajah, The International Law on Foreign Investment (2nd ed., CUP 2008) at 149 'Within the context of the rules on expropriation, the issue whether full compensation represents international law has remained a contested proposition.'

proceed on the basis of customary international law but will be premised on specific treaty language on what constitutes a lawful expropriation in any particular case. An investment tribunal acting under a particular treaty will not – in the absence of a specific mandate – be competent to determine the modalities of a *lawful* expropriation; the language in the treaty on what constitutes a lawful expropriation will only serve the purpose of providing a benchmark for deciding whether a certain impugned state measure in a particular case constitutes an *unlawful* expropriation or not.

§4.04 THE MANNER IN WHICH INVESTMENT TREATIES DEAL WITH EXPROPRIATION

Paradoxically, investment protection treaties do include, without exception, more or less elaborate guidelines for the determination of the value of expropriated assets in cases of *lawful* expropriation. However, on the subject of unlawful expropriation, the treaties remain silent.

From this follows the odd consequence that investment tribunals are not provided with any guidance in the treaty text on how to deal with different questions which arise from a finding of an expropriatory measure's unlawfulness. The language which is provided on the subject of lawful expropriations in the treaty can be used only for purposes of determining whether certain state conduct complained of in a particular case fits the bill for lawfulness or not. It *does not* provide guidance to determine compensation in case of unlawful expropriations. This gives rise to a series of quandaries as regards the standard of valuation, choice of valuation methodology, time of valuation and a host of related issues.

In view of the treaties' silence, these quandaries have to be resolved by seeking out principles of customary international law, which, in turn, raises issues where customary international law does not provide clear-cut answers. Examples of such questions are: what methodology shall be applied to satisfy the criterion of 'reparation' or 'fair market value'? Do criteria such as 'going concern', 'track record of profit generation', 'proven' or 'speculative' projections affect the choice of methodology? At what date shall the valuation take place? Is there a right of choice between different dates of valuation open to the investor? May parties refrain from asking for fulfilment of the primary remedy of restitution under international law? Can a hypothetical sale of the investment by the investor to a third party serve as a proper measure of 'reparation'? What about issues such as currency of compensation, principles and rates of interest accrual? May circumstances *post factum* occurring or coming to light after the event(s) of expropriation be taken into consideration?

This state of things may explain the diversity of approaches that tribunals have chosen when confronted with a kaleidoscope of issues unfolding in different sets of factual circumstances.

§4.05 LAWFUL EXPROPRIATION IN AN INVESTMENT TREATY CONTEXT

Investment tribunals need not take a position on the lawfulness of expropriations under customary international law. The reason for this is that the criteria for lawfulness are, unexceptionally, laid down in the investment treaty itself (which of course also is the instrument that vests the tribunal with jurisdiction). It is these criteria which have to be reviewed for purposes of determining the (un)lawfulness of the state measure (this is mostly a distinction without substance as investment treaties reflect what their drafters perceive as the position of customary international law).

It may be described as a remarkable fact that investment protection treaties do not deal with unlawful expropriation at all. Instead, such treaties, as stated above, unexceptionally include language that describes, in lesser or greater detail, what is required for an expropriation to be *lawful*.

An example of criteria for a lawful expropriation articulated in a treaty text may be taken from the Finland-Brazil BIT:

> **Article 5**
>
> Expropriation (1) Investments of investors of each Contracting Party shall not be nationalized, expropriated or subjected to measures having a similar effect (hereinafter referred to as 'expropriation') in the territory of the other Contracting Party, unless the measures are taken in the public interest on a non-discriminatory basis, under due process of law and provided that provisions have been made for effective, prompt and adequate compensation. (2) Such compensation shall amount to the fair market value of the investment, immediately before the measures of expropriation or impending expropriation was taken or became public knowledge, whichever is earlier. The compensation shall be effected in a freely convertible currency and it shall also include interest at London Interbank Offered Rate (Libor) from the date of expropriation until the date of payment. (3) When a Contracting Party expropriates assets of a company or an enterprise in its territory, which is constituted under its laws, and in which investors of the other Contracting Party own shares, stocks or other interests or rights, the provisions of this Article shall apply to ensure prompt, adequate and effective compensation for those investors for any impairment or diminishment of the market value of such investment resulting from the expropriation.

So, the important conclusion to make is that the jurisdiction of an investment tribunal, acting under an investment treaty, does not extend to the adjudication of the economic consequences of a *lawful* expropriation. The description of what constitutes a lawful expropriation, found in any treaty, only serves the function as a point of reference for purposes of deciding whether certain state action constitutes a lawful or an unlawful expropriation.

§4.06 THE THRESHOLD ISSUE OF THE LAWFULNESS OF THE EXPROPRIATORY MEASURE

As a result of the treaties' structural approach to dealing with allegations concerning unlawful expropriations will limit the avenues open to the tribunal: The threshold issue with which a tribunal is faced is to determine if whatever conduct the state has conducted reaches the level of unlawfulness and, hence, engages the state's responsibility under international law. This enquiry may eventuate in a finding of lawfulness – according to the criteria laid down in the particular treaty – which puts an end to the enquiry or unlawfulness, in which case the enquiry has to be continued. Importantly, the treaty language does not mandate the tribunal to decide – in the place of the host state – what the fair market value (or any other substantive requirement) should be in order to render the expropriation lawful. If the tribunal does not agree with the host state's assertion regarding the impugned state measures' lawfulness, it may only conclude that the expropriatory act was unlawful and proceed accordingly.

§4.07 DOES ABSENT COMPENSATION RENDER THE EXPROPRIATION UNLAWFUL?

Expropriation cases are almost without exception brought to the attention of investment tribunals because state interference leading to impairment or extinction of the investor's business has not been assuaged by compensation, let alone an offer of payment. Not to put too fine a point on it, one may assume that the average investor is less concerned about formal defects in the expropriation process (such as public purpose or due process) as long as it considers itself adequately compensated.

A question that has arisen in adjudicatory practice is if the absence of 'prompt, effective and adequate compensation' (or whatever equivalent description is used in the particular treaty) still makes the expropriation (conditionally) lawful. One would think that the requirement laid down in the investment treaty compels the conclusion that this renders the expropriation unlawful. This has also been concluded in a line of cases.[6]

However, scholars have not seldom argued that expropriations only wanting compensation should still be considered legal. If an expropriation were to be considered illegal as soon as no compensation is granted, then the consequence, according to a prominent legal scholar, would be that in cases in which an expropriation meets all the conditions for a legal expropriation except for a determination of the tribunal that the host State had not paid market value for the property expropriated such an expropriation would have to be considered 'illegal' and compensation would therefore be awarded not on the basis of the valuation standard in the treaty but on the basis of the Chorzów Factory principle and customary international law. It is suggested that such a result would not accord with the intention of the Contracting Parties, as

6. *Wena v. Egypt*, para. 100; *Vivendi v. Argentina*; *Rumeli v. Kazakhstan*.

evidenced by the treaty text.[7] There are also exceptions to this clear reading of the treaty language applied by investment tribunals.

For instance, in the *Goetz* case, lack of payment did not render the expropriation unlawful.[8] This case concerned the revocation of a licence to process precious metals in a free trade area of Burundi. The treaty (Belgium-Burundi BIT) included a customary expropriation provision, stating, specifically, that compensation should reflect the market value of the assets (if the investor could not establish a higher value) and that payment was to be effected 'without delay' in transferable currency.[9] Although no payment was offered, let alone paid by Burundi (the revocation occurred on 29 May 1995, and the award (confirming a settlement between the Parties) was issued on 29 January 1999), the tribunal opined[10] that the matter of lawfulness remained suspended ('*reste en suspens*''] awaiting the state's decision to either effect payment or to reinstate the licence. One may well question this view, pragmatic as it may be, considering that payment had certainly not been made 'without delay' and that the unlawfulness was, therefore, already perfected.[11]

In *Tidewater*, which concerned revocation of rights to operate a deep-water oil exploration, the tribunal arrogated to itself the right to determine the value of the expropriated assets on the assumption that the expropriation was lawful despite the absence of compensation. It differed from other cases insofar as an offer had been made by the state to compensate the 'book value' of the operations which, in the claimant's view, did not represent 'adequate' compensation. The tribunal concluded that 'an expropriation wanting only a determination of compensation by an international tribunal is not to be treated as an illegal expropriation'.[12] The tribunal considered that such determination fell within its jurisdiction on the basis of Article 8 of the Barbados-Venezuela BIT.[13]

However, the requirements laid down in Article 5 of the BIT, among others that compensation shall amount to the 'market value of the investment' to be paid on a 'prompt, adequate and effective' basis, are objective criteria to be used by the tribunal for determining the(un)lawfulness – they are not matters for the tribunal to give substantive content (i.e., determine the scope of the state's primary obligations). This applies, *a fortiori*, in this case, as the dispute resolution provisions provide that '[t]he arbitral award shall be limited to determining whether there is a breach by the Contracting Party concerned of its obligations under this Agreement, whether such breach of obligations has caused damages to the national concerned, and if such is the case, the amount of compensation'.[14,15]

---

7. Jeswald W. Salacuse, The Law of Investment Treaties (Oxford University Press 2009), 328.
8. *Goetz et al. v. Burundi*, Case No. ARB/95/3, Award 10 February 1999 (the 'Goetz Award').
9. Belgium-Burundi Treaty, Art. 4(1)(c) and Art. 4(2).
10. The Goetz Award, para. 131.
11. As the Parties settled the case, one may also question why a pronouncement by the tribunal on the state action's (un)lawfulness was necessary in the first place.
12. *Tidewater et al. v. Venezuela*, Award, 13 March 2015, ICSID Case No. ARB/10/5, para. 140 (the 'Tidewater Award').
13. The Tidewater Award, para. 82.
14. Barbados-Venezuela BIT, Article 8(3).

As another example may be quoted he proposition advanced by the tribunal in the Venezuela Holdings case:[16]

> 301. It is not disputed that the Claimants did not receive compensation and that Venezuela did not fulfil its obligation to pay compensation in accordance with Article 6(c) of the BIT. However, the mere fact that an investor has not received compensation does not in itself render an expropriation unlawful.

According to the applicable treaty (the Netherlands-Venezuela BIT), Art 6 (c), payment was to be effected 'without delay'.

The above findings of absent payment not rendering an expropriation unlawful may be contrasted with the *Crystallex v. Venezuela* Award:[17]

> 716. Finally, pursuant to Article VII(1) of the Treaty, expropriation must be accompanied by 'prompt, adequate and effective compensation'. It is undisputed that no such compensation was either paid or offered to Crystallex. When a treaty cumulatively requires several conditions for a lawful expropriation, arbitral tribunals seem uniformly to hold that failure of any one of those conditions entails a breach of the expropriation provision.

Fortunately, the Crystallex award is only one of a long line of cases which have concluded - in line with the 'ordinary meaning'[18] of the treaty language - that the absence of compensation renders the expropriation unlawful.[19]

The question of whether, under customary international law, the absence of payment may not render an expropriation unlawful may be left to the side. A tribunal will have to seek guidance in the relevant treaty. If that treaty includes the customary

15. While treating the expropriation as a lawful one (e.g., the Award, para. 162) the tribunal proceeded to determine compensation on a DCF basis with an, in all likelihood, materially appropriate outcome.
16. *Venezuela Holdings v. Venezuela*, ICSID Case No. ARB/07/27, Award of 9 October 2014.
17. ICSID Case No. ARB(AF)/11/2.
18. Article 31(1) of the Vienna Convention on the Law of Treaties (VCLT).
19. *See, e.g., Funnekotter et al. v. Zimbabwe*, ICSID Case No. ARB/05/6, Award, 22 April 2009, para. 98 ('The Tribunal observes that the conditions enumerated in Article 6 are cumulative. In other terms, if any of those conditions is violated, there is a breach of Article 6.'); *Saluka Investments BV v. Czech Republic*, PCA/UNCITRAL, Partial Award, 17 March 2006, para. 266 (noncompliance with one or more of the conditions set out in Article 5 of the treaty would lead to the conclusion that the respondent has breached Article 5 of the Treaty); *Kardassopoulos v. Georgia*, ICSID Case Nos ARB/05/18 and ARB/07/15, Award, 28 February 2010, para. 390 (noting that absence of due process is sufficient to support a finding that the expropriation was wrongful); *Compañía de Aguas del Aconquija SA and Vivendi Universal SA v. Argentina*, ICSID Case No. ARB/97/3, Award, 20 August 2007, para. 7.5.21 (lack of compensation makes an expropriation unlawful); *Siag and Vecchi v. Egypt*, ICSID Case No. ARB/05/15, Award, 11 May 2009, para. 428; *Unglaube v. Costa Rica*, ICSID Case Nos ARB/08/1 and ARB/09/20, Award, 16 May 2012, para. 305; *Gemplus and Talsud v. Mexico*, ICSID Case Nos ARB(AF)/04/3 and ARB (AF)/04/4, Award, 16 June 2010, para. 8-25 ('The Tribunal concludes that these expropriations were unlawful under the BITs and international law, given the facts found by the Tribunal and the further fact that the Respondent did not meet the condition required by Article 5 of both treaties regarding the payment of adequate compensation.').

'prompt, adequate and effective' (or equivalent) language[20] as regards compensation, the absence of payment will, without further, render the expropriation unlawful. One cannot, either, ignore the paramount importance of this requirement to the investor, who may be less concerned about the public purpose or due process requirements of any particular course of conduct pursued by the host state.

There are rare cases where the host state actually offered compensation[21] but where the payment was not made, for instance, because the investor did not accept the amount for not, in its estimation, adequately compensating its loss. One would consider that such a situation would constitute a breach as the ensuing situation is not one where 'prompt'[22] payment occurs.

However, it is reasonable to accept as best practice what has been summarized in the Goetz Award that, if all other conditions for a lawful taking have been met, the failure to pay prompt and adequate compensation does not suffice 'to taint this measure as illegal under international law'.[23] Ripinsky and Williams state that 'a good faith offering of, or provision for, compensation (even if not in a sufficient amount, as long as not manifestly unreasonable) should render the expropriation lawful'. Marboe concludes: 'While earlier the mere "promise" of a State to pay any sum at any time was not enough for the lawfulness of an expropriation, today there seems to be consensus that it is sufficient, if a State, at the time of the expropriation, offers compensation or provides for the determination of compensation ... .' One may, therefore, conclude that according to arbitral practice and scholarly writing, 'the mere existence of a dispute about the amount of compensation does not render the expropriation unlawful'.[24] Cf. the position where the State makes no offer of compensation at all[25] or offers an amount that is so negligible as not to be in made in good faith (as in *Rumeli v. Kazakhstan*: 'the valuation [...] was manifestly and grossly inadequate', eventuating in a finding that the expropriation was unlawful.[26]

§4.08 THE CONSEQUENCES OF AN UNLAWFUL EXPROPRIATION UNDER INTERNATIONAL LAW

If an investment tribunal concludes that the host state's act amounts to an unlawful expropriation, it has to determine the legal consequences that this finding gives rise to.

20. This language is culled from a diplomatic note from US Secretary of State Cordell Hull to his Mexican counterpart Eduardo Hay in 1938 as a response to widespread expropriations carried out in the course of the Mexican land reform.
21. The Tidewater Award, para. 135.
22. '8. Compensation will be deemed to be "prompt" in normal circumstances if paid without delay. [...]' (World Bank Guidelines).
23. The Goetz Award, para. 130 ('Le Tribunal ne considère toutefois pas que cette circonstance suffit à entacher d'illicéité internationale la mesure litigieuse.').
24. *Mondev v. USA*, para. 71.
25. *Wena v. Egypt*, para. 100; *Vivendi v. Argentina* (Resubmission).
26. *Rumeli et al. v. Kazakhstan*, ICID Case No. ARB/05/16, Award of 29 July 2008, para. 706; Salacuse, The Law of Investment Treaties (Oxford University Press 2009) 328; Thomas Wälde and Borzu Sabahi, 'Compensation, Damages and Valuation' in Peter Muchlinski, Federico Ortino and Christoph Schreuer (eds), The Oxford Handbook of International Investment Law (OUP, 2008), 1070.

As the treaties do not offer any guidance on this important question, the answer needs to be sought out on the basis of customary international law. In this regard, investment tribunals frequently rely on the *Factory at Chorzow* case,[27] which is universally held to articulate those principles in the constantly quoted declaration that 'reparation must, as far as possible, wipe out all the consequences of the illegal act and re-establish the situation which would, in all probability, have existed if that act had not been committed'.[28] The principle thus enunciated is neither surprising nor controversial. The challenge consists in the application of this lofty principle to the facts of each particular case.

Just as frequently, reliance is placed on the provisions of the Responsibility of States for Internationally Wrongful Acts ('the ILC Articles') elaborated by the International Law Commission. The ILC Articles deal with so-called secondary rules on the international responsibility of states (i.e., not the substantive, 'primary', rules on what constitutes wrongful conduct, but what consequences the breach of such substantive rules will give rise to). These articles were adopted by the ILC in 2001 and, in that same year, 'commended [...] to the attention of Governments without prejudice to the question of their future adoption or other appropriate action'[29] by the UN General Assembly.

For guidance, the ILC has also provided a commentary on the ILC Articles ('the ILC Commentary').

The ILC Articles do not have the force of law, and they are not binding on the states or other international actors by force of treaty or otherwise. However, they possess great authority in view of the eminent scholarly effort that has gone into their drafting.

Article 31 of the ILC Articles spells out the fundamental rule that '[t]he State is under an obligation to make full reparation for the injury caused by the internationally wrongful act'. Article 34 is captioned 'Forms of reparation' and deals with the ways in which 'full reparation' may be achieved; of importance, in an investor-state dispute settlement (ISDS) context is to note the fact that the primary remedy is *restitution*, i.e., an obligation to reinstate the situation that existed before the impugned act was committed (if materially possible and not out of all proportion, Article 35(a) and (b)).

In an investor-state context, the remedy of restitution is usually not a meaningful or even feasible remedy. It has also been stated on more than one occasion that

27. Chorzow is a city centrally located in Poland, today with a population of approximately 100,000. The Chorzow factory was established before World War I with German ownership. The factory produced fertilisers and explosives, commodities of strategic importance. According to the Geneva Convention the German ownership of the factory was to continue. However, in 1922, after an uprising in the eastern part of Silesia, Chorzow was ceded to Poland and the factory was taken over by the Polish state. The German Reich espoused the factory owners' claims and the parties submitted to the jurisdiction of the Permanent Court of International Justice (PCIJ), which resulted in the *Factory at Chorzow* case.
28. Case concerning the *Factory at Chorzow (Germany v. Poland)*, 1927 PCIJ, Series A, No. 9 (Jurisdiction); 1928 PCIJ, Series A, No. 17 (Merit) [hereinafter Chorzów Factory], Award, pp. 47-48.
29. General Assembly Resolution 56/83, para. 3; 12 December 2001.

ordering a state party to effect such specific performance might be an illicit encroachment on the state's sovereignty.[30] However, it is far from infrequent that investment treaties confer on the tribunal an express mandate to order specific performance.[31] Restitution has been pleaded (initially by the respondent) in the odd instance, e.g., *Funnekotter*, concerning farmers having been deprived of their farmlands in Zimbabwe.[32] Also, in a strikingly analogue case to *Funnekotter*, the claimants in the *Pezold* case requested restitution of farmlands, and the tribunal so ordered.[33]

If the remedy of restitution is not available, Article 36(1) of the ILC Article imposes the obligation 'to compensate for the damages caused thereby', an obligation which comprises (Article 36(2) 'any financially assessable damage'.[34]

In line with the above, the dichotomy of lawful and unlawful expropriation may be summarized as follows.

Lawful Expropriation	*Unlawful Expropriation*
The valuation takes place at the date of expropriation (or before the expropriation became public knowledge).	The valuation takes place at the date of the Award.
The valuation is objective (determining the fair market value), i.e., it does not consider the specific adverse consequences to the particular investor.	The valuation takes into consideration the circumstances of the particular investor.
The valuation only considers circumstances known at the time of the expropriation.	The valuation takes into consideration subsequent facts (and prior facts coming to light *post factum*.
Objective determination of fair market value	Actual loss to the particular investor (including incidental cost)

30. 'It is obvious that this Tribunal cannot substitute itself for the Indonesian Government, in order to cancel the revocation and restore the license: such actions are not even claimed, and it is more than doubtful that this kind of restitution could be ordered against a sovereign state.' Also, *LG&E Energy v. Argentina*, Award, para. 87 '[...] The judicial restitution in this case would imply modification of the current legal situation by annulling or enacting legislative or administrative measures that make over the effect of the legislation in breach. The Tribunal cannot compel Argentina to do so without a sentiment of undue reference with its sovereignty. [...]'
31. For example, NAFTA, Art. 1135(1): '... the Tribunal may award, separately or in combination, only [...]restitution of property, in which the award shall that the disputing Party may pay monetary damages and any applicable interest in lieu of restitution [...]'
32. *Funnekotter et al. v. Zimbabwe*, ICSID Case No. ARB/05/6, para. 68.
33. *von Pezold et al. v. Zimbabwe*, ICSID Case No. ARB/10/15.
34. The ILC Articles, Art. 37, also include the remedy of 'satisfaction' which is a non-economic consequence that is not relevant in an investor-state context.

§4.09 THE LAWFUL/UNLAWFUL DICHOTOMY IN INVESTMENT ARBITRATION PRACTICE

In many cases - particularly in the early 2000s - it does not appear that the tribunals attributed any relevance to whether the expropriation was lawful or not as regards valuation methodologies or fixing a point in time for the valuation.[35] This can have many explanations, such that the parties were in agreement on how valuation was to be approached (e.g., fair market value at the time of expropriation) or that the tribunal just assumed that the treaty's provision on lawful expropriation also applied to unlawful acts.[36] In the *Crystallex* arbitration,[37] the parties agreed on the date of expropriation. This was also the case in the *Saint-Gobain v. Venezuela* case,[38] and, in many cases, these choices, in all likelihood, did not have appreciable economic consequences.[39]

There are also awards where it appears that the tribunals, in fact, noted the distinction between law and unlawful expropriation but did not let this categorization play into the valuation process.

Actually, the first case which very clearly opted in favour of selecting the date of the Award as the relevant date for assessing reparation following an unlawful expropriation was the *ADC* case.[40]

The *ADC investment* case concerned an airport outlet concession which was frustrated by state intervention. In ADC's view, this was a clear-cut case of unlawful expropriation. The tribunal agreed. It noted succinctly, that 'Since the BIT does not contain any *lex specialis* rules that govern the issue of the standard for assessing damages in the case of an unlawful expropriation, the Tribunal is required to apply the default standard contained in customary international law in the present case'.[41] As for the point in time at which damages should be determined, the tribunal made the pragmatic observation that previous tribunals had opted for the date of the expropriation because there had been a decline in the value of the investment after regulatory interference.[42] The *ADC* case, however, was described by the tribunal as almost unique 'since the value of the investment after the date of expropriation (1 January 2002) had

35. Metalclad, Award of 30 August 2000, para. 118; Wena Hotels, Award 8 December 2000, para. 118; Middle East Cement, Award 12 April 2000, paras 144, 146; Tecmed, Award 29 May 2003, paras 151, 187-188; Rumeli Telekom, Award 29 July 2008, para. 785; ASistem Muhendislik Insaat Sanayi ve Ticaret, Award 9 September 2009; Occidental Petroleum, Award 5 October 2012, para. 707; Abengoa y Cofides, Award 5 October 20213, para. 681; SAUR, Award 22 March 2014, para. 85; *Tenaris and Talta v. Venezuela*, Award 29 January 2016.
36. *Yukos Universal Ltd v. Russia*, PCA Case No. AA 227, Final Award 18 July 2014, para. 1571.
37. *Crystallex v. Venezuela*, Award 4 April 2016, para. 854.
38. Decision on Liability and the Principles of Quantum of 30 December 2016, paras 611-614.
39. However - occasionally - the choice of date as of the expropriation or as of the date of the award could have significant consequences: The *Yukos* tribunal noted [the Yukos Award, para. 1826,] that a valuation at the earlier date would yield approx. USD 22 billion while a valuation at the award date would represent slightly in excess of USD 66.5 billion.
40. *ADC v. Hungary*, ICSID Case No. ARB/03/16, Award of 2 October 2006 ('ADC Award').
41. ADC Award, para. 483.
42. *Ibid.*, para. 496.

risen very considerably ...'.[43] So, in this particular case, the tribunal concluded that '[h]owever, in the present, *sui generis*, type of case the application of *the Chorzow Factory* standard requires that the date of valuation should be the date of the Award and not the date of expropriation, since this is what is necessary to put the Claimants in the same position as if the expropriation had not been committed'.[44]

For purposes of a fair summary of the respective characteristics of the lawful/unlawful divide, the following quote may serve: 'This distinction also has crucial practical implications. Compensation is calculated by determining the "objective" fair market value of an investment at the time of expropriation [...] whereas damages are usually assessed by ascertaining the actual loss of the investor at the time of the decision, as laid down in the so-called Chorzow factory standard [...]'.[45]

There is definitely a trend in contemporary adjudicatory practice to use the date of the award as the appropriate point in time where the value of the expropriated assets shall be determined. This is also expressed in a number of cases,[46] and it is also taken for a given assumption in modern scholarly works.[47]

Using the date of the award and *post factum* data accumulated until that date for purposes of valuation has been criticized because it allows enterprise value to be determined by exogenous factors – e.g., market fluctuations – which bear no relation to the breach and by such circumstances that could not have been foreseen at the time of expropriation. The timing of the award and, hence, the valuation will be fortuitous, and the attribution of a value to the (hypothetical) business enterprise will constantly be in a flux of changing economic circumstances.

However, these empirically well-recognized considerations do not give cause for concern. Certainly, putting a value on a business enterprise which is a going concern will always be chasing a moving target. Its value will vary over time depending on a number of business-specific and macroeconomic factors. However, it is at the time of rendering the award that the damages to be compensated are quantified, reflecting – at least in theory – the possibility of seeking alternative investment opportunities under comparable market conditions.

As regards the matter of foreseeability, what was possible to foresee at the time of the breach is not a relevant circumstance when it comes to satisfying the requirement of full reparation for an unlawful expropriation.[48]

43. *Ibid.*
44. *Ibid.*, para. 497.
45. August Reinisch and Christoph Schreuer, International Protection of Investments (CUP 2020), para. 118.
46. In the *Quiborax* case it is explicitly stated by the [majority of] the tribunal that the valuation shall use data at the date of the award.
47. *See, e.g.*, Marboe, pp. 3.266 & seq.
48. *Amco Asia Corporation v. Republic of Indonesia*, ICSID Case No ARB/81/1 (Resubmitted Case), Award (31 May 1990); para. 186 'foreseeability [...] would anyway be an inappropriate test for damages that approximate to *restitutio in integrum*'.

§4.10 SELECTING THE DATE OF VALUATION

It is clear that in the event of a lawful expropriation, under customary international law, the determination of the fair market value shall be carried out as per the date of the expropriation (or, rather, immediately before the action was undertaken or when the intention to undertake the action became public knowledge). From this point in time, the investor is entitled to interest (only).[49]

However, this rule does not apply to any unlawful expropriation. In order to assess the adverse economic consequences suffered by the investor, it is necessary that the valuation is carried out in close proximity to the date of the award, irrespective of whether the value has risen or fallen after the expropriatory act. Normally – as in the *ADC* case – the impugned state measure will put paid to the enterprise for good, and any lingering effects of the expropriation will not be an issue. However, in case the enterprise somehow continues – e.g., because the regulatory intervention frustrates only one of multiple lines of operations of the investment – the valuation date still has to be the date of the award, but any adverse effect of the expropriation existing at the valuation date will have to be discounted. In such cases, the matter of causation attracts importance or, in the words of one tribunal, '... it is necessary to exclude the effects of actions taken by the nationalizing state in relation to the enterprise which actions may have depressed its value.'[50]

In earlier investment arbitration practice, tribunals have more or less programmatically (and consistently) declared that an unlawfully expropriated asset should (just as in the case of a lawful expropriation) be valued at the time of the expropriation and not, for example, at the date of the award.[51] This practice has in all likelihood been driven by the very pragmatic fact that the asset represented a higher value at the time of the expropriation as compared to later due to a degradation of to business environment as a consequence of the action. This quite arcane circumstance appears to have excluded consideration of any other date of valuation, such as the award date, in a number of cases. In other cases the parties have simply been in agreement that the date of breach be used, or, occasionally, that the tribunal mistakenly has assumed that the prescribed features of a lawful expropriation of the treaty also applies to an unlawful expropriation.

---

49. Once the indemnifiable amount has been fixed in judicial order, the investor's exposure to commercial risks will be excluded, leaving only the time element of any outstanding payment to be compensated.
50. *American International Group v. Iran* 4 Iran-US CTR (1983) 96, 107.
51. *See, e.g., Sedco, Inc v. NIOC and Iran,* Interlocutory Award (27 March 1986) reprinted in 25 ILM 629 (1986); *Tippetts, Abbett, McCarthy, Stratton v. TAMS-AFFA Consulting* Engineers of Iran, Iran, and others, Award (29 June 1984) reprinted in 6 Iran-US CTR 219; *American International Group, Inc v. Iran,* Award (19 December 1983) reprinted in 4 Iran-USCTR 96; *Antoine Goetz et al. v. Burundi,* ICSID Case No ARB/95/3, Award (29 January 1999) paras 124, 135; *Wena Hotels Ltd v. Egypt,* ICSID Case No ARB/98/4, Award (8 December 2000) para. 118; *CME Czech Republic BV v. Czech Republic,* UNCITRAL, Partial Award (13 September 2001) para. 619; *Middle East Cement v. Egypt,* ICSID Case No. ARB/99/6, Award (12 April 2002) para. 107; *Tecmed v. United Mexican States,* ICSID Case No ARB(AF)/00/2, Award (29 May 2003) para. 187; *CMS Gas Transmission Company v. Argentina,* ICSID Case No. ARB/01/8, Award (12 May 2005) para. 410; *Azurix v. Argentina,* ICSID Case No. ARB/01/12, Award (14 July 2006) paras 420, 424.

There is definitely a trend in contemporary adjudicatory practice to use the date of the award as the appropriate point in time where the value of the expropriated assets shall be determined.

Using the date of the award and post-factum data accumulated until that date has occasionally been criticized because it allows enterprise value to be determined by exogenous factors which bear no relation to the breach and by such circumstances that could not have been foreseen at the time of expropriation.[52] The timing of the award and hence the valuation will be fortuitous and the attribution of a value to the (hypothetical) business enterprise will constantly be in a flux of changing economic circumstances.

However, these empirically well recognized considerations do not give cause for concern. Certainly, putting a value on a business enterprise which is a going concern will always be chasing a moving target. Its value will vary over time depending on a number of business-specific and macroeconomic factors. However, it is at the time of rendering the award that the damages to be compensated are quantified, reflecting – at least in theory – the possibility to seek alternative investment opportunities under comparable market conditions.

As regards the matter of foreseeability, it merits mentioning that what was possible to foresee at the time of the breach is not a relevant circumstance when it comes to satisfying the requirement of full reparation for an unlawful expropriation.[53]

§4.11 PRINCIPLES OF VALUATION AND METHODOLOGY

Obviously, there is no controversy as to the propriety of the principle of 'full reparation' as spelt out in the ILC Articles in cases where a state has incurred responsibility for an internationally wrongful act. However, the transformation of this principle in any given set of circumstances into hard and fast numbers is an entirely different matter.[54]

International law (whether customary or treaty-based) does not prescribe any particular methodology for purposes of determining the fair market value or the amount of compensation, respectively, to be paid for an expropriated asset. Methods that are used may be described as asset-based, income-based or market-based. Tribunals are at liberty to select the method they consider appropriate in the circumstances of the particular case.

As a general overview, a brief summary may be made.

Book value is, generally speaking, a very poor means of determining enterprise value as it represents an actuarial, historical accounting method. It starts with the acquisition value of an asset and reduces that amount by depreciation (as calculated

52. *See, e.g.*, Prof. Stern's strong dissent in the *Quiborax* case.
53. *Amco Asia Corporation v. Republic of Indonesia*, ICSID Case No. ARB/81/1 (Resubmitted Case), Award (31 May 1990); para. 186 'foreseeability [...] would anyway be an inappropriate test for damages that approximate to *restitutio in integrum*'.
54. In any particular treaty context it may be argued that a lawful expropriation requires something less than 'full reparation', e.g., the Respondent's position in the Von Pezold case (Award, para. 753) that the tribunal should consider '[the Respondent's] ability to pay any compensation ordered', implying that any such amount should be 'just'.

over the asset's useful economic life or as allowed by accounting conventions). It says nothing about the investment's potential to generate future income.

Historic value differs from book value only in that the historic acquisition costs are restated with no allowance made for depreciation (whether to distribute the cost over the life-cycle of the asset or in order to adhere to accountancy dictates). Similarly to the book value, the historic cost is a poor indicator of the value of a going concern business enterprise. Still, in the absence of a track record of profitable operations, investment tribunals have occasionally resorted to this measure.

Book value and historic value are retrospective, while enterprise value necessarily has to be forward-looking.

Liquidation value relates to the value that the assets would represent in the context of an orderly liquidation of the enterprise. The liquidation value does indeed provide a definitely relevant measure in cases where the invested assets do not constitute a 'going concern' for purposes of valuation.

Replacement value represents the cost – at the time of expropriation – of acquiring the asset(s) of which the investor may have been deprived by expropriatory action. The method may yield a more adequate outcome for the investor than other base-asset approaches but shares the weaknesses of those alternatives as a poor measure of the investment's 'real' value based on its income-generating potential.

Stock market value, more properly defined as the market capitalization of a company, is hardly ever an available metric in expropriation cases as foreign investment regularly constitutes a subset of any listed company's operations, regularly also held by a wholly-owned SPV ('Special Purpose Vehicle') registered in the host state.

Peer valuation: Comparing the investment's income generation potential by comparing it to a number of 'peers' – i.e., what prices other, similar enterprises fetch in a market with buyers acting on a voluntary basis in like circumstances – is certainly an excellent method. The problem is, however, that it is usually impossible to find comparable 'peers' that may be used for purposes of such a valuation.

The DCF methodology estimates the future earning potential of an asset over a number of years and discounts the aggregate amount to its present value by a discount factor determined by the time value of money and business risk. The DCF methodology is by far the optimal methodology for valuation of a 'going concern'.[55] There are really no objections of principle that can be raised against it on a theoretical level, although, in its practical application, it can lead to significant under- or over-valuation depending on the degree of realism of the different factors that are put into the formula, not least the risk factor (of a multifarious nature) which affects the outcome of the calculation.

55. The World Bank Guidelines on the Treatment of Foreign Direct Investment define 'going concern' as 'an enterprise consisting of income-producing assets which has been in operation for a sufficient period of time to generate the data required for the calculation of future income and which could have been expected with reasonable certainty, if the taking had not occurred, to continue producing legitimate income over the course of its economic life in the general circumstances following the taking by the State'.

The DCF methodology has, at least initially, encountered notable headwinds in scholarly writings[56] as well as in case law.[57]

There can hardly be any doubt that the DCF methodology is the one that is most appropriate for calculating a fair market value of income-generating assets. Occasionally, the method has come under criticism, but this can hardly relate to the methodology as such but to its application. It cannot be denied that spreadsheets displaying DCF projections convey an alluring image of scientific exactitude that can be deceptive. However, these projections are not better than the assumptions that are fed into the formula (if a number of unrealistic assumptions are used, this even compounds the under- or overshoot of the result).

When weighing the pros and cons of different valuation methodologies, it is important to consider that in an increasingly technologically sophisticated and specialized business environment, the value of physical, balance sheet-eligible assets becomes increasingly decoupled from the wealth-creating potential of many types of business operations. To illustrate this phenomenon with a striking – but maybe not run-of-the-mill example – one may take the example of Microsoft Corporation which shows an asset value on its balance sheet of USD 365 billion but a market capitalization of almost USD 2 trillion (2023).

Sunk costs represent expenditure which has not been possible to recapture because the intended venture was stopped by governmental interference before it could be brought to fruition or because the venture in the end was simply not susceptible to profitable operation.

If no case can be made at all for future profitability – the project was, for instance, brought to a premature halt by illicit state intervention – it would appear appropriate to award sunk costs. Such an amount would certainly not represent a 'fair market value'

56. *See* ILC's Commentary in relation to Art. 36 of the ILC Articles: 'The discounted cash flow (DCF) method has gained some favour, especially in the context of calculations involving income over a limited duration, as in the case of wasting assets. Although developed as a tool for assessing commercial value, it can also be useful in the context of calculating value for compensation purposes. But difficulties can arise in the application of the DCF method to establish capital value in the compensation context. The method analyses a wide range of inherently speculative elements, some of which have a significant impact upon the outcome (e.g. discount rates, currency fluctuations, inflation figures, commodity prices, interest rates and other commercial risks). This has led tribunals to adopt a cautious approach to the use of the method. Hence, although income-based methods have been accepted in principle, there has been a decided preference for asset-based methods.'
57. *Metalclad Corporation v. United States of Mexico* (ICSID Case No. ARB(AF)/97/1), Award of 30 August 2000, at para. 118; *Southern Pacific Properties (Middle East) Limited v. Arab Republic of Egypt* (ICSID Case No. 84/3), Award of 20 May 1992; *Wena Hotels Ltd. v. Arab Republic of Egypt* (ICSID Case No. ARB/98/4), Award on Merits of 8 December 2000; *Marvin Roy Feldman Karpa v. United Mexican States* (ICSID Case No. ARB(AF)/99/1), Award of 16 December 2002, at para. 194; *Tecmed*, at para. 186; Rumeli, at para. 811; *Tidewater*, at paras 139, 144, 152-165 and 185. Also in the Iran-US Claims Tribunal practice a reserved posture has been adopted as regards the DCF method. *See, e.g.*, the following Iran-US Claims Tribunal awards: *Phillips Petroleum Co. v. Iran*, 21 Iran-US CTR 79 at para. 79, Partial Award No. 425-39-2, 29 June 1989; *American International Corp. v. Iran*, 4 Iran-US CTR 96 at 106, Award No. 93-2-3, 19 December 1983; *INA Corp. v. Iran*, 8 Iran-US CTR 373 at 380, Award No. 184-161-1, 13 August 1985; *James M. Saghi et al. v. Iran*, 29 Iran-US CTR 20 at para. 79, Award No. 544-298-2, 22 January 1993.

of the funds invested, but it would represent a measure of damages arguably indemnifiable under international law as it would, in some sense, represent 'reparation'. If, on the other hand, the business venture proved unprofitable for reasons unrelated to any inappropriate state intervention, the compensation that could be determined should be based on the value of the assets in the context of an orderly liquidation of the business venture.[58] In that context, 'sunk costs' are not relevant at all.

Loss of opportunity has been relied on by some tribunals where the investment was, as it were, nipped in the bud and effectively prevented by state interference from bringing its operations on stream (whether profitably or unprofitably) before accumulating a sufficient track record allowing any assumptions as to its income-generating potential.[59] This is really nothing else than a variant of the market value approach, recognizing that ventures based on such flimsy underpinnings are regularly traded by willing actors in the M&A markets.

'Lucrum cessans and damnum emergens'

The age-worn compensation measure based on *lucrum cessans* and *damnum emergens* may safely be dismissed as unhelpful in a valuation context. It is, indeed, a quite primitive tool, built on a cash-based rather than accrual-based cash flow basis. It may at best be used (if at all) in a contract breach context in a civil law setting.

It is '... based on an anachronistic method of valuation, one that separated out *damnum emergens* and *lucrum cessans*, rather than modern financial terms. Chorzów Factory's valuation formulas reached their expiration date decades ago.'[60] It has also been described as 'economically anachronistic',[61] and discussion of the concept has recommended that 'the dichotomy of *damnum emergens* and *lucrum cessans* should be abandoned in this context'.[62]

§4.12 USING DATA OCCURRING OR COMING TO LIGHT AFTER THE EXPROPRIATORY EVENT?

When using the date of expropriation, tribunals have been faced with the query of whether they may assess data that have occurred or come to light after the event. It

58. This conclusion is also supported by the recommendations issued by the World Bank in its Guidelines on the Treatment of Foreign Direct Investment (Article 6): '(i) for a going concern with a proven record of profitability, on the basis of the discounted cash flow value; (ii) for an enterprise which, not being a proven going concern, demonstrates lack of profitability, on the basis of the liquidation value; (iii) [...]'.
59. *See Sapphire International Petroleum v. National Iranian Oil Company*, 35 ILR 136 (1963); *Southern Pacific Properties (Middle East) v. Egypt* (ICSID Case No. ARB/84/3), Award of 20 May 1992; compare, in contract relations, Art. 7.4.3(2) of the Principles of International Commercial Contracts.
60. Steven E. Ratner, Compensation for Expropriations in World of Investment Treaties: Beyond the Lawful/Unlawful Distinction (2017), Law & Economics Working Papers 131, 9.
61. WQ Michael Reisman and Robert D. Sloane, Indirect Expropriation and Its Valuation in the BIT Generation (OUP 2004), 137.
62. Irmgard Marboe, *Calculation of Compensation and Damages in International Investment Law* (1st edn, OUP 2009).

would seem obvious that in order to arrive at the most appropriate level of 'reparation', all information available at the time of adjudication should be applied to the enquiry.

Reasons that have been given for disregarding *post factum* events are, essentially, that circumstances affecting valuation *post factum* may not have been foreseeable and that such circumstances are external to the breaching act as such. However, foreseeability is not a relevant factor affecting valuation in case of a breach. One may recall that the primary remedy under international law is restitution, and the obligation to restitute property is unaffected by what the parties may have foreseen. By the same token, the duty to pay damages remains unaffected by the foreseeability of further intervening events up to the date of the award.

However, this problem cannot arise on a proper approach to the quantification issue, putting that calculus at the time of the award. All information – irrespective of whether it pertains to events *ex ante* which have become known after the event or whether they concern subsequent, unforeseen events (they may relate to unexpected changes in the pricing of input factors, market conditions, technological development, competitive patterns, regulatory issues) – shall be used in order to arrive at the amount required to effect reparation. It is important to underscore in this regard that the expectations of the parties to the arbitration at the time of the expropriatory event are irrelevant for quantification purposes. For the same reason, one cannot attach relevance to what a willing seller and a willing buyer, acting under no compunction at the time of the expropriatory act, would accept as the fair market value of the investment as those (hypothetical) parties will not be in possession of possibly relevant *post factum* data.

Fixation of the amount of damages in as close proximity as possible to the point in time at which the amount is quantified and susceptible of enforcement must in all instances optimally fulfil the function of 'full reparation' to which the aggrieved investor is entitled.

§4.13 WHAT IF THE INVESTMENT REPRESENTS A LOWER VALUE AT THE TIME OF THE AWARD: DOES THE INVESTOR GET TO CHOOSE?

It has happened in a number of investment cases that a valuation of a business enterprise at the date of the award yields a lower monetary amount than one undertaken at the date of the breach (even disregarding any adverse economic effects inflicted on any remaining part of the business after the expropriation by the unlawful state conduct). Should this circumstance call for a departure from the principle of valuation as per the award date? In other words, should such a situation give rise to an entitlement on the part of the investor to choose the most favourable outcome (in these cases, by opting for the date of breach)?

An intuitive response to this question is that such a choice cannot reasonably be on offer. Damages following an international breach have to be quantified in terms of one monetary amount and cannot very well be represented by two different amounts. Still, in those investment cases where enterprise value has declined at the time of the award, the investor has invariably been given the right to choose the higher value that applied at the time of the expropriation.[63] Remarkably, this position has been taken for granted, and no *ratio decidiendi* has been ventured in these cases. A typical reference will read: 'The Tribunal also holds that, in the case of an unlawful expropriation, as in the present case, Claimants are entitled to select either the date of the expropriation or the date of the award as the date of valuation'.[64]

How can that be? It has been argued, for instance, that expropriation is a special case because, here, the investor would have been entitled to compensation in all circumstances (i.e., also in the event of a lawful expropriation). 'This part of the damage is, therefore, not causally linked to the valuation'.[65] But one cannot look at it in that way: in the context of a damage calculation, *all funds* awarded in a case of unlawful expropriation derive from its illegality; there are no 'spill-over' effects from the contrafactual lawful measure which is based on a different methodology.

An argument has also been raised that choice should be motivated by an interest to discourage states from engaging in overbearing conduct.[66] This is not a valid motive. While investment cases claiming damages for unlawful acts hopefully have a sobering effect on the state's conduct of its affairs, this cannot be accepted, under international law or otherwise, as a valid justification for offering the investor more than what represents reparation at the time of the award. Even if, in a given instance, this would represent a lower amount than what follows from the fair market value at the time of expropriation, it will surely be sufficient to act as a deterrent against untoward actions. And, in any event, investment tribunals are not tasked with meting out retribution in instances of untoward state conduct.

There exists no logical justification to allow the investor (or the state, for that matter) to choose between the most favourable valuation that can be achieved at the time of expropriation and the time of the award, respectively. This may produce a result where the investor is afforded damages in an amount which is less than what has followed from a lawful expropriation. However, there is nothing remarkable in that; as the methodologies to apply in respect of lawful and unlawful expropriations are quite distinct, there is nothing remarkable that they may yield different outcomes.

One can understand the spontaneous sentiment expressed in doctrine and in many investment cases that a state having attracted responsibility for an unlawful act

63. *ADC v. Hungary*, ICISD Case No. ARB/03/16, Award of 2 October 2006; *Kardassopopulos v. Georgia*, ICSID Case No. ARB/05/18, Award of 3 March 2010; *Hulley Enterprises et al v. Russia*, PCA Cases Nos 227 and 228, Award of 18 July 2014; *Unglaube v. Costa Rica*, ICSID Cases Nos ARB/08/01 and ARB/09/20, Award of 16 May 2012; *ConocoPhillips et al. v. Venezuela*, ICSID Case No. ARB/07/30, Decision on Jurisdiction and Merits (3 September 2013) and Award (8 March 2019); *Hulley* (n. 34); *Yukos* (n. 34) *v. Russia*; *Veteran Petroleum* (n. 34); *Gold Reserve v. Venezuela*, ICSID Case No. ARB(AF)/09/1, Award (22 September 2014); *Pezold and others v. Zimbabwe*, ICSID Case No. ARB/10/15, Award (28 July 2015); *Teinver et al. v. Argentina*, ICSID Case No. ARB/09/1, Award (21 July 2017); *OperaFund v. Spain* (n. 8).
64. Yukos Award, para. 1763.
65. I. Marboe, 3.332.
66. *See, e.g.*, Conoco award, para. 242, end: 'However, a damages award that returns the plaintiff to its economic position at the date of the injury, but leaves the defendant with a gain as a result of his action may not be appropriate and not deter future unlawful acts'.

should not be able to escape the consequences at a lower price than what would follow from a lawful act. This reaction certainly is understandable but defies logic: the approaches in the two instances are different and may certainly yield these results on a proper application. There is also a forbidding element in the proposition that the investor may pick the best outcome: The purpose is to offer reparation for a certain wrongful act, and such an amount (whether considered right or wrong) is the one that, by definition, reflects the damages sustained. It is mildly surprising that the investor's entitlement to choice has not met with some pushback in more recent case law and writings.[67]

§4.14 DIVESTITURE OF THE INVESTMENT AS A RELEVANT PARAMETER?

A reason put forward by some tribunals for a higher valuation than would otherwise follow is that the investor could have divested itself of the enterprise at some earlier time and, if so, secured a higher amount of reparation than at the time of the award. The *Yukos* tribunal – as an argument why any depreciation of the value cannot be at the expense of the investor – explained that '[...] in the absence of the expropriation the investor could have sold the asset at an earlier date at its previous higher value. [...]'.[68] Generally speaking, there can be no presumption in favour of the hypothesis that an investor entertains such plans – the traditional role of the investment is to secure future income for the long haul. In order for the investor to vindicate the higher value that a hypothetical divestiture of the investment would bring, it would require compelling evidence that such a sale was consummated by the investor or at least imminent in the particular instance.

The *Unglaube* case is also interesting in that the tribunal assumed that the investor would have sold the investment just prior to the peak in real estate prices in the intervening period.[69] No allegation that the investor actually had intended to sell the investment was on the record, however.

§4.15 A MANDATE TO DETERMINE FAIR MARKET VALUE

The *Santa Elena* is sometimes quoted as the authority for the proposition that the absence of payment does not render an expropriation unlawful.[70] However, it is important to note that this arbitration was *not* based on an investment treaty but on an *ad hoc* agreement to submit to arbitration prompted by the US Helms Amendment and

67. However, a poignant critique of what has been termed as the 'Asymmetrical Approach' may be found in a recent paper by Pacôme Ziegler and Cristian Gallorini, The Case for the Ex-post Valuation of Damages under International Investment Law, Journal of Investment & Trade 24 (2023), 115-265.
68. Yukos Award, para. 1768.
69. *Unglaube et al. v. Costa Rica* (ICSID Cases Nos ARB/08/1 and ARB/09/20), Award 16 May 2012, para. 318.
70. The Tidewater Award, para. 135.

that the parties did not argue in terms of lawful/unlawful expropriation; they simply wanted to have the matter of compensation finally settled. Additionally, the Parties were in agreement that 'international law' was to apply and that the investor was entitled to 'the fair market value' of the property. The only bone of contention was the valuation date, whether at the time of the expropriation (1978) or the then 'current value' (1998).

In the *Santa Elena* case, compensation had not been paid, although many years had elapsed since the expropriation.

The *Santa Elena* case concerned an investor who acquired a property in Costa Rica with a view of developing it into a tourist resort. This happened back in 1970. In 1978, Costa Rica issued an expropriation decree in respect of the property in order to create a natural preserve in view of the region's 'dazzling variety of flora and fauna'.[71] At the time, Costa Rica offered to pay the equivalent of USD 1.9 million for the property. The offer was turned down by the investor who believed that USD 6.4 million would come closer to the truth. Thereafter, a period of twenty years ensued, during which the compensation issue remained unsettled. Finally, the US prevailed upon Costa Rica to submit the compensation issue to international arbitration before an ICSID tribunal. This was in 1995. In the arbitration, the investor upped the ante and asked for USD 41.2 million.[72]

In the event, the tribunal settled for a valuation as per the time of expropriation and identified, on this basis, an amount of USD 4.15 million. Adding to this amount (compound) interest accruing up to the date of the award, the tribunal awarded a flat amount of USD 16 million in all. This is, then, a strict application of the *Factory at Chorzow* rule of FMV at the date of the taking plus interest from that date and Article 38(1) of the ILC Articles (which, of course, deals with reparation).

In this context - i.e., when an investment tribunal is mandated to determine the fair market value of a lawful expropriation - it is worth mentioning that there are still in existence some investment treaties (essentially with China and former Soviet Union republics) which leave it to international arbitration to determine 'the amount and modalities of payment' only once a domestic court in the host state has determined that an expropriation has taken place. The value of such a treaty will be illusory to the investor - a domestic court of, e.g., a former Soviet Union republic would hardly declare that foreign-held assets (even if such were in existence) had been subject to expropriation.[73]

71. Santa Elena Award, para. 15.
72. *Ibid.*, para. 29.
73. *See*, on this topic, August Reinisch, How Narrow Are Narrow Dispute Settlement Clauses in Investment Treaties?, Journal of International Dispute Settlement 2(1) (2011), 115-174, which raises the issue 'whether it is the proper role of investment tribunals to correct the meaning of dispute clauses they qualify as use- or senseless or whether such remedial action should remain reserved to the State Parties' (p. 174).

While a majority of tribunals have recognized this limitation as regards the scope of jurisdiction,[74] a few tribunals have arrogated to themselves, nonetheless, the authority to decide whether there has been an expropriation or not.[75]

§4.16 DEPARTING FROM THE PRINCIPLE OF FULL COMPENSATION?

During the gestation process leading up to the ILC Articles, extensive discussions were conducted on whether there should be a departure from the principle of full compensation in cases of, as it was called, 'crippling compensations'. Such an accommodation did not follow from any elevated principle of sovereignty as much as making a virtue out of necessity; states simply not being able to suffer the harrowing consequences of indemnifying a larger investor collective in the context of any all-out nationalization.

Although strong sympathy was expressed for such a possibility in many quarters, in the end, it was not reflected in the ILC Articles. The ILC Articles being declaratory of the status of international law, one can, therefore, say that 'full compensation' is the invariable compensation standard in cases of lawful expropriation under international customary law.[76]

In any event, if a tribunal has to decide on the lawfulness of an expropriation, it does not have to consider this issue: If the treaty requires 'full compensation', this will constitute the relevant criterion in terms of compensation for a lawful expropriation irrespective of any view on this matter in customary international law.

§4.17 CAUSATION

Normally, the matter of causation is not an issue in expropriation cases. The expropriation has caused the demise of the business, full stop, and no further enquiry as to causation is required. However, in other cases, such an enquiry is necessary, e.g., when overbearing regulatory activity has only partially stymied the operations of the business entity. This raises the spectre of cause and effect. It is uncontroversial that not all effects of a breach - however accidental and fortuitous - shall be compensated, but only such having an adequate 'nexus' to the expropriatory act. The question is only by what means investment tribunals shall fix those limits of causal events. Tribunals have struggled with this nexus between the act and the effect by resorting to terms of

74. *Vladimir and Moise Berschader v. The Russian Federation*, SCC Case No. 080/2004, Award 21 April 2006; *RosInvestCo UK Ltd. v. The Russian Federation*, Award on Jurisdiction 2007, SCC Case No. Arb V079/2005 'does not include jurisdiction over the questions whether an expropriation occurred and was legal'. 21 (para. 114); *Austrian Airlines AG v. The Slovak Republic*, UNCITRAL Final Award, 9 October 2009.
75. *European Media Ventures SA v. Czech Republic*, Judgment of the High Court of England and Wales, 5 December 2007, (2007) EWHC 2851 (Comm); *Renta 4 S.V.S.A et al. v. Russian Federation*, Award on Preliminary Objections, 20 March 2009, SCC No. 24/2007.
76. *See*, on this topic, Martins Paparinskis, Crippling Compensation in the International Law Commission and Investor-State Arbitration (ICSID Review, 37(1-2) (2022), 289-312.

'foreseeability', 'proximate cause', 'sufficient causal link', 'too remote', 'a natural consequence' and similar.[77]

These terms are in all likelihood useful tools to arrive at a satisfactory limitation of effect that may have followed a certain breach in any specific case. There is also a theory of 'adequate causation' which may give rise to liability in cases of remoteness or absent foreseeability (only requiring that a typical consequence of the conduct that can be established with the help of all relevant expertise that can be mustered).[78] However, in the context of an unlawful expropriation, one must exclude from the range of limiting factors what the parties reasonably may (or may not) have foreseen at the time of expropriation. Even if the effect was not foreseeable, it is indemnifiable if it was adequately caused by the expropriatory act.[79]

On the subject of causation, it may be mentioned that it has been argued[80] that a more nuanced approach should be adopted by analysing the economic implications of any specific breach of the prerequisites for a lawful expropriation in the particular case. That is, if an expropriation was unlawful because of the absence of a public purpose, due process and compensation, the economic consequences should be different from a situation where unlawfulness follows from, e.g., absent compensation only: in the former case, the investor would be entitled to *restititio in integrum* (because the expropriation was not supposed to happen at all), while in the latter (where a right to expropriate was present) only the adverse consequences of absent payment would be subject to damage assessment.

Despite the seeming attractiveness of this proposition, it is not likely that it can be argued from the way in which treaties are currently structured. Having regard to the way in which the conditionalities of a lawful expropriation are structured, the absence of any single criterion renders the act unlawful – and this mere fact removes the state's act from the realm of lawfulness into a situation where the interest of full reparation has to be satisfied. A different order could certainly be envisaged where the investment treaty would provide for a mandate to tribunals to determine fair market value without prejudice to the act's lawfulness, but such a solution is not on offer in current treaty practice.

---

77. For an illustrative discussion of the topic of causation in the ISDS context, *see SD Myers v. Canada*, Second Partial Award of 21 October 2001 (a NAFTA arbitration under the UNCITRAL Rules), paras 140-160.
78. David Khachvani, Compensation for Unlawful Expropriation: Targeting the Illegality, ICSID Review, 32(2) (2017), 385-403 (394 & seq.).
79. *See, e.g.*, the S D Myers Award, para. 159.
80. Pacôme Ziegler and Cristian Gallorini, The Case for the Ex-post Valuation of Damages Under International Law, Journal of Investment & Trade 24 (2023) 115-165 DOI: 10.1163/22119000-12340286.

CHAPTER 5
Re-examining the Approach to Factual Witness Evidence in International Arbitration

Matthew Saunders, Emma Johnson & Harsh Hari Haran

Every man's memory is his private literature.

– Aldous Huxley

§5.01 INTRODUCTION

The concept of witnesses having a central role in the determination of legal disputes is as old as the law itself and is a constant across all major legal systems. But the way in which witness evidence is assessed, the primacy it plays (or does not play) and how it is deployed and verified differs significantly, not least between the civil and common law systems. One author notes that 'few differences between common law and civil law procedure are as striking as the attitudes toward the testimony of witnesses'.[1] Although civil and common law legal systems adopt different approaches to witness evidence, they share a common goal – that of seeking to arrive at what is most likely to be the truth. This task is by no means straightforward; science has demonstrated that human memory is easily distorted and often inaccurate.[2]

Generally speaking, common law jurisdictions adopt an adversarial approach to witness evidence, placing a focus on what the witness says and that testimony being open to probing and challenge through processes such as cross-examination. In

1. John M. Townsend, Siegfried H. Elsing, *Bridging the Common Law and Civil Law Divide in Arbitration* (Arbitration International, vol. 18, 2002), 4 DOI: 10.1023/a:1014200908066.
2. ICC Commission, *The Accuracy of Fact Witness Memory in International Arbitration Report* (International Chamber of Commerce, 2020) 1.5(a).

contrast, civil law jurisdictions tend to place greater emphasis on documentary evidence and the adoption of an inquisitorial approach where witnesses are subject to relatively limited questioning by a judge or other decision-maker instead of by an opposing party's counsel. (These are, of course, generalisations and significant diversity of approach sits within common law and civil law systems.)

It is in the nature of court-based national legal systems that there is relatively little opportunity for 'cross-pollination' from other legal systems since rules on the right to appear in a national court mean that the legal profession participants (judge and counsel) will be from the same legal 'culture' and their practising experience will commonly be quite narrow. (There are of course exceptions where a legal system is a 'hybrid' or where a particularly high volume of international work means that more diverse cultural approaches are experienced.)

The position in international arbitration is quite different, with an ever-broadening diversity of practitioners, many of whom have very significant experience of different legal systems. Such diversity of background and approach has supported a 'reconciliation' of approaches through 'soft' laws such as the IBA Rules on Taking of Evidence in International Arbitration that provide parties with a flexible framework for management of witness evidence. It is notable (at least for a common law author, albeit one with plenty of time spent arguing before civil law tribunals) that common practice in international arbitration reflects predominantly the common law approach with frequent use of lengthy written witness statements often prepared with significant assistance of lawyers. It is striking that the adoption of a common law practice of written witness statements has taken place just as criticism of the 'cottage industry' of witness statement preparation has taken root in London, with 'an impression shared by a substantial majority of the judges of the Commercial Court that factual witness statements were often ineffective at performing their core function of achieving best evidence at proportionate cost in Commercial Court trials'.[3]

This chapter looks at a little history behind the current position in international arbitration and suggests steps that may be taken to ensure that the world of international arbitration benefits from the diversity of approaches that underpin it in its use of witness evidence rather than using an approach that is increasingly criticised in the legal system from which it was largely copied.

§5.02 ORIGIN OF THE CIVIL AND COMMON LAW DIVIDE

Reforms introduced by Henry II (who was the King of England from 1154 until 1189) marked the start of the common law divergence from the Romanist jurisdictions on the Continent.[4] (With Scotland taking a slightly different approach as it has to this day.) Such reforms included the creation of a group of royal judges and the introduction of

3. Witness Evidence Working Group, *Factual Witness Evidence in Trials Before the Business and Property Courts* (https://www.judiciary.uk/wp-content/uploads/2019/12/Witness-statement-working-group-Final-Report-1-1.pdf), 1.
4. Arthur R. Emmet, *Towards the Civil Law?: The Loss of 'Orality' in Civil Litigation in Australia* (University of New South Wales Law Journal, 2003).

the jury in civil cases.[5] Due to the increased quality of justice that was considered to be dispensed by the royal judges, the old local courts were abandoned by litigants.[6] Thus, 'England adopted an adversarial system of trial by jury, together with a qualitative system of evidence, under which – though many types of evidence were excluded – the weight attributed to that which was admitted was not mechanically fixed but submitted in each case to the judgment of a group of lay men'.[7] By contrast, the Continental jurisdictions adopted an inquisitorial system of trial by public officials[8] and a system of evidence under which everything was admitted but was allowed only a fixed weight.[9]

§5.03 THE COMMON LAW APPROACH TO WITNESS EVIDENCE

Common law jurisdictions generally adopt an adversarial system of justice where the role of a judge is to mediate, superintending the lawyers as they adduce their competing versions of the facts and the law.[10] Therefore, one of the aims of witness evidence is to persuade the judge and, in achieving that objective, witness evidence forms a central part of a hearing.

Historically, the rule in England was that witnesses gave oral testimony at trial. It was thought that the 'best evidence is often obtained by a traditional examination-in-chief, when witnesses are giving their evidence in their own words and give a more genuine version of their recollection'.[11] This approach changed in 1986 with the introduction of Order 38, Rule 2A of the Civil Procedure Rules, which saw written witness statements introduced into certain parts of the High Court[12] and was extended to the general courts of the Queen's Bench Division of the High Court in 1988.[13] In 1995, it was further provided that in the absence of any order to the contrary, 'every witness statement shall stand as the evidence in chief of the witness concerned'.[14] This change has been described in the notes to the White Book as 'an outstanding and far-reaching change in the machinery of civil justice'.[15] It may come as a surprise to civil law practitioners that written witness statements are a relatively recent innovation in the common law.

5. Emmet, *supra* n. 4.
6. R.C Van Caengegem, *Judges, Legislators and Professors: Chapters in European Legal History* (Cambridge University Press, 1987), 114.
7. Julius Stone and W.A.N Wells, *Evidence: Its History and Policies* (Butterworths North Ryde, 1991), 29 in Emmet, *supra* n. 4.
8. Stone and Wells, *supra* n. 7 in Emmet, *supra* n. 4.
9. Emmet, *supra* n. 4, 2.
10. John H. Langbein, *Historical Foundations of the Law of Evidence: A View from the Ryder Sources* (Cambridge Law Journal, 1999), p. 1169.
11. Witness Evidence Working Group, *supra* n. 3, 6.
12. Order 38, Rule 2A of the Civil Procedure Rules applied to any cause or matter which is proceedings in the Chancery Division, the Commercial Court, the Admiralty Court or as official referees' business.
13. James Hope, *Witness Statements in International Arbitration: The Cost of 'Gilding the Lily'*, Commercial Dispute Resolution, 17 June 2014, 4.
14. Practice Direction, *Civil Litigation: Case Management* (1995, 1 WLR 262), 3.
15. Hope, *supra* n. 13, 5.

The primary reasons for requiring written witness statements were to ensure 'fair and expeditious disposal of proceedings and the saving of costs'[16] and encourage a '"cards on the table approach" which would in some cases promote settlement and in other cases make for a fairer trial'.[17] Such was the perceived success of the reforms that other common law jurisdictions quickly followed suit and replaced examination in chief (also known as direct examination, the process whereby the witness gives his or her 'story' orally and where leading questions are generally not permitted by counsel).

§5.04 THE CIVIL LAW APPROACH TO WITNESS EVIDENCE

Civil law jurisdictions are generally based on an inquisitorial system where the role of investigating and adjudicating sits primarily with professional judges, although lawyers play a significant role in guiding and limiting judicial enquiry.[18] Witnesses are considered to be evidentiary sources of the court, and it is the judge, not the parties, who decides which witnesses are to be heard and will be in charge of their examination. Additionally, in many civil law jurisdictions, the parties' counsel are not supposed to talk to the witnesses before the trial and witness preparation is regarded as uncomfortably close to manipulation of evidence.[19] The courts also tend to give higher regard to written documents as evidence rather than overly polished witness statements.[20]

In our experience, witness evidence takes a relatively lesser role overall in civil law proceedings, and it is commonly advanced in the form of direct examination at trial rather than formal witness statements. Perhaps most surprising to common law practitioners is the fact that opposing counsel can and often do contact a party's witnesses in advance of the trial. Furthermore, cross-examination is often not confrontational, with no 'putting' of positive cases to the witness, and it is not uncommon for evidence to be challenged in post-hearing submissions despite relevant questions not having been asked of the witness at the hearing. Indeed, a civil law judge or arbitrator may well take a dim view of 'aggressive' cross-examination. Such approaches raise a practical issue for a common law advocate (and one the author has experienced in Stockholm) where the ethical obligation to 'put' a proposition to a witness such that she or he has a chance to respond is criticised by a tribunal as 'arguing with the witness'.

§5.05 CURRENT PRACTICE RE-WITNESS EVIDENCE IN INTERNATIONAL ARBITRATION

Deploying witness statements has become standard practice in international arbitration and in our experience wherever the arbitration takes place and under whatever

16. White Book, note 38/2A/2.
17. Lord Justice Jackson, *Review of Civil Litigation Costs: Preliminary Report (Volume Two)* (TSO (The Stationary Office), 2009), 403.
18. Emmet, *supra* n. 4.
19. Dr Andreas Respondek, *How Civil Law Principles Could Help to Make International Arbitration Proceedings More Time and Cost Effective* (Singapore Law Gazette, February 2017), 3.
20. Respondek, *supra* n. 19.

applicable law. It is striking that, with few exceptions, the manner in which such witness statements are prepared and deployed follows the practice prevalent in common law jurisdictions, such as simultaneous exchange, rules as to the citing and exhibiting of documents referred to, albeit without the safeguards applied in many litigation systems such as requirements that the witness statement contain a 'statement of truth' confirming that the facts stated in the witness statement are true[21] (proceedings for contempt of court may be brought if a statement of truth is found to have been false[22]) and that the witness statement is in the witness' own words.[23] The prevalence of common law practices is likely due in significant part to the fact that common law seats such as London, Singapore and Hong Kong have, according to one international survey,[24] become the preferred global seats (but it should be noted that the survey was undertaken by a London based academic institution in the English language, and so may not properly reflect a truly global picture). Another survey undertaken by the same academic institution also found that a key reason for the choice of seat was the law governing the substance of the dispute. [25] It is suggested that another factor supporting the adoption of common law practices may be the extent to which many English and US law firms became global firms from the 1990s onwards, influencing the adoption of English and US practices. London law firms had historically dominated international shipping work, which sector had been using international arbitration for decades before its wide scale adoption for international projects and a myriad of international commercial transactions.

§5.06 CRITICISMS OF THE COMMON LAW APPROACH

While the common law approach to witness evidence largely dominates within international arbitration, it is facing mounting criticism in the jurisdictions from whose court systems the practices derive and from an array of different sources. Leading arbitration practitioners have commented that:

> Written witness statements can bear little relation to the independent recollection of the factual witness, with draft after draft being crafted by the party's lawyer or the party itself, with the witness's written evidence becoming nothing more than special pleading, usually expressed at considerable length. It rarely contains the actual unassisted recollection of the witness expressed in his or her own actual words.[26]

---

21. Practice Direction 32, para. 20.2.
22. Civil Procedure Rule 32.14.
23. Practice Direction 32, paras 18.1 and 19.1(8).
24. Queen Mary University London, *International Arbitration Survey: Adapting Arbitration to a Changing World* (Queen Mary University London and School of International Arbitration, 2021), 8.
25. Queen Mary University London, *International Arbitration Survey: Improvements and Innovations in International Arbitration* (Queen Mary University London and School of International Arbitration, 2015), 11.
26. Laurent Levy and V.V. Veeder, *Arbitration and Oral Evidence* (Kluwer Law International, 2004), 7.

Pieter Sanders, who is often referred to as the father of the New York Convention,[27] has stated:

> Drawn up with the party or its legal advisers the witness may be influenced in formulating his or her Statement which has to be signed and affirmed by him or her as being the truth. In my opinion, the Witness Statements preceding the hearings of the witnesses in person are not in accordance with the expectations of many parties in international arbitration.[28]

It is striking that some of the most trenchant criticism of witness statements comes not from arbitration practitioners but from national judges. In *Ceviz v. Frawley & Anor*, the High Court of England and Wales criticised both the written and oral evidence of the witnesses of fact, stating that '[the witness statement] was 22 pages long, comprised 111 paragraphs and contained a great deal of comment and commentary that has no place in a witness statement'.[29]

In fact, in March 1994, just eight years after written witness statements were introduced, the Lord Chancellor, a senior member of the Cabinet who, prior to the Constitutional Reform Act 2005, was also the head of the judiciary,[30] appointed Lord Woolf to 'review the rules of civil procedure with a view to improving access to justice, reducing the cost of litigation and removing unnecessary complexity'.[31]

Lord Justice Jackson made similar statements when he reviewed civil litigation in England and Wales some fifteen years later. On 3 November 2008, Sir Anthony Clarke MR appointed Lord Justice Jackson to lead a 'fundamental review into the costs of civil litigation'.[32] The review was requested as Sir Anthony Clarke MR was 'concerned at the costs of civil litigation and believe[d] that the time [was] right for a fundamental and independent review of the whole system'.[33] In his review, Lord Justice Jackson identified a number of problems regarding witness statements:

> To prepare an effective witness statement in a complex case, substantial input is required from the witness. The lawyer must spend sufficient time with a witness so that he understands what the witness is trying to say. This in itself can rack up costs and this is before several iterations of the statements have been drafted and comments from the witness, counsel and the rest of the solicitor team have been taken into account. Often what appears to happen is that a witness statement

27. J. William Rowley KC, *The New York Convention at 50: Pieter Sanders – A tribute*, https://globalarbitrationreview.com/article/the-new-york-convention-50-pieter-sanders-tribute (accessed 17 April 2023).
28. Pieter Sanders, *Quo Vadis Arbitration?: Sixty Years of Arbitration Practice* (Springer Netherlands, 1999), 262.
29. *Ceviz v. Frawley & Anor* [2021] EWHC 8 (Ch), 3, 10.
30. UK Parliament, https://www.parliament.uk/site-information/glossary/lord-chancellor/, (accessed 17 April 2023).
31. A.A.S. Zuckerman, *Lord Woolf's Access to Justice: Plus ça change* (The Modern Law Review, 1996), 773.
32. Lord Justice Jackson, *Review of Civil Litigation Costs, Final Report*, TSO (The Stationary Office), 2010), 27.
33. Lord Justice Jackson, *supra* n. 32.

> simply repeats what is already in the documents and it ends up being a carefully crafted court document more akin to submissions than the story of a lay person.[34]

So, some thirty years after the witness statement became an integral part of English court proceedings on the basis that they would save time and costs – they have come under challenge as failing to deliver this and, instead, have increased costs and served to obscure what the evidence of the witness, in fact, is, replacing it with a lawyer's version of what that evidence should be. The extent of judicial criticism, from the same judicial sources responsible for the introduction of witness statements in the first place, suggests that reform is necessary. And if reform in the courts is necessary, it would be surprising if the position in international arbitration was fundamentally different.

§5.07 PURPOSE OF WITNESS STATEMENTS AND CHALLENGES IN PRESENTING WITNESS EVIDENCE

In order to understand and attempt to resolve the criticisms levelled against witness statements, it is important first to understand their fundamental purpose (which is no different as between court litigation and international arbitration). There is the general consensus, at least in England, that witness statements are intended to promote the 'fair and expeditious disposal of proceedings and the saving of costs'.[35] However, the current practice as to the lawyer-led preparation of witness statements has given rise to 'a real concern [...] that sometimes the use of witness statements, instead of saving costs and promoting fairness, has the opposite effect'.[36]

At the meeting of the Commercial Court Users Committee – the principal channel for the flow of information between the Court, litigants and lawyers[37] – in March 2018, concerns regarding the effectiveness of witness statements were raised. As a result, a working group was set up to consider ways in which the current practice could be improved (the 'Witness Evidence Working Group'). It was tasked with assessing factual witness evidence in trials before the Business and Property Courts in England and Wales.

The Witness Evidence Working Group found that only 6% of survey participants thought that the current system of witness statements 'fully' achieved the aim of producing the best evidence possible, with 45% of participants considering that it did so only partly or not at all.[38] Of those who gave reasons as to why witness statements did not fulfil their purpose,[39] 68% thought that they were too long, 73% felt they included legal arguments, and 55% thought that witness statements failed to reflect

34. Lord Justice Jackson, *supra* n. 17, 403.
35. White Book, *supra* n. 16.
36. Lord Justice Jackson, *supra* n. 17, 401.
37. HM Courts & Tribunals Service, *The Business and Property Courts of England & Wales, The Commercial Court Guide* (Eleventh Edition, 2022), paras A3.1 and A3.2.
38. Witness Evidence Working Group, *supra* n. 3, 9.
39. Seventy-five per cent of all participants that responded gave reasons as to why witness statements did not fulfil their purpose.

witnesses' own evidence.[40] The Witness Evidence Working Group outlines that a consistent theme emerges: the 'over-lawyered nature of witness statements'.[41]

At the same time, it seems clear that the answer is not to dispense with written witness statements altogether. In fact, a survey conducted by the School of International Arbitration at Queen Mary University of London and White & Case LLP found that 92% of respondents opposed eliminating witness evidence.[42] The answer, therefore, lies in changing the process by which witness statements are prepared in regard to the science of memory; here lies the true challenge in preparing witness statements.

The ICC Commission's Report on the Accuracy of Fact Witness Memory in International Arbitration (the 'ICC Report') notes that a witness' exposure to pre and post-event information can change the witness' memory of the event.[43] The ICC Report highlighted four areas of concern.

[A] The Impact of Phrasing on Responses to Questions

The ICC Report references studies which demonstrate that qualifying descriptors in a question can heavily influence the answer given. In one study, participants who were asked to estimate 'How long was the movie?' answered with an average of 130 minutes, compared with those who were asked 'How short was the movie?' who responded with 100 minutes on average.[44] This shows that the specific wording used in witness interviews can materially change the evidence that a witness recounts. However, standard practice in the preparation of witness statements involves a witness being questioned or interviewed by a lawyer who may go on to prepare a first draft of a witness statement based on the answers given by the witness. Therefore, the manner in which a witness is questioned can potentially have a material impact on his evidence.

[B] The Misinformation Effect

The misinformation effect is 'a phenomenon where typically misleading information which participants are exposed to after an event interferes with or impairs their original memory of that event'.[45] Studies have shown that where two subjects viewed somewhat different versions of an incident and discussed the events subsequently, they unwittingly transmitted misleading information to each other, which can substantially alter a witness' memory and report. The ICC Report even found that people 'tend to incorporate details of other witnesses' memory reports into their own memory

40. Witness Evidence Working Group, supra n. 3, 9.
41. Witness Evidence Working Group, *supra* n. 3, 9.
42. Queen Mary's University London, *International Arbitration Survey: Current and Preferred Practices in the Arbitral Process* (Queen Mary University London and School of International Arbitration, 2012), 29.
43. ICC Commission, *supra* n. 2, 2.5.
44. ICC Commission Report, *supra* n. 43, 11.
45. ICC Commission Report, *supra* n. 43, 11.

reports, even if that information contradicts what they have observed'.[46] In the arbitration context, this means that evidence given by witnesses may not be accurate as a result of prior discussions between the witness and others involved in the dispute.

[C] False Memories

At its extreme, the 'misinformation effect' has been shown to result in individuals 'recalling' entire fabricated events which happened to them personally. False memories can also arise from manufactured evidence. In one experiment, participants were asked to corroborate that they had seen another participant cheating. Those participants shown a false video were more likely to provide corroboration than those who had not seen the video despite the video showing something that had not happened.[47]

[D] The Impact of Retelling on Subsequent Recall

Research has shown that taking a particular perspective after an event can later lead to a biased recollection of the event. Participants in one study were provided with a story regarding an interaction with two roommates during their first week of a new year at college. One group was asked to write a letter complaining about the roommates, the second group was asked to write a positive letter about the roommates and the final group was merely asked to write about the roommates. When their memory was later tested, the participants' recollection of events was materially influenced by the stance they had been asked to take when writing the letters.

The ICC Report demonstrates that in the context of a commercial dispute, where a witness is often engaged in telling his or her story from a particular perspective, there is a real risk of a biased retelling.[48]

§5.08 A SUGGESTED WAY FORWARD

Although the ICC Report sets out a number of measures that could be taken to reduce distorting influences and their effects in international arbitration, the report concluded that it would not be appropriate to 'systematically take some or all [of the steps] to ensure that the memories of the witnesses who give evidence are as accurate as can be'.[49]

The ICC Report arrived at this conclusion because: (i) witness evidence does not always depend on accuracy, for example, where it is used to provide context, background or technical explanations; and (ii) even where accuracy is important, it is

46. ICC Commission Report, *supra* n. 43, 12.
47. ICC Commission Report, *supra* n. 43, 13.
48. ICC Commission Report, *supra* n. 43, 13.
49. ICC Commission Report, *supra* n. 43, 26.

not advisable to change current practices which ensure, for example, witnesses are prepared and provide helpful evidence.[50]

The authors would agree with the ICC Report's conclusion that there is no need for a 'systemic' change. However, the following steps can be taken in appropriate cases to ensure that witness evidence is necessary, accurate, helpful, and prepared without unnecessary costs being incurred.[51]

[A] Is Witness Evidence Necessary?

The starting point is for parties and counsel to consider whether or not witness evidence is necessary. In the experience of the authors, there is an increasing trend for witness statements simply to repeat what is set out in contemporaneous documents. This is unnecessary and leads to costs being incurred needlessly.

Generally, witness statements are required to: (i) prove disputed facts which cannot be proven by other documentary evidence; (ii) explain the context of certain documents, e.g., a telephone conversation which preceded an email exchange; (iii) provide background, e.g., explaining the efforts made by the founders of a company which led to goodwill in the market; and (iv) providing technical experience – although this would typically be the subject of expert evidence.[52]

The authors would suggest that arbitration practitioners should not shy away from following the civil law traditions of placing reliance upon documentary evidence where such evidence is clear. Certainly, in our experience, arbitral tribunals (even those from common law backgrounds) do not favourably consider witness statements that simply repeat the contents of documents already on the record.[53]

[B] Is Accuracy Important, and Is There a Risk of Contamination?

Counsel should consider taking alternative approaches to drafting witness statements depending on the extent to which: (i) accuracy in a witness' evidence is important; and (ii) there is a risk of contamination.

Accuracy is likely to be important where there are disputed facts and limited contemporaneous documents, such as where negotiations have taken place over a telephone call. But if there is a low risk of contamination because there is only one individual with the relevant information, then it may not be proportionate or appropriate to take all of the steps set out below.

50. ICC Commission Report, *supra* n. 43, section VI, 26 and 27.
51. *See also*: ICC Commission Report, *supra* n. 43, section V, 20.
52. ICC Commission Report, *supra* n. 43, section IV.B, 17.
53. *See also*: Appendix to CPR Practice Direction 57AC, paras 3.4 and 3.5, 3.

[C] Limited Direct Evidence

One of the benefits of practising in international arbitration is the ability to adopt practices deriving from different legal systems. The authors have experienced the practice in Stockholm of allowing some limited direct evidence from a witness, as well as using a witness statement. Not only does this give some 'colour' to the written testimony but it also means the witness is more 'invested' in the process of giving evidence and so less likely to delegate the exercise of preparing a witness statement to lawyers. Knowing that a witness will also be giving direct evidence (which can never be fully controlled by the lawyer in a way that written statements can) should serve to instil some caution and mean that written statements more closely align with the witness' factual knowledge. This approach also has the virtue of being straightforward to deliver on and not to require changes of any dramatic nature to existing protocols.

[D] Witness Summaries

The Report of the Witness Evidence Working Group, which considered the practice of factual witness evidence before the Business and Property Courts in England and Wales, has suggested the use of witness summaries instead of full witness statements. Under this approach:

> each witness would briefly outline the facts within his/her knowledge that are relevant to the issues in dispute, but would not go into extensive detail and would not refer to all of the documents (although it may be difficult for the witness to tell his/her story without reference to the key documents). Such an approach would mean that evidence-in-chief would need to be restored, in order that the witness can supplement his/her summary.[54]

The authors do not consider that witness summaries should replace witness statements. Properly drafted witness statements are of significant utility to an arbitral tribunal, particularly where unsophisticated witnesses, or witnesses whose first language is not the same as that of the arbitration (a common occurrence), are concerned. It is also a significant consideration that arbitrations are commonly more time-constrained than court trials, with much less capacity to accommodate lengthy direct examination (or for the adjournments necessary to accommodate cross-examination preparation if there is no advance notice of what a witness is going to say).

Instead, the authors are of the view that it may be appropriate to consider whether a witness should be first asked to prepare a summary of his evidence, which then forms the basis of interviews with lawyers according to which a witness statement can be prepared. Such an approach draws on the practice in the Supreme Court of Victoria, where witness statements are not 'ordered as a matter of course for commercial cases'[55] but where the court may order the provision of a witness outline which must 'clearly identify the topics in respect of which evidence will be given and the

54. Lord Justice Jackson, *supra* n. 17, 407.
55. Hope, *supra* n. 13, 17.

substance of that evidence. A witness outline must be directed only to matters in issue'.[56]

The preparation of witness summaries in the way proposed by the authors would minimise risks of inaccuracies in witness recollection and would allow for the preparation of a witness statement that seeks to clarify rather than alter or interfere with a witness' evidence.

The authors also consider, drawing on their previous experience of limited direct evidence from witnesses of fact in Stockholm arbitrations, that adopting this practice would bring significant benefits.

[E] Witness Interviews

Bearing in mind that witness statements were intended to replace lengthy direct examination,[57] it is logical that witness interviews are conducted in a manner that is similar to a direct examination. This would mean using open-ended and not leading questions to minimise the impact of phrasing on responses,[58] interviewing witnesses individually to minimise contamination of memory and keeping an accurate record of the interview so that any subsequent witness statement can accurately reflect the witness' evidence.[59]

[F] Preparation of Witness Statements

In England, trial witness statements are now to be prepared in accordance with the Statement of Best Practice, which forms part of Practice Direction 57AC of the Civil Procedure Rules. This requires that 'The preparation of a trial witness statement should involve as few drafts as practicable'[60] because 'Any process of repeatedly revisiting a draft statement may corrupt rather than improve recollection.'[61] Witness statements should also be as far as possible in the witnesses' own words[62] and should be based on the record of the interviews with the witness and the witness summary.[63] Witness statements should not contain commentary, speculation, argument or any narrative about disclosed documents.[64]

56. The Commercial Court of the Victoria Supreme Court (Practice Note No. 10 of 2011), 38.
57. In fact, para. 2.1 of PD57AC states 'The purpose of a trial witness statement is to set out in writing the evidence in chief that a witness of fact would give if they were allowed to give oral evidence at trial without having provided the statement.'
58. ICC Commission Report, *supra* n. 43, section II.A; Appendix to CPR Practice Direction 57AC, para. 3.10.
59. ICC Commission Report, *supra* n. 43, section V.A.(ii).
60. Appendix to CPR Practice Direction 57AC, *supra* n. 53, para. 3.8.
61. Appendix to CPR Practice Direction 57AC, *supra* n. 53, para. 3.8.
62. Appendix to CPR Practice Direction 57AC, *supra* n. 53, para. 3.6.
63. Appendix to CPR Practice Direction 57AC, *supra* n. 53, paras 3.9 and 3.12.
64. Appendix to CPR Practice Direction 57AC, *supra* n. 53, para. 3.5.

[G] Use of AI and Similar Technologies

The focus of recent months on the use of artificial intelligence tools such as ChatGPT has yet to feed into the debate about the use of witness statements, but the stated intentions of certain EU states to legislate to contain the use of AI reflect a set of concerns that will doubtless be expressed by judges and arbitrators; what credibility can ever be attached to a statement that is machine produced rather than the product of a witness' work? Soon enough, we can expect to see express prohibitions on the use of AI to draft statements, easily introduced in institutional rules or by tribunals in procedural orders. However, the authors can see no foolproof way of policing such restrictions.

§5.09 ENFORCEMENT CHALLENGES

Reforms such as Practice Direction 57AC which implement changes in relation to factual witness evidence in national courts are strictly enforced by the courts, including by way of orders which require non-compliant sections of the witness statements to be revised.[65]

The authors do not consider such a strict approach appropriate in international arbitration and concur with the ICC Task Force's view that the preparation of witness statements should not become subject to enquiry by the Tribunal.[66] Such an approach is only likely to result in unnecessary delay and costs. Instead, similar to the approach under the London Maritime Arbitrators Association Rules ('LMAA Rules'), the advancing of needless, irrelevant and prolix witness evidence could be a factor which the Tribunals can consider in apportioning costs.[67] In that context, it is worth noting that the LMAA Rules include a Checklist in the Fourth Schedule which also addresses the manner in which factual evidence should be presented to the Tribunal. The authors suggest that there is a great deal of more scope generally for efficiencies in the conduct of arbitrations to be fostered by the use of more discerning orders for costs (including at various stages during the proceedings) that reflect more fully how parties respectively have run an arbitration.

§5.10 CONCLUSION

Civil and common law jurisdictions have over the centuries developed their own practices in relation to factual witness evidence. Both approaches have their advantages and disadvantages, but international arbitration enjoys the privileged position of being able to choose on an 'á la carte' basis the best elements of each. Practices such as greater use of a discerning approach taken to how witness statements are to be

65. *Blue Manchester Limited v. (1) Bug-Alu Technic GmbH & (2) Simpsonhaugh Architects Limited* [2021] EWHC 3095 (TCC), 3, 6.
66. ICC Commission Report, *supra* n. 53 para. 6.9.
67. LMAA Terms 2021, Schedule 2, para. 19(b).

prepared and deployed, usefully drawing from the experience of reforms in national court systems, including recent English reforms, should be encouraged. Arbitration practitioners – particularly tribunals – should increasingly challenge lazy assumptions as to how witness evidence should be deployed efficiently and fairly, exploiting to the fullest degree the flexibility that is said to be one of international arbitration's greatest strengths.

CHAPTER 6

Stating the Obvious and Connectivity to Self*

Carita Wallgren-Lindholm

§6.01 TAKING THINGS FOR GRANTED VERSUS MANAGING REFLEXES IN A MIX OF LEGAL TRADITIONS

Numerous are the surprised, and even suspicious, reactions to an arbitrator asking about the meaning that counsel ascribe to a commonly used concept in international arbitration. Does the arbitrator not know what "cut-off date" means? Or understand that s(he) obviously can rule on the parties' claims in any order that s(he) feels is appropriate or convenient? How about the arbitrator's ability to "massage" the claim if it does not lend itself to a ruling or award as written? And everyone of course knows without asking that direct examination is a "no-no" beyond warm-up, and no one of course can call his or her own witnesses to be heard or cross-examined beyond the four corners of a witness statement.

Everyone "in the know" knows about these matters, and it is not worth spending time on them, let alone writing about them, in a procedural order.

Whatever the merit of these rather trivial examples, it is my view that too much is often taken for granted by too many at the beginning of an arbitration. And too little time is usually allocated at the outset to explore what exactly participants read into the quite standard documentation and the standard terminology, homegrown somewhere and then imported into new settings.

These thoughts I have entertained and also uttered many times before, so some of you may find them neither novel nor original. It is also true that matters that we have been passionate about for long risk appearing worn, repetitive and maybe even

* This chapter only addresses commercial arbitration, and makes scattered observations on arbitrating in Sweden with Swedes and others.

outdated. However, with the risk of yet again stating the obvious, it is not possible to look away from the fact that so much is taken for granted, especially in fora—like Sweden—with long arbitral traditions, developed arbitration practices and experienced arbitration counsel. Content is provided by a commonly shared vision, and gaps are filled in a uniform manner by counsel on both sides (if they are Swedish). In quoting an oft-quoted late American politician, it can be difficult for a non-Swedish arbitrator to know what it is that s(he) does not know or can take account of (*unknown unknowns*). And even where the arbitrator would be prone to conduct the proceedings in his/her household style, the efficiency of the arbitration is not enhanced when participants have partly differing models and structures in their heads that they act upon and see as the default position (failing directions to the contrary).[1]

Another question that could be asked more frequently by arbitrators is *do we really need all this in this case.* It is not an overstatement to say that proceedings are quite often unnecessarily inflated procedurally. Even where an arbitrator is confident enough not to fear looking inexperienced, questioning the necessity to use all proposed procedural tools could risk an appearance of disrespect or come out as belittling the importance of the case at hand. However, cumulation of procedural tools from different legal systems is, necessarily, bound to result in increased time and cost. The driver behind some cumulation may also be counsel's view of their ethical obligations under their own Bar Rules. While my observation is that Swedish arbitral counsel are well versed—and comfortable—in their deontological duties, which in my experience seldom appear to have clashed with how international arbitration is usually conducted, this may not be the case regarding all counsel coming from outside of Sweden. But in order for a discussion to be held, e.g., regarding the necessity for comprehensive oral testimony, everyone obviously needs to recognize that what may be a mandatory, or at least a best-practice, exercise before a national (foreign) court may not be a necessity in an international arbitration, e.g., in Stockholm. And even where it is recognized that procedural fairness in proceedings governed by Swedish *lex arbitri* may not require all the moves that counsel are used to seeing as compulsory, a mental barrier may exist on an individual level that can constitute a limitation to act outside of one's customary pattern or practice.[2]

So what can the aforesaid boil down to in practice, and how can arbitrators initiate a meaningful discussion that is conducive to leaner procedures without interfering with parties' right to use counsel of their choice? Maybe it would be useful to have an initial discussion (instead of interference in the examination of witnesses later on) to the effect that a Nordic-chaired arbitration would mostly be happy to have clearly worded documents speak for themselves (without witness mirroring, interpretation or corroboration), that we will assume that documents are not forged, and witnesses speak the truth (unless contra-indications exist) and that less text is often

1. I obviously recognize that (best) practices in international commercial arbitration are standardized in many respects, largely as a result of so-called soft law. This, however, does not in my view mean that there is one overriding uniform practice across continents and regions.
2. I have chosen generally not to give examples in order to maintain the discussion on an abstract, principled level.

more in terms of clarity. Swedish counsel, I will note, are mostly commendably good at brevity. And while also in Sweden, famous respondents' counsel have been known for their skills in muddying the waters, in Sweden, you can as a rule expect, and can as a tribunal indicate that you expect, symmetrical pleadings in the sense that arguments of opposing counsel are addressed head on (instead of offering an alternative narrative that never meets the other party's case).

Any such initial discussion between the arbitral tribunal and the parties is not only to set ground rules but also a tone. To increase predictability, it is also only fair for a tribunal to articulate up front its general expectations. While obviously a tribunal cannot and should not interfere with who does what in a party's counsel team, principled dialogue may at least plant a thought in the participants to (re)think roles in the team. Relative closeness to the context of the dispute and the legal tradition of the seat are of a nature to increase efficiency, as is obviously the best concrete knowledge in the team of the substantive question at hand. It is unfortunate when a chair needs to intervene in counsel's activities during oral testimony for time management or in order to shield a witness.

Also, the volume of documents and their character can, and often should, be discussed initially in an effort to coin the principle that, while some context obviously is necessary and useful, it is oftentimes sufficient to exhibit written evidence only for matters as and when those matters are in dispute instead of submitting, for all eventualities, everything related to the transaction underlying the dispute. It is not uncommon in Sweden that the aggregate number of exhibits does not exceed by much what we know as the bundle of core documents for the hearing. The tribunal could explain that it can be trusted to allow submission of documents later in the proceedings should a new point of disagreement arise that was not foreseen at the outset. While access to the opposing party's documents as a procedural right is seen as fundamental in certain procedural cultures, with ensuing obligations also for counsel, this of course is not true in others. And on a practical level, Nordic counsel would traditionally lean back if a moving party cannot substantiate its allegations instead of asking for document production to disprove a mere allegation. It is certainly the case that refraining from trying to disprove allegations that have not been corroborated by evidence or dispensing with proving what is fundamentally not in dispute (to provide context) are measures that keep the dispute centered on its core elements, not only saving time and money but also providing clarity to the adjudicators. While we all know the benefits of repetition in the learning process, counsel should assume that arbitrators pick up arguments after one or two presentations and that repetition also can have a numbing and distracting effect.

In order for a meaningful exchange to take place between all participants in the arbitration, it is of course important that we all fundamentally respect and accept other legal traditions as at least being adequate. In addition to a certain humility in all, taking the time to understand the rationale and functioning, as well as context, of the procedural measures proposed to be used will assist in identifying presumptions and tacit expectations and weed out cumulative procedural steps. We may all find novel ways to secure access to justice, due process and equal treatment; there is really no acquired right to do things a certain way. From an arbitrator's perspective, the readiness of counsel to downshift and streamline procedures often reflects mastery of and confidence in the case.

All the above softly argues in favor of allowing conversational time at the outset of an arbitration in order to save time going forward. This may not only hopefully decrease the volume of materials on the record and time generally but also avoid constant interruptions due to disagreement down the road on matters that can arise from opposing legitimate expectations. There is of course no great wisdom in this observation but only common sense for an arbitrator to first endeavor to understand that (s)he may not share the parties' paradigm and then have the courage to ask for clarification. It will also require that counsel is sufficiently comparatively versed to take a healthy distance from his/her own jurisdictional habitat or, indeed, his/her own perception of what constitutes "best practices in international arbitration" to be able to explain what he/she deems applicable absent agreed or ordered regulation for the arbitration at hand. It is of course not efficient to have arbitrators manage procedural measures, the function and operation of which they do not understand.

Above, I have been advocating for more procedural discourse for clarity in the arbitral proceedings. In a somewhat different vein, I may advocate for less explanation of the basic elements of the law applicable to the merits, which sometimes occurs where legal argument is handled by quite junior lawyers (in a big team). Here, I would warn against underestimating arbitrators' general understanding of the law, even if foreign. Arbitrators' grasp of the law is not infrequently broad and holistic, especially in arbitrators of some seniority. It would be wise for a counsel team to have a senior lawyer well versed, e.g., in Company Law, Securities, or other Market Law, draft/plead necessary sections of submissions/pleadings. This would not only be useful to avoid potential irritation amongst the arbitrators but also to save time and money. Especially if arguments consist in explaining to foreign lawyers technicalities of local business laws, too junior a presentation will come out as—yes—technical and uninformed from the perspective of arbitrators who may have broad experience in cross-border transactions and will recognize patterns in regulation. While it is of course important not to overestimate an arbitrator's understanding of other trades, it is a fair assumption that he/she has a basic understanding of the functioning of the law generally. Reading an arbitrator's CV may help in the relevant respect. Seniority (partner) driven top-down structured cases tend to be more compelling than bottom-up structures.

It will have become obvious that I believe in communication and in an effort to actively listen and try to understand the expectations and tacit presumptions of all participants in an arbitration prior to agreeing or ordering the sequences thereof. This, of course, also presupposes the ability of the tribunal to identify and act upon a situation where prerequisites for consensual solutions do not exist. And I obviously do not need to qualify by further developing given limitations to openness and transparency that follow from the nature of adjudication.

§6.02 IS SWEDEN FORMALISTIC?

As surprising as many, especially among the Swedes, may find, I would like to answer in the affirmative. Swedish arbitration practitioners tend to be remarkably formalistic in certain respects relating to procedure, often drawing from civil law procedure in the courts. One area where I have also discerned a certain formalism is tribunal deliberations and the related procedure. While obviously deliberation for a final award requires some structure, my (anecdotal) perception is that Swedish arbitrators do not necessarily expect to discuss the case or the testimony as it proceeds but await a formal deliberation at the end. This is a phenomenon that I am still somewhat struggling to align with considering what we (Finns) have seen as a conversational tradition and a very open climate of debate in Sweden. A strong fear of prejudging the case may explain the restraint in discussing it as it proceeds.

§6.03 OUTSIDE PERCEPTIONS COUNT

I stated above that my impression is that Swedish counsel have good compasses when it comes to their deontological duties, something that I have noted also in other societies where ethical rules are largely principle-based and not casuistic. I also believe Sweden has and has had an open conversational climate regarding the duties of advocates. It is also obvious and attractive—to see the cordiality and collegiality that Swedish advocates pay to one another and the trust they place in each other's promises. I believe that the awareness among professionals that you are only as good as your word is even stronger in small societies such as Sweden (and Finland). And because Swedish counsel place trust in each other, they obviously—and rightly so—believe they are worthy of the same trust themselves. However, while Swedish advocates in Sweden are trusted to have friends plead before them or to be dissociated from close relationships high up the echelon of Swedish corporates when dealing with their cases, these situations may not look like arms' length relationships to parties or counsel from other cultures and legal traditions. While I, as a neighbor, am familiar with the respectful professional climate that exists inside the legal profession in Sweden—including the judiciary and academia—I believe that we Nordic lawyers need to pay particular attention to the reactions that may be prompted abroad from the fact that we are seen as closely knit and all know and liaise with one another professionally and otherwise. We should especially not be offended when particulars are asked about our relationships with one another, and we should be ready to engage in related discussions and disclosure (as far as our professional duties allow).

§6.04 SWEDISH PRACTITIONERS OF INTERNATIONAL ARBITRATION: ANECDOTAL

Having observed Swedish arbitration practitioners for long I find them generally very accomplished, well versed in law, including comparative law, and proficient languagewise (with the small caveat mentioned above that sometimes there exist assumptions regarding the way forward shared among "those in the know" which are not always visible to those from outside of Sweden).[3] Swedes are also, as a rule, good at oral advocacy (something that we Finns admire, being less so). Whether prompted by peer pressure/observation or culture, I find that we can expect Swedish counsel to be sincere and truthful. And truth, even if farfetched, is compelling as we know. I already referenced above a skill of brevity, which often translates into clarity. And brevity and clarity often come out as confidence, also in the case at hand. As a Finn, I obviously also relate well to a capacity to lower the voice in order to be heard. And the Swedes will hopefully forgive a Finn for revealing that we often in Finland say that the Swedes, underneath their pleasant demeanor, are ultimately much tougher—and even more merciless—than us Finns. And I will not deny that I have made similar observations.

When I was a partner in a big law firm on both sides of the millennium (and on both sides of the sea that separates us), we thought that one of our biggest challenges was to be able to remain lead counsel in transactions involving our country(ies) and to be able to take the lead also in international arbitrations seated in the Nordic region. This was at the time when many international law firms were landing on our shores to establish themselves or to practice here. Though I cannot claim to have my finger on the pulse any longer, it seems to me that Sweden has done well and managed to foster and retain a corps of practitioners who are internationally competitive and deliver international products. I also think Finland has benefited from the Swedish arbitration world and ongoing cross-fertilization between practices in the two countries. And I hope there is more to come; even though the formal joint legislative projects between our countries are not as active as in the past, our joint traditions, also in arbitration, are well worth preserving and fostering.

3. Non-Nordic practitioners have been known to sometimes say that *arbitration in Sweden is very Swedish.*

CHAPTER 7

Emergency Arbitration Meets the Courts

Cameron Sim

§7.01 INTRODUCTION

First encounters often do not go entirely as expected. This is particularly the case where there has been much trepidation prior to the meeting. Often, this turns out to have been both unnecessary and counterproductive. After initial contact, it may become clear, sometimes immediately, that there was nothing to be concerned about. Fear may morph into empowerment as a bright and certain future suddenly emerges.

When emergency arbitration first appeared in international arbitration, serious doubts, and at times vociferous opposition, were expressed in some quarters as to the viability of the procedure, and whether courts would, or even should, recognize and enforce decisions issued by emergency arbitrators. It is fair to say that the enforceability debate has dominated emergency arbitration jurisprudence. However, as has been identified, enforceability is 'the wrong debate'.[1] The debate has given rise to negative perceptions about emergency arbitration, with the focus on negative risks (viz. a court refusing enforcement) as opposed to positive outcomes (viz. obtaining urgent relief, with reported high levels of party compliance, thus avoiding the need to go to court).[2] The debate has also seen other contentious and complex issues in emergency arbitration not receive the attention they deserve, including most prominently, the role of the seat of emergency arbitration, applicable laws, and the application of due process norms.

Inevitably, emergency arbitration decisions have appeared before domestic courts. As emergency arbitration has found itself the subject of judicial consideration in

1. Diana Paraguacuto-Mahéo and Christine Lecuyer-Thieffry, *Emergency Arbitrator: A New Player in the Field – The French Perspective*, 40(3) Fordham International Law Journal 749, 761 (2017).
2. *See, e.g.*, ICC Commission Report: Emergency Arbitrator Proceedings (International Chamber of Commerce, April 2019), para. 202.

jurisdictions across the globe, a clear trend appears to be emerging. For the most part, courts have shown themselves to be willing to adhere to the expectations of international arbitration users, give efficacy to their use of the procedure, and display comity towards emergency arbitrators. In so doing, courts have also demonstrated their commitment to due process and to vindicating the rights of all parties involved in the proceedings. Broadly, with minor exceptions, the first encounters of emergency arbitration meeting the courts have been relatively uneventful and ought to have assuaged much of the apprehension surrounding the rise of the procedure.

After outlining the basics and benefits of emergency arbitration, this chapter explores how courts in several jurisdictions have reacted to key issues concerning emergency arbitration. These issues include the jurisdiction of the emergency arbitrator, the operation of the principle of concurrent jurisdiction between emergency arbitrators and courts, the application of due process norms, and the enforceability of emergency arbitration decisions.[3] Whilst there has been some inconsistency in approach, overall, courts have strengthened the foundations of emergency arbitration. In turn, this has reinforced party autonomy in international arbitration, and is likely to ensure the longevity and popularity of the procedure. There remain other key issues which still require further exploration in the courts. This chapter concludes by identifying those issues and how courts may choose to deal with them.

§7.02 THE BASICS AND BENEFITS OF EMERGENCY ARBITRATION

Emergency arbitration is a relatively recent innovation in international arbitration. Whilst the parties may be embroiled in rapid and escalating developments at the time of commencement of proceedings, somewhat paradoxically, arbitrations often get off to a slow start as the parties engage in the tribunal formation process. This can be lengthy, depending on the size of the tribunal, the process for arbitrator nomination and confirmation, the speed at which the arbitral institute operates, whether agreement can be reached between the parties and any challenges that are raised. During this period, it may become necessary for a party to apply for urgent interim relief to protect their rights pending the ultimate determination of their claims by the arbitral tribunal. Without such protection, it may be that the respondent's dissemination of assets, destruction of evidence or property, dissemination of confidential information, or engagement in some other form of harm or wrongdoing may defeat the purpose of pursuing claims and obtaining relief where it may end up being futile.

Prior to the advent of emergency arbitration, a party requiring urgent relief during the period required for tribunal formation could only turn to domestic courts for assistance.[4] Where emergency arbitration is available under the applicable arbitration rules, a party may now seek relief during that period from an emergency arbitrator. In 1999, the first emergency arbitration rules appeared in the Commercial Arbitration

3. Emergency arbitration rules refer variously to both awards and orders. For ease of reference, the term emergency arbitration decision is adopted to include both awards and orders.
4. Subject to instances where the parties have agreed on the availability of other fora for pre-tribunal relief, such as before a dispute board, or before a referee under the ICC Pre-Arbitral Referee Rules.

Rules of the American Arbitration Association (AAA), which included opt-in 'Optional Rules for Emergency Measures of Protection'.[5] In 2006, the International Centre for Dispute Resolution (ICDR) adopted out-out emergency arbitration rules.[6] Over the coming decade, many arbitral institutes worldwide followed suit. Emergency arbitration rules now appear in many of the leading international arbitration rules. The majority are on an opt-out basis with retroactive application.[7]

The reasons emergency arbitration may be preferable to seeking relief from courts reflect the reasons parties choose arbitration in the first place. The confidentiality of arbitral proceedings extends to emergency arbitrations, and parties may wish to retain confidentiality over all aspects of their dispute. The parties may also have concerns about the quality of decision-making in courts of competent jurisdiction, or even the neutrality of justice available, and may instead prefer to have an emergency arbitrator, potentially specialized in the relevant industry, determine the application for urgent relief. Equally, the parties may wish to avoid procedural complexity. This may arise if several courts need to be approached for interim relief, which in turn may require the application of different laws (and engagement of multiple legal teams), create the risk of inconsistent decisions between courts, and even lead to the issuing of incompatible forms of relief. Court judgments may also be subject to appeal, which risks causing delay. In contrast, emergency arbitration may present a streamlined method to obtain the relief that is required before a single decision-maker. In addition, there may be a risk that courts will prejudge the merits of the parties' claims, whereas an emergency arbitrator should only consider whether the claimant has a *prima facie* case, or reasonable prospects of success, on the merits of the underlying claims.

In summary, an emergency arbitration runs as follows. The applicant files an application with the relevant arbitral institute. Under most emergency arbitration rules, the respondent is notified of the proceedings, although some rules permit ex parte proceedings.[8] The arbitral institute appoints the emergency arbitrator in short order, typically within one day,[9] two days,[10] or three days.[11] The emergency arbitrator has

5. American Arbitration Association Commercial Arbitration Rules and Mediation Procedures (1999) Optional Rules for Emergency Measures of Protection, O-1 to O-8.
6. International Centre for Dispute Resolution International Arbitration Rules (2006) Art. 37(c).
7. *See, e.g.*, Commercial Rules of the American Arbitration Association (2013) (AAA Rules), R-38(d); Arbitration Rules of the Australian Centre for International Commercial Arbitration (2021) (ACICA Rules), Art. 2.4; China International Economic and Trade Arbitration Commission Arbitration Rules (2015) (CIETAC Rules), Arts 4(2)-4(3); Hong Kong International Arbitration Centre (2018) (HKIAC Rules), Art. 1.4; International Chamber of Commerce Arbitration Rules (2021) (ICC Rules), Art. 29(6)(a); International Centre for Dispute Resolution International Arbitration Rules (2021) (ICDR Rules), Art. 1(1); Arbitration Rules of the London Court of International Arbitration (2020) (LCIA Rules), Art. 9.16; Swiss Chambers' Arbitration Institution, Swiss Rules of International Arbitration (2021) (Swiss Rules), Art. 1(2); Arbitration Institute of the Stockholm Chamber of Commerce Arbitration Rules (2017) (SCC Rules), Preamble; Arbitration Rules of the Singapore International Arbitration Centre (2016) (SIAC Rules), Rule 1.2.
8. Swiss Rules, Arts 29(3), 43(1); Arbitrators' and Mediators' Institute of New Zealand Arbitration Rules (2017) (AMINZ Rules), Art. 50.2.
9. *See, e.g.*, AAA Rules, R-38(c); ACICA Rules, Schedule 1, para. 2.1; ICDR Rules, Art. 7(2); SCC Rules, App. II, Art. 4(3).
10. *See, e.g.*, CIETAC Rules, App. III, Art. 3; SIAC Rules, Schedule 1, para. 5.
11. *See, e.g.*, HKIAC Rules, Schedule 4, para. 7; ICC Rules, App. V, Art. 3(1); Swiss Rules, Art. 43(4).

wide procedural discretion over the conduct of the proceedings, including as to the number and form of submissions, and whether a hearing is required.[12] In determining the application, the central issue is urgency and, specifically, whether the relief sought could await the constitution of the arbitral tribunal.[13] Other issues often include those typically arising for consideration in applications for interim measures, including whether the claimant has demonstrated a risk of irreparable harm,[14] a prima facie case or reasonable prospects of success on the merits of its substantive claims,[15] and that the balancing of the parties' interests militates in favour of the imposition of relief.[16]

Under most rules, the emergency arbitrator must issue a decision within a prescribed timeframe, ranging from five days[17] to fourteen days[18] to fifteen days,[19] although some rules are silent as to the permitted timeframe.[20] To sustain the application for emergency measures, and subject to the applicable rules, the applicant is required to file a notice of arbitration and thereby commence arbitration on the merits either prior to or simultaneously with,[21] or within a short period after filing for emergency arbitration (typically seven to ten days),[22] or within a longer thirty-day period.[23] The arbitral tribunal, once constituted, is not bound by the emergency arbitrator's decision, and is typically empowered to modify, terminate or annul it.[24]

§7.03 JURISDICTION OF THE EMERGENCY ARBITRATOR

The principle of Kompetenz-Kompetenz applies in emergency arbitration. This entails that the emergency arbitrator reaches a determination on their own jurisdiction. Many emergency arbitration rules expressly specify this to be the case.[25]

12. *See, e.g.*, CIETAC Rules, App. III, Art. 5(1); ICC Rules, App. V, Art. 5(2); LCIA Rules, Art. 9.7; SIAC Rules, Schedule 1, para. 14; SCC Rules, App II, Art. 7; Swiss Rules, Art. 43(6).
13. *See, e.g.*, CIETAC Rules, App. III, Art. 1(1); HKIAC Rules, Schedule 4, para. 2(d); ICC Rules, Art. 29(1) and App. V, Art. 1(3)(e); ICDR Rules, Art. 7(1)(b).
14. *See, e.g.*, AAA Rules, R-38(e); ACICA Rules, Schedule 1, para. 3.5(a).
15. *See, e.g.*, ACICA Rules, Schedule 1, para. 3.5(c); HKIAC Rules, Schedule 4, para. 11.
16. *See, e.g.*, ACICA Rules, Schedule 1, para. 3.5(b); HKIAC Rules, Schedule 4, para. 11.
17. *See, e.g.*, ACICA Rules, Schedule 1, para. 3.1; SCC Rules, App. II, Art. 8.
18. *See, e.g.*, HKIAC Rules, Schedule 4, para. 12; LCIA Rules, Art. 9.8; SIAC Rules, Schedule 1, para. 9.
19. *See, e.g.*, CIETAC Rules, App. III, Art. 6(2); ICC Rules, App. V, Art. 6(4); Swiss Rules, Art. 43(7).
20. *See, e.g.*, AAA Rules; ICDR Rules.
21. *See, e.g.*, ACICA Rules, Schedule 1, para. 1.2(b); ICDR Rules, Art. 7(1); LCIA Rules, Art. 9.5; SIAC Rules, Schedule 1, para. 1.
22. *See, e.g.*, HKIAC Rules, Schedule 4, para. 21; ICC Rules, App. V, Art. 1(6); Swiss Rules, Art. 43(3).
23. *See, e.g.*, SCC Rules, App. II, Art. 9(4)(iii).
24. *See, e.g.*, AAA Rules, R-38(f); ACICA Rules, Schedule 1, para. 5.2; CIETAC Rules, App. III, Art. 6(4); HKIAC Rules, Schedule 4, para. 11; ICC Rules, Art. 29(3); ICDR Rules, Art. 7(5); LCIA Rules, Art. 9.11; SCC Rules, App. II, Art. 9(4)(i); SIAC Rules, Schedule 1, para. 10; Swiss Rules, Art. 43(8).
25. *See, e.g.*, AAA Rules, R-38(d); HKIAC Rules, Schedule 4, para. 10; ICC Rules, App. V, Art. 6(2); LCIA Rules, Art. 9.14; SIAC Rules, Schedule 1, para. 7.

In *GD v. HY*,[26] the Hong Kong High Court accepted implicitly that the principle of Kompetenz-Kompetenz applies in emergency arbitration but disagreed with the emergency arbitrator's assessment of jurisdiction. The claimant had obtained an emergency arbitration award (albeit the Court's judgment does not specify under which rules the emergency arbitration took place). This included typical interim relief in the form of an order restraining the respondent from dissipating its assets and requiring the respondent to disclose a list of its assets. Unlike most jurisdictions which have yet to amend their arbitration laws following the advent of emergency arbitration, the Hong Kong Arbitration Ordinance expressly recognizes the enforceability of emergency arbitration awards, and permits *ex parte* enforcement of them.[27] The High Court granted the claimant leave for enforcement on such an *ex parte* application, following which the respondent applied to set aside the enforcement order on the basis that the emergency arbitrator did not have jurisdiction.

The emergency arbitrator had concluded that he had jurisdiction on the basis of an extension letter to a loan agreement. The extension letter contained an arbitration agreement, whereas the loan agreement contained an exclusive jurisdiction clause in favour of the Hong Kong courts. The loan agreement contained a stock standard variation provision, which required the written agreement of all parties to any variation of the terms of the loan. The extension letter had been signed by both the claimant and the respondent to the emergency arbitration, but it had not been signed by all parties to the loan agreement. In setting aside the enforcement order, the High Court held that this was fatal and that, as a matter of contractual interpretation, the loan agreement could only be varied by a written instrument signed by all parties.[28]

In reaching this decision, the High Court applied the test under Hong Kong law for the court to review and be satisfied as to the correctness of an arbitral tribunal's ruling on its own jurisdiction.[29] It is striking that in conducting this assessment, the Court did not call into question the status of the emergency arbitrator or query the power of the emergency arbitrator to rule on their own jurisdiction. This was taken for granted. The issue, instead, was whether the emergency arbitrator had reached the correct legal decision in the same manner in which the court would assess whether an arbitral tribunal had reached the correct legal decision on its jurisdiction.

§7.04 CONCURRENT JURISDICTION BETWEEN EMERGENCY ARBITRATORS AND COURTS

Concurrent jurisdiction refers to the principle of co-existence that remains between courts and arbitral tribunals when it comes to issuing interim measures in support of arbitral proceedings. Even where parties have agreed to arbitrate their disputes, in most circumstances, arbitral tribunals do not have exclusive jurisdiction to issue

26. *GD v. HY* [2021] HKCFI 3900.
27. Hong Kong Arbitration Ordinance (Cap. 609) section 22B(1).
28. *GD v. HY* [2021] HKCFI 3900, paras 10 to 12.
29. *S Co v. B Co* [2014] 6 HKC 421.

interim measures, and where appropriate, parties may also turn to courts for assistance. The principle of concurrent jurisdiction has been described as 'deeply-engrained' in the framework of international arbitration.[30]

[A] The Tensions Inherent in Concurrent Jurisdiction

Inevitable tensions arise where two decision-making bodies have jurisdiction over the same or similar issues. In the emergency arbitration context, this issue is whether interim measures are required prior to the constitution of the arbitral tribunal. Emergency arbitration rules generally expressly preserve the principle of concurrent jurisdiction. Several rules specify that an application to the court for interim measures is not to be deemed incompatible with the applicable emergency arbitration rules,[31] with some going further and stipulating that such an application should not be deemed incompatible with the parties' arbitration agreement and should not be deemed a waiver of the right to arbitrate.[32] Along similar substantive lines, other emergency arbitration rules stipulate that the availability of emergency arbitration should not prejudice or affect a party's right to apply to a court for interim measures[33] or that this availability is not intended to prevent a party from seeking interim measures from a court.[34]

It is likely that, on many occasions, we will see courts grappling with the principle of concurrent jurisdiction arising in different scenarios. These include whether they should exercise their jurisdiction to issue interim measures in support of arbitration where emergency arbitration is an available option, where an emergency arbitration is already underway, or where the claimant has already been unsuccessful in an emergency arbitration. Whilst emergency arbitration rules are intended to preserve the principle of concurrent jurisdiction, there has already been some judicial reluctance to act where the principle is engaged. Equally, emergency arbitrators will likewise grapple with the question as to whether they should issue interim measures in circumstances where a like application is being pursued simultaneously or has already failed in the courts.

[B] The Decision in Gerald Metals

In *Gerald Metals SA v. Timis*, the High Court of England and Wales considered the principle of concurrent jurisdiction in the context of the LCIA Rules and their interaction with the *Arbitration Act 1996* (UK).[35] Section 44(3) of the Act empowers the court 'on the application of a party or proposed party to the arbitral proceedings, [to]

30. Gary Born, *International Commercial Arbitration* (3rd edn, Kluwer Law International 2020) p. 2639.
31. *See, e.g.*, AAA Rules, R-38(h); ICDR Rules, Art. 7(7); Swiss Rules, Art. 43(8).
32. *See, e.g.*, ICC Rules, Art. 29(7); SCC Rules, App. II, Art. 1(2); SIAC Rules, Rule 30.3.
33. *See, e.g.*, ACICA Rules, Schedule 1, para. 7.1; CIETAC Rules, App. III, Art. 5(4).
34. *See, e.g.*, ICC Rules, Art. 29(7).
35. *Gerald Metals SA v. Timis* [2016] EWHC 2237 (Ch).

make such orders as it thinks necessary for the purpose of preserving evidence or assets', but provided that 'the case is one of urgency'.[36] This power is limited by section 44(5) of the Act, which provides that 'the court shall act only if or to the extent that the arbitral tribunal, and any arbitral or other institution or person vested by the parties with power in that regard, has no power or is unable for the time being to act effectively.'[37] Article 9B of the LCIA Rules contains an emergency arbitration procedure. This permits a party 'in the case of emergency at any time prior to the formation or expedited formation of the Arbitral Tribunal' to apply for the appointment of an emergency arbitrator.[38]

The claimant in *Gerald Metals* applied pursuant to the LCIA Rules for the appointment of an emergency arbitrator to seek an order to prevent a trustee from disposing of a Cayman trust's assets. The trustee provided various undertakings aimed at obviating the need for urgent relief. The LCIA rejected the application for the appointment of an emergency arbitrator. The claimant then approached the High Court for relief pursuant to section 44.

The Court dismissed the claimant's application. This was on the basis that courts are only empowered to act pursuant to section 44 if the expedited tribunal formation or emergency arbitration provisions are 'inadequate' to address the situation[39] or 'where the practical ability is lacking to exercise those powers'.[40] The Court acknowledged that there may be instances where emergency arbitration is 'insufficient' for a claimant, and court assistance may be required.[41] Nonetheless, the Court rejected the claimant's contention that the LCIA 'ha[d] taken a narrower view of the extent of its own powers' in declining to appoint an emergency arbitrator, and dismissed the notion that this led to 'a gap in the practical ability of a party in the position of [the claimant] to obtain relief'.[42] Instead, the Court considered there was no gap in these circumstances on the basis that the LCIA must have deemed that the claimant had not met the requisite urgency thresholds to justify expedited tribunal formation or the appointment of an emergency arbitrator.[43]

The Court also stated that the 'obvious purpose' of the expedited tribunal formation procedure and emergency arbitration provisions contained in the LCIA rules was 'to reduce the need to invoke the assistance of the court in cases of urgency by enabling an arbitral tribunal to act quickly in an appropriate case'.[44] Similarly, the Court held that whilst the emergency arbitration rules were 'not intended to prevent a party from exercising a right to apply to the court' for interim measures,[45] their

36. Arbitration Act 1996 (UK) section 44(3).
37. Arbitration Act 1996 (UK) section 44(5).
38. LCIA Rules, Art. 9B.
39. *Gerald Metals SA v. Timis* [2016] EWHC 2237 (Ch), para. 8.
40. *Ibid.*
41. *Ibid.*, para. 6.
42. *Ibid.*, para. 9.
43. *Ibid.*
44. *Ibid.*, para. 7.
45. *Ibid.*, para. 10.

availability does 'not prevent the power of the court on such an application from being limited as a result of the[ir] existence'.[46]

In *Gerald Metals*, the claimant had applied for the appointment of an emergency arbitrator pursuant to the 2014 version of the LCIA Rules. These provide that the availability of emergency arbitration 'shall not prejudice any party's right to apply to a state court or other legal authority for any interim or conservatory measures before the formation of the Arbitration Tribunal; and it shall not be treated as an alternative to or substitute for the exercise of such right'.[47] Whilst one may have been forgiven for considering this to be a clear embrace of the principle of concurrent jurisdiction, the High Court appeared to consider otherwise. Notably, following the decision in *Gerald Metals*, the next iteration of the LCIA Rules (2020) now provides that notwithstanding the availability of emergency arbitration, 'a party may apply to a competent state court or other legal authority for any interim or conservatory measures before the formation of the Arbitral Tribunal; and Article 9B shall not be treated as an alternative to or substitute for the exercise of such right.'[48] This amended language reinforces the principle of concurrent jurisdiction and should be interpreted as a clear expression of the maintenance of the principle, even where emergency arbitration is an available option.

[C] The Decision in *Ashwani Minda*

In *Gerald Metals*, the claimant had not failed in an application before an emergency arbitrator but instead had failed to persuade the LCIA to appoint one. The case of *Ashwani Minda* before the Delhi High Court concerned the scenario where a claimant approaches the court for relief after an emergency arbitrator has rejected an application for interim measures.[49] Initially, in an emergency arbitration seated in Japan pursuant to the JCAA rules, the claimant had sought interim measures aimed at restraining the respondent's conduct in respect of a joint venture or alternatively requiring the respondent to transfer the shares in the joint venture to the claimant. The emergency arbitrator declined to grant the requested relief.

The claimant turned to the Indian courts for assistance and sought substantially the same relief as had been rejected by the emergency arbitrator. Section 9(1) of the Arbitration and Conciliation Act 1996 permits the grant of interim measures 'before or during arbitral proceedings'.[50] The Delhi High Court declined to assist the claimant. The Court held that in agreeing to arbitration under the JCAA rules, which include 'a detailed mechanism for interim and emergency measures', the parties had clearly evinced their intention to exclude the section 9(1) route to relief.[51] Relevant to this

46. *Ibid.*
47. LCIA Rules (2014), Art. 9B, para. 9.12.
48. LCIA Rules (2020), Art. 9B, para. 9.13.
49. *Ashwani Minda v. U-Shin Ltd*, OMP (I) Comm 90/2020 (Delhi High Court, 12 May 2020).
50. Arbitration and Conciliation Act 1996 (India) section 9(1).
51. *Ashwani Minda v. U-Shin Ltd*, OMP (I) Comm 90/2020 (Delhi High Court, 12 May 2020), para. 54.

determination is that the JCAA rules do not expressly recognize the principle of concurrent jurisdiction, and even stipulate that interim measures issued by an emergency arbitrator are 'deemed to be Interim Measures granted by the arbitral tribunal when it is constituted'.[52] However, the Court also considered that the claimant had 'consciously chosen to tread on a path and cannot turn around only because [it was] unsuccessful'.[53] On one reading, this may be taken as an indication that if the claimant had not already sought and failed to obtain interim measures from an emergency arbitrator, it may have been more sympathetic to an application brought before the court in the first instance.

In addition, the Delhi High Court criticized the claimant for seeking to 'take a second bite of the cherry' by seeking interim measures from the Court which the emergency arbitrator had already deemed were not required.[54] As an expression of comity, it is striking that the Court also ventured that the Court could not 'sit as a Court of Appeal to examine the order of the Emergency Arbitrator'.[55]

[D] Other Decisions on Concurrent Jurisdiction

In *Airbus v. Asian Sky Group*, the Toulouse Court of Appeal also had the opportunity to consider the principle of concurrent jurisdiction in the emergency arbitration context. The Court identified that the ICC Rules enable parties to seek relief from an emergency arbitrator. Article 29(7) of the ICC Rules provides that the availability of emergency arbitration is 'not intended to prevent any party from seeking urgent interim or conservatory measures from a competent judicial authority at any time prior to making an application for such measures, and in appropriate circumstances even thereafter'.[56] The Court noted that emergency arbitration 'was only one of the options available' to obtain interim relief prior to the constitution of the arbitral tribunal, and accepted that this option 'did not prevent [a party] from applying to the competent judicial authority' for relief whilst awaiting tribunal formation.[57]

In *Mer Telecom Ltd. v. Sint Maarten Telephone Company N.V.*, the Tel Aviv District Court considered the principle of concurrent jurisdiction also in the context of the ICC emergency arbitration rules.[58] The applicant applied to the Tel Aviv District Court for an interim injunction, but, in so doing, informed the Court that it intended to apply for the appointment of an emergency arbitrator pursuant to the ICC Rules. The applicant stated that it was seeking relief from the court pending such time as either the emergency arbitrator or arbitral tribunal could reconsider whether the injunction

52. Japan Commercial Arbitration Association Commercial Arbitration Rules (2015) (JCAA Rules), Art. 72(5).
53. *Ashwani Minda v. U-Shin Ltd*, OMP (I) Comm 90/2020 (Delhi High Court, 12 May 2020), para. 56.
54. *Ibid.*
55. *Ibid.*
56. ICC Rules, Art. 29(7).
57. *Airbus v. Asian Sky Group*, Case. No. 17/3754, 30 April 2018 (Toulouse Court of Appeal).
58. O.M. (Tel-Aviv) 56844-10-19 *Mer Telecom Ltd. v. Sint Maarten Telephone Company N.V.* (Nevo, 17.3.2020).

should remain in place. The Court issued a temporary injunction (an available remedy under Israeli law) but subsequently rejected the application for an interim injunction on jurisdictional grounds, namely on the basis that once an arbitration had been commenced, the Israeli court could not continue proceedings. In reaching this conclusion, the Court did not refer to Article 29(7) of the ICC Rules and the principle of concurrent jurisdiction it expressly preserves.

The principle of concurrent jurisdiction has not, however, been universally accepted. In Romania, the Bucharest Court of Appeal held that the Romanian Civil Procedure Code confers exclusive jurisdiction on Romanian courts to determine applications for interim measures made prior to the constitution of the arbitral tribunal and that an emergency arbitration order issued in a Romanian-seated emergency arbitration would violate mandatory laws and public policy under Romanian law. On this basis, the Court annulled an emergency arbitration order that had been issued under the 2018 version of the Arbitration Rules of the Court of International Commercial Arbitration of the Chamber of Commerce and Industry of Romania.[59] The decision has been criticized on several bases, including that there is simply no valid reason under Romanian law for the courts to enjoy exclusive jurisdiction to determine applications for interim measures filed before tribunal formation.[60] In focusing on the primacy of the courts, and riding roughshod over the autonomy of the parties to consent to emergency arbitration, the approach of the Bucharest Court of Appeal appears to be an outlier.

Overall, the manner in which courts have approached the application of the principle of concurrent jurisdiction in the emergency arbitration context is a slightly mixed bag. Courts have both respected the operation of the principle, but some courts have also seen the availability of emergency arbitration as limiting the rights of parties to access the courts for assistance pending tribunal formation. However, it is particularly striking that where concurrent jurisdiction has arisen for consideration, courts have not been seeking to sidestep emergency arbitration provisions and compel or encourage parties instead to apply to courts for relief. Instead, courts have been seeking to respect the autonomy of the arbitral process and have not cast doubt on emergency arbitration as an inferior procedure which parties should strive to avoid. On the contrary, courts have evinced a reluctance to act where parties have the option of seeking the appointment of an emergency arbitrator, or where an emergency arbitrator has already rejected an application for interim measures, or an arbitral institute has rejected the application for the appointment of an emergency arbitrator.

If the principle of concurrent jurisdiction is to be upheld, this overcautious approach, whilst understandable, is unwarranted. Courts will not be riding roughshod over parties' rights by entertaining applications for interim measures where emergency arbitration is available, as emergency arbitration rules are not intended to confine parties to that forum. However, where emergency arbitration has been attempted, and a party has failed to obtain the desired interim measures, there is scope for that failure

59. *Civil Decision No. 76 of 25 July 2019* (Bucharest Court of Appeal).
60. Cristina Ioana Florescu, 'Emerging Tools to Attract and Increase the Use of International Arbitration', 10(2) Juridical Tribune 255, 268-270 (2020).

to impact a court's subsequent determination of an application for like or similar interim measures, subject to the applicable law and the reasons the emergency arbitrator rejected the application for relief.

§7.05 APPLICATION OF DUE PROCESS NORMS

Due process is a fundamental concept firmly embedded in the framework of international arbitration. Due process ensures procedural fairness by mandating that parties must be notified of proceedings and permitted to respond to claims raised and for determination of those claims to be made by an impartial and independent arbitral tribunal.[61]

[A] Due Process in Emergency Arbitration

In arbitral proceedings, all parties must be given an opportunity to be heard. The contours of what this requires can be difficult to define. Article 18 of the UNCITRAL Model Law provides that '[t]he parties are to be treated with equality and each party shall be given a full opportunity of presenting his case'.[62] However, a 'full opportunity' does not entail that arbitral tribunals must accommodate even unreasonable demands made by parties.[63] The Hong Kong Court of Appeal has observed that having the opportunity to present a case 'cannot mean that a party is entitled to present any case it pleases, at any time it pleases, no matter how long the presentation should take'.[64] Instead, as noted by the Singapore Court of Appeal, the parties must be treated with fairness and equality in having the opportunity to present their cases.[65]

Emergency arbitration rules require parties to have a reasonable opportunity to be heard, albeit this is expressed differently across leading rules. No rules stipulate that parties to an emergency arbitration must be afforded a full opportunity to present their cases. Instead, the opportunity to be heard is qualified by reference to reasonableness,[66] fairness,[67] or equality.[68] The urgent nature of an emergency arbitration does not entail that due process norms are suspended.

61. Gary Born, *International Commercial Arbitration* (3rd edn, Kluwer Law International 2020) section 15.04[B].
62. UNCITRAL Model Law on International Commercial Arbitration (2006) Art. 18.
63. Howard M. Holtzmann and Joseph E. Neuhaus, *A Guide to the UNCITRAL Model Law on International Commercial Arbitration: Legislative History and Commentary* (Kluwer 1995) 550.
64. *Pacific China Holdings Ltd (In Liquidation) v. Grand Pacific Holdings Ltd* [2012] 4 HKLRD 1, para. 68.
65. *China Machine New Energy Corp v. Jaguar Energy Guatemala LLC* [2020] SGCA 12, paras 1,97.
66. *See, e.g.*, AAA Rules, R-38(d); HKIAC Rules, Schedule 4, para. 10; ICDR Rules, Art. 7(3); Swiss Rules, Art. 43(6); SIAC Rules, Schedule 1, para. 7.
67. *See, e.g.*, Korean Commercial Arbitration Board International Arbitration Rules (2016) (KCAB Rules), App. 3, Art. 5.
68. *See, e.g.*, SCC Rules, Art. 23(2).

[B] The Decision in *CVG v. CVH*

In *CVG v. CVH*,[69] the Singapore High Court considered an application to set aside an emergency arbitration award issued by an ICDR emergency arbitrator in proceedings seated in Pennsylvania, United States. The dispute concerned a Singapore franchisee's termination of agreements governing its franchise operations.[70] After the franchisor filed for bankruptcy protection in the United States, another company acquired it and installed new executives. After disputes arose, the franchisor provided the franchisee with a notice of default under the agreements, following which the franchisee terminated the agreements on the basis of material breach and/or anticipatory repudiation. The franchisee took steps to de-identify the franchise stores (as post-termination, it was no longer entitled to use the franchisor's proprietary trademarks), and the franchisor removed the franchisee's access to its worldwide ordering system, cancelled various pending orders, and started selling its products directly in Singapore. Subsequently, the franchisor commenced arbitration pursuant to the ICDR rules to seek relief pertaining to post-termination provisions in the agreements. At the same time as filing its demand for arbitration, the franchisor also sought emergency measures of protection pursuant to the ICDR rules.

The emergency arbitration proceeded swiftly. On 27 May 2022, the ICDR appointed the emergency arbitrator. On the same day, the emergency arbitrator issued a procedural order setting out a schedule for submissions and a hearing. After the respondent filed its response submission and the applicant its reply submission, an oral hearing took place on 6 June 2022, i.e., ten days after the appointment of the emergency arbitrator.[71] On the day after the hearing, the emergency arbitrator emailed the parties a list of issues and requested post-hearing submissions to be filed by the following day.

One of the issues raised by the emergency arbitrator was whether the claimant considered the franchise agreements to have been terminated. At the time of the hearing, the claimant's position was that the agreements had been terminated, albeit allegedly without cause, and the claimant was seeking to enforce post-termination provisions in the agreements. In its post-hearing submission, the respondent based its defence on the claimant's case that the agreements had been terminated, as presented in the claimant's application and at the hearing. In the claimant's post-hearing submission, the claimant put forward an alternative position that it did not consider the agreements to have been terminated. The emergency arbitrator issued an award on the basis that the claimant's case was that the agreements had not been terminated and imposed relief aimed at restoring the status quo of the parties to the position they had been in pre-termination. In short, the emergency arbitrator granted relief on the basis of a new case that only emerged in the claimant's post-hearing submission.

Section 31(2)(c) of the Singapore International Arbitration Act 1994 permits a court to refuse enforcement where there has been a breach of the rules of natural

69. *CVG v. CVH* [2022] SGHC 249.
70. *Ibid.*, paras 4-11.
71. *Ibid.*, paras 11-14.

justice, including if the party against whom enforcement is sought demonstrates that it 'was otherwise unable to present [its] case in the arbitration proceedings'.[72] Here, the High Court concluded that was precisely what had occurred.[73] The respondent had been denied the opportunity to make submissions that the claimant was precluded from adopting the position that the agreements were not terminated, to adduce factual evidence in support, and to address the question of relief on the basis of the claimant's new case.[74]

It is unclear from the judgment as to whether, following the filing of post-hearing submissions, the respondent had requested to have the opportunity to respond to the claimant's new case. If the respondent had made such a request and it had been denied, this would clearly have amounted to a violation of the respondent's due process rights, as the emergency arbitrator would be determining the application based on a case in respect of which the respondent had not had a reasonable opportunity to be heard. If the respondent had not made such a request, then the position may be less clear-cut, depending on the speed at which the emergency arbitrator issued the decision following receipt of the post-hearing submissions. If a respondent has sufficient time to identify that a claimant has put forward a new case and chooses to remain idle and not raise this issue with the emergency arbitrator, then in some circumstances, it may be possible to conclude that the respondent was not denied a reasonable opportunity to be heard, as it did not seek to have such an opportunity. However, in this scenario, the prudent course for the emergency arbitrator would always be to ensure the respondent had been offered a reasonable opportunity to be heard prior to issuing a decision.

The emergency arbitrator also has another procedural tool which may be deployed to seek to narrow the issues in the case and ensure that all parties have been heard as to their expectations for the conduct of the emergency arbitration. It is open to an emergency arbitrator to hold a brief case management conference prior to the issuing of the timetable for the proceedings or even thereafter. Holding such a conference may also assist the emergency arbitrator in identifying what the key contentious issues in the proceedings are likely to be. This may help to concentrate both the emergency arbitrator's and also the parties' minds on the key issues on which submissions need to be made and ultimately determinations reached.

Unlike the majority of emergency arbitration rules, the ICDR rules do not stipulate a timeframe within which the emergency arbitrator must issue a decision. In an analysis of the first eighty-seven emergency arbitrations conducted pursuant to the ICDR rules, the average length of emergency arbitration proceedings was approximately three weeks.[75] The speed at which the emergency arbitrator acted in this case, despite the absence of a stipulated timeframe for the conduct of proceedings, is impressive. However, it is conceivable that an early case management conference may have assisted in identifying and narrowing the issues in dispute, potentially even

72. International Arbitration Act 1994 (Singapore) section 31(2)(c).
73. *CVG v. CVH* [2022] SGHC 249, paras 52-56.
74. *Ibid.*, para. 54.
75. Martin F. Gusy and James M. Hosking, A Commentary to the ICDR International Arbitration Rules (2nd edition, Oxford University Press 2019) para. 6.04.

avoiding the need for post-hearing submissions and ultimately avoiding the due process error.

In any event, the Singapore High Court's decision does not undermine the autonomy of emergency arbitration. If anything, the Court's decision provides reassurance to parties that where, as will happen on occasion, due process violations are committed by emergency arbitrators, they will not be overlooked and that parties' rights will be protected. Ultimately, this should be seen as supportive of emergency arbitration by ensuring the procedure does not fall into disrepute. Equally, though, courts should be mindful not to second-guess emergency arbitrators on each and every procedural decision and to pay due regard to the wide procedural discretion under which emergency arbitrators operate. The Court's judgment also sounds like a warning to claimants that they should not seek to take advantage of potential due process violations, as this might create difficulties if it becomes necessary to seek enforcement of an emergency arbitration decision.

§7.06 ENFORCEMENT OF EMERGENCY ARBITRATION DECISIONS

Whilst the enforcement debate in emergency arbitration may have already garnered significant attention, it would be remiss not to explore how courts have reacted to the question of enforcement of emergency arbitration decisions.

[A] Enforcement in India

The question of the enforceability of emergency arbitration decisions has made its way to the Supreme Court of India.[76] This occurred in a protracted dispute between Amazon and the Future Group. In 2019, Amazon had invested in the Future Group subject to several conditions. These included that Future Group would not transfer its retail assets without Amazon's consent or transfer its assets to a list of restricted parties, including the Reliance Group. In 2020, following Future Group's announcement that it had agreed to sell assets amounting to USD 3.4 billion to the Reliance Group, Amazon commenced SIAC arbitration seated in New Delhi against Future Group pursuant to an arbitration agreement contained in the underlying shareholders' agreement.

At the outset, Amazon applied for emergency relief from an SIAC emergency arbitrator to seek to restrain Future Group's sale of assets to the Reliance Group. The emergency arbitrator issued various relief in support of Amazon's application. This included injunctive relief aimed at preventing Future Group from taking any steps in furtherance of the sale or taking any steps in respect of its retail assets without Amazon's prior written consent.

Despite the emergency arbitrator's orders, the Future Group decided to proceed with the sale to Reliance Group and, in so doing, described the award as a nullity, even

76. *Future Coupons Private Ltd. v. Amazon.com NV Investment Holdings LLC*, Civil Appeals Nos. 4492-4493 of 2021.

venturing that the emergency arbitrator was *coram non judice*.[77] The Future Group filed a civil suit before the Delhi High Court and requested an interim injunction to restrain Amazon from placing reliance on the emergency arbitrator's order before statutory authorities, alleging this would amount to tortious interference with its civil rights.[78] The Court declined to grant the requested interim relief.

Amazon filed a petition in the Delhi High Court to seek to enforce the emergency arbitrator's order. Amazon did so pursuant to section 17(2) of the Indian Arbitration Act 1996. The Court held that an emergency arbitration award constitutes an award under section 17(1) of the Act and that such an award is enforceable as an order pursuant to section 17(2). The Court stated in clear terms that '[t]he Emergency Arbitrator is an Arbitrator for all intents and purposes'.[79] Future Group appealed the decision to the Supreme Court of India.

The Supreme Court upheld the High Court's decision. The Supreme Court referred to the principle of party autonomy 'as being one of the pillars of arbitration in the Arbitration Act'.[80] The Supreme Court noted that '[t]here is nothing in the Arbitration Act that prohibits contracting parties from agreeing to a provision providing for an award being made by an Emergency Arbitrator.'[81] The Court further noted that the words 'arbitral proceedings' in the Arbitration Act 'are not limited by any definition and thus encompass proceedings before an Emergency Arbitrator'.[82] The Court also stated that an emergency arbitrator's order 'is exactly like an order of an arbitral tribunal once properly constituted'.[83]

To be sure, the Supreme Court's observations constitute robust support for emergency arbitration. The Supreme Court did not cast a shred of doubt on the viability and legitimacy of the procedure. Instead, in concluding that an emergency arbitrator's order is 'exactly like' an arbitral tribunal's order, the Supreme Court made clear that emergency arbitrators do not constitute a second-class tribunal within the arbitral process. These observations from a court at the highest appellate level once again constitute evidence of courts displaying comity towards emergency arbitrators and strengthening the foundations of emergency arbitration.

The Supreme Court also suggested, once again in strong terms, that it is not open to a party after agreeing to arbitrate under rules that permit emergency arbitration and then participating in an emergency arbitration, that it is then not bound by the emergency arbitrator's decision; in other words, that an estoppel arises. In the Supreme Court's words, 'it cannot lie in the mouth of a party to ignore an Emergency Arbitrator's award by stating that it is a nullity when such party expressly agrees to the binding nature of such award from the date it is made and further undertakes to carry out the

77. *Ibid.*, para. 2.6.
78. *Ibid.*
79. *Future Coupons Private Ltd. v. Amazon.com NV Investment Holdings LLC*, Delhi High Court (18 March 2021), para. 188.
80. *Future Coupons Private Ltd. v. Amazon.com NV Investment Holdings LLC*, Civil Appeals Nos. 4492-4493 of 2021, para. 14.
81. *Ibid.*, para. 17.
82. *Ibid.*, para. 19.
83. *Ibid.*, para. 35.

said interim order immediately and without delay'.[84] The Court referred in this regard to paragraph 12 of Schedule 1 of the SIAC Rules, which provides that '[t]he parties agree that an order or Award by an Emergency Arbitrator [...] shall be binding on the parties from the date it is made, and undertake to carry out the interim order or Award immediately and without delay.' This is a typical provision which appears along similar lines in most emergency arbitration rules.

The Supreme Court's judgment also paid heed to the public policy reasons for supporting emergency arbitration. The Court noted that the Arbitration Act 1996 is 'a statute which favours the remedy of arbitration so as to de-clog civil courts'.[85] The Court saw emergency arbitration orders as 'an important step in aid of decongesting the civil courts and affording expeditious interim relief to the parties'.[86] This may be so, although ultimately, the vindication of parties' rights in private law should not depend on whether the courts obtain some collateral benefit. If parties have consented to emergency arbitration, they should not be permitted to avoid the consequences of doing so, irrespective of whether that benefits the courts in the respective jurisdiction where proceedings may otherwise have been pursued.

Whilst the Court identified that several other jurisdictions have adopted provisions to provide expressly for the enforceability of emergency arbitration decisions, this did not take matters any further. This was because, on a proper interpretation of the Arbitration Act, the Court concluded that an award or order issued by an emergency arbitrator would be covered by section 17.[87]

[B] Enforcement in Singapore

Singapore is one of the jurisdictions that has amended its arbitration law to recognize the development of emergency arbitration. Section 2(1) of the International Arbitration Act now provides that the term 'arbitral tribunal' includes 'an emergency arbitrator'.[88] In the context of enforcement, it was already clear that emergency arbitration awards or orders issued in Singapore-seated emergency arbitrations were enforceable, as this definition applied to Part 2 of the International Arbitration Act which concerns domestic awards. However, this definition did not expressly apply to Part 3 of the Act, which governs foreign awards.

In the case of *CVG v. CVH*, the Singapore High Court confirmed that the reference in Part 3 of the Act to arbitral awards includes emergency arbitration awards and that Singapore courts are empowered to enforce foreign awards issued by emergency arbitrators.[89] The respondent submitted that the lack of an express reference in Part 3 of the Act to emergency arbitrators or emergency arbitration evidenced the legislature's

84. *Ibid.*, para. 36.
85. *Ibid.*, para. 38.
86. *Ibid.*, para. 41.
87. *Ibid.*, para. 62.
88. International Arbitration Act 1994 (Singapore), section 2(1).
89. *CVG v. CVH* [2022] SGHC 249.

intention to exclude emergency arbitration awards from enforcement (with the consequence that an emergency arbitration award issued by a foreign-seated tribunal could not be enforced in Singapore). According to the respondent, if the legislature had intended for emergency arbitration awards issued by foreign-seated tribunals to be enforceable, it would also have amended Part 3 of the Act to expressly refer to emergency arbitration awards. The Court disagreed and held that on a purposive interpretation of the Act, the term '*arbitral award*' in section 27(1) of the Act applies to foreign awards by emergency arbitrators.[90] In so doing, the Court avoided creating an artificial distinction between awards issued by Singapore-seated emergency arbitrators, and awards issued outside of Singapore.

[C] Enforcement in the United States of America

In the United States, the Federal Arbitration Act confers United States district courts with original jurisdiction over 'action[s] or proceeding[s] falling under the [New York] Convention'.[91] US district courts have both ordered and refused enforcement of emergency arbitration decisions.

In *Al Raha Group v. PKL Services*, the District Court for the Northern District of Georgia declined to enforce an award issued by an ICDR emergency arbitrator. The respondent had announced its intention to terminate a contract with the claimant, and the claimant obtained an injunction to prevent the respondent from doing so. The emergency arbitrator noted that in accordance with the ICDR Rules, the award could be subject to reconsideration, modification, or vacatur of parts or in its entirety by the arbitral tribunal once constituted. The Court deemed the award was not sufficiently final to be capable of enforcement and held that it was 'a placeholder that did not purport to resolve finally any of the issues submitted to arbitration'.[92] The Court also pointed to the emergency arbitrator's acknowledgement that the award had been granted pending the constitution of the arbitral tribunal to justify its conclusion.

Along similar lines, in *Chinmax Medical Systems Inc v. Alere San Diego, Inc.*, the District Court for the Southern District of California declined to enforce an award issued by an ICDR emergency arbitrator. The parties had entered into a distribution agreement for various products and had failed to reach an agreement on the process for product registration renewals despite confirming that it was in their mutual interests to ensure that these renewals were made. The emergency arbitrator ordered the respondent to provide various documents into an escrow and to provide relevant registration documents to the claimant in order to enable the claimant to respond to inquiries raised by authorities regarding the renewals. The emergency arbitrator also identified that the order would remain in effect pending its review by the arbitral tribunal once constituted. The Court dismissed the enforcement petition on the basis that the emergency arbitrator had not intended the interim order issued to be final because the emergency

---

90. *Ibid.*, paras 28-35.
91. Federal Arbitration Act, 9 U.S.C. para. 203.
92. *Al Raha Group v. PKL Services* [2019] WL 4267765.

arbitrator 'stated that the interim order was issued to facilitate a conservancy order by the full arbitration panel'.[93] The Court concluded that the power of the arbitral tribunal, following its formation, to modify or vacate the emergency arbitrator's decision meant that it lacked sufficient finality to be enforceable.

The Court's observations in *Al Raha* and *Chinmax* do not demonstrate that the respective emergency arbitrators had erred in identifying that, once the respective arbitral tribunals had been constituted, their decisions could be revisited. The point of emergency arbitration is not to circumvent the powers of arbitral tribunals once they have been formed but simply to provide a mechanism for parties to obtain pre-tribunal relief to protect their rights on an interim basis until the arbitral tribunal has had the opportunity to consider matters further. These decisions overlook the self-evident point that the emergency arbitrator's decision on whether relief is required before the arbitral tribunal is in place is a decision in itself and resolves the time-sensitive issue as to whether immediate and urgent relief is required to preserve the claimant's position.

In contrast to these judgments, other US district courts have held that emergency arbitration decisions entail sufficient finality to be capable of enforcement because they resolve the issue as to whether interim measures are required before the arbitral tribunal has been formed.[94]

In *Blue Cross Blue Shield of Michigan v. Medimpact Healthcare Systems*, the District Court for the Eastern District of Michigan confirmed an emergency arbitration award issued under the AAA rules on the basis that interim awards can resolve 'separate independent' claims as regards the need for interim relief.[95] The emergency arbitrator had ordered the respondent to continue to perform its obligations under an agreement for pharmacy benefit managing services. As occurred in *Al Raha* and *Chinmax*, the emergency arbitrator expressly identified that the relief was only intended to remain in place until an arbitral tribunal was in place and considered the need for the relief to continue. The Court did not see this acknowledgement as preventing enforcement of the emergency arbitrator's award because it resolved the separate and independent issue as to whether the respondent in the interim should continue to perform its contractual obligations.

In *Draeger Safety Diagnostics v. New Horizon Interlock*, the District Court for the Eastern District of Michigan observed that an interim award, such as an emergency arbitration award, which 'finally and definitely disposes of a separate and independent claim [i.e., a claim that interim measures are required before the constitution of the arbitral tribunal] may be confirmed notwithstanding the absence of an award that finally disposes of all the claims that were submitted to arbitration'.[96] In that case, the Court confirmed an emergency arbitration award issued under the AAA rules. The emergency arbitrator ordered the respondent to return to the claimant various records, data and reports that it had retained after the termination of a manufacturing

93. *Chinmax Medical Systems Inc. v. Alere San Diego Inci* [2011] WL 2135350.
94. *See, e.g., Air Center Helicopters, Inc. v. Starline Investments Ireland Limited*, Case No. 4:18-cv-00599; *Sharp Corp v. Hisense USA Corp*, 292 F Supp 3d 157 (2017).
95. *Blue Cross Blue Shield of Michigan v. Medimpact Healthcare Systems* [2010] WL 2595450.
96. *Draeger Safety Diagnostics v. New Horizon Interlock* [2011] WL 653651.

agreement, which provided for such return within five days of termination. The claimant had alleged that the respondent's failure to comply with this obligation was preventing it from complying with statutory monitoring and reporting requirements, which risked revocation of its business licence. The Court, however, declined to enforce the emergency arbitrator's award of costs of the proceedings on the basis that the arbitral tribunal had the power to determine the final apportionment of the costs of the emergency arbitration.

In *Vita Pharmaceuticals v. PepsiCo Inc*, the District Court for the Southern District of Florida likewise deemed an emergency arbitration award issued under the AAA Rules to be sufficiently final to be capable of enforcement. The emergency arbitrator issued an order for the respondent to abide by the terms of a distribution agreement and to stop selling products to customers for whom the claimant had exclusive distribution rights. The Court held that the emergency arbitrator's order 'resolve[d] the issue of whether the parties [were] required to maintain the status quo and continue to perform their contractual obligations during the pendency of the arbitration'[97] and that confirmation of the order preserved the claimant's right to seek relief from the arbitral tribunal without rendering the emergency relief 'meaningless'.[98] The Court also deemed that a provision in the underlying contract permitting appeals against the arbitral tribunal's decision did not apply in respect of a decision issued by an emergency arbitrator.[99]

Along similar lines, in *Yahoo! v. Microsoft*, the District Court for the Southern District of New York identified that 'if an arbitral award of equitable relief based upon a finding of irreparable harm is to have any meaning at all, the parties must be capable of enforcing or vacating it at the time it is made'.[100] The AAA emergency arbitrator had ordered the respondent to complete a migration of search and search ad services. The Court declined the respondent's application to vacate and instead confirmed the award, noting that the relief granted was sufficiently final.

Evidently, there is no uniform approach to the enforcement of emergency arbitration decisions in US district courts. The form of relief granted does not appear to have influenced courts' decisions to either grant or refuse enforcement. Instead, the debate has focused on the nature of the relief granted and whether it is sufficiently final to be capable of enforcement.

§7.07 ANTICIPATED DEVELOPMENTS

Whilst courts have already encountered several key issues concerning emergency arbitration, there are two key issues relating to emergency arbitration which are yet to make their way before the courts.

First, whether the courts of the seat of emergency arbitration have any role to play in respect of challenges to the emergency arbitrator. Emergency arbitration rules

97. *Vital Pharmaceuticals v. PepsiCo Inc*, Case No. 20-Civ-62415-Rar (2021).
98. *Ibid.*, at 1310.
99. *Ibid.*, at 1309.
100. *Yahoo! v. Microsoft*, 983 F Supp 2d 310 (2013).

typically contain procedures for challenging the emergency arbitrator before the respective arbitral institute. These mirror the procedure for challenging an arbitrator, although the timeframes are often narrowed to reflect the fast-track nature of an emergency arbitration. Arbitration laws often permit parties to petition the courts of the seat of arbitration to remove an arbitrator (usually only after a party has exhausted all available avenues with the respective arbitral institute). It is possible that a party whose challenge to an emergency arbitrator fails before the arbitral institute may attempt to take that challenge to the courts of the seat of emergency arbitration.

Second, whether the courts of the seat of emergency arbitration are empowered to annul emergency arbitration decisions. Emergency arbitration rules typically permit the arbitral tribunal, once constituted, to modify or terminate the emergency arbitration decision. As such, a party may prefer to await tribunal formation before seeking annulment of the decision before the courts of the seat of arbitration. This is particularly the case in circumstances where it may be unclear whether the courts of the seat have the power to annul emergency arbitration decisions. Currently, there are no specific annulment procedures available with respect to emergency arbitration decisions issued in the seat of emergency arbitration. If an emergency arbitration decision is seen to constitute an arbitral award under the law of the seat of emergency arbitration, and there is an available annulment procedure in respect of arbitral awards, then it is possible that a court may conclude that it is empowered to annul an emergency arbitration decision.

§7.08 CONCLUSION

Broadly, the first encounters of emergency arbitration with the courts have been positive. Increasingly, trepidation regarding the use of the procedure is becoming less warranted and eventually should become unnecessary. Over time, the development and application of legal norms in emergency arbitration will create greater certainty for all parties concerned. While, as is always the case in the law, exceptions may exist, for the most part, courts have been, and will continue to be, receptive to the procedure.

As several cases to date demonstrate, courts have sought to give efficacy to parties' consent to and use of emergency arbitration. At the same time, courts have acted to prevent the infringement of parties' rights where emergency arbitrators have committed errors impugning the integrity of the emergency arbitration decision. It will be of immeasurable benefit to international arbitration users if this respectful and constructive approach continues in future encounters between emergency arbitration and the courts.

CHAPTER 8

The Accused Arbitrator: New Roles and Dilemmas in the Era of Arbitration Litigation

Mads Bryde Andersen

§8.01 A NEW TREND TO CHALLENGE ARBITRAL PROCEEDINGS?

The risk that arbitral awards are set aside or denied recognition or enforcement is a frequent topic for discussion among arbitrators. In the absence of formal statistics,[1] it is uncertain whether such litigation is actually on the rise. A short glance into the case portal serviced by the Stockholm Chamber of Commerce[2] displays a significant number of such cases from the Swedish *Svea Hovrätt*, of which some indeed come out successful. In *Denmark*, the number of such cases is lower, but still more frequent than before, if you look into the cases reported in Ugeskrift for Retsvæsen.[3] However, during

1. All the Nordic arbitration institutes—the Danish Institute of Arbitration (DIA), the Finnish Institute of Arbitration and the arbitration institute at the Stockholm Chamber of Commerce (SCC) produce statistical information on their own case handling, just as the ICC Court of Arbitration (ICC) and the London Court of International Arbitration (LCIA) do. But since those institutes may not even know of the litigation, because it involves other parties, they do not produce official statistics on challenge litigations. And even *if* such statistics was produced by the arbitration institutes, it would not show the full picture, since it would not include cases litigated as ad hoc arbitration.
2. https://www.arbitration.sccinstitute.com/Swedish-Arbitration-Portal/start/. In SvJT 2023, pp. 108 ff., *Anne Kuttenkeuler & Anders Lundberg* has analyzed the examination of arbitral awards conducted by Swedish high courts in challenge litigations. The authors studied sixty-five such cases decided in the period from 2014 to May 2022 of which only a few came out successful for the plaintiffs. According to the overview in *SOU 2015/37*, at pp. 79-81, ten arbitral awards (equaling 6% of the total cases litigated on that issue) were set aside by Swedish courts in the previous period from 2004 to 2014.
3. That is, the Danish Weekly Law Report, section A of which reports case law, in the following abbreviated as "U." Under the subject title "Retspleje 28.5—Voldgiftskendelsers gyldighed" (the invalidity of arbitral awards) such cases may be retrieved.

the last many years, none of these (reported) cases have held arbitral awards invalid by Danish courts.

There may also be a trend to involve arbitrators personally in challenge litigations. In some cases, arbitrators have been called as witnesses (against their will) to testify on the *proceedings* and *deliberations* of the tribunal. In other cases, arbitrators are even claimed to be *liable* for their alleged wrongdoings.[4]

In such litigation, the defendant tribunal, arbitrator or arbitration institute "stands accused", directly or indirectly, for not having conducted the proceedings in accordance with due process principles, mandatory rules and the arbitrators' other duties. The same accusation is in the air when arbitrators are called as witnesses to testify.

Such litigation differs substantially from those disputes that may bring arbitral tribunals in contact with state courts as part of the proceedings, e.g., when under applicable *lex arbitri* rules disputes on conflicts of interest or arbitrator's fees are referred to state courts. Lawsuits that include claims to *set aside* arbitral awards are typically raised against the successful party in the arbitration. *Liability* litigation may either be raised against individual arbitrators, against the tribunal as such, and/or against an arbitration institute.

It is therefore unknown whether a possible increase in the number of court cases about setting aside awards is proportional to the increase in arbitration cases in total, or whether there *is* indeed a growing "trend" to challenge arbitral awards. It is also difficult to conclude whether challenge litigations are today raised against other types of *defendants*, and on the basis of other types of *allegations* than earlier. Furthermore, we do not know *what kinds* of awards are most often challenged. Are, for example, arbitral awards rendered after rudimentary procedures challenged more often than awards with no stone left unturned—or is it rather the other way around? And are arbitral awards in international cases more exposed to such litigation than awards in domestic arbitrations?

To start the discussion, I will introduce Danish arbitration as an example of how various arbitration cultures can develop with different traditions for challenging awards. On this basis, I will try to identify some factors here that may affect this possible trend.

§8.02 THE DIVERSE DANISH ARBITRATION LANDSCAPE

The term "arbitration" is broad. It usually refers to any *out of court* procedure aiming at a *final* and *legally binding* settlement of a dispute according to procedural rules that are agreed upon, or at least known to, the parties. Arbitration comprises *any* out-of-court dispute resolution procedure that leads to this result, i.e., both *rudimentary* procedures decided by non-lawyers after a few hours of case presentations and with a

4. *See* for an overview of this practice, *Sarah Schæffer*: Approaches to Arbitrators' Liability: Immunity or Liability (Printed as Chapter 14 of Stockholm Arbitration Yearbook 2020, pp. 249-271, and (in Danish) in Erhvervsretligt Tidsskrift 2020, pp. 45 ff.).

focus on technical inspections of a subject matter and what I will refer to as "*high-end* commercial arbitration," in which hundreds or even thousands of hours are spent on the case, both on the parties' side and on the tribunal's.

The *finality* of arbitration implies that the award may be enforced under the 1958 New York Convention. Mediation and conciliation are, due to their different scopes, beyond this topic.[5] The requirements for recognition and enforcement of awards listed in *Article V* of this convention have indeed motivated tribunals to provide due process.

In Denmark, the position of arbitration in the legal system has changed substantially over time. In the 1683 Code of Denmark (Article 1-6-1),[6] the competence of the arbitrator was based on a *proxy* theory, according to which parties to a dispute might leave it to "honorable men" ("*Dannemænd*") who would then be empowered to decide it, subject to any other decision made by the king. These umpires were regarded as someone to be *trusted*, regardless of what procedural safeguards they offered the disputing parties.

Up through the twentieth century, most Danish arbitration cases were conducted under the presidency of a *state court judge* who, to a large extent, would conduct the proceedings as if the Danish Administration of Justice Act applied (which it did not, unless specifically agreed by the disputing parties). Hearings would even take place in state court buildings against pre-fixed payment to the court administration. Apart from the fact that the co-arbitrators would typically not be state court judges, it was difficult from the outside to see the difference between such arbitration and state court proceedings.

Coming back to the topic of the present contribution, the presence of a state court judge as president of a panel of arbitrators may indeed have had a demotivating effect on parties considering initiating a court case on setting aside the award. Not only would his or her presence give the parties reason to presume that the arbitration was conducted under the same high procedural standards as in the judiciary system. The prospect that counsels might meet the judge in court later on in other cases might also make them reluctant to litigate against judges.[7]

In 2006, the Danish Court Procedures Act was amended so that a maximum on what state court judges could earn in addition to their ordinary salary came into force. After that, many "arbitration-popular" state court judges often had to decline nominations as presidents to arbitral tribunals to be replaced by prominent attorneys or law

5. *See* for a further discussion of this, *Andreas Ehlers:* Blaming the Unblameable? On the Liability of Mediators. Nordic Journal of Commercial Law Issue 2014#1, available at https://journals.aau.dk/index.php/NJCL/article/view/2887/2433).
6. "Dersom Parterne voldgive deris Sag og Tvistighed paa Danne-mænd, enten med Opmand, eller uden, da hvad de sige og kiende, saa vit deris Fuldmagt dennem tillader at giøre, det staar fast og kand ej for nogen Ret til Underkiendelse indstævnis, dog Kongen sin Sag forbeholden."
7. This trend also seems to have been predominant in England and Wales. In his book "The Fall of the Priests and the Rise of the Lawyers" (2016), p. 222, *Philip R. Wood KC* makes the point that in the twentieth century, commercial arbitration grew under inspiration from state courts as a "close cousin of justices—a kind of privatized judiciary": Just as it was presumed that a such judge would conduct the proceedings in the same way as in a state court, it would be unlikely to hold an arbitrator liable for his or her alleged misconduct, as it would be to hold a state court liable.

professors. More or less at the same time (i.e., around the turn of the century), international commercial arbitration came to Denmark, which—for various historical reasons[8]—happened much later than in Sweden.

Before that happened, a number of quite special arbitration systems had developed. Some of these special arbitration procedures still exist and have deep historical roots. They were—and are—"special" in many ways. First, because they only provide dispute resolution services to specific types of professional parties. Second, because they relied on procedural rules substantially different from what one would today perceive as "commercial arbitration."

An example hereof is the *Copenhagen Adjudication and Arbitration Committee for Grain and Feedstuff Trade*, which has performed its services for well over a hundred years.[9] According to its website (https://www.copenhagencontracts.dk), the committee consists of approximately thirty-five members (in addition to a President and three to six Vice Presidents), who all work in the Danish and Swedish grain and feedstuff sector and who all offer their expertise and time on a voluntary basis. It hears disputes in the grain and feedstuff trade, which may arise between seller and buyer in relation to the quality or condition of the goods or other issues, and where the parties have agreed on arbitration before it.

The procedure of this committee differs in many ways from what one would expect in contemporary arbitration: Under Clause 5(5), the parties are not informed in advance of which members of the committee will take part in the hearing of the case. Nevertheless, the system works. At least none of the challenge decisions reported by the Danish legal database ("Karnov") displays decisions from this committee.

Another predominant particularity of Danish arbitration is the *Building and Construction Arbitration Board*, which for almost a century has heard disputes arising from the commonly applied Danish standard contracts for building contracts, including presently the "AB18."[10] The procedural rules of such arbitration are also quite different from what one would expect in contemporary commercial arbitration. One special characteristic is the practice of appointing technical experts without a legal background as arbitrators.[11] Another is its widespread use of state court justices as presidents of tribunals, all selected from an existing list.[12] But also, this system seems to work. Apart

8. Among those reasons are (1) the Danish industrial culture which all through the twentieth century mainly consisted of small or medium-sized industries, (2) the fact that Sweden was seen as a neutral country, whereas Denmark much earlier than Sweden was part of both NATO and the EU.
9. *See, e.g.*, the Supreme Court decision reported in U 1907.586 H.
10. *See* for further references, https://voldgift.dk/?lang=en. The predecessor of the said arbitration board was an arbitration board which since 1927 had been operated by the Danish Association of Engineers and referred to in previous versions of "AB 18."
11. A challenge procedure on this particular point was decided in *U 2015.1192 V:* In this case the Danish High Court for the Western Circuit upheld such an award decided by an architect as sole arbitrator, since both parties had agreed to his appointment.
12. This practice, however, has made it easier for the parties to accept that the said tribunals also decide cases that involve multiple parties, e.g., a client, several contractors and subcontractors, as well as consultants. In doing that, all parties can be heard in one place at the same time on the basis of their agreement, and their disputes be resolved collectively.

from the 2015 decision mentioned in footnote 11, there is no reported case law claiming that such awards should be set aside.

A third, albeit less "commercial," Danish arbitration specialty has for over a century decided labor disputes in so-called industrial arbitration (*"faglig voldgift"*) and under rules substantially different from other kinds of arbitration. The co-arbitrators of an industrial arbitration panel will typically be party representatives employed by the organizations that represent the parties to the dispute. Their presence as such is not seen as a conflict of interest. Not surprisingly, they often file dissenting opinions. Therefore, such awards are usually rendered by the president alone.[13]

§8.03 DANISH COURT PRACTICE ON CHALLENGE CLAIMS

These very different kinds of arbitration take place on a day-to-day basis and are considered relatively safe and reliable by the disputing parties, although they do not in all respects live up to the procedural standards of contemporary international commercial arbitration.[14] With a view to the present topic, it is noteworthy that challenge litigations are both rare and, when they occur, unsuccessful.

A likely explanation for this widespread willingness to deviate from predominant arbitration standards is that the applied procedural rules (and shortcomings) are fully transparent to the parties and, indeed, combined with other kinds of advantages: Legal costs remain modest considering that the tribunal possesses knowledge on both technical issues and business customs, and when much of this litigation can be put in the hands of in-house legal counsels.

None of the said characteristics apply to such types of arbitration that have been subject to the most recent Danish Supreme Court practice where arbitral awards have been challenged. Noteworthy, the two most recent cases decided by the Danish Supreme Court involved high-end international commercial arbitrations.

The first one was decided in 2022 (*U 2022.1117 H*). It concerned claims in the magnitude of EUR 20 million arising out of a contractual relationship for the delivery of ship engines from the respondent (Skaugen Marine) to the claimant (MAN Diesel). It transpires from the case that the reported challenge litigation was one among several challenge litigations pending between the parties related. The award was rendered by an international panel with an Italian president and co-arbitrators from Germany and Norway, and under the rules of the DIA. The unsuccessful respondent challenged the award on grounds of procedural errors for not having had a reasonable opportunity to present its case. A panel of nine Supreme Court justices found no such violation since all procedural orders had sufficient basis in the procedural rules applicable in the arbitration.

13. The 2005 Danish Arbitration Act exempted industrial arbitration of labor market from the act, cf. Art. 1(5), just like disputes decided by arbitration under other statutory rules were. They still operate outside the scope of the act.
14. *See* for a further discussion on this *Sylvie Cécile Cavaleri*: Danish construction arbitration: civil proceedings in disguise?, printed in Marianne Roth & Michael Geistlinger (eds.): Yearbook on International Arbitration and ADR (2019), pp. 99-117.

The same result was the outcome of the Supreme Court decision reported in *U 2016.1558 H* on a claim of MDKK 170 arising out of a contract for the delivery of windmill components.

As said, both cases fall into the category of high-end international commercial arbitration. The 2022 case was decided by an international panel of arbitrators. The 2016 case was also international but arbitrated by Danish counsels and decided by a panel of Danish arbitrators (the president being a well-esteemed law professor).

In both cases, the Supreme Court assumed a wide margin of appreciation to the tribunal, thus relying on the generally recognized ban against material revision (cf. Article 34 of the UNCITRAL Model law), which only leaves a narrow scope for setting aside arbitral awards. Subsequent high court practice has followed this path.

As said, and unlike the reported practice from *Svea Hovrätt*, no recent Danish Supreme Court decision has set aside an arbitral award for neither its content nor for the procedure provided by the tribunal's decisions. In the absence of such court practice, no monetary claims have been presented towards arbitrators or arbitration institutions.

§8.04 MONETARY CLAIMS AGAINST ARBITRATORS

A successful court case by which an arbitral award is set aside may in principle be succeeded by monetary claims presented towards the arbitral tribunal, individual arbitrators, and/or arbitration institutes. Such monetary claims may either take the form of claims for the reimbursement of arbitrator's fees or as professional liability claims for compensation for the parties' losses caused by undue arbitral proceedings.

It is clear that a failed arbitration may cause damage to the parties: If an award is set aside, new procedural costs arise in the retrial proceedings. Additional costs may also occur if an arbitrator with no legitimate cause resigns the day before the main hearing should take place, thus causing re-scheduling costs. The parties may also suffer losses if arbitrators reveal trade secrets. It may even be that the tribunals fail to identify (and thereby facilitate) corruptive practices and thereby cause various kinds of sanctions.[15]

Arbitrators are not immune to such liability: In a civilized society, everybody has—and should have—the privilege to take their legal complaints to courts or other competent bodies, e.g., to claim compensation. In general, the scope of such liability depends on the kind of mistake that gave rise to the claim. The more negligence the tribunal exercises, the more likely it is that it will be subject to liability.

The reported case law that I am aware of indeed seems to pertain to quite significant procedural errors.

In *Roulas v. Professor J Tepora* (decision of January 31, 2005), the Finnish Supreme Court held an arbitrator liable for having accepted appointment in a dispute

15. Article 24 of the Whistleblower Directive (2019/1937) establishes that its rights and remedies "... cannot be waived or limited by any agreement, policy, form or condition of employment, including a pre-dispute arbitration agreement."

where he had provided an expert opinion to one of the parties prior to and during the arbitration proceedings without disclosing that to the other party. The claim for liability was raised after the Helsinki Court of Appeal had set the award aside. The Court found that Professor Tepora had not complied with the arbitrator's duty to disclose circumstances, which may give rise to justifiable doubts regarding the arbitrator's impartiality or independence. This lack of disclosure resulted in a monetary compensation of EUR 81,000 to the parties.

In a *Netherlands Supreme Court* judgment of September 30, 2016, in the matter "*The Qnow* case," an arbitrator was held liable for a procedural error (the president neglected to have the award signed by his fellow arbitrators). The ruling follows the principle set forth in a 2009 case (*Greenworld*), according to which liability might occur in relation to an annulled award if the arbitrator intentionally or knowingly acted recklessly or with a gross misjudgment in fulfilling his duties.

A judgment of February 15, 2015 of the *Spanish Supreme Court* (102/2017) in the *Puma* case set aside an award that had been conducted contrary to the principle of arbitral collegiality because one of the arbitrators had not participated in the final deliberation. The party could therefore recover arbitrator fees paid to two arbitrators.

As said, there is no reported Danish case law on arbitrators' liability. However, in a case from the Danish High Court for the Eastern Circuit, reported in *U 2011.2407 Ø*, an expert witness ("*syn- og skønsmand*") was held liable towards one of the parties for damages caused by his flawed conduct, including excess of his mandate. Damages were awarded on a discretionary basis to DKK 10,000.

In all the reported four cases, the arbitrators (respectively, the expert witness) had acted with more than simple negligence. So far, these cases might be seen as a support to a general assumption that arbitrator liability may only be relevant under *qualified* circumstances so that claims for *liability* are only relevant if the actions or omissions of the arbitrator qualify as gross negligence. In relation to claims for reimbursement of fees, a similar harsh standard should apply. At the same time, there is no basis for assuming that arbitrators, etc., are as such *immune* to liability or repayment claims—just as little as state court judges are.

This legal situation seems to be reflected in the legislation which has been adopted in those jurisdictions that have regulated arbitrator's liability.

One such example is *section 29 of the English Arbitration Act 1996*, which reads as follows (with emphasis added):

> Immunity of arbitrator.
> (1) An arbitrator is not liable for anything done or omitted in the discharge or purported discharge of his functions as arbitrator *unless the act or omission is shown to have been in bad faith.*
> (2) Subsection (1) applies to an employee or agent of an arbitrator as it applies to the arbitrator himself.
> (3) This section does not affect any liability incurred by an arbitrator by reason of his resigning (but see section 25).

A similar bad faith reservation is included in section 21(1) of the Spanish Arbitration Act 2003, which reads as follows (again, with emphasis added):

> Liability of arbitrators and arbitral institutions. Provisioning funds
> 1. Acceptance requires arbitrators and, as appropriate, the arbitral institution, to comply with their commission in good faith. If they fail to do so, they will be liable for any damages resulting from *bad faith, recklessness or mens rea*. In arbitration commissioned from an institution, the damaged party may file suit directly against it, irrespective of any action for indemnity lodged against the arbitrators. Arbitrators or arbitral institutions on their behalf will be bound to take liability insurance or equivalent security for the amount established in the rules. Public entities and arbitral systems integrated in or under the aegis of governmental authorities are exempted from this obligation.

As I will discuss below in §8.06[B], similar provisions are adopted by a number of arbitration institutes.

A different attitude, and indeed one that seems more akin to what applies to state representatives under international law, is reflected in *section 21(a) of the ICSID Convention*. The provision provides that arbitrators "shall enjoy immunity from legal process with respect to acts performed by them in the exercise of their functions, except when the Centre waives this immunity." Furthermore, Rule 31 of the *ICSID Rules* (under the title "Waiver of Immunities") states that "the Secretary-General may waive the immunity of the Centre; (...) and the Chair may waive the immunity of the Tribunal" when immunity impedes the cause of justice and that such waiver would not prejudice the interest of the Centre. As said, this provision seems to be rooted in the law of diplomacy rather than in arbitration law.

An adverse reading of the quoted statutory acts seems to presume that arbitrators might in principle be held liable for substantial wrongdoings that have caused harm to the parties (or at least one of them). Such reservations are also reflected in the contractual practice that I will discuss below in §8.06[B].

Personally, I find such a rule quite reasonable. If it applies, arbitrators may not have anything to worry about.

But does it? Can we assume that the requirements for the arbitrator's liability remain as high as indicated by the quoted case law? The answer to this is not known until we have more practice in which arbitrators are claimed liable for less severe misconduct than what transpires from the said cases. Nothing can be excluded, and for parties that are prepared to pursue their claims at all costs, it may very well be that we will see more such litigation.

In §8.06 below, I will offer my views on some of the strategic considerations that this possible risk will present prospective arbitrators with before they accept nominations.

§8.05 WITNESS EXAMINATIONS OF ARBITRATORS

As said above in section 1, arbitrators may be summoned as a witness of fact to testify in challenge litigations on why and how the award was decided and procedural decisions made. Mindful that such witness examinations will take place in a public courtroom with the risk of compromising the arbitrator's duty of confidentiality, any arbitrator should be cautious against it unless both parties agree.

In Danish court practice, such witness examinations happen now and then, and apparently with no objections, neither from the parties to the dispute nor from the called arbitrators.

An example hereof is the Supreme Court decision reported in *U 2010.802 H* where the president of an arbitral tribunal (being a Supreme Court justice himself) testified as a witness of fact in a challenge litigation. In the aforementioned *U 2016.1558/2 H,* the president of the tribunal (a law professor) also testified.

Some of the reported Danish cases have dealt with whether court judges or arbitrators are obliged to appear as witnesses. In all circumstances, the obligation to do so resumes that there is a need to hear the said testimony.

This practice is illustrated by the following Danish cases:

> In the high court decision reported in *2013.687 ØLK* the testimony (to which both parties agreed) was held not to be "clearly" unimportant to the litigation. Therefore, the plaintiff's request to hear the president of an arbitral tribunal on whether the tribunal had considered certain legal allegations was allowed. The city court had denied this witness examination as unimportant to the outcome.

The result was otherwise in the high court decision reported in *U 2022.923 ØLK,* which held that the testimony of the president of an arbitral tribunal was unnecessary during enforcement proceedings during which the court found no basis for setting the award aside.

A similar result was reached in *U 2020.2413 ØLK*, where an assistant judge could not be called as a witness to comment upon a judgment he had rendered which was not under appeal.

I do not know of any Danish case law where arbitrators have been requested to appear as witnesses against their will in regard to cases handled by them. In its decision in the case of CZT v CZU [2023] SGHC(I) 11 of 28 June 2023, the Singapore International Commercial Court has explored the policy considerations behind keeping an arbitral tribunal's deliberations confidential in the context of a setting aside application. The court confirmed that it would "take a very compelling case" to overcome these underlying policy considerations. The Italian president of the tribunal who rendered the award that was challenged in the case reported in *U 2022.1117 H* (and discussed before on page 119) has informed me that he was asked by one of the disputing parties to appear as a witness at the Danish High Court for the Eastern Circuit when the litigation was prepared here. He refused, and the requesting party did not insist—perhaps so because the request was made when the COVID-19 crisis was on the rise in February-March 2020.

Therefore, Danish courts have not considered whether Article 169(1) of the Danish Administration of Justice Act might be applied in such a situation. That provision exempts "officials or other individuals acting in public or equivalent positions" from the obligation to testify. Since this provision might be applicable by analogy to arbitrators in relation to the tribunal's deliberations, unwilling arbitrators might consider invoking it towards such witness requests should they be summoned to testify.[16]

§8.06 STRATEGIC ISSUES

[A] Choice of Law Issues

The above presentation has identified a number of points where arbitrators may face a risk of liability claims.

The likeliness of that risk depends on a number of factors, among which the prevailing court practice of setting aside arbitral awards is most important. Lawsuits challenging the validity of enforcement of awards may be raised in any jurisdiction in the world. Therefore, it will always be uncertain what level of invalidity will prevail in such litigations.

When it comes to the arbitrator's risk of facing liability, the law of the seat of the arbitration (the *lex arbitri*) will also be the law under which the claim for liability shall be decided. This choice of this jurisdiction is under the full control of the arbitrators when they accept appointments or agree to the terms of reference (or other procedural rules) applicable to the arbitration. When they accept appointment, they also accept this choice of jurisdiction. That choice therefore comprises the first and most fundamental strategic decision for prospective arbitrators who want to manage their risk of facing personal liability claims.

[B] Contractual Solutions

Having said that, the contractual framework for the arbitration is another crucial factor to rely on to manage the risk of claims for liability. It is thus the prevailing view in Nordic legal theory that the tribunal and the parties take part in a sui generis "procedural association" with its basis in the arbitration clause, i.e., a contractual phenomenon.[17]

16. The document that the DIA request prospective arbitrators to sign includes the following statement on the issue:

> Arbitrators have from time to time been summoned before the Danish courts to give witness testimony, for instance in cases about setting aside of the arbitral award. Usually, arbitrators have voluntarily accepted to give testimony in such cases. However, it is presently unclear under Danish law whether an arbitrator has a duty to give testimony (and to what extent) if the arbitrator does not voluntarily accept to give testimony.
>
> If a claim for damages is raised against an arbitrator, the arbitrator may be covered by the DIA's liability insurance for arbitrators. For more information, contact the Secretariat of the DIA.

17. *See, e.g., Stefan Lindskog:* Skiljeförfarande. En kommentar, 3. upplagan (2020), p. 395, and *Jakob Juul & Peter Fauerholdt Thommesen:* Voldgiftsret, 3. udg. (2017), p. 203.

If you follow that theory, the basis for a claim raised by the parties to the dispute against the arbitrators must necessarily be contractual. On *one* side, this means that applicable standards of contractual negligence apply, which in turn will depend on the contractual provisions agreed. On the *other* side, the door will also be open for contractual provisions limiting or prescribing that liability.

Provisions of the latter kind have been applied by most arbitration institutes. Article 41 of the 2021 ICC Rules thus provides that the arbitrators, any person appointed by the arbitral tribunal, the emergency arbitrator, the Court and its members, ICC and its employees, and the ICC National Committees and Groups and their employees and representatives shall not be liable to any person for any act or omission in connection with the arbitration, *except to the extent such limitation of liability is prohibited by applicable law.*

Also, Article 51 of the 2021 DIA Rules provides that "The members of the Arbitral Tribunal, the secretary of the Arbitral Tribunal, or other persons appointed by the DIA or the Arbitral Tribunal, and the DIA, including the members of the Council of Representatives, the Board, the Chair's Committee, the Secretariat and the Secretary-General shall not be liable for any act or omission in connection with commencement of an arbitration, the processing of an arbitration or an award made by the Arbitral Tribunal, *except to the extent such limitation of liability is prohibited by applicable law.*"

Article 52 of the 2017 SCC rules provides that neither the SCC, the arbitrator(s), the administrative secretary of the Arbitral Tribunal, nor any expert appointed by the Arbitral Tribunal is liable to any party for any act or omission in connection with the arbitration, *unless such act or omission constitutes willful misconduct or gross negligence.*

And finally, Article 31.1 of the 2014 LCIA rules provides that none of the LCIA (including its officers, members and employees), the LCIA Court, the LCIA Board, any arbitrator, any Emergency Arbitrator, any tribunal secretary and any expert to the Arbitral Tribunal shall be liable to any party howsoever for any act or omission in connection with any arbitration, save: (i) where the act or omission is shown by that party to constitute conscious and deliberate wrongdoing committed by the body or person alleged to be liable to that party; or (ii) to the extent that any part of this provision is shown to be *prohibited by any applicable law.*

All these contractual disclaimers do not apply to accusations that may be characterized as recklessness or gross negligence or as a result of *bad faith*. This reservation is in line with Nordic court practice, under which wide and general contractual disclaimers are often held to be unfair and invalid in such situations.

It should be noted that Danish courts are more favorable towards contractual disclaimers that include caps on claims, e.g., maximized to the fee paid or to an insurance maximum. Such clauses thus stand a better chance against allegations of contractual invalidity. I have never seen such provisions used in arbitration practice. The arbitration institutes seem to favor the broader liability exclusions. But nothing should prevent such provisions, which are applied by a number of professions (e.g., technical consultants).

This will typically be the case in high-end commercial arbitration conducted by large teams of counsels. It is likely that such arbitrations provide a lucrative business case from the counsel's perspective. Just like in M&A transactions, no stone is left unturned. Huge teams of lawyers focus on different aspects of the dispute, and with *clients* with deep pockets, there may be a similar incentive to pursue post-award claims in order to give the losing party a "second chance."

The roles are different in more simple disputes on legal matters where the court holds expertise and where the facts of the case are being established in the course of the main hearing.

If the trend to accuse tribunals of procedural failures, etc., in various forms increases, there may, therefore, be a particular need to reconsider the way high-end arbitrations are conducted.

One relevant issue to discuss is the use of so-called administrative secretaries in arbitral tribunals. Formally, the use of secretaries is restricted to administrative tasks. It is, however, difficult to understand why arbitrators should not be able to rely on (separately payable) *legal* assistance in the preparation of the case, just as judges in state courts do.

I am well aware that this idea is seen by many arbitration professionals as quite controversial. As said above in footnote 11, a Danish high court has accepted the use of a legal secretary in an arbitration conducted by the Danish *Building and Construction Arbitration Board* where the sole arbitrator had no legal background. Other cases outside Denmark have also touched upon the topic.[18] Although no final decision has been rendered in these cases, the jury is out on the issue, and the debate is thus ongoing.

Regardless of how this legal question is finally decided, discussions and viewpoints articulated within the arbitration community may play a role in its outcome.

So far, the arbitration community has not been open to such a practice, possibly because the arbitrator's task is still seen as a personal vocation and not a business. But perhaps the time is up to initiate such a debate.

I refer to "the arbitration community" because arbitrators as such are not in general seen as individuals that belong to an "arbitration profession." Both attorneys, academics, and judges are part of their own professions. But arbitrators are not, due to the simple fact that they are being recruited from these other, different professions.

This may explain why there has never been an ideological framework for what arbitrators do other than the framework applicable to each profession. When new

18. One example hereof is the decision of 24 April 2023 by Belgian Supreme Court in the case *European Commission v. Emek Inşaat Şti and WTE Wassertechnik* in which it was held that arbitral secretaries may draft arbitral awards, provided that arbitrators do not delegate their decision-making powers to them. Reference is made to https://arbitrationblog.kluwerarbitration.com/2023/08/08/green-light-for-secretaries-to-assist-in-drafting-arbitral-awards-so-long-as-tribunals-call-the-shots-nothing-new-under-the-belgian-sun/. Another example is the decision rendered by the Court of Appeal of The Hague in February 2020 in the *Yukos* case which held that there was no evidence that an administrative secretary to the tribunal had participated in the decision-making process. See for a further presentation of the case https://www.ibanet.org/article/B55CB7F1-01C6-4BDF-9383-90F567C17147.

debatable issues come up, they are only occasionally discussed, e.g., at the many conferences that are being held on arbitration issues. Indeed, some arbitration associations (e.g., the Swiss Institute and the Chartered Institute of Arbitrators) promote rule-making for arbitration. So does UNCITRAL. But not in their capacities of "professional" bodies. One notable example of an international professional body which—despite its name—does not exclusively organize members of the legal profession is the International Bar Association, whose 2014 *Guidelines on Conflicts of Interest in International Arbitration* is perhaps the best example of an attempt to self-regulate arbitration practitioners.[19]

Therefore, it is still hard to claim that arbitration is indeed "a" profession with its own values, ethics, and rulemaking, given the many different kinds of arbitration we have. Instead, emerging topics may be discussed in the many yearbooks, tribute books, and periodicals we have (like the present one) and at conferences on various arbitration issues.[20]

But perhaps the arbitration community, or at least some of the arbitration institutions, could agree on the viewpoint that arbitrators in high-end disputes should call for specific considerations and be seen as other high-end service providers. Such perception would make it easier to initiate discussions that would, for example, leave it open to the tribunal to use the same kind of setup as counsels in such cases. It would thus be adequate that the disputing parties and the arbitrators negotiate some of the issues I have raised above, including the basis for possible liability, insurance issues and the use of both administrative and legal secretaries.

Such negotiating and contracting practices may in all circumstances reduce the risks of disappointments in the arbitral procedure.

19. *See* for a further discussion on this point, *Luca G. Radicati di Brozolo and Flavia Ponzano:* The need for arbitration-specific rules on ethics: a plea for a collective effort. Printed in Mohamed S. Abdel Wahab et al. (eds.): "Leadership, Legitimacy, Legacy, A tribute to Alexis Mourre" (2022), pp. 105-119.
20. The thoughts that I share here, have already been made at my presentation in September 2022 on the *Copenhagen Arbitration Day*.

CHAPTER 9

Beyond the Myth of the Bermuda Triangle: A Swedish Perspective on Conflicts of Interest in the Context of Third-Party Funding in International Arbitration

Johan Skog & Carl Persson

§9.01 INTRODUCTION

The issue of potential conflicts of interest in cases involving third-party funding (TPF) has been widely debated since TPF emerged in the 2000s. The most discussed issue relating to conflicts of interest has been the situation where an arbitrator may have a previous or existing relationship with a funder. However, it has also been argued that TPF can give rise to potential conflicts of interest emanating from the relationship between the funder and a funded party, counsel, or the funded party's opposite party.

In §9.02 of this chapter, we examine what actually constitutes a conflict of interest, how the contractual TPF relationship is usually structured in Sweden, and whether it can generally be said that conflicts of interest are inevitable, or highly likely, to arise for funders and counsel involved in a funded dispute. In §9.03 of this chapter, we provide an overview of rules and best practices regarding conflicts of interest and disclosure in relation to arbitrators in funded international arbitrations seated in Sweden.

§9.02 CONFLICT OF INTEREST ISSUES RELATING TO FUNDERS, COUNSEL AND FUNDED PARTIES

[A] Introduction

This first section of the chapter focuses on potential and alleged conflicts of interest other than those involving arbitrators, mainly related to the funder and counsel. The perceived danger of conflicts of interest arising in TPF has been frequently raised by international authors and commentators, sometimes even by pioneering funders themselves. For example, Selvyn Seidel, co-founder of Burford (later with Fulbrook), states that:

> real problems exist and are troublesome. One such problem is conflicts. The relationship among the claimant, its lawyer, and the investor, is fraught with potential conflicts and dangers, like the Bermuda Triangle. They can be managed, but first they have to be identified, and then governed.[1]

This remark, even if made in a short introductory booklet (which admittedly does not allow for a deep dive into the subject), can be regarded as somewhat characteristic of discussions on TPF.

Common themes in such discussions are that (i) the broad and vague term 'conflicts' is used in an unspecified and undefined manner; (ii) reference is made to a triangular relationship (unclear whether contractual or not); (iii) it is stated that TPF involves dangers; and, after those remarks have been made, (iv) no effort is shown to provide for a clear and systematic analysis of circumstances which would actually constitute such alleged conflicts. Below, we discuss and present our view on these topics.

[B] Brief Comments on the Term *Conflict of Interest*

In order to properly discuss issues regarding conflicts of interest, as with any other analysis relating to a legal concept, it is of course important to clearly set out what is meant by such a term.

Naturally, any discussion regarding conflicts of interest in international arbitration would at some point rely on and refer to the IBA Guidelines on Conflicts of Interest in International Arbitration (the 'IBA Guidelines'). However, the purpose and focus of the IBA Guidelines is to identify and avoid potential conflicts of interest with respect to the *arbitrator*, rather than any other participant in arbitral proceedings. Thus, for the purposes of a *general* understanding of what constitutes a conflict of interest, the IBA

1. Selvyn Seidel, *Snapshot. Contemporary Litigation Finance*, p. 30 (Lambert Academic Publishing, 2019). The reference to the Bermuda Triangle when discussing the relationship between funder, funded party and counsel has been taken up and used by others, *see, e.g.*, Jonas von Goeler, who refers to Luke Eric Peterson who, in turn, cites Selvyn Seidel. Jonas von Goeler, *Third-Party Funding in International Arbitration and Its Impact on Procedure*, p. 97 and footnote 187 (Kluwer Law International, 2016). *See also, e.g.*, Charles Kaplan, who states that 'the three-cornered relationship must inevitably give rise to potential conflicts ...'. Charles Kaplan, *Issues for Counsel*, p. 75 (Bernardo M. Cremades and Antonias Dimolitsa (eds), *Third-Party Funding in International Arbitration*, ICC Dossier, Kluwer Law International, 2013). On potential conflicts of interest, *see, e.g.*, also Lucy Pert, Anthony Sebok, *Third-Party Litigation Financing and Lawyers' Ethical Obligations*, p. 76 (Steven Friel (ed.), *The Law and Business of Litigation Finance*, Bloomsbury Professional, 2020); Adriana Cordina, *Is It All That Fishy? A Critical Review of the Concerns Surrounding Third Party Litigation Funding in Europe*, p. 277 (Erasmus Law Review, Vol. 14, No. 4, 2021) DOI: 10.5553/elr.000211 (stating that: 'Given the assumption of self-interest, TPF arrangements inevitably give rise to the possibility of conflicting interests between the funder, the claimant and the lawyer.' (p. 275).

Guidelines are not sufficient, as their primary purpose in this regard is to ensure that the individual sitting as arbitrator is impartial and independent (which is further discussed in the second section of this chapter). In this section, we are instead dealing with potential conflicts of interest arising mainly for funders and counsel – who are not and cannot be disinterested as to the outcome of the dispute.

According to Black's Law Dictionary, a conflict of interest means the following: '1. A real or seeming incompatibility between one's private interests and one's public or fiduciary duties. 2. A real or seeming incompatibility between the interests of two of a lawyer's clients, such that the lawyer is disqualified from representing both clients if the dual representation adversely affects either client or if the clients do not consent.' This definition is well reflected in both the Code of Conduct for European Lawyers[2] and the Swedish Bar Association Rules,[3] and it is clear that professional obligations and fiduciary duties[4] are key to understanding the concept of *conflict of interest*. This is well-explained in an EU report on conflict of interest:

> CoI [i.e., Conflict of Interest] as a legal concept has a long agreed-upon meaning in law used to regulate fiduciaries – individuals entrusted to serve the interest of another party or to serve a designated mission – who are held to the highest legal standards of conduct. Generally, these laws and codes do not permit fiduciaries to promote their own interests or the interests of third parties. Instead, they require fiduciaries to be loyal to the party they serve, to act prudently and diligently, and to account for their conduct.[5]

It is important to note that words such as *conflicting* or *competing interests*, as generally used in ordinary language, do not have the same meaning as the more narrow legal concept of *conflict of interest*.[6] All business arrangements almost inevitably give rise to competing interests between the contracting parties. There is nothing inherently harmful about that. At the core of the term *conflict of interest* is instead the compromise of professional or fiduciary duties, or the risk of such duties being compromised. The natural step for anyone who is in a conflict of interest is generally to resign or withdraw from further participation entirely or to discontinue at least one of the relations which give rise to the conflict of interest situation.[7]

---

2. The Code of Conduct for European Lawyers, items 3.2.1-3.2.3.
3. The Swedish Bar Association Rules, item 3.2.1.
4. *Fiduciary duty* is, according to Black's Law Dictionary, generally understood to mean the following: 'A duty of utmost good faith, trust, confidence, and candor owed by a fiduciary (such as a lawyer or corporate officer) to the beneficiary (such as a lawyer's client or a shareholder); a duty to act with the highest degree of honesty and loyalty toward another person and in the best interests of the other person (such as the duty that one partner owes to another).'
5. The European Parliament's Policy Department for Citizens' Rights and Constitutional Affairs, *The Effectiveness of Conflict of Interest Policies in the EU Member States*, p. 38 (2020).
6. This has been pointed out in a previous article by one of us, *see* Johan Skog, *Illusory Truths and Frivolous Claims: Critical Reflections on a Report on Litigation Funding by the European Parliamentary Research Service* (Eva Storskrubb (ed.), *YSEC Yearbook of Socio-Economic Constitutions 2022*, Springer, 2023).
7. If the person in a conflict of interest situation is a legal counsel, he or she should cease to act for the client (the Code of Conduct for European Lawyers, item 3.2.2 and the Swedish Bar Association Rules, item 3.4) and if being a judge, he or she should recuse himself or herself from adjudicating the matter, which is generally provided for under national procedural law.

In light of the above, we understand the term *conflict of interest* to mean the compromise of professional or fiduciary duties, or the risk thereof, arising *for* a certain party (not *between* parties). We will use the term accordingly in this chapter.

[C] The Contractual Relationships in a Swedish TPF Deal

As noted above, TPF arrangements have been referred to as a Bermuda Triangle of dangers. Such language is no doubt eye-catching, but for the purposes of any conflict of interest analysis, it is important that it is made perfectly clear how the relationships are actually structured and under which specific circumstances a conflict of interest would arise.

In some TPF markets, particularly common law jurisdictions, funders may enter into a contractual relationship with the funded party's counsel, either directly as a party to the litigation funding agreement ('LFA') or under a separate contract (as an ancillary agreement to the LFA),[8] with negative effects of intricate fiduciary and/or contractual duties for counsel.

However, these types of structures are in our experience not reflected in Swedish TPF practices.[9] On the contrary, in Sweden, where the authors of this chapter are primarily active, funders would not require – and counsel would generally not accept – that any contractual relationship be established between the two.[10] In our view, such a contractual relationship would under Swedish conditions expose counsel to situations involving challenging ethical issues, for example, if counsel would itself be contractually obligated to disclose to the funder any negative developments in a case, and at the same time be instructed by its client not to do so. Thus, Swedish funders typically enter into an LFA with the funded party only, with no ancillary agreements involving the funded party's counsel.

As will be demonstrated below, it turns out that many of the allegedly difficult 'conflict' situations discussed in much of the literature on TPF actually evaporate when counsel do not expose themselves by entering into a contractual relationship with the funder, and when the funder refrains from requiring counsel to do so. A key factor for our conflict of interest analysis with respect to TPF in Sweden is the presumption that the funder is not a client of the funded party's counsel and that it has not entered into any contract with counsel. It is equally important to remind oneself that, similarly, the funded party is not a client of the funder, as the funder is generally not a service

8. Alex Lempiner, Jonathan Barnes, *The Litigation Funding Agreement*, p. 145, para. 6.4 (Steven Friel (ed.), *The Law and Business of Litigation Finance*, Bloomsbury Professional, 2020); Jonathan Barnes, *Regulation and Legislation: England*, p. 34, para. 4.45 (Steven Friel (ed.), *The Law and Business of Litigation Finance*, Bloomsbury Professional, 2020); Max Volsky, *Investing in Justice: An Introduction to Legal Finance, Lawsuit Advances and Litigation Funding*, pp. 128 and 141-142 (The Legal Finance Journal, 2013); Lisa Bench Nieuwveld and Victoria Shannon Sahani, *Third-Party Funding in International Arbitration*, Second Edition, p. 26 (Wolters Kluwer, 2017).
9. Johan Skog and Carl Persson, *Tvistfinansiering*, p. 108 (Norstedts Juridik, 2022).
10. *See also* Stefan Kirsten and Alexander Foerster, *Sweden*, p. 230 (Steven Friel and Jonathan Barnes (eds), *Litigation Funding*, Lexology GTDT, 2023).

provider but an investor,[11] and thus under no fiduciary obligations vis-à-vis the funded party.[12]

It has now been explained that (i) a *conflict of interest* means the compromise of professional or fiduciary duties, or the risk of thereof; (ii) the funder is not a client of the funded party's counsel or in a contractual relationship with counsel; and (iii) the funded party is not a client of the funder. The next section will apply these findings when examining some of the situations which have been raised as being particularly 'dangerous' from a conflict of interest perspective.

[D] Situations Often Discussed with Respect to Conflicts of Interest

[1] Initial Comments

In the sections below, we discuss some of the situations that are often mentioned in the context of TPF and conflicts of interest and analyse them on the assumption that a conflict of interest means the compromise of professional or fiduciary duties, or the risk thereof, for a certain party.[13]

[2] The Funder

[a] General

As mentioned above, it is an important fact that litigation funders are *investors* – not service providers – and thus, the funded parties are not their clients. Yet, this is often overlooked or forgotten in writings on TPF, where the funded party is frequently referred to as a 'client' of the funder.[14] Regrettably, such ignorance has a bearing on the

11. Lempiner and Barnes, p. 143, para. 6.1; Cordina, p. 277; the EPRS study, p. 5, footnote 13; Mohamed F. Sweify, *Third Party Funding in International Arbitration. A Critical Appraisal and Pragmatic Proposal*, p. 4, stating that 'Rather than providing a service in exchange for a fee, funders invest in the lawsuit.' (Edward Elgar Publishing, 2023); Susanne Augenhofer and Adriani Dori, *The Proposed Regulation of Third Party Litigation Funding – Much Ado About Nothing?*, p. 32 (Zeitschrift für das Privatrecht der Europäischen Union, Vol 20, Issue 5).
12. It should however be noted that in September 2022, the European Parliament adopted a resolution which includes a proposal for a directive regulating TPF in the EU, in which it is set out that member states shall ensure that TPF agreements 'are based on a fiduciary relationship', requiring funders 'to act in the best interests of a claimant', and that 'the litigation funder shall commit to placing the interests of the claimants [...] above its own interests.' *European Parliament resolution of 13 September 2022 with recommendations to the Commission on Responsible private funding of litigation (2020/2130(INL))*, Draft Art. 7. Such language is at odds with the fact that the funder is an investor, not a service provider to the funded party. Augenhofer and Dori state the following regarding the proposed directive's language on conflict of interest: 'These provisions focus on the relationship between the funder and the claimant. They neglect the fact that in Europe, as mentioned, the wronged party is hardly ever the client of the funder.' (p. 32) The European Commission has stated that it will carry out a study on TPF within the EU before taking any action in relation to the proposed directive.
13. Except for arbitrator conflicts of interest, which are discussed in §9.02 below.
14. *See, e.g.*, Nick Rowles-Davies, *Third Party Litigation Funding*, p. 66 f., para. 3.37 f. (Oxford University Press, 2014); Bench Nieuwveld and Shannon Sahani, p. 12; Solas, p. 261.

analysis carried out with respect to the relationship between the funder and funded party (as a client is owed fiduciary duties not owed to other business partners) and to what extent – if at all – there are any risks of conflicts of interest arising. Our view is that a funder owes no fiduciary duties to the funded party (but it is, of course, under a general obligation of contractual loyalty under the LFA).

[b] Funder Control

As regards potential conflicts of interest due to funder control in relation to the funded party, such concerns often relate to the understanding that the funder may wish to see or withhold certain procedural actions, including seeking an earlier settlement.

In common law jurisdictions, funders are generally careful not to take control over the proceedings, as such arrangements may not be allowed. However, in civil law jurisdictions, where doctrines of maintenance and champerty have generally not been applied and where claims may be freely assigned, the issue of control is of less significance. This is explained by Willem van Boom as follows:

> Whether 'steering the case' is considered unlawful or unethical depends heavily on the foundations of assignment of claims and debts. If, under a particular legal system, the law of assignment is unproblematic and fully permits such legal transfer, it is unlikely that any ethical problems will be experienced when a TPF funder is permitted to take control with the claimant's consent. It is, however, important to note that, depending on the rules of professional conduct applicable to client-counsel relationships, issues of conflict of interest may quickly arise if the lawyer is retained simultaneously by the claimant and the TPF funder.[15]

Sweden is such a jurisdiction where claims may be freely assigned and where the parties can agree as they wish with respect to the level of control by the funder. However, it should be stressed that unless the LFA confers the right on the funder to exercise control in a certain situation, such as a settlement, the funder will not have any right or possibility to take control or require certain action by the funded party. The funded party – and not the funder – is and should be the only client of the law firm; the funder can have no possibility or right to steer the dispute other than as explicitly set out in the LFA – and the funded party's counsel should never under Swedish conditions be 'retained simultaneously' by the funder, as put by van Boom in the above quote.[16]

15. Willem van Boom, *Litigation Costs and Third-Party Funding*, p. 25 (van Boom (ed.) *Litigation, Costs, Funding and Behaviour. Implications for the Law*, Routledge, 2017).
16. In a Swedish context, the funded party might delegate the management of the case to the funder, but counsel should of course only accept and follow instructions from the funder as long as such delegation has not been withdrawn. With respect to the issue of funder control, von Goeler makes the following remark: 'To the extent the funded party agrees with the litigation funder on a free and informed basis to cede control to the latter, it is difficult to see how this could be an issue. Why should a commercially experienced and legally advised party in international arbitration *not* be able to exercise its private autonomy by delegating case management to a third person?' (von Goeler, pp. 97 et seq., emphasis in original.) This is a truly continental or north European approach, which – due to the historical doctrines of champerty and maintenance – is almost unthinkable to find in US and UK works on TPF, most commonly utterly concerned with the issue of control.

Counsel should and must take instructions from the funded party, irrespective of whether such instructions would be in breach of the funded party's obligations to the funder under the LFA. The funder can never be allowed to direct counsel against the will of the funded party. The funder can thus only require that the funded party complies with its obligations under the LFA with respect to instructions to counsel.[17] Should that not be the case, the funded party would be in breach of the LFA, and the funder could take action accordingly.[18]

If the LFA contains no right for the funder to require that the funded party shall take or refrain from certain actions, including settling the case at a certain level, the funded party will be able to proceed as it sees fit. Thus, the parties have either identified the relevant situation in advance and dealt with it in the LFA, which may allow the funder to require certain actions by the funded party, or the situation is not dealt with in the LFA, which allows the funded party to act as it wishes. The fact that the parties may have competing interests regarding such matter, as at what time or at what level to settle, does not mean that either of them has a conflict of interest in either situation, as there is no risk of professional or fiduciary duties being compromised.[19] That would be the case also if the funded party acted in breach of the LFA by not taking the required action.

[c] Excessive Pricing

It is sometimes argued that funders may provide funding in return for an excessive share of any recovery to the benefit of the funder itself and at the expense of the funded party and that this may constitute a conflict of interest.[20] However, we do not consider that to constitute a conflict of interest issue within the legal meaning of the term and as we use such term in this chapter. Of course, the parties have competing interests as to the amount of the recovery which should be paid out to the funder. But this is a pricing issue that is fully reflected in the terms of the LFA. The concerns one may have relating to alleged excessive remuneration would rather be an issue of potentially unlawfully charged rates or payment terms, something which is not the subject of this chapter.

17. von Goeler notes in plain language that '[t]he litigation funding agreement may expressly entitle the litigation funder to exercise control over certain decisions of the funded party. The appointment of counsel and arbitrator by the funded party as well as decisions relating to settlement are situations that immediately spring to mind.' (von Goeler, p. 35.) From a Swedish perspective, this is not controversial, particularly as no common law doctrines of champerty or maintenance exist, as claims may be freely assigned and as funders will not enter into any contractual relationship with the funded party's counsel.
18. For a more detailed account of alleged conflicts of interest in settlement situations, *see* Skog (2023), sections 5.2 and 5.3.
19. Here, a comparison may be made with respect to the intervention in the attorney-client relation that follows under many insurance liability arrangements. Bench Nieuwveld and Shannon Sahani: '... in situations ... where a traditional liability insurance arrangement is involved, the client usually retains little or no control over the direction of the case.' Bench Nieuwveld and Shannon Sahani, p. 9.
20. For example, these issues are mentioned by the EPRS, p. 22. *See also, e.g.*, Cordina, p. 276 and Solas, p. 278.

[d] A Funder's Relation with the Funded Party's Opposite Party

It is a banal truism that a funder's interest is in fundamental conflict with the funded party's opposite party in the dispute. Even so, this issue has been addressed by commentators,[21] public bodies[22] and EU regulators,[23] and is understood by some to raise certain concerns within the context of conflicts of interest.

In the EPRS report, for example, it is stated that 'the third party intervention may lead to conflicts of interests between the funder and the defendant'.[24] Naturally, it is unavoidable in every funded case that there will be competing interests between a funder and the funded party's opposite party. From our perspective, this does not raise any issues of interest for further analysis, particularly as there are no duties (fiduciary or other) whatsoever arising between the funder and the funded party's opposite party, and no conflict of interest (as the term is understood in this chapter) would thus arise for a funder in relation to the funded party's opposite party. Some brief comments should nevertheless be made.

What appears to be the most common point of discussion with respect to the relationship between the funder and the funded party's opposite party is so-called revenge funding, where a funder provides capital to a party in order to pursue a claim not for commercial reasons but for the purpose of harming a competitor or other legal or natural person – irrespective of whether there is a sound legal claim. However, the risk that any professional funder managing its investors' capital should carry out a TPF deal for anything other than business purposes is presumably non-existent.[25] Any revenge funding arrangements that might potentially be carried out by other parties are outside the scope of this chapter.

Two other related situations that are sometimes discussed in this context are when a funder is backing a claim against (i) a competitor; or (ii) a respondent on whom the funder is dependant. For example, the EU Representative Actions Directive provides as follows:

> 1. Member States shall ensure that, where a representative action for redress measures is funded by a third party, [...] conflicts of interests are prevented and that funding by third parties that have an economic interest in the bringing or the outcome of the representative action for redress measures does not divert the representative action away from the protection of the collective interests of consumers.

---

21. *See, e.g.*, Solas, who in a specific section of his book under the heading 'Conflicts between Funders and Counterparties', states that '[i]t may also be possible that conflictual situations concern the funder in relation to the counterparty of the funded party.' Solas, p. 263.
22. EPRS-report, Annex, p. 78.
23. The Representative Actions Directive, Art. 10. See also the European Parliament's proposal for a directive regulating TPF, Art. 5.1 (c) and Art. 13.2 (b).
24. EPRS report, Annex, p. 78. See also the European Parliament's proposal for a directive regulating TPF (suggested to apply also in arbitration), Art. 5.1 (c), where it is set out that member states shall ensure that funders 'have established internal procedures to prevent a conflict of interest between themselves and the defendants in proceedings involving the litigation funder'.
25. Solas also correctly notes that there are mechanisms in place in most jurisdictions with respect to summary dismissal of vexatious claims. Solas, p. 263.

2. For the purposes of paragraph 1, Member States shall in particular ensure that:
   (a) [---];
   (b) the representative action is not brought against a defendant that is a competitor of the funding provider or against a defendant on which the funding provider is dependent.[26]

With respect to the situation involving a 'competitor', it should be noted that, by definition, this means that the funder and the respondent must be in the same line of business, as they have to be competitors. Thus, in the case of professional TPF, such a situation can only arise if a funder funds a claim against a competing funder. We are aware of no such case to date, and it may strongly be questioned whether any such case would ever materialize.

As regards the situation of a dispute against a respondent on which the funder is dependent (Representative Actions Directive, Article 10.1(b)) or by whom the funder is controlled,[27] that would mean that a funder would be providing capital for a claim against its own parent company or major individual shareholder. We cannot foresee that such a situation would ever arise in practice, as no management or investment committee of a funder would propose or accept that such an investment be made.

Now, the EU Representative Actions Directive discussed above may not be directly relevant to international arbitrations. However, it should be stressed that there are regulatory proposals at the EU level which suggest that language similar to that contained in the referenced Directive be adopted in a Directive specifically regulating TPF – which should apply to arbitration as well.[28] Thus, the draft Directive provided in a report by the Committee on Legal Affairs, the so-called Voss Report, and adopted as a proposed Directive by the European Parliament sets out as follows:

> Member States shall require litigation funders to disclose to a claimant and intended beneficiaries in the third-party funding agreement all information that may reasonably be perceived as having the potential to give rise to a conflict of interest. Litigation funders' disclosures shall include at least the following: (a) [...]; (b) details of any relevant connection between the litigation funder and a defendant in the proceedings, in particular in relation to any situation of competition.[29]

26. Directive (EU) 2020/1828, Art. 10. *See also, e.g.*, the EPRS report, where the following is set out: 'For example, a conflict of interests may arise: [...] b. when the funder provides financing for an action against a defendant who is a competitor of the funder or against a defendant by whom the funder is controlled ("revenge funder").' EPRS, p. 75.
27. EPRS, p. 75, *ibid.*
28. *European Parliament resolution of 13 September 2022 with recommendations to the Commission on Responsible private funding of litigation (2020/2130(INL))*, draft Art. 3 (c) and (e), which set out that the term 'court' includes 'arbitral body' and that 'proceedings' include 'arbitration procedure'.
29. *European Parliament resolution of 13 September 2022 with recommendations to the Commission on Responsible private funding of litigation (2020/2130(INL))*, draft Art. 13. See also *Committee on Legal Affairs, Proposal for a Directive of the European Parliament and of the Council on the regulation of third-party litigation funding*, Art. 13 (*Annex to Report with recommendations to the Commission on Responsible private funding of litigation (2020/2130(INL))*, July 2022. As mentioned above, the European Commission has stated that it will carry out a study on TPF within the EU before taking any action in relation to the proposed directive.

As stated above, it is difficult to even imagine a situation where a funder should provide funding for a claimant to take legal action against a respondent in which the funder has a financial or other interest (in lack of which there could be no conflict of interest). Therefore, such suggested conflicts of interest situations would presumably be non-existent or close to non-existent, particularly with respect to the professional practice of commercial funding. However, should such a situation nevertheless arise, it would of course be important for the funded party that such information be disclosed.

[3] *The Counsel*

[a] *Control*

Much of the focus with respect to conflicts of interest for counsel relates to the level of control of the proceedings that is exercised by the funder.[30] These concerns partly stem from the common law doctrines of maintenance and champerty.[31] In Sweden, as in continental European civil law jurisdictions, there are no such doctrines to take into consideration. Even so, situations may also arise in a Swedish context which warrant careful and due consideration by counsel in order not to run into conflicts.

Any risk for counsel to compromise professional or fiduciary duties with respect to issues of control would mainly arise if and when counsel has entered into some form of contractual relationship with the funder, under which it is obliged to follow instructions directly from the funder. As has been argued above, counsel should be careful not to put itself in such a position.[32] Thus, the funding agreement should be entered into between the funder and the funded party only, and counsel should not agree to enter into any ancillary agreements with the funder. Even though the funder may have influence over the funded party with respect to the instructions the funded party is to provide to its counsel, the funder must not have any right to control or directly instruct counsel, nor to receive any information, against the will of the funded party. This would generally be the case in a standard TPF deal involving a Swedish funder and counsel. If this basic premise is upheld, there should be limited – if any – need for concern, as this arrangement provides for a simple and straightforward conflict of interest analysis.

Considering the influence exerted by legal insurance companies on counsel representing the insured, a well-established and accepted arrangement in most jurisdictions, it is intriguing that the issue of control in the TPF context is deemed by some to be so difficult and controversial. As a Swedish-style TPF arrangement does not provide for the funder to have any direct influence over counsel, a traditional insurance situation may indeed be considered to give rise to more concerns with respect to issues of control.

30. Rowles-Davies, p. 12; Pert and Sebok, p. 77, para. 4.46.
31. Lempiner and Barnes, p. 147, para. 6.13; Bench Nieuwveld and Shannon Sahani, p. 43.
32. *See, e.g.*, von Goeler, who notes that 'counsel will need to make sure that it is not representing conflicting interests, similarly to the situation where an insurer becomes involved.' von Goeler, p. 99.

[b] *Counsel Acts for the Funder in Another Matter*

[i] Counsel Acts for the Funder in a Matter Related to the Funded Case

A situation that may raise certain concerns is where a counsel is engaged by a funder to perform an initial case assessment in relation to a dispute and, either during or after the engagement, is asked to represent one of the parties to the dispute.[33]

As a result of the engagement relating to the initial case assessment, a client relationship arises between counsel and the funder in relation to that case. Due to this client relationship, it is of course not possible for counsel to simultaneously represent the opposing party of the party seeking funding in the dispute, given that counsel has a client relationship with the funder in relation to the same case.[34]

As regards the possibility for counsel to represent the potentially funded party in the same case, a distinction should be made between the situation (i) where counsel would represent the funder and the potentially funded party at the same time; and (ii) where counsel's engagement for the funder has ended when it is asked to represent the potentially funded party.

In the first situation, there is a conflict of interest. Counsel would be acting for different clients in the same or a related matter at a stage where their interests could be considered to be conflicting in that the funder wants the case assessment to be as illuminating as possible, whilst the potential funded party has an interest in ensuring that the case assessment does not deter the funder from funding the dispute.[35] Therefore, counsel should refrain from representing both parties because the dual representation adversely affects both clients.

In the second situation, i.e., where counsel's engagement with the funder has ended, a conflict of interest could arise due to a residual duty of loyalty for counsel in relation to the funder.[36] For example, the funder may have intended to continue using counsel's services to assess the dispute at a later stage. This would no longer be

33. A more detailed account of the matters addressed in this section from a Swedish Bar rules perspective can be found in section 14.3.2 of our full-length book on TPF, *see* Skog and Persson.
34. In view of the risk of a breach of confidence, and the undue advantage that the new client could gain as a result of the previous engagement, counsel would be barred from taking on such assignment also if the engagement for the funder has come to an end. Section 3.2.3 of the Code of Conduct for European Lawyers provides that '[a] lawyer must also refrain from acting for a new client if there is a risk of breach of a confidence entrusted to the lawyer by a former client or if the knowledge which the lawyer possesses of the affairs of the former client would give an undue advantage to the new client.' Even if counsel's engagement for the funder has been completed, there can still be a risk of a breach of a confidence entrusted to counsel by the funder. The knowledge obtained by counsel during the engagement for the funder (e.g., regarding strategy and evidentiary issues) could also give the new client an undue advantage.
35. Section 3.2.1 of the Code of Conduct for European Lawyers provides that '[a] lawyer may not advise, represent or act on behalf of two or more clients in the same matter if there is a conflict, or a significant risk of a conflict, between the interests of those clients.' If counsel represents both the funder and the funded party, there would be a significant risk of a conflict between the interests of the two clients.
36. *See* section 3.2.3 of the Code of Conduct for European Lawyers. *See also* Council of Bars and Law Societies of Europe, *Charter of Core Principles of the European Legal Profession & Code of Conduct for European Lawyers*, commentary to principles (c) and (e).

possible if counsel accepts instructions from the funded party, as the situation would then be the same as in the first situation described above. Depending on whether it is deemed to be the same or a related matter, counsel would either have to decline one assignment (if the matter is deemed to be the same) or inform both clients of the situation and the potential implications that may arise from this, and obtain the clients' approval (if the matters are only considered to be related).

Even if such approval is given, a conflict of interest may arise for counsel with respect to its advice as to how the funded party should conduct the dispute if such advice is at odds with the advice counsel may have given to the funder as to what case strategy and procedural actions that would best suit the funder's purposes. Consequently, where counsel has previously represented a funder, it should always carefully consider whether it is appropriate to accept an engagement for a party being funded by the same funder, as situations may arise in which the funder and the funded party could have different interests.[37] Thus, some prudence is required in this respect.

[ii] Counsel Acts for the Funder in a Matter Unrelated to the Funded Case

A related question is whether a counsel could represent a client in a dispute ('Dispute 1') in which the funder is considering investing (a matter in which counsel has not been engaged by the funder) at the same time as, or after, counsel performs a case assessment or other work on behalf of the funder in another dispute ('Dispute 2'). Thus, this would be a situation in which counsel would act for both the funder and the funded party, but in relation to two different cases.

It cannot be excluded that a conflict of interest could arise in such a situation. That could for example be the case if there is a risk that knowledge gained by counsel through its work for the funder in relation to Dispute 2 could be relevant to counsel's work for the client in Dispute 1, or that counsel in some other way could be prevented from acting in the client's best interests in Dispute 1 due to its relationship with the funder.[38]

An example of such a situation could be that counsel as part of its assignment in Dispute 2 has gained certain confidential information of the funder's business, and is thereafter asked to negotiate the funding agreement with the funder on behalf of the party seeking funding in Dispute 1. In such case, counsel should not accept to represent the party seeking funding in the negotiations of the funding agreement or any questions relating to the funding agreement unless the funder grants its approval to counsel to do so (and assuming that counsel is not prevented from acting in the client's best interests

37. Cf. David Riskin, *Third-Party Litigation Financing: Ethical Issues for Attorneys*, p. 9 (Practical Law, accessed on 29 March 2023).
38. *See* section 3.2.3 of the Code of Conduct for European Lawyers, pursuant to which a lawyer must refrain from acting for a new client if there is a risk of breach of a confidence entrusted to the lawyer by a former client or if the knowledge which the lawyer possesses of the affairs of the former client would give an undue advantage to the new client.

in some other way).[39] In any case, considering the risk of a conflict of interest, a simple and practical way to deal with the situation could be for the party seeking funding in Dispute 1 to engage other counsel for the task of representing such party in the negotiations of the funding agreement and subsequent issues that may come up in relation to the funding agreement.

However, it should be noted that the preparation of a case assessment or other type of work for the funder in Dispute 2 would not necessarily provide counsel with such knowledge pertaining to the funder that would be relevant to the negotiation of the funding agreement in Dispute 1.[40] It should also be noted that, in the context of a dispute, the funding agreement is only a secondary matter of minor importance in relation to the engagement as such, which is to represent the client in a dispute against another party.[41]

Having said this, it should be borne in mind that the negotiation of the funding agreement is just one area where a conflict of interest could arise. The situation and example described above may be varied, depending on, among other things, the timing of the assignments in relation to each other (for example, counsel might already be representing the party in Dispute 1 when asked to assist the funder in relation to Dispute 2). Whether or not counsel could accept the second assignment would then have to be assessed on a case-by-case basis, taking into account what knowledge counsel has gained and whether or not counsel could be prevented from acting in both clients' best interests due to its relationship with the other client.

[c] Disclosure of Case Information

One issue that is sometimes raised in relation to the question of whether counsel runs the risk of conflict of interest when representing a funded party is that of disclosure of

39. As the LFA arguably benefits counsel (as it relates to payments to be made to the counsel), it can sometimes be recommendable for the party seeking funding from the funder to engage separate counsel for the task of negotiating the LFA also in situations where the counsel who is to represent the client in the dispute has not previously been engaged by the funder. External counsel can in such situations negotiate (i) the legal budget between counsel and the party seeking funding and (ii) the LFA between the funder and the party seeking funding. If the party seeking funding does not engage other counsel, it is important to bear in mind that counsel, when negotiation the LFA, has a strict duty of loyalty against the client and that it is the client's interests that counsel must safeguard (and not its own interest to take on the matter). *See also* section 3.2.3 of the Code of Conduct for European Lawyers.
40. Counsel's case assessment should reasonably relate to the chance of winning the case and other legal assessments relating to the dispute, not to matters concerning the funding agreement.
41. Similarly, if the relationship between the funded party and the funder becomes strained during the course of the proceedings in the case between the funded party and its opposite party and a dispute arises between the funder and the funded party over the interpretation of the funding agreement, it is important that counsel ensures that it can fully represent the funded party in discussions with the funder, notwithstanding the fact that counsel is acting or has acted for the funder in another matter. Where counsel, or counsel's law firm, has an ongoing relationship with the funder, the lawyer should also inform the funded party of this relationship and obtain approval from the funded party to be represented by the law firm, notwithstanding its relationship with the funder. (Riskin, p. 8 f.) Therefore, some prudence is required in this respect as well.

case information to the funder.[42] In a chapter on TPF in Sweden, Stefan Kirsten and Alexander Foerster provide the following explanation regarding this concern:

> Notably, it is advisable for an advocate to exercise caution when agreeing to an obligation to disclose information to the funder. If the obligation is too extensive, the advocate runs a risk of ending up in a conflict of interest in relation to his or her client. It is conceivable, in certain situations, that the disclosure of information to the funder is not necessary in the client's best interest. Therefore, an advocate should insist that he or she is given a right to continuously test, in each individual situation, whether a disclosure is compatible with his or her fiduciary duty towards the client.[43]

Kirsten and Foerster thus suggest that there is a potential risk of conflict of interest for counsel with respect to disclosure of case information. However, the argument presumes that it should be an issue for counsel (rather than for the funded party) to decide on or agree to a disclosure obligation to the funder. This, in turn, implies a specific arrangement between counsel and funder under which counsel has certain contractual obligations towards the funder. We are not aware of such practices by local funders operating on the Swedish TPF market, even though some international funders from other jurisdictions that are also occasionally active in Sweden may require that counsel enter into an adherence agreement or other direct arrangement with a funder.

Under a typical Swedish TPF arrangement, it may well be that the funded party is required to release counsel from its confidentiality obligation and instruct counsel to disclose any and all relevant information about the dispute directly to the funder. Such agreement does not allow counsel to decide whether to agree or refuse to follow its client's (i.e., the funded party's) instruction that the information be disclosed to the funder. If the LFA contains an obligation that the funded party must provide for full disclosure by counsel to the funder, and the funded party has also instructed counsel to make such disclosure, it would be contrary to the client's instruction if counsel were to second guess the effects of disclosure of specific information and not to provide such information to the funder (acting in breach of direct client instructions). Of course, there may be information which the funded party would have preferred that the funder was unaware of. However, when negotiating the terms of the LFA, the funded party has generally allowed the funder to have full access to the file in exchange for the provision of funding.

In light of the above, it is difficult to understand how counsel could 'insist' that it should have the right to assess in each case whether disclosure should be made.[44] If the funded party were to allow counsel to do so, it would directly be in breach of the LFA under which it has agreed to instruct counsel to fully disclose information in the file. In any event, it is difficult to conceive why counsel should be in a conflict of interest if it complies with the client's instructions on disclosure (which the client

42. Solas, p. 261.
43. Kirsten and Foerster, p. 229.
44. *Ibid.*

agreed to provide to its counsel in order to have its dispute funded). It is not even clear to us what the conflicting interests would be,[45] or which party that would act or risk acting contrary to any fiduciary or ethical duty (under Bar rules or otherwise).[46]

Thus, under a Swedish TPF arrangement, we can see no reason why the disclosure of information from counsel to funder – of course, only with the funded party's consent – should amount to a conflict of interest for counsel.

[d] Fee Arrangements

An issue which is sometimes raised with respect to fee arrangements and potential or alleged conflicts of interest is the fact that counsel's fees are often being paid directly to counsel by the funder.[47] However, that situation does not seem to be significantly different from the situation in which an insurer picks up the bill for counsel fees on behalf of the insured (who is the client of counsel) under a regular liability or legal fees expense insurance policy.[48] Most dispute resolution lawyers on the Swedish market have represented insured parties under such arrangements without any significant reports of noncompliance with Bar rules or any other rules relating to conflicts of interest. However, if counsel were to adjust their advice to their client in order to better serve the goals of a funder (or other type of third party, e.g. an insurer), that would indeed constitute a serious conflict of interest and breach of fiduciary duty. This follows directly from applicable Bar rules and does not require a particularly sophisticated analysis which would have to take account of the specifics of TPF; rather, it is a general and fundamental principle to which all lawyers should always adhere.

[4] The Funded Party

To our knowledge, it is rarely, if ever, suggested by arbitration academics or practitioners that the funded party should risk finding itself in a potential conflict of interest

45. A specific situation which would put counsel in a very difficult situation is if a funded party in breach of the LFA would instruct counsel not to disclose certain negative information to the funder, or even instruct counsel to inform the funder as part of the regular updates on the proceedings that no negative developments have occurred. Such actions by counsel, knowingly providing false and misleading information to the funder in order not to have the funder cease its payments for counsel's services under the LFA, would presumably be in breach of the bar rules in most countries.
46. The analysis in this regard may of course be different if counsel has entered into a US/UK style tripartite TPF arrangement. As explained above, we strongly recommend against such arrangements.
47. For example, the EPRS has stated the following: 'The existence of a conflict of interests between the claimant and the funder places the lawyer in a very sensitive position, as the latter is contractually obliged towards the claimant but his or her fees are paid by the funder.' Poncibò and D'Alessandro, p. 72.
48. Another situation which may come to mind is the relatively common M&A situation where a SPA provides for a specific indemnity by the seller in relation to the outcome of a dispute to which the target company is a party, and where such seller is entitled to disclosure and steering power in relation to the dispute and the target company's counsel representing the target company in the dispute.

situation due to the funding arrangement. The discussions are solely focused on the funder and the counsel. Following our understanding of the term conflict of interest, as set out above, we have also not identified any situation which could potentially imply a conflict of interest for the funded party that warrants any comment in this chapter.

[5] Summary and Concluding Comments

Even though TPF is now an established commercial practice which is widely used – often in international arbitration – it is still approached with suspicion by some commentators, particularly as regards discussions regarding potential conflicts of interest. Bench Nieuwveld and Shannon Sahani have stated the following in this respect: 'Despite the debates and obvious confusion, which creates a sort of mystery around third-party funding in ethical circles, it appears to be a market that is only growing. Therefore, eventually these ethical mysteries will require a resolution.'[49]

As we have explained above, to penetrate any such perceived mystery with respect to conflicts of interest, it is important to be careful with the terminology used. Our position is that, preferably, any legal commentary on conflicts of interest should set out what is meant by the term *conflict of interest*; whether the parties are in a fiduciary or another type of relationship with each other, which would imply that conflict of interest rules could be relevant; what the potentially conflicting interests consist of; and why they are in conflict.

As set out above, in our view: (i) a conflict of interest means the compromise of professional or fiduciary duties or the risk thereof; (ii) a conflict of interest may arise for a party, not between parties; (iii) the funder is not a client of the funded party's counsel and should not be in a contractual relationship with counsel; and (iv) the funded party is not a client of the funder.

Following such analysis and principles, many of the alleged or perceived dangers and conflicts of interest – stemming from the presumed Bermuda Triangle trope of a tripartite contractual arrangement – disappear, or, at least, they can be easily resolved or assessed using existing rules on conflicts of interest. Thus, we have found that, at least in a Swedish context, there are no 'ethical mysteries' in TPF which necessitate any specific solutions that are not already available. What remains after the fog has cleared are mainly situations to which traditional tools and methods can be applied.[50] We will now turn to the issue of potential conflicts of interest for arbitrators in funded international arbitrations.

49. Bench Nieuwveld and Shannon Sahani, p. 72.
50. Pert and Sebok, p. 65.

§9.03 ARBITRATOR CONFLICTS OF INTEREST AND DISCLOSURE[51]

[A] Introduction

As mentioned in the introduction to §9.01, this second section of the chapter will provide a Swedish perspective on rules and best practices regarding arbitrator conflicts of interest and disclosure in funded international arbitrations, focusing on the Swedish Arbitration Act (SAA) and the Arbitration Rules of the SCC Arbitration Institute (the 'SCC Rules').

Initially, it is worth noting that arbitrators tend to be practising lawyers who can be active in both arbitrator and counsel assignments. As a result, contacts between arbitrators and funders can be numerous. For reasons set out below, this could be problematic given that funders may be treated as a party to proceedings for conflict of interest purposes. Accordingly, the risk of conflicts of interest must be carefully assessed in arbitration proceedings when a funder is involved.

If an arbitrator has to be released from his or her appointment due to a conflict of interest, this will typically lead to significant delays in the arbitration proceedings.[52] Even more serious is the fact that if a conflict of interest only becomes apparent after arbitration proceedings have been concluded, this may constitute grounds for setting aside the arbitral award.[53] In addition to constituting grounds for challenge, a conflict of interest may also constitute grounds for refusing to enforce the arbitral award in accordance with the rules of the New York Convention.[54]

In light of the above, issues relating to conflicts of interest and the duty of disclosure in arbitration proceedings are of great importance to both the funded party, the funder and the arbitrator, as will be set out in the following.

---

51. This section of the chapter is based on Chapter 16 in our book on TPF in Sweden, *see* Skog and Persson, but further develops relevant aspects of our reasoning, in particular with regard to corresponding foreign rules and regulations, such as the IBA Guidelines, and the rules adopted by other arbitration institutes than the SCC Arbitration Institute.
52. *See* sections 10 and 16 of the SAA and Arts 19-21 of the SCC Rules. Art. 21(3) of the SCC Rules states that if an arbitrator has been replaced, the newly composed arbitral tribunal should decide whether and to what extent the proceedings are to be repeated.
53. It should be noted that the time limit for challenging arbitral awards seated in Sweden is no more than two months. If a challenge is not brought within that time limit, the ground of challenge is precluded. Whether the losing party did not become aware of the ground of challenge until after the expiry of the time limit is irrelevant to the issue whether the challenge was timely made. *See* section 34, para. 1, subsection 6 of the SAA; Lars Heuman, *Skiljemannarätt*, p. 656 (Jure, 1999); Stefan Lindskog, *Skiljeförfarande*, p. 990 (Norstedts Juridik, 2020).
54. Article V.(b) of the New York Convention on the Recognition and Enforcement of Foreign Arbitral Awards.

[B] Arbitrator Conflicts of Interest

[1] General Comments on Arbitrator Conflicts of Interest under the Swedish Arbitration Act

According to the general rule under Article 8, paragraph 1 of the SAA, an arbitrator must be impartial and independent. This means that arbitrators must be independent of both the parties and the case. If any circumstances exist that may diminish the confidence in the arbitrator's impartiality or independence, the arbitrator must be released from his or her appointment at the request of a party.

Section 8, paragraph 2 of the SAA sets out an illustrative list of circumstances that are considered to always diminish confidence in the arbitrator's impartiality or independence in such a way that an arbitrator must be released from his or her appointment.[55] If any of the circumstances listed in the provision are present, there is a presumption of a conflict of interest that cannot be remedied.[56]

Although impartiality is ultimately a mental attitude of an arbitrator, the assessment of an arbitrator's impartiality is objective in nature. This means that it is to be made based on external observable circumstances that typically pose a risk to an arbitrator's impartiality. Accordingly, it is not necessary for an arbitrator to be aware of or actually influenced by the circumstances giving rise to diminished confidence.[57]

A conflict of interest often arises where there is a relationship between an arbitrator and a party. A conflict of interest will exist if an arbitrator is in some kind of state of dependence in relation to a party, e.g., if the arbitrator is indebted to or paid by the party or if an arbitrator is employed by a company that has an ongoing business relationship with a party.[58]

Additional circumstances become relevant to the assessment if the arbitrator is also a practising counsel, as alluded to in the introduction. If a party is, or recently has been, a client of the arbitrator or of a counsel practising at the same law firm as the arbitrator, there is a conflict of interest. It is irrelevant that the client matter has no

55. Section 8, para. 2 of the SAA lists the following circumstances:

    1. if the arbitrator or a person closely associated with the arbitrator is a party to the dispute or otherwise stands to gain or be prejudiced by the outcome of the dispute;
    2. if the arbitrator or a person closely associated with the arbitrator is a director of a company or other entity which is a party to the dispute or otherwise acts as a representative of a party or of another person who stands to gain or be prejudiced by the outcome of the dispute;
    3. if the arbitrator has taken on a position in the dispute as an expert or otherwise, or has assisted a party in the preparation or conduct of its case in the dispute; or
    4. if the arbitrator has received or reserved remuneration in breach of section 39, paragraph 2.

56. Lindskog, p. 451.
57. *Ibid.*, pp. 449 and 454.
58. *Ibid.*, pp. 459 et seq.; Government Bill 1998/99:35, p. 85; case reported on p. 347 in NJA 1900.

connection with the arbitration.[59] This is also the case if a party, or a party's counsel's law firm, has appointed the same arbitrator in several previous arbitrations.[60]

In addition to the provision of the SAA described above, the Swedish Supreme Court has stated that when considering issues relating to conflicts of interest, it can be appropriate to look not only to the provisions of the SAA but also to consider foreign rules and guidelines. In a case reported at NJA 2007 p. 841, which concerned an arbitration between two Swedish parties, the Swedish Supreme Court found that there were circumstances that could have given rise to diminished confidence in an arbitrator's impartiality or independence, adding that its assessment was supported by, *inter alia*, the IBA Guidelines.[61]

Accordingly, case law indicates that Swedish courts and arbitrators may, and possibly should, draw guidance from international frameworks such as the IBA Guidelines when deciding on conflict of interest issues.[62] Therefore, it is worth looking more closely at these leading guidelines for advice on how to deal with TPF when section 8 of the SAA is at issue. However, before proceeding with the discussion of the IBA guidelines, something should first be said about the SCC Rules.

[2] General Comments on Arbitrator Conflicts of Interest under the SCC Rules

Article 18 of the SCC Rules sets out a similar conflict of interest provision as the SAA, stating that '[e]very arbitrator must be impartial and independent.'[63] According to Article 19 of the SCC Rules, a party may challenge an arbitrator if circumstances exist that give rise to justifiable doubts as to the arbitrator's impartiality or independence, or if the arbitrator does not possess the qualifications agreed by the parties. Any such challenge will be decided by the board of directors of the SCC Arbitration Institute.

In making its assessment, the SCC will consider a variety of sources, such as the SAA (assuming the seat of arbitration is Sweden), previous decisions of the SCC and the IBA Guidelines.[64] For an arbitration seated in Sweden, an assessment under the SAA and the SCC Rules can be expected to produce the same result.[65] As is also the case under the SAA, Article 19 of the SCC Rules does not require that the circumstances have actually influenced the arbitrator.[66] Thus, the examples of breaches of trust described

59. Lindskog, p. 461.
60. Case reported on p. 317 in NJA 2010.
61. The Supreme Court also referred to the IBA Guidelines in the case reported on p. 317 in NJA 2010.
62. According to Lindskog, the significance of the IBA Guidelines should lie primarily in the fundamental values expressed therein. However, Lindskog further states that, at a detailed level, the IBA Guidelines should hardly be attributed much importance; the court must always make its own assessment of whether a conflict of interest within the meaning of section 8 of the SAA exists. Lindskog, pp. 447 et seq.
63. Article 18(1) of the SCC Rules.
64. Ragnwaldh et al., *A Guide to the SCC Arbitration Rules*, p. 63 (Kluwer, 2019).
65. Lindskog, p. 446.
66. Ragnwaldh et al., p. 65.

above in relation to the SAA are also relevant in SCC arbitrations, and both sets of rules allow for guidance to be drawn from the IBA Guidelines.

[3] General Comments on Arbitrator Conflicts of Interest under the IBA Guidelines

From a general perspective, the IBA Guidelines contain similar provisions as the SAA and the SCC Rules in that arbitrators are required to be impartial and independent. If an arbitrator has any doubt as to his or her ability to be impartial or independent, the arbitrator must decline the appointment or (if the proceedings have already commenced) refuse to continue to act as an arbitrator.[67]

The IBA Guidelines become of particular relevance when considering the issue of conflicts of interest in the context of TPF. This is because neither the SAA nor the SCC Rules specifically address TPF. In contrast, the IBA Guidelines contain specific provisions on TPF, which may be relevant for determining conflicts of interest under both the SAA and the SCC Rules.

Of particular importance is General Standard 6(b) of the IBA Guidelines, which states:

> If one of the parties is a legal entity, any legal or physical person having a controlling influence on the legal entity, or a direct economic interest in, or a duty to indemnify a party for, the award to be rendered in the arbitration, may be considered to bear the identity of such party.[68]

The meaning of the provision is that a party with a direct economic interest in the outcome of the dispute – e.g., a funder – can be equated with the relevant party in the proceedings for the purposes of a conflicts of interest analysis. This is also explicitly stated in the commentary on said provision:

> Third-party funders [...] may have a direct economic interest in the award, and as such may be considered to be the equivalent of the party.[69]

67. General Standard 2(a) of the IBA Guidelines.
68. General Standard 6(b) of the IBA Guidelines.
69. The commentary to General Standard 6(b) reads in full as follows: 'When a party in international arbitration is a legal entity, other legal and physical persons may have a controlling influence on this legal entity, or a direct economic interest in, or a duty to indemnify a party for, the award to be rendered in the arbitration. Each situation should be assessed individually, and General Standard 6(b) clarifies that such legal persons and individuals may be considered effectively to be that party. Funders and insurers in relation to the dispute may have a direct economic interest in the award, and as such may be considered to be the equivalent of the party. For these purposes, the terms "funder" and "insurer" refer to any person or entity that is contributing funds, or other material support, to the prosecution or defence of the case and that has a direct economic interest in, or a duty to indemnify a party for, the award to be rendered in the arbitration.' It is worth noting that an entity which has funded an action for other than commercial reasons, e.g., for social, political or indirect economic purposes (without any right to part of the recovery), falls outside the scope of the provision (cf. 'a direct economic interest in the award').

Therefore, the question of whether a funder may be considered to bear the identity of the funded party must be assessed on a case-by-case basis. Given how the commentary has been drafted, the provision should apply to a commercial funder since its remuneration is generally directly dependent on the outcome of the case. Accordingly, the funder can be considered to have a direct economic interest in the award, and there are compelling reasons for equating the funder with a party to the proceedings, as provided for under the IBA Guidelines.

[4] *Arbitrator Conflicts of Interest That May Arise in the Context of Funded Arbitrations*

[a] *Introduction*

The general position in relation to arbitrator conflicts of interest under the SAA and the SCC Rules has been described above. The question that arises is if, and to what extent, these considerations also apply to the relationship between an arbitrator and a funder.

As mentioned above, it is the Swedish Supreme Court's position that foreign rules and guidelines should be considered when assessing conflict of interest issues. As also explained above, a funder can be equated with a party in the proceedings for such purposes under the IBA Guidelines. As this is the case, there is reason to believe that a funder can be considered a party from a conflict of interest perspective under the SAA (even though it is not settled law). The same applies to the SCC Rules, given that the Board of the SCC will take the IBA Guidelines into consideration when assessing a challenge of an arbitrator. As a result, a variety of situations may arise in which parties, funders, counsel and arbitrators will have to carefully assess whether TPF may give rise to circumstances that could constitute a conflict of interest. Some of the situations that may arise are discussed in the following.

[b] *The Arbitrator Is or Has Been Acting on Behalf of the Funder*

As stated above, it is considered a conflict of interest under the SAA if an arbitrator has a remunerated engagement from a party if the engagement is ongoing during the arbitration or if such engagement has been concluded shortly before the arbitration begins. A typical example in the context of TPF would be when a counsel has provided a second opinion on a dispute on behalf of a funder, and the same counsel is then asked to be an arbitrator in another dispute in which one of the parties' claim is funded by the same funder. If the second opinion engagement is ongoing or has recently ended, the prospective arbitrator (and counsel) should decline the arbitrator appointment or, at the very least, inform the parties of the situation if and when accepting the appointment.[70]

70. In the case of a minor engagement, the existence of a conflict of interest may be questioned, according to the reasoning of the Swedish Supreme Court in case Ö 5308-17, paras 26 and 27.

If the prospective arbitrator, or his or her law firm, is acting for the funder, it means that counsel most likely cannot accept an appointment as arbitrator in a dispute in which a party is funded by the same funder. This is because, as stated above, it is considered a conflict of interest if an arbitrator is employed by a company that has an ongoing business relationship with a party.

In light of the above, if a counsel is acting as an arbitrator and becomes aware that a party's claim is funded by a funder, it is important that the funder is also registered as a party in the law firm's conflict of interest management system. By doing so, it is possible to avoid the situation that a colleague of the arbitrator agrees to act on behalf of the funder or a party funded by the funder during the proceedings without any knowledge of the relationship. If this happens, a conflict of interest may exist since the arbitrator would then be working for a law firm which has an ongoing business relationship with someone who can be equated with a party. This, of course, presupposes that the legal position actually is such that a funder is to be equated with a party. However, in view of the foregoing and the potentially draconian effects in the form of the risk of an arbitral award being set aside if a conflict of interest is subsequently discovered, the relationship should, in any event, be disclosed and the arbitrator should carefully consider whether he or she can continue as arbitrator.

[c] *The Arbitrator, or His or Her Colleague, Is Acting as Counsel for a Party in Another Dispute Whose Claim Is Funded by the Same Funder That Is Funding a Party to the Arbitration*

Another problematic situation can arise if a lawyer, or his or her colleague, is acting as counsel for a funded party in a dispute ('Dispute 1'), while the lawyer, or his or her colleague, is at the same time asked to be arbitrator in another unrelated dispute ('Dispute 2'), where one of the parties is being funded by the same funder.[71]
The above example may be varied, depending on, among other things, the timing of the different situations in relation to each other. However, the fact that the fees for the representation in Dispute 1 are paid by the funder (even if it is not a client or principal per se) raises significant concerns about the lawyer's suitability as arbitrator in Dispute 2. As mentioned above, a party with a direct economic interest in the outcome of the dispute – e.g., a funder – may be equated with the relevant party in the proceedings for the purposes of a conflicts of interest analysis.

If this situation arises, the lawyer should in our view decline the arbitrator appointment in Dispute 2 or, at the very least, inform the parties of the situation if and when accepting the appointment.[72] If the lawyer has already been appointed as arbitrator in Dispute 2 and subsequently becomes aware that a party is receiving funding from the funder, the arbitrator should inform the parties of the situation and carefully consider whether he or she can continue as arbitrator.

71. The example, which has been slightly modified, has been taken from International Council for Commercial Arbitration, *Report of the ICCA-Queen Mary Task Force on Third-Party Funding in International Arbitration*, pp. 112 et seq. (The ICCA Reports No. 4, 2018).
72. See also footnote 72 above.

[d] *The Arbitrator Has Been Appointed on Several Occasions by Parties Who Have Received Funding from the Same Funder*

As set out above, it is considered a conflict of interest if a party or a law firm frequently appoints the same arbitrator in several different disputes, as this can give the impression that the arbitrator has ties to the party or the firm. It may also constitute a conflict of interest if parties funded by the same funder repeatedly appoint the same arbitrator.[73] The IBA Guidelines state that a repeat appointment exists if an arbitrator during the last three years has either been appointed on at least two occasions by the same party, or an affiliate of the party,[74] or more than three times by the same counsel or law firm.[75] Both of these situations are included in the so-called 'Orange List' of the IBA Guidelines, meaning that the arbitrator would be under a duty to disclose such situations. If no timely objection is made after disclosure, the parties will be deemed to have accepted the arbitrator.[76]

The legal position as to whether these rules should be applied by analogy to an underlying funder in Sweden is unclear. It should be borne in mind that the funder rarely has a formal right under the funding agreement to control the appointment of the arbitrator but that it is common for discussions on this issue to take place between the funded party, its legal counsel and the funder.

In order to avoid conflict of interest issues in this respect, a funder should keep records of the number of times each arbitrator in its funded cases has been appointed by a party funded by the funder over the past three years. Since it is in the interest of the funder to avoid conflict of interest issues that could delay the proceedings or give rise to a challenge, a funder should seek to avoid, as far as possible, recurrent appointments of the same arbitrator by the parties it funds in a manner that could be inconsistent with the IBA Guidelines.[77]

[C] Disclosure Obligations in Funded Arbitrations

[1] *Initial Comments*

As we have just seen, there are various situations where conflicts of interest can arise for arbitrators under the SAA and the SCC Rules in the context of funded arbitrations. This, in turn, raises the question of what duty of disclosure arbitrators and parties have under the SAA and SCC Rules. This question will be addressed in the following.

73. The ICCA Reports No. 4, pp. 48 et seq.
74. Situation 3.1.3 of the IBA Guidelines (Part II: Practical Application of the General Standards).
75. Situation 3.3.8 of the IBA Guidelines (Part II: Practical Application of the General Standards).
76. Paragraph 3 of the IBA Guidelines (Part II: Practical Application of the General Standards).
77. According to the case reported on p. 317 in NJA 2010, an overall assessment must be made with respect of conflicts of interest, which in this context should mean that a conflict of interest cannot automatically be deemed to exist on the grounds that a funder has funded parties who have appointed the same arbitrator, especially if the arbitrator in question receives a large number of requests every year and the funder funds a large number of parties who in turn appoint just as many arbitrators.

However, before going into detail on these issues from a Swedish perspective, it is worth mentioning a few words regarding disclosure obligations in relation to TPF from an international perspective, focusing on some of the more well-known arbitral institutions and frameworks.

[2] TPF Disclosure Obligations from an International Perspective

Starting with the IBA Guidelines, General Standard 7(a) requires a party to, on its own initiative and at the earliest opportunity, disclose 'any relationship, direct or indirect, between the arbitrator and the party (or another company of the same group of companies, or an individual having a controlling influence on the party in the arbitration), or between the arbitrator and any person or entity with a direct economic interest in, or a duty to indemnify a party for, the award to be rendered in the arbitration.'[78] As explained in the commentary to the provision, the '[d]isclosure of such relationships should reduce the risk of an unmeritorious challenge of an arbitrator's impartiality or independence based on information learned after the appointment.'[79]

Several arbitral institutions have adopted similar mandatory disclosure requirements. Both the ICC Arbitration Rules[80] and the HKIAC Administered Arbitration Rules[81] require funded parties to disclose the existence of a funding agreement and the identity of the funder. SIAC has adopted a slightly different approach, whereby tribunals are empowered to order parties to disclose the existence of a funding arrangement and/or the identity of the funder and, where appropriate, details of the funder's interest in the outcome and if the funder has committed to undertake adverse costs liability.[82] Under the CIETAC International Investment Arbitration Rules, a party must disclose the existence and nature of the funding arrangement and the name and address of the funder, and the tribunal can also order the disclosure of any relevant information about the funding arrangement.[83]

Most recently, the latest version of the ICSID Arbitration Rules that came into effect on 1 July 2022 also introduced a mandatory duty for parties to file a written notice stating the name and address of any non-party who has provided funding through a donation or grant, or in return for remuneration dependent on the outcome of the proceedings.[84] If the funder is a juridical person, the notice shall also include the names of the persons and entities that own and control that juridical person. Furthermore, a

78. General Standard 7(a) of the IBA Guidelines.
79. Explanation to General Standard 7 of the IBA Guidelines.
80. Article 11(7) of the 2021 ICC Arbitration Rules provides the following: 'Each party must promptly inform the Secretariat, the arbitral tribunal and the other parties, of the existence and identity of any non-party which has entered into an arrangement for the funding of claims or defences and under which it has an economic interest in the outcome of the arbitration.'
81. Article 44 of the 2018 HKIAC Administered Arbitration Rules.
82. Rule 24(l) of the 2017 SIAC Investment Arbitration Rules. *See also* Singapore International Arbitration Centre, *Practice Note PN – 01/17 on Arbitrator Conduct in Cases Involving External Funding for Administered Cases under the SIAC Arbitration Rules*, para. 5 (2017).
83. Article 27 of the 2017 CIETAC International Investment Arbitration Rules.
84. Article 14(1) of the 2022 ICSID Arbitration Rules.

tribunal may order the disclosure of further information regarding both the funding agreement and the funder.[85]

Based on the above, the general trend considered from an international perspective seems to point towards the adoption of mandatory rules requiring parties to disclose whether their claims are funded by a funder. Bearing this in mind, we will now proceed to examine the disclosure obligations of both arbitrators and parties from a Swedish perspective.

[3] *Arbitrator Disclosure Obligations under the Swedish Arbitration Act*

Under section 9 of the SAA, a prospective arbitrator must immediately disclose any circumstances that might be considered to prevent him or her from acting as an arbitrator (e.g., the circumstances discussed above in relation to arbitrator conflicts of interest).[86] Further, the arbitrator must also inform the parties and the other arbitrators as soon as the arbitrator becomes aware of any new relevant circumstance after the commencement of the arbitration proceedings.[87]

In addition, an appointed arbitrator most likely has a certain duty of disclosure with regard to conflicts of interest. An arbitrator must consider the areas in which such a conflict may exist, including whether any previous position could constitute an impediment. If there is any indication that there is a conflict of interest, an arbitrator must take further investigative steps.[88] More specifically, an arbitrator's duty of investigation may include asking the parties whether any of them are receiving TPF. Such a duty most likely exists if there is any indication that a party is receiving funding, in which case the arbitrator should inquire about this no later than at the first case management conference.

If it turns out that one of the parties is receiving TPF, the arbitrator will have to proceed to investigate whether this may give rise to a conflict of interest and then inform the parties of this. The information should be as exhaustive as possible to enable the parties themselves to make an adequate assessment of whether or not there are grounds for requesting that the arbitrator be released from his or her appointment.

[4] *Arbitrator Disclosure Obligations under the SCC Rules*

Article 18 of the SCC Rules addresses the arbitrator's duty of disclosure and states that an arbitrator must submit a signed statement confirming his or her impartiality and

85. Article 14(4) of the 2022 ICSID Arbitration Rules.
86. The disclosure obligations under section 9 of the SAA in effect correspond to those set out in General Standard 3 of the IBA Guidelines.
87. Lindskog, p. 477.
88. Government Bill 1998/99:35 p. 86, and Lindskog, p. 476. *See also* General Standard 7(d) of the IBA Guidelines which states as follows: 'An arbitrator is under a duty to make reasonable inquiries to identify any conflict of interest, as well as any facts or circumstances that may reasonably give rise to doubts as to his or her impartiality or independence. Failure to disclose a conflict is not excused by lack of knowledge, if the arbitrator does not perform such reasonable inquiries.'

independence. The statement must contain disclosures of any circumstances that may give rise to justifiable doubts as to the arbitrator's impartiality or independence. Further, an arbitrator must immediately inform the parties and the other arbitrators if any circumstances that may give rise to justifiable doubts as to the arbitrator's impartiality or independence arise during the course of the arbitration.[89] Similar duties of disclosure exist in all established institutional rules.[90]

In order to avoid a circumstance giving rise to a conflict of interest coming to light at a late stage or after the conclusion of the arbitration proceedings, it is advisable for a requested arbitrator to check with the party seeking the appointment of the arbitrator whether any of the parties' claims are funded by a third party, at least if there is any circumstance that leads the arbitrator to believe that this may be the case. If any party is in fact receiving TPF, the funder should also be taken into account when the arbitrator conducts his or her conflict of interest assessment and subsequently submits the statement confirming his or her impartiality and independence to the SCC. As stated above, the arbitral tribunal should also follow up on this issue at a later stage once it has been constituted and ask the parties to disclose any TPF.

[5] Party Disclosure Obligations under the Swedish Arbitration Act

There is no obligation for a party to disclose TPF on its own initiative under the SAA. Although General Standard 7(a) of the IBA Guidelines states that '[t]he parties are required to disclose any relationship with the arbitrator' and a funder can be equated with a party according to General Standard 6(b) of the IBA Guidelines, the IBA Guidelines cannot be considered binding on the parties in this respect (unless agreed otherwise between the parties).

The above means that unless the arbitral tribunal orders the parties to disclose any TPF, there is a risk that, in an ad hoc arbitration under the SAA, there may be a third party with a direct economic interest in the outcome of the dispute without the arbitral tribunal being informed of that fact. As TPF is becoming increasingly more common, arbitral tribunals should, therefore, in our view, be proactive in this respect and require the parties to disclose any TPF. Such an order should only relate to the identity of the funder and not to the funding agreement as such.[91] The arbitral tribunal should preferably do this when the tribunal is constituted or at the time of the first case management conference.

From an international perspective, it is sometimes argued that an arbitrator cannot be considered to have a conflict of interest if the arbitrator is not actually aware of the underlying circumstance and that, consequently, there is no need to disclose the existence of TPF.[92] This conclusion presupposes that the assessment of whether there

89. Article 18 of the SCC Rules.
90. *See, e.g.*, Art. 11(1)-(3) of the 2021 ICC Arbitration Rules and Art. 5.3-5 of the 2020 LCIA Arbitration Rules.
91. The ICCA Reports No. 4, p. 81.
92. *Ibid.*, p. 86. It should be noted that the authors of the ICCA Report do not support such an analysis.

is a conflict of interest is based on a subjective perception. However, as mentioned above, the assessment under Swedish law is objective in nature – meaning that it is irrelevant whether the arbitrator is unaware of the circumstance giving rise to a conflict of interest. Instead, the only relevant factor is whether there are external observable circumstances that constitute a conflict of interest.[93]

As mentioned initially, if the TPF relationship is discovered later in the proceedings, and if there is a conflict of interest due to any relationship between the funder and one of the arbitrators, it may constitute a conflict of interest under the SAA. In such a situation, the arbitrator, whose impartiality has been compromised, may have to be released from his or her appointment – which typically leads to significant delays in the arbitration. A conflict of interest that only becomes apparent after the arbitration has been concluded may constitute grounds for challenge and setting aside of the arbitral award or refusal to enforce the arbitral award in accordance with the rules of the New York Convention.

Given this fact, although there is no such obligation under the SAA, a funded party and a funder take a significant risk if the funded party fails to inform the arbitral tribunal that its claim is being funded by a third party. Consequently, the question of whether the arbitral tribunal should be informed of the TPF in order to prevent the existence of an *ex post facto* conflict of interest from becoming apparent must be carefully considered by the funded party.

If the funded party for some reason chooses not to disclose the TPF to the tribunal, it is important that the party and its legal counsel at the very least discuss the composition of the tribunal with the funder to ensure that no conflict of interest exists. For example, the funded party's counsel should inquire whether the funder has invested in any other dispute in which any of the arbitrators has also been appointed. It should also inquire whether there is any type of employment or consultancy relationship between the funder and any of the arbitrators or (where applicable) their law firms or whether the arbitrators have any corporate links with the funder. As mentioned above, failure to do this carefully and correctly could, in the worst case, result in the setting aside or unenforceability of a subsequent arbitral award.

[6] Party Disclosure Obligations under the SCC Rules

As set out above, the general international trend seems to point towards arbitral institutions adopting mandatory rules requiring parties to disclose if their claims are funded by a third party. In contrast, following their latest revision in 2023, the SCC Rules do not contain any duty for a party to disclose that its claim is being funded by a third party. At the same time, the SCC has adopted a non-binding policy on the duty of disclosure applicable to third parties with an interest in the outcome of the dispute.[94]

93. Lindskog, pp. 449 and 454.
94. SCC Policy – Disclosure of Third Parties with an Interest in the Outcome of the Dispute, adopted by the Board of the SCC on 11 September 2019.

The SCC's policy states that each party in an SCC arbitration is encouraged to disclose the identity of any third party with a significant interest in the outcome of the dispute in its first submission, including but not limited to funders and parent companies. The parties are also encouraged to promptly disclose during the arbitration the identity of any third party who acquires a significant interest in the outcome of the dispute.[95] The information should be provided to the arbitral tribunal, the institution and the other party.

The SCC's policy does not impose any explicit obligation on the parties to disclose such information, and as the policy is not binding, no sanction is imposed on a party that does not comply with the policy. However, a funded party that derogates from the policy should carefully consider the risk that a circumstance giving rise to a conflict of interest might come to light at a later stage.

[7] Summary and Concluding Comments Regarding Arbitrator Conflicts of Interest and Disclosure in Funded Arbitrations

As we have seen in §9.02 of the chapter, TPF arrangements can give rise to conflicts of interest under certain circumstances. However, even though TPF arrangements may give rise to new situations where such issues become of relevance, these situations could generally be managed using the general framework for conflicts of interest set out in the SAA and the SCC Rules. This is so even if neither the SAA nor the SCC Rules contain any rules specifically dealing with TPF. While the scope of existing general conflict of interest rules may be extended to funders as a result of the fact that funders may be equated to parties under the IBA Guidelines, this also means that there already are mechanisms to handle such situations, even if increased attention will need to be given to such matters from all parties involved, in particular with regard to the disclosure of relevant circumstances.

As is the case in other jurisdictions and under established institutional rules, arbitrators acting in Swedish and/or SCC arbitration proceedings are under an obligation to disclose circumstances that could give rise to justifiable doubt as to their impartiality and independence. Even without the explicit mention of TPF in this regard, funding arrangements should certainly be considered to be a circumstance that is of relevance to that assessment.

The assessment under Swedish law is objective in nature, meaning that it is irrelevant for the assessment whether an arbitrator actually had knowledge of or was influenced by a certain circumstance. However, arbitrators can of course only disclose circumstances of which they are aware. This means that in the context of TPF, the onus of disclosure with regard to funding arrangements is effectively moved to the parties themselves, as the parties are the only ones who are in a position to disclose whether a case is funded.

95. SCC Policy – Disclosure of Third Parties with an Interest in the Outcome of the Dispute, paragraph A.

As set out above, there is no general obligation for a party under the SAA or the SCC Rules to disclose whether its case is being funded. However, due to the objective nature of the assessment and the risks inherent in a conflict of interest only becoming apparent later on, parties in funded arbitrations should nevertheless have strong incentives to disclose any funding arrangements (at least to the extent necessary for the determination of potential conflicts of interest) even in the absence of mandatory disclosure obligations. By doing so, the parties avoid the risk of delays to the proceedings or even setting aside or refusal of enforcement of an award due to a conflict of interest.

CHAPTER 10

Submitting New Evidence after the Cut-Off Date: When Are Exceptional Circumstances Present?

Helen Lehto & Laura Parkkisenniemi

§10.01 INTRODUCTION

Evidence plays a key role in any arbitration; no party will succeed without it. As both parties develop their case, it is common for further evidence to be submitted along the way as the proceedings move forward. However, in order to maintain procedural efficacy, parties should not be allowed to hinder the proceedings by submitting new evidence or facts at an inconveniently late stage when they could and should have submitted it before.

That is why it is common in arbitration to agree on a *cut-off date*. A *cut-off date* is generally defined as a date after which the parties cannot present new facts, arguments or evidence,[1] as the case may be.[2] Its main purpose is to prevent a party from producing such new evidence or facts at a late stage in the proceedings, in a worst-case scenario at the hearing, which could derail the proceedings and harm the other party.[3]

1. Mika Hemmo, *Prosessitoimia rajoittavat määräajat ja niiden poikkeukset välimiesmenettelyssä*, p. 39 (2022), available at https://www.edilex.fi/artikkelit/27108.pdf.
2. In the following article, we will mostly focus on and refer only to 'evidence' when discussing what a party wishes to submit after the passing of the cut-off date. However, it is equally possible that a party may wish to submit new facts, allegations, grounds, or claims (as the case may be), and a cut-off date may well take these into account; but this is not the main focus of this article.
3. This type of conduct is also problematic in terms of parties' equal treatment, as the other party might not have sufficient possibility to be able to comment on such new evidence (and/or produce rebuttal evidence) unless the arbitral tribunal grants the responding party an extension of time, potentially causing even more procedural delays. Such reasoning by a sole arbitrator

In the past, a cut-off date was often recommended to be used in pending cases only where it was already evident that a party was constantly amending its claims or the grounds thereof, or where a party kept producing new evidence, leading to complicated and delayed proceedings. Nowadays, the cut-off date is normally agreed upon soon after the arbitrator has received the case file, for example, at the case management conference. This provision is typically inserted into the procedural timetable even when there is no reason to suspect that one party will keep bringing up new claims, grounds, or evidence throughout the process. However, agreeing on a cut-off date at the outset will likely increase the chances of mutual adherence to the procedural timetable.[4]

Nevertheless, sometimes, even the most diligent parties may face a situation where they have an unexpected need to submit new evidence or rely on new facts after the cut-off date. If the other party objects, it must be determined by the arbitral tribunal whether new facts and/or new evidence is nevertheless permitted. Sometimes, arbitration rules (or the procedural orders, timetables or terms of reference where the cut-off date is agreed upon) state that new evidence is not permitted after the cut-off date unless the arbitral tribunal in *exceptional circumstances* decides otherwise.

But when are the circumstances exceptional?

In this chapter, we aim to address this question. In doing so, we will first conduct a brief overview of certain arbitration rules and practices related to cut-off date provisions. Thereafter, we will discuss some situations in which the circumstances could be found to be exceptional. We present our findings at the end of the chapter.

§10.02 CUT-OFF DATES IN ARBITRATION RULES

Despite the fact that cut-off dates are widely recognised and encouraged to be used, not many of the major arbitration rules contain an explicit article concerning cut-off dates.[5] Instead, the rules merely tend to grant the tribunal the authority to conduct the proceedings in an efficient manner, from which the use of the necessary tools, such as cut-off dates, will follow.[6] Often, the authority to impose cut-off dates will flow from

---

regarding, e.g., parties equal treatment is found in case law, *see, e.g.*, *Supplier (Xanadu) v. Reseller (Utopia)*, (SCC Case No. 2018/127), Final Award, 14 November 2019, in Stephan W. Schill (ed.), ICCA Yearbook Commercial Arbitration 2020 – Volume XLV, para. 185 (2020), as available at Kluwer Law International.

4. On a related note, the provision regarding a cut-off date was explicitly introduced into the Arbitration Rules of the Finland Chamber of Commerce in 2013 to support swift and cost-efficient dispute resolution. Regarding the aim of introducing the cut-off provision and the intention for its usage, please *see* Mika Savola, *Guide to the Finnish Arbitration Rules*, pp. 297-298 (2015).
5. Mika Hemmo, *Prosessitoimia rajoittavat määräajat ja niiden poikkeukset välimiesmenettelyssä*, p. 41 (2022), available at https://www.edilex.fi/artikkelit/27108.pdf. Despite the fact that not all arbitration rules include an explicit provision on the use of a cut-off date, its use is widely accepted. *See, e.g.*, ICC Commission on Arbitration and ADR, *ICC Commission Report: Controlling Time and Costs in Arbitration*, para. 73 on p. 14 (2018) and Gustav Flecke-Giammarco et al., (eds), *The DIS Arbitration Rules: An Article-by-Article Commentary*, p. 432 (2020).
6. The Supreme Court of Finland has also confirmed that cut off-dates may be used in arbitration, as long as the provision is clear and has been accepted by the parties. *See* Finnish Supreme Court case KKO 2018:48, para. 17.

clauses in arbitration rules, which state that submissions shall be made and evidence shall be provided within the time limits set by the arbitral tribunal. The same also arguably follows from the application of the IBA Rules on the Taking of Evidence, where such rules apply.[7]

By way of example, the rules of the Danish Institute of Arbitration (DIA) state that documents or other evidence must be submitted in accordance with the set time limits and that failure to comply with this may cause the arbitral tribunal to reject admission unless the arbitral tribunal considers the failure justified, or if 'special circumstances' exist.[8]

One set of rules which specifically mentions a cut-off date is the Arbitration Rules of the Finland Chamber of Commerce (the 'FAI Rules') which has had a provision concerning the cut-off date since 2013. At the outset, the provision was part of an article concerning the taking of evidence more generally. However, as part of the rule amendments in 2020, the cut-off provision was separated into its own article, while the wording remained the same. It reads as follows:

> The arbitral tribunal may, after consulting with the parties, set a cut-off date prior to the commencement of any hearing referred to in Article 36 and order that after the cut-off date, the parties will not be allowed to present any new claims, arguments or documentary evidence on the merits of the dispute, or to invoke any new witnesses not previously nominated, unless the arbitral tribunal in *exceptional circumstances* decides otherwise.[9] (emphasis added)
>
> An explicit provision mentioning a cut-off date is also included in the Prague Rules.[10] Article 3.3. states that 'the arbitral tribunal shall consider imposing a cut-off date for submission of evidence and not accepting any new evidence after that date, save for under *exceptional circumstances*' (emphasis added).[11]

Despite the fact that explicit cut-off articles are not present in all arbitration rules, cut-off dates are widely agreed upon in procedural orders, timetables and/or terms of

7. *See IBA Rules on the Taking of Evidence in International Arbitration*, Art. 3.1 on p. 10 and Art. 4.1 on p. 13 (2020). Arbitration rules also tend to include clauses on closing of the proceedings, which effectively lead to the same outcome as a cut-off date, however, at a later stage in the proceedings. For example, *see ICC Rules of Arbitration* (2021), Art. 27: '(...) After the proceedings are closed, no further submission or argument may be made, or evidence produced, with respect to the matters to be decided in the award, unless requested or authorized by the arbitral tribunal.'
8. The Rules of Arbitration of the Danish Institute of Arbitration (2021), Art. 34: 'The parties shall produce documents or other evidence in support of their claims and give the other party or parties and the Arbitral Tribunal notice of the witness(es) and expert(s) that the party wishes to give testimony, in accordance with the time limits set by the DIA or the Arbitral Tribunal. Failure to comply with a time limit may cause the Arbitral Tribunal to reject admission of the corresponding evidence, unless the Arbitral Tribunal considers the failure justified or if special circumstances exist.'
9. The Arbitration Rules of the Finland Chamber of Commerce (2020), Art. 35.
10. It shall be noted that the Prague Rules have been developed to provide guidance for arbitral tribunals and parties on how to increase efficiency in arbitral proceedings by encouraging more active case management by the arbitral tribunals. Nevertheless, the Prague Rules are not intended to replace the rules of arbitration institutes, but rather to be used to supplement the procedure. Rules on the Efficient Conduct of Proceedings in International Arbitration (Prague Rules) (2018), p. 3.
11. Rules on the Efficient Conduct of Proceedings in International Arbitration (Prague Rules) (2018), Art. 3.3.

reference. Especially in cases where the rules do not provide any specific guidance on how to potentially word the cut-off date provision, it is of essence to carefully consider and specify the scope of the cut-off date ultimately agreed upon with the parties. For example, in the FAI Rules, the scope is extensive, covering 'new claims, arguments or documentary evidence on the merits of the dispute, or to invoke any new witnesses not previously nominated'. In comparison, the Prague Rules and DIA Rules only refer to 'evidence'.[12] As such, the tribunal should be mindful of the wording of both the underlying rules, if any, as well as its own chosen expressions when drafting a cut-off provision.

It could be argued that a tribunal must have jurisdiction to draft a cut-off provision which is narrower in scope than what the rules envisage (e.g., the FAI Rules state that the arbitral tribunal 'may' set a cut-off date concerning the issues mentioned in Article 35, not that it 'must' or 'shall' set such a date). However, it is a bit more unclear whether a tribunal has jurisdiction to set a cut-off date which is more far-reaching than what the rules envisage. In practice, this is unlikely to be a recurring problem, as institutional rules rarely contain restrictive wording to this effect, to the extent that they contain any such wording at all. In any event, party agreement and involvement are the keys to any successfully worded cut-off date.

Often, arbitrators tend to interpret cut-off provisions strictly based on their wording. By way of example, when a dispute concerning the scope of the cut-off arose in SCC case 2018/127, the arbitrator concluded that the cut-off date provision in the case at hand referred only to the submissions of additional documentary evidence and legal texts, and as such did not refer to oral witness testimonies. Thus, new oral testimony was admissible even after the cut-off date, as the provision was clear in its meaning and could not be interpreted against its plain wording to encompass oral testimony of fact witnesses.[13]

12. The DIA rules also mention 'documents', which arguably would fall under the category of 'evidence'. The ICC commission report also envisions a similar scope: 'In advance of any evidentiary hearing, consider setting a cut-off date after which no new documentary evidence will be admitted unless a compelling reason is shown.' ICC Commission on Arbitration and ADR, *ICC Commission Report: Controlling Time and Costs in Arbitration*, para. 73 (2018).

13. In the case at hand, Procedural order No. 1 included the following provision on cut-off date: 'After the cut-off date mentioned in Section (1) of the Procedural Timetable, the parties are not permitted to submit any additional documentary evidence or legal texts. The Arbitral Tribunal will not accept any late submission unless the Arbitral Tribunal in exceptional circumstances decides otherwise upon a party's reasoned request showing sufficient cause for the delay.' *Supplier (Xanadu) v. Reseller (Utopia)*, (SCC Case No. 2018/127), Final Award, 14 November 2019, paras 38, 161-170, in ICCA Yearbook Commercial Arbitration 2020 – Volume XLV (2020), as available at Kluwer Law International. Similarly, in SCC case 2018/a, the arbitrator found that a party had the right to claim interest also after the cut-off date: 'According to Article 30 of the SCC Rules, a party may amend or supplement its case prior to the close of the proceedings, pursuant to Article 40. The proceedings were not closed on [date X], and the claim for interest is comprised by the arbitration agreement. In the opinion of the arbitrator, the general cut-off date does not exclude the application of Article 30 in the SCC Rules', *Company (Xanadu) v. Company (Sweden)*, (SCC Case No. 2018/a), Final Award, 30 January 2020, para. 562, in ICCA Yearbook Commercial Arbitration 2021 – Volume XLVI (2021), as available at Kluwer Law International.

As demonstrated by the examples above, quite often, cut-off date provisions either state that new evidence may only be submitted after the cut-off date in *exceptional circumstances* or use similar wording to the same effect. Such wording allows for multiple arguments, but the use of the word 'exceptional' in and of itself suggests that such circumstances should not materialise often.[14] Therefore, it is worthwhile to consider what might constitute such exceptional circumstances. In the following, we will delve into the main topic of this article and discuss in what instances evidence may be submitted even after the relevant cut-off date has passed; i.e., when might the 'exceptional circumstances' threshold be met?

§10.03 WHAT MIGHT CONSTITUTE 'EXCEPTIONAL CIRCUMSTANCES'?

When considering whether to admit new evidence or facts after the cut-off date, the FAI Rules and the Prague Rules both refer to *exceptional circumstances*.[15] The DIA Rules similarly refer to a 'justified' failure to submit evidence or to the existence of 'special circumstances', while the ICC commission has used the wording 'compelling reason'.[16] Similar wording has also been used in many procedural orders and timetables, as well as terms of reference drafted by arbitral tribunals worldwide. Therefore, we will discuss what type of standard is required. In other words, when could such exceptional circumstances be present, which would allow new evidence to be submitted after the cut-off date?

In conducting this evaluation, it must first be established what the content and scope of the agreed cut-off date is. Ultimately, this comes down to the wording of the clause itself. Have the parties intentionally agreed on either a high or a low threshold for when new evidence can be submitted? Could it be argued that a 'justified reason' constitutes a lower threshold for the submission of evidence than a 'compelling reason' or an 'exceptional circumstance'? In this article, our focus is on 'exceptional circumstances' as mentioned in the FAI Rules, but in a real-life scenario, the use of different – and perhaps less strict – wording in the actual cut-off date provision could be of significant importance when determining whether new evidence can be submitted.

At the outset, it should be noted that the arbitral tribunal will not need to rule on what might constitute exceptional circumstances should all of the parties agree that the new evidence in question may be submitted despite the passing of the cut-off date. However, when the other party objects, the arbitral tribunal must decide whether to declare the evidence admissible. In taking such a decision, the arbitral tribunal has

14. A similar interpretation has been presented by Finnish professor Mika Hemmo. Mika Hemmo, *Prosessitoimia rajoittavat määräajat ja niiden poikkeukset välimiesmenettelyssä*, footnote 16 (2022), available at https://www.edilex.fi/artikkelit/27108.pdf.
15. The Arbitration Rules of the Finland Chamber of Commerce (2020), Art. 35. Rules on the Efficient Conduct of Proceedings in International Arbitration (Prague Rules) (2018), Art. 3.3.
16. The Rules of Arbitration of the Danish Institute of Arbitration (2021), Art. 34. ICC Commission on Arbitration and ADR, *ICC Commission Report: Controlling Time and Costs in Arbitration*, para. 73 on p. 14 (2018).

wide discretionary powers unless the parties have agreed otherwise or more specifically agreed on what should be regarded as 'exceptional circumstances'.[17]

Moving to the question at hand, we will address different aspects considered by tribunals as potential 'exceptional circumstances' in the evaluation of the admissibility of a certain piece of evidence after the cut-off date.

First, tribunals would typically consider whether the party has had an opportunity to submit it before the cut-off date. If such evidence has not been reasonably available earlier, it has been considered not to be fair to preclude its submission.[18] Such situations could arise with regard to, e.g., financial statements or judgments that have been issued after the cut-off date.[19] As such, the availability or materialisation of certain evidence only after the cut-off date has passed could be seen to constitute exceptional circumstances which may lead to the evidence being admissible.

Second, it might sometimes happen that, at the outset of a dispute, a party considers a certain piece of documentary evidence to be redundant. At this stage, it may appear to only be relevant for a point which is wholly undisputed by the opposing party. However, if the opposing party later turns out to dispute such a point, either in written submissions or even as late as at the hearing, it might then be justified to request that the tribunal allow the submission of such evidence, even if the cut-off date has passed. These circumstances could arguably be seen as 'compelling' or 'justified', but it might be somewhat more unclear whether they would rise to the level of being 'exceptional', considering that the party will have had said evidence in its possession throughout the duration of the dispute. The question then becomes whether a party should pre-emptively submit any and all loosely related documentary evidence to the tribunal at its earliest convenience in order to not take the risk of having to argue in favour of its right to submit such evidence at a later stage, after the passing of the cut-off date. However, submitting excessive documentary evidence to the tribunal will hinder procedural efficiency and render the case overly burdensome, which is why a certain degree of restraint should be exercised in this respect.[20] In deciding how to

---

17. The FAI Rules do not provide guidance on what could be regarded as exceptional circumstances, and therefore, it likely falls on the tribunal to determine this. *See* Mika Savola: *Guide to the Finnish Arbitration Rules*, p. 298 (2015).
18. Nikolas Pitkowitz, *Chapter II: The Arbitrator and the Arbitration Procedure, The Vienna Predictability Propositions: Paving the Road to Predictability in International Arbitration* in Christian Klausegger et al. (eds), Austrian Yearbook on International Arbitration 2017, p. 137 (2017), as available at Kluwer Law International. Generally, the evaluation has centered upon whether the party is able to provide sufficient reasons for why the evidence has not been submitted earlier, *see, e.g.*, Jakob Ragnwaldh, Fredrik Andersson, Celeste E. Salinas Quero, *Chapter 5: The Proceedings Before the Arbitral Tribunal*, in *A Guide to the SCC Arbitration Rules*, p. 103 (2019), as available at Kluwer Law International: 'The Arbitral Tribunal's determination as to whether to admit the new evidence will, in general, turn on factors such as whether the party in question can convincingly explain why the evidence has not been able to be submitted before and the weight and materiality of the evidence.'
19. Mika Hemmo, *Prosessitoimia rajoittavat määräajat ja niiden poikkeukset välimiesmenettelyssä*, p. 51 (2022), available at https://www.edilex.fi/artikkelit/27108.pdf.
20. *See, e.g.*, Mika Hemmo, *Prosessitoimia rajoittavat määräajat ja niiden poikkeukset välimiesmenettelyssä*, pp. 49–50 (2022), available at https://www.edilex.fi/artikkelit/27108.pdf.

proceed, it is necessary to carry out a careful balancing act of the various interests that are affected.

By way of example, in ICC case No. 18671, the claimant's new evidence was admissible despite the cut-off date having already passed, as the respondent had presented vague and contradicting arguments in the proceedings. The sole arbitrator stated, e.g., that 'the Sole Arbitrator has the power to admit documentary evidence after the cut-off date in exceptional circumstances, if appropriate in view of all relevant circumstances. When assessing all relevant circumstances of the case, the Sole Arbitrator particularly focuses on (i) the relevance of the evidence submitted and (ii) the reasons why it was not submitted within the ordinary exchange of briefs as per Timetable.'[21]

The sole arbitrator found that the submitted evidence could be relevant, as it related to a substantive issue of the case, i.e., which version of the contract was the correct one. Pursuant to the arbitrator's decision, exceptional circumstances were present as the respondent had submitted two directly contradictory explanations with respect to the relevant contract versions and had additionally raised a counterclaim based on a contractual relationship – even though it had also disputed the existence of such a contractual relationship. Additionally, the need for the submitted evidence appeared only after the respondent had pleaded inconsistent factual arguments. As such, the sole arbitrator considered that exceptional circumstances were present, allowing the submission of new evidence past the cut-off date.[22]

Third, a similar situation might also arise regarding witness evidence, and the same points could be argued with respect to a sudden need to supplement the witness list with additional witnesses. However, witness evidence also presents some further challenges as compared to the submission of documentary evidence: in addition to the late recognition of a need to call a certain witness to testify, issues might arise with respect to witness availability and/or the witness's willingness to cooperate.

For example, one could envisage a situation where a witness who has previously been uncooperative suddenly decides to engage in the proceedings. At the outset, no witness statement might have been submitted on the witness's behalf, but the possibility to do so might later present itself after the relevant cut-off date has passed. In such a situation, it might be somewhat more difficult to argue that this would constitute '*exceptional*' circumstances, assuming that the relevance of the witness' statements was known to the parties already well before the passing of the cut-off date. Additionally, and depending on the judicial system, a party to an arbitration might also be able to enlist the help of the national courts in compelling a reluctant witness to give evidence.[23] Although parties are understandably reluctant to go to such lengths, in situations where this option exists, a party could arguably have availed itself of such an

21. *Buyer (Taiwan) v. Seller (Germany), Final Award, ICC Case No. 18671*, in Albert Jan van den Berg (ed.), *ICCA Yearbook Commercial Arbitration 2017* – Volume XLII, para. 23 (2017), as available at Kluwer Law International.
22. *Buyer (Taiwan) v. Seller (Germany), Final Award, ICC Case No. 18671*, in Albert Jan van den Berg (ed.), *ICCA Yearbook Commercial Arbitration 2017* – Volume XLII, paras 15-33 (2017), as available at Kluwer Law International.
23. *See, e.g.*, the Finnish Arbitration Act (23.10.1992/967), section 29.

option sooner, in case it was aware of the reluctance of a certain witness to testify coupled with the relevance of the testimony already before the passing of the cut-off date.

However, a party might more easily be able to meet a lower threshold for the submission of new witness evidence after the cut-off date, arguing, e.g., that 'justified' circumstances exist for calling a new witness although the cut-off date has passed. Yet again, the wording of the cut-off clause is central in this respect: does it envisage that exceptional circumstances have to be present for new evidence to be submitted, or does it allow for the submission of new evidence on the basis of a lower threshold? Is there even any wording included in the clause which would concern witness evidence and/or the threshold for submission of evidence after the passing of the cut-off date?

Another potential situation could arise where a certain witness has been called to testify and may already have submitted a written witness statement before the cut-off date but is then unable to appear at the hearing despite being called to be examined and/or cross-examined. If a party is unable to compel the witness to arrive, the question becomes whether this could amount to exceptional circumstances which would allow a party to call a new replacement witness after the cut-off date. The argument seems easier to make if the witness is severely ill or has, in fact, died, but in cases where the witness is simply reluctant to cooperate, and the assistance of the courts could be available but the party calling the witness is reluctant to resort to this measure, meeting the threshold of 'exceptional circumstances' might prove to be difficult.[24]

In our experience, some arbitral tribunals have also admitted new written evidence where a party had requested to submit it in order to prove that a witness' oral testimony at the hearing was contradictory and/or that the witness allegedly was lying. For instance, such tribunals have concluded that the threshold of 'exceptional circumstances' had been met, as the relevance of the evidence allegedly only became clear to the party at the hearing when it stated that a witness was giving contradictory testimony, and the new evidence was considered to be of essential relevance to the credibility of such a witness.[25]

Fourth, technical difficulties might also meet the threshold of 'exceptional circumstances', allowing for the late filing of evidence. In a judgment by the Svea Court of Appeal, the court addressed a case in which the arbitral tribunal had deemed a submission admissible after the cut-off date when the party who made the filing had suffered from technical difficulties and the submission was filed 1 hour and 52 minutes late (at 1.52 am), with some appendices being filed around noon on the same day. The parties had scheduled a hearing for roughly two weeks from the filing, and the opposing party objected to the late filing. However, the Svea Court of Appeal did not

24. This situation also raises the related point of whether the written witness statement in and of itself could be considered sufficient evidence without any direct examination or cross-examination of the witness at the hearing, but this is outside the scope of this article and would, in any event, largely depend on the wording of the procedural orders in the case at hand.
25. On this topic, *see, e.g.*, Mika Hemmo, *Prosessitoimia rajoittavat määräajat ja niiden poikkeukset välimiesmenettelyssä*, pp. 55-59 (2022), available at https://www.edilex.fi/artikkelit/27108.pdf.

assess the arbitral tribunal's decision to accept the submission, as it deemed that the opposing party had waived its right to object to the decision by not raising the issue again at a later stage of the arbitration, after a short discussion on the first day of the hearing in which it was left to the said party's discretion to request a measure to mitigate the problem, such as adding more time to the hearing or submitting another submission.[26] Thus, one could argue that technical issues might constitute exceptional circumstances, but only for a very limited period of time after the cut-off date. Proving such technical difficulties may be challenging, but in order to meet the standard of 'exceptional circumstances', some evidence might arguably need to be provided in support of the notion that technical difficulties (such as a network disruption) have actually occurred to an extent which hindered the timely filing of the evidence. It may also be relevant whether the technical difficulties in question were foreseeable and/or within the control of the party making the submission.

In all instances mentioned above, the materiality and the weight of the evidence which a party wishes to submit after the passing of the cut-off date plays a key role. It would arguably not be necessary to file any such evidence which only relates to a minor point – or where the relevance of the evidence is unclear – after the passing of the cut-off date, and finding exceptional circumstances to be at hand in such an instance might prove more difficult.

In many cases, tribunals have also considered whether the opposing party can and should be afforded an opportunity to rebut the evidence submitted after cut-off. In case a late filing is allowed, tribunals have often attempted to ensure that the other party has such a possibility, whether it be through the opportunity to file rebuttal evidence or simply the right to comment on the substance of the new evidence.[27]

§10.04 CONCLUSION

In light of the above, we conclude that exceptional circumstances may be present in a variety of different situations, such as where a certain piece of evidence did not exist or was not in the possession of a party wanting to submit it prior to the cut-off date, where its relevance was not previously known to the party that now wishes to submit it, or where technical difficulties have prevented the timely submission of evidence.

However, the final answer as to what can constitute exceptional circumstances is not straightforward, as it will always depend on an assessment of the facts of the case at hand taken as a whole. In particular, the wording of the cut-off clause is of central

26. Judgment of the Svea Court of Appeal, 16 December 2015 regarding SCC Case No. V 2012/171, *Doan Technology Pty Ltd. and Mr. Binh Doan v. Uretek Worldwide Oy*, to the extent summarised in English, available at Jus Mundi.
27. Such considerations, which relate to equal treatment of the parties and the parties' right to present their case, have been taken into account in several cases mentioned in this article. *See, e.g.*, Judgment of the Svea Court of Appeal, 16 December 2015 regarding SCC Case No. V 2012/171, *Doan Technology Pty Ltd.* and *Mr. Binh Doan v. Uretek Worldwide* Oy, para. 154, to the extent summarised in English, available at Jus Mundi. *Supplier (Xanadu) v. Reseller (Utopia)*, (SCC Case No. 2018/127), Final Award, 14 November 2019, in Stephan W. Schill (ed.), ICCA Yearbook Commercial Arbitration 2020 – Volume XLV, para. 169 (2020).

importance when assessing what evidence can be submitted after the passing of the cut-off date, as well as the materiality and weight of the proposed new evidence.

Some commentators have argued that arbitrators should adopt a restrained approach when considering whether to allow new evidence to be presented after the cut-off date. As it is not mandatory to impose a cut-off date, in cases where such a date has been inserted into a procedural timetable or a procedural order, the parties have presumably consented to such inclusion. As such, the cut-off date will usually constitute a party agreement. Therefore, it has been argued that subsequent derogation from such agreement at the insistence of only one party should not be permitted lightly.[28] Indeed, depending on the wording of the agreement, this may not even be possible.

Be that as it may, the question of when to accept new evidence after the cut-off date is of essential importance, as it may give grounds for a party to attempt to challenge the subsequent arbitral award. If the tribunal considers that extraordinary circumstances exist and thus allows the submission of new evidence that affects the outcome of the case, the losing party may seek to contest the arbitral award, stating that the tribunal has exceeded its mandate or that a procedural error has occurred when it allowed new evidence after the cut-off date.[29]

However, should the tribunal instead reject the admissibility of the new evidence, the party whose evidence was rejected could try to set aside the award, claiming that the arbitral tribunal did not allow that party a sufficient opportunity to present its case.[30] It follows that the arbitral tribunal must diligently consider the admissibility of the new evidence, taking into consideration such things as the equal treatment of the parties as well as the enforceability of the award.

---

28. *See, e.g.*, Irene Welser, Samuel Mimnagh, 'Chapter II: The Arbitrator and the Arbitration Procedure, An Arbitrator's Imperative – How to Avoid Disappointing the Parties, Preventing Surprises and Enabling Efficient and Progressive Arbitral Proceedings', in Christian Klausegger et al. (eds), Austrian Yearbook on International Arbitration, Volume 2021, p. 150 (2021), as available at Kluwer Law International.
29. *See, e.g.*, Judgment of the Svea Court of Appeal, 16 December 2015 regarding SCC Case No. V 2012/171, *Doan Technology Pty Ltd. and Mr. Binh Doan v. Uretek Worldwide Oy*, to the extent summarised in English, available at Jus Mundi.
30. *See, e.g.*, Mika Hemmo, *Prosessitoimia rajoittavat määräajat ja niiden poikkeukset välimiesmenettelyssä*, p. 62 (2022).

CHAPTER 11

A Matter of Characterisation Distinguishing Issues of Arbitral Jurisdiction and Admissibility of Claims

Fabricio Fortese

§11.01 INTRODUCTION

It is axiomatic that arbitration is a matter of contract and, therefore, the legitimacy of arbitration depends on the fundamental premise that parties are not required to arbitrate without their consent.[1] Arbitrators enjoy dispute resolution authority only when the parties have validly agreed to submit their disputes to arbitration.

Disputes often arise regarding the existence, validity, or enforceability of an alleged agreement to arbitrate. Those disputes impact on and imperil the arbitrators' jurisdiction. But some disputes that at first glance appear to involve a jurisdictional challenge might, in fact, relate to the *admissibility* of the substantive claims. Consider, for example, the scenario presented by escalation clauses. Escalation clauses are contractual provisions setting forth more than one dispute resolution method to operate in sequential order. They require compliance with the first agreed method (e.g., mediation) before initiating the next one (e.g., arbitration). Disputes that a party has failed to comply with one of those contractual pre-arbitration requirements present a question of characterisation. They could be characterised as 'jurisdictional', 'admissibility', or 'procedural' issues.

1. *See, e.g.*, George A. Bermann, The 'Gateway' Problem in International Commercial Arbitration, 37 *Yale Journal of International Law* (2012), p. 5. For a discussion about arbitration 'without consent', *see also*, Gabrielle Kaufmann-Kohler et al., *Formula 1 Racing and Arbitration: The FIA Tailor-Made System for Fast Track Dispute Resolution*, 17 *Arbitration International*, no. 2 (2014), pp. 173-210 DOI: 10.1023/a:1011250312120.

They could be understood as *jurisdictional issues* based on the argument that the arbitration agreement does not provide arbitrators with authority (jurisdiction) until the pre-arbitration dispute resolution methods have been complied with. Complying with them would be viewed as a condition precedent to the parties' consent to arbitrate.

The same claims could, also, be characterised as *admissibility* defences. The argument would be that although the arbitration agreement vests arbitrators with jurisdiction, it does not permit the assertion of substantive claims until after the agreed pre-arbitration requirements have been satisfied.

Like the admissibility defences, if the pre-arbitration requirements were characterised merely as part of the *procedural steps*[2] for the resolution of the dispute, failure to comply with them would not affect the jurisdiction of an arbitral tribunal to decide the substantive dispute. This characterisation can be assimilated to admissibility (or, more generally, non-jurisdictional) issues because it would usually not affect the 'adjudicative power' of the arbitral tribunal to decide the substantive dispute. They would affect the temporal aspect of the exercise of that power.

Before proceeding, it is important to make here a caveat. For the sake of simplicity and the sole purpose of this chapter, procedural steps and admissibility defences will be treated together under the term 'admissibility' to distinguish them from jurisdictional issues.

In that understanding, the correct characterisation of an issue as jurisdictional (or not) matters in terms of the allocation of competence to decide that controversy. It also matters regarding the standard of court review where arbitrators have preliminarily decided that issue.[3] This chapter addresses that characterisation and distinctions. It starts with a brief description of the competence-competence principle, its source, extent, and limitations (§11.02). It then introduces a closely linked principle: separability (§11.03), before discussing the challenges of identifying disputes concerning the jurisdiction of arbitrators and the admissibility of the claims (§11.04). The final section contains the concluding remarks (§11.05).

§11.02 COMPETENCE-COMPETENCE

It is uncontroversial that arbitrators have the authority to rule on their own jurisdiction. This is known as the competence-competence principle, and it operates as a tool to foster the efficacy of commitments to arbitrate and procedural efficiency in arbitration.

2. *Westco Airconditioning Ltd v. Sui Chong Construction & Engineering Co. Ltd*, [1998] HKCFI 946, Hong Kong Court of First Instance, 3 February 1998, para. 12: Failure to comply with preliminary steps does not render the arbitration agreement null and void, inoperative or incapable of being performed. The court referred the parties to arbitration, to complete the agreed preliminary procedural steps.
3. George A. Bermann, The Role of National Courts at the Threshold of Arbitration, *International Arbitration and the Rule of Law: Contribution and Conformity, ICCA Congress Series*, no. 19 (2017), pp. 450-451.

In practical terms, competence-competence channels a policy choice against dilatory manoeuvres.[4] Without it, a challenge to the arbitral tribunal's jurisdiction would stall arbitration proceedings until a national court settles the objection. It would transform the promise to arbitrate into an illusion because even 'the most feeble challenge would abort the proceedings, and the parties (...) would be thrown into the courts when that is exactly contrary to their bargain.'[5]

The competence-competence principle is as commendable as uncontroversial in contemporary arbitration law and practice. It is such a fundamental feature of arbitration that it has found normative recognition almost universally, including national arbitration legislation,[6] institutional arbitration rules, international conventions,[7] and case law.[8] Article 16(1) of the UNCITRAL Model Law ('Model Law') articulates the competence-competence principle in these terms:

> The arbitral tribunal may rule on its own jurisdiction, including any objections with respect to the existence or validity of the arbitration agreement.

The principle is aligned with the Model Law's purpose because it fosters efficiency in dispute resolution as 'it impedes unmeritorious tactical challenges, which would otherwise flourish like weeds.'[9] The Model Law's preparatory works further reveal that the drafters of Article 16(1) discussed and rejected a suggestion to start the paragraph with the phrase 'unless otherwise agreed by the parties'.[10] This rejection is not simply anecdotal but instructive of how some textual 'silences' should be interpreted in the context of the Model Law, especially given the clear and specific consideration that the drafters paid to the instrument's wording. The textual silence is not an oversight but a deliberate choice against language that carries a specific meaning and legal effect. That drafting decision and the principle's fundamental role in the

4. *See, e.g.*, the Report of the Secretary-General: Possible Features of a Model Law on International Commercial Arbitration, A/CN.9/207 (14 May 1981), para. 88.
5. Jan Paulsson, *The Idea of Arbitration* (Oxford University Press, 2013), p. 54.
6. For example, Swedish Arbitration Act, section 2; Hong Kong Arbitration Ordinance (Cap. 609), section 34; Switzerland Private International Law Act, Art. 186(1); Singapore Arbitration Act, Art. 16(1) (Model Law); English Arbitration Act (1996), section 30; Germany Arbitration Act (Book 10 ZPO), section 1040(1); Mexico Commercial Code, Art. 1432; Peru Arbitration Law, Art. 41(1), Spain Consolidated Arbitration Law, Art. 22(1), France, Code of Civil Procedure (Decree 2011-48), Art. 1465; Mauritius International Arbitration Act (2008), section 20; amongst many others.
7. For example, the European Convention on International Commercial Arbitration (1961), Art. V(3); ICSID Convention, Art. 41; Inter-American Convention on International Commercial Arbitration (Panama Convention, 1975), Art. 3, refers to the Inter-American Commercial Arbitration Commission, which in its Art. 18.1 explicitly provides for the competence-competence principle.
8. *See* §11.05 below.
9. Paulsson, *The Idea of Arbitration* (*supra* n. 5) p. 57.
10. Summary Records of the 315th Meeting, A/CN.9/246, annex; A/CN.9/263 Add.1-2, A/CN.9/264 (10 June 1985), paras 24-26. Nevertheless, States may deviate from the model when adopting it and permit parties to exclude (or limit) the arbitrators' competence-competence. *See*, Report of the United Nations Commission on International Trade Law on the Work of its Eighteenth Session, A/40/17 (21 August 1985), para. 151.

effective functioning of arbitration led some authorities to suggest that competence-competence features a mandatory character.[11] And one scholar even stated that the principle forms part of transnational public order.[12]

Although with two textual dissimilarities, the text of Article 16(1) was modelled on Article 21(1) of the UNCITRAL 1976 Arbitration Rules. According to the Rules, '[t]he arbitral tribunal shall have the power to rule on objections that it has no jurisdiction'. The Model Law uses the phrase 'may rule' instead of 'shall have the power to rule', and it does not refer to 'objections' but to the arbitrators' power to rule over their own jurisdiction ('The arbitral tribunal may rule on its own jurisdiction'). However, these textual differences do not carry a significant degree of disparity in their interpretation and application.[13]

The New York Convention does not contain a provision like the one in the UNCITRAL Model Law and the Arbitration Rules. It does not explicitly address the competence-competence principle, and its scant legislative history shows that its drafters did not debate the matter. Still, nothing in its text or legislative history indicates that the Convention prevents arbitrators from determining jurisdictional disputes. On the contrary, recognition of the competence-competence principle can be inferred from the language of Article V.

Two of the Convention's grounds to resist the recognition and enforcement of foreign awards relate to the validity (Article V(1)(a)) and scope of the parties' agreement to arbitrate (Article V(1)(c)). At least impliedly, the Convention assumes that arbitrators render awards on the substantive dispute despite the parties having challenged their jurisdiction. Had the arbitrators found in favour of a jurisdictional objection, there would be no award on the merits or at least on the dispute outside the scope of the arbitration. By the same logic, if the party aggrieved by the invalidity or scope of the arbitration agreement failed to raise its challenge during the arbitral proceedings, and, therefore, there is an arbitral decision on the substantive matter, then this would (generally) be taken as the party having relinquished its jurisdictional objection.

Competence-competence is not a novel device exclusive to the realm of arbitration. As Bermann noted, the principle achieves for arbitration what we practically assume in litigation: national courts determine by themselves whether they have jurisdiction over a given case.[14] But despite the high degree of recognition and acceptance of the competence-competence principle, there are different visions regarding its source. The following section then addresses the source of the arbitrators' competence to determine their jurisdiction.

---

11. Howard M. Holtzmann et al., *A Guide to the UNCITRAL Model Law on International Commercial Arbitration* (Kluwer Law International, 1989), p. 480 ('The principle of Kompetenz-Kompetenz is a mandatory one in the Law, that is, the parties cannot agree to limit the power of the arbitral tribunal to rule on its jurisdiction.').
12. Pierre Lalive, Ordre Public Transnational (ou réellement international) et Arbitrage International, *Revue de l'Arbitrage*, no. 3 (1986), p. 350, para. 352.
13. *See* Commission Report A/40/17, para. 152.
14. George A. Bermann, *International Arbitration and Private International Law: General Course on Private International Law* (Martinus Nijhoff, 2017), pp. 103, 107.

[A] The Source of the Competence-Competence Principle

In the Model Law context, competence-competence is a non-contractual, statutory construct. It is counter-intuitive to argue that the arbitrators' power to rule on their jurisdiction derives from the agreement whose existence or validity is disputed or uncertain. Consequently, the arbitrators' authority does not originate from the putative arbitration agreement but from the statutes (based on Article 16(1) Model Law) that recognise it and the New York Convention.

Distinctively, competence-competence in the United States (a non-Model Law jurisdiction) has a contractual basis. As a default rule, jurisdictional matters are reserved for national courts, not the arbitrators, unless the parties have clearly and unmistakably intended to delegate the decision of jurisdictional issues to arbitrators.[15] This is also the case in Israel (another non-Model Law jurisdiction), where the arbitration law does not recognise in arbitrators the authority to decide jurisdictional disputes. However, parties can explicitly and specifically authorise them to do so.[16]

Some authors describe competence-competence as an inherent power of the arbitrators' adjudicatory role and essential to them carrying out their tasks properly.[17] Other authors describe competence-competence as a 'legal fiction'[18] rooted in policy considerations favouring arbitration. Its pragmatic purpose is to defeat the logic and circularity of the argument that bases arbitral competence-competence on an arbitration agreement that is contended.[19]

Others acknowledge that although competence-competence is one of the effects of the (even putative) arbitration agreement, the basis of such a power is not the arbitration agreement itself nor the principle of *pacta sunt servanda*. Its source is found in arbitration legislation. First, the arbitration law of the seat of the arbitration 'and, more generally, the laws of all countries liable to recognise an award made by arbitrators concerning their own jurisdiction'.[20] Somewhat similar, another scholar has

15. *See, e.g., AT&T Technologies, Inc. v. Communications Workers,* 475 U.S. 643, United States Supreme Court, 7 April 1986, p. 649 ('Unless the parties clearly and unmistakably provide otherwise, the question of whether the parties agreed to arbitrate is to be decided by the court, not the arbitrator.'); reiterated in *First Options of Chicago, Inc. v. Kaplan,* 514 U.S. 938, US Supreme Court, 22 May 1995, p. 939.
16. Daphna Kapeliuk-Klinger, 'National Report for Israel', in *ICCA International Handbook on Commercial Arbitration,* ed. Bosman (Kluwer Law International, 2019), p. 26.
17. Nigel Blackaby et al., *Redfern and Hunter on International Arbitration,* 6th ed. (Oxford University Press, 2015), pp. 339-340. Also, Emmanuel Gaillard et al., 'Negative Effect of Competence-Competence: The Rule of Priority in Favour of the Arbitrators', in *Enforcement of Arbitration Agreements and International Arbitral Awards: The New York Convention in Practice,* ed. Emmanuel Gaillard and Domenico di Pietro (Cameron May, 2008), p. 259.
18. Julian D.M. Lew et al., *Comparative International Commercial Arbitration* (Kluwer Law International, 2003), p. 333, paras 14-16; Stavros Brekoulakis, The Negative Effect of Competence-Competence: The Verdict Has to Be Negative, *Austrian Arbitration Yearbook* (2009).
19. Brekoulakis, *ibid.* pp. 239, 251.
20. Philippe Fouchard et al., *Fouchard Gaillard Goldman on International Commercial Arbitration* (Kluwer Law International, 1999), pp. 399-400, para. 658.

stated that the arbitrators' jurisdictional power derives from national laws and institutional arbitration rules.[21]

A more nuanced assessment of the source of arbitral authority distinguishes between jurisdictional grounds. Born, for example, takes the position that an agreement to arbitrate could be the source of the arbitrator's competence-competence in cases where the existence or validity of the agreement is not disputed (e.g., challenges to the scope of the agreement). In those cases, the decision-making powers would be part of the arbitrator's inherent adjudicatory attributes.[22] However, where the jurisdictional question concerns the existence or validity of the agreement to arbitrate, the arbitrators' competence-competence rests 'on the positive force of national, and international, law.'[23]

Born also concedes that virtually all national arbitration regimes 'presume' arbitral competence-competence, as part of the 'basic objectives of the arbitral process and the inherent powers and mandate of an adjudicatory tribunal'.[24] Reflecting on the wide acceptance of competence-competence in practice (regardless of the applicable law), the author suggests that it could be considered 'a general principle of international law and an inherent power (absent contrary agreement) of an arbitral tribunal'.[25]

The Model Law (and statutes that adopt it) dissipates these potential controversies by codifying the competence-competence principle with broad, comprehensive language. It does not distinguish between disputes concerning the agreement's existence, validity, or scope. The inclusive wording of Article 16(1) stretches to cover all those disputes: '[t]he arbitral tribunal may rule on its own jurisdiction, including any objections with respect to the existence or validity of the arbitration agreement'. But the arbitrators' power to rule on their jurisdiction is limited. The limitations are addressed in the next section.

[B] Limits to the Arbitrators' Authority

A contextual reading of Article 16(1) of the Model Law impacts the arbitrators' competence-competence, which is not exclusive nor conclusive. It is correct to qualify this important principle as the arbitrators' authority to consider and determine their own jurisdiction as *'provisional'* or *'preliminary'*. At least regarding the decisions

21. William W Park, 'The Arbitrator's Jurisdiction to Determine Jurisdiction', in *International Arbitration 2006: Back to Basics?*, ed. Albert Jan van den Berg, ICCA Congress Series (Kluwer Law International, 2007), p. 59.
22. Gary B. Born, *International Commercial Arbitration*, 3rd ed., vol. 1 (Kluwer Law International, 2021), p. 1167.
23. *Ibid.*
24. *Ibid.*, p. 1152. Professor Park, instead, suggests that agreements to submit jurisdictional questions to arbitrations must be honoured but not presumed. *See*, Park, *The Arbitrator's Jurisdiction* (*supra* n. 21) p. 62.
25. Born, *International Commercial Arbitration* (*supra* n. 22) p. 1162.

where the arbitrators decide against the objections and find they do enjoy jurisdiction to resolve the substantive dispute.[26]

The arbitrators' decision on jurisdiction is provisional because it is reviewable at different stages and by different courts. At the seat of the arbitration, the judiciary could decide the issue immediately after the arbitrators have assumed jurisdiction in a preliminary ruling (Article 16(3) Model Law). This could also be done at the end of the proceedings, should the arbitrators have answered the jurisdictional question together with the award on the merits (Article 34 Model Law). A court other than the ones at the seat of the arbitration could also review the arbitrators' jurisdiction in an action for recognition and enforcement of the award (Article 36 Model Law and Article V New York Convention).

Further, jurisdictional issues may arise and need to be determined by national courts before any arbitral proceedings have started (or even whilst they are in course), in the context of a substantive court action covered by an arbitration agreement (e.g., Articles 8 Model Law and II(3) New York Convention).[27]

A basic understanding of arbitration requires reiterating an essential expression of the principle of 'party autonomy'. All the scenarios of judicial determination mentioned above are hypothetical because national courts do not have a spontaneous obligation to review the arbitrators' jurisdiction. Given that the disputing parties may opt to wave their jurisdictional objections, the court review and determination materialise only at a party's request. But there are exceptions to this general rule. Matters concerning arbitrability and public policy affect arbitral jurisdiction and limit party autonomy, and national courts could review them ex officio where a party files a substantive action or seeks the recognition or enforcement of an arbitral award.

Some authorities argue that the competence-competence principle is limited regarding the effects it produces. It is undisputed that competence-competence produces a *positive* effect. But for some authors, the principle also triggers a *negative* one.[28]

That arbitrators enjoy the authority to determine their own jurisdiction is known as the *positive* effect of the competence-competence principle. The *negative* effect moves the spotlight away from the arbitral tribunal and focuses it on national courts.[29] In a nutshell, the negative effect encapsulates the idea that vesting arbitrators with competence-competence necessarily entails divesting national courts of the authority to *conclusively* determine jurisdictional questions at the threshold of an arbitration.[30]

26. The decisions whereby the arbitrators find that they lack jurisdiction are final, not provisional. These are discussed below.
27. The extent of the court review of jurisdictional issues before or after the arbitrators have preliminarily decided the matter may vary depending on several factors (e.g., the ground for the challenge, the national approach, the instance at which the challenge is brought to court, etc.). This chapter does not embark on that discussion.
28. The strongest voices behind this argument are Fouchard et al., *International Commercial Arbitration* (*supra* n. 20) p. 401, para. 660.
29. *See, e.g.*, Gaillard et al., *Negative Effect of Competence-Competence* (*supra* n. 17) p. 260 ('[A] court that is confronted with the question of the existence or validity of the arbitration agreement must refrain from hearing substantive arguments as to the arbitrators' jurisdiction until such time as the arbitrators themselves have had an opportunity to do so.').
30. For example, Art. 8(1) of the Model Law, Art. II(3) of the New York Convention.

Therefore, in that scenario, the crucial feature of the negative dimension of the competence-competence principle is that it establishes a rule of priority in favour of arbitrators.

In the context of the Model Law, whether the language of Article 16(1) shadows the powers of national courts (Article 8(1)) is controversial. Some authorities conclude that recognising the negative effect 'best fits with the Model Law's legislative history, its basic structure and underlying principles'.[31] There are equally strong views that do not recognise the negative aspect of competence-competence.[32]

Whether the Model Law allows or imposes the negative effect is a thorny and thought-provoking question. Judge Judith Prakash wittily compared that question and the dichotomy of the prima facie or full merits standard of review that it entails with the brain teaser in the question: Which came first, the chicken or the egg?[33] But its answer exceeds the scope of this chapter, which is limited to a closely related but distinct matter: the characterisation of challenges aimed at the jurisdiction of arbitrators or at the admissibility of the parties' substantive disputes.

§11.03 SEPARABILITY

In addition to the competence-competence principle, some laws codify another essential tool related to jurisdictional disputes: the *separability* presumption. For example, the second and third sentences of Article 16(1) of the Model Law provide that, in determining whether the arbitral tribunal has jurisdiction:

> [A]n arbitration clause which forms part of a contract shall be treated as an agreement independent of the other terms of the contract. A decision by the arbitral tribunal that the contract is null and void shall not entail *ipso jure* the invalidity of the arbitration clause.[34]

The separability presumption complements the competence-competence principle. While competence-competence recognises the arbitrators' power to determine their own jurisdiction, separability permits isolating the arbitration clause. It protects it from *automatically* running the same fate as the contract in which it appears. It then follows that the arbitration agreement may be valid even where the rest of the contract

31. *See, e.g.*, Frédéric Bachand, Does Article 8 of the Model Law Call for Full or *Prima Facie* Review of the Arbitral Tribunal's Jurisdiction?, 22 *Arbitration International*, no. 3 (2006), p. 465 DOI: 10.1093/arbitration/22.3.463.
32. *See, e.g.*, Brekoulakis, *The Negative Effect of Competence-Competence* (*supra* n. 18) p. 238. Bermann, *International Arbitration* (*supra* n. 14), p. 15; Paulsson, *The Idea of Arbitration* (*supra* n. 5) p. 58 (The negative effect of competence-competence 'is not an inevitable corollary of allowing the arbitral tribunal to proceed when faced with a jurisdictional objection'.).
33. *Malini Ventura v. Knight Capital Pte Ltd and others*, [2015] SGHC 225, Singapore High Court, 27 August 2015, paras 1, 19.
34. The separability presumption in the Model Law was modelled on its parallel in Art. 21(2) of the UNCITRAL 1976 Arbitration Rules. *See*, Secretariat Report A/CN.9/207, para. 54, Report of the Working Group on International Contract Practices, on the Work of its Third Session, A/CN.9/216 (23 March 1982), para. 34, and approved at an early drafting stage, according to the Report of the Working Group on International Contract Practices, on the Work of its Fourth Session, A/CN.9/232 (10 November 1982), paras 47-48.

is not, as long as the grounds for invalidity do not directly affect the arbitration clause itself.[35]

That arbitration clauses are separable from the rest of the contract has become a vital presumption for determining jurisdictional challenges. It is considered a part of the 'generally accepted principles of arbitration'[36] and a common-sense tool in applying legal rules to recognise the parties' intention,[37] even a transnational rule of international commercial arbitration.[38] Having achieved such a status, the separability presumption is not a tool exclusively reserved for arbitrators. It is equally available for national courts, which rely on it when deciding on arbitral jurisdiction.[39] It is, therefore, also useful for the characterisation contest between jurisdiction and admissibility.

§11.04 JURISDICTION VERSUS ADMISSIBILITY

The terms 'jurisdiction' and 'admissibility' are not used consistently. They are often used interchangeably as if they were synonyms. They are not, and the distinction between them matters. It matters not because of terminological fussiness but regarding the allocation of competence to decide them and their effect over substantive disputes. It matters also in terms of the reviewability of the arbitrators' decisions: national courts can review jurisdictional but not admissibility decisions.

The distinction bears special relevance at the threshold of an arbitration when interpreting Article 8(1) of the Model Law and Article II(3) of the New York Convention. Non-jurisdictional matters invariably trigger the court referral to arbitration that those articles provide for.

This section introduces a conceptual description of those issues, explains why the distinction mentioned above matters, and highlights the determining factor to distinguish jurisdictional objections from non-jurisdictional ones.

35. Analytical Commentary on the Draft Text of a Model Law on International Commercial Arbitration: Report of the Secretary-General, 18th session, A/CN.9/264 (25 March 1985), para. 2.
36. *See, e.g.*, *Enrique C. Wellbers S.A.I.C. A. G. v. Extraktionstechnik Gesellschaft für Anlagenbau M.B.M. s/ Ordinario*, La Ley, 1989-E-302, National Court of Appeals (Comm), Argentina, 26 September 1988 ('[T]he principle of the autonomy of the arbitration clause is internationally accepted and, as such, incorporated in the Model Arbitration Law (Article 16(1)). ... the Model Law (...) generally reflects accepted principles in the matter and can be considered to make up for the absence of a specific national norm.').
37. *Comandate Marine Corp. v. Pan Australia Shipping Pty. Ltd*, [2006] FCAFC 192, Federal Court of Australia, 20 December 2006, para. 228.
38. Fouchard et al., *International Commercial Arbitration* (*supra* n. 20) p. 202, para. 398.
39. One of the earliest and leading decisions oft-cited and studied internationally is that of the Supreme Court of the United States, in the *Prima Paint* case, where the Court confirmed that '(...) except where the parties otherwise intend - arbitration clauses as a matter of federal law are "separable" from the contracts in which they are embedded'; *Prima Paint Corp. v. Flood & Conklin Mfg. Co.*, 388 U.S. 395, 405 (1967), United States Supreme Court, 12 June 1967, para. 402. *See also*, Holtzmann et al., *A Guide to the Model Law* (*supra* n. 11) p. 305, where the authors explain that not only arbitrators but also courts can rely on the separability presumption when deciding jurisdictional issues.

[A] Jurisdiction

Jurisdiction is a prerogative to hear and settle disputes.[40] Jurisdictional issues, then, relate to the arbitrators' (legal) *authority* to settle substantive disputes. Jurisdiction determines, essentially, 'whether an adjudicatory body has authority to entertain a claim'.[41]

Given that party agreement is the foundation of arbitration, the notion of jurisdiction (legal authority) is closely linked to 'party consent'. In the absence of consent to arbitrate, arbitrators are not vested with jurisdiction.[42] Hence, jurisdictional challenges usually relate to the very *existence* of a *valid* agreement to arbitrate (and of its scope). That happens, for example, when the arbitration agreement is so poorly drafted that it is impossible to determine the parties' intention to settle disputes in arbitration. These 'pathologically incurable' clauses take aim at the forum where the parties should ventilate their controversies (arbitration or litigation) and at the decision-maker who should settle them (arbitrator or judge).

There are other defective[43] arbitration clauses that, notwithstanding their shortcomings, reveal the parties' intention to arbitrate. This happens, for example, when parties have entered into a 'blank clause',[44] or an arbitration clause that mistakenly refers to non-existent arbitral institutions or appointing authorities, or contains defective choice-of-law clauses, or other defects.[45] Although these defective or imperfect clauses do not call into question the parties' intention to arbitrate, they, too, constitute jurisdictional matters because they cast doubts on the effectiveness or validity of the agreement.[46]

40. When addressing the distinction between questions of jurisdiction and admissibility, arbitrators Professor Vaughan Lowe Q.C, Judge Charles N. Brower and Christopher Thomas, Q.C concluded that '[j]urisdiction is an attribute of a tribunal and not of a claim, whereas admissibility is an attribute of a claim but not of a tribunal'; *Hochtief AG v. The Argentine Republic, Decision on Jurisdiction*, ICSID Case No. ARB/07/31, 24 October 2011, para. 90.
41. ALI, Restatement (Third), U.S. Law of International Commercial and Investor-State Arbitration § 2.8 – Reporter's Notes.
42. Bermann, *The Role of National Courts* (*supra* n. 3) p. 450.
43. Born prefers and suggests using the term 'convalescent' rather than 'pathological' arbitration clauses. He supports that idea on the large number of authorities that rely on the application of the 'validation principle' and of 'effective interpretation' approach to give effect to commercial parties' intention to resolve their international disputes by arbitration. *See*, in general, Gary Born et al., 'Rethinking "Pathological" Arbitration Clauses: Validating Imperfect Arbitration Agreements', in *Finances in International Arbitration: Liber Amicorum Patricia Shaughnessy*, ed. Sherlin Tung et al. (Kluwer Law International, 2019).
44. That is, a clause that 'does not specify either the method for appointing the arbitrators or the number of arbitrators comprising the tribunal'. For example: 'The parties agree to resolve their disputes in arbitration', or 'In case of any dispute, arbitration.' Fouchard et al., *International Commercial Arbitration* (*supra* n. 20) p. 497.
45. *See, e.g.*, *Insigma Technology Co Ltd v. Alstom Technology Ltd*, [2009] SGCA 24, Singapore Court of Appeal, para. 31: '[W]here the parties have evinced a clear intention to settle any dispute by arbitration, the court should give effect to such intention, even if certain aspects of the agreement may be ambiguous, inconsistent, incomplete or lacking in certain particulars.'
46. Arbitration agreements are not recognised and enforced if they are inoperative or incapable of being performed; according to, e.g., Art. II(3) New York Convention and Art. 8(1) Model Law.

Other common jurisdictional disputes relate to the identity of the parties bound by the arbitration agreement, whether the dispute can be determined in arbitration, and (or) whether it falls within the scope of the agreement.[47]

In sum, jurisdictional issues relate to the arbitration agreements' existence, validity, and scope. However, the parties' agreement and other factors may trump the possibility of commencing (or continuing) arbitral proceedings without calling the arbitrators' jurisdiction into question. Instead, these would be matters of admissibility.

[B] Admissibility

Admissibility refers to the existence of constraints on the parties' right to file their claims.[48] Those constraints prevent the arbitrators from exercising their authority (jurisdiction) to hear and settle substantive disputes.[49] Admissibility issues, then, focus on the claims and not on the decision-maker or forum where the claims will be discussed. Typically, they question the enforceability of the claim and relate it to its nature or particularities.[50] Examples could include whether the claim has been affected by a statute of limitation. This happens where statutory time limits bar actions that seek (e.g.) compensation for damages, regardless of the forum (arbitration or litigation).[51] Claims may also be affected by a contractual time limitation. For example, where the parties' agreement provides that in case of a dispute, the same must be brought to arbitration not later than [e.g., thirty days or any other period] or not before the expiry of a period of time from the moment the dispute arose.[52]

47. *BBA and others v. BAZ and others*, [2020] 2 SLR 453, Singapore Court of Appeal, 28 May 2020, para. 78: '... arguments as to the existence, scope and validity of the arbitration agreement are invariably regarded as jurisdictional, as are questions of the claimant's standing to bring a claim or the possibility of binding non-signatory respondents'. Also, *see, e.g., MS 'Emja' Braack Schiffahrts KG, v. Wärtsilä Diesel Aktiebolag*, Case No. Ö 3175/95, Supreme Court of Sweden, 15 October 1997, where the Swedish Supreme Court found that a party that succeeds both the rights and obligations of another in a contract cannot be permitted to circumvent a related arbitration clause.
48. Park, *The Arbitrator's Jurisdiction* (*supra* n. 21) p. 74.
49. *Ibid.*; Michael Hwang et al., 'The Chimera of Admissibility in International Arbitration', in *Jurisdiction, Admissibility and Choice of Law in International Arbitration: Liber Amicorum Michael Pryles*, ed. Neil Kaplan and Michael Moser (Kluwer Law International 2016), pp. 287-288: '[a] decision on admissibility is nothing more than a decision on the procedure of the arbitration undertaken by the tribunal in the exercise of its discretion'.
50. *BBA v. BAZ*, [2020] 2 SLR 453 para. 79: '[A]dmissibility ...asks whether a tribunal may decline to render a decision on the merits for reasons other than a lack of jurisdiction ....'
51. CIArb, 'Jurisdictional Challenges', in *International Arbitration Practice Guideline* (Chartered Institute of Arbitrators, 2015), para. 6 of the Preamble and Art. 3.
52. *See, e.g., Grandeur Electrical Co. Ltd v. Cheung Kee Fund Cheung Construction Co. Ltd*, [2006] HKCA 305, Hong Kong Court of Appeal, 25 July 2006 p. 27 ('Notwithstanding the expiry of the [contractual] time limit, the arbitration agreement remains operative, as it remains possible for the Plaintiff to proceed to arbitration, and to apply to the arbitrator for an extension of time within which to refer the matter to arbitration.'). The Swiss Federal Supreme Court drew the opposite conclusion in DFT 4P.284/1994, reported in 14 ASA Bulletin 673 (1996).

Other admissibility issues include whether the claimant waives its right to arbitrate the dispute, involves determinations of res judicata issues,[53] or whether the claim is 'ripe' (or stale) for arbitral decision. The latter is usually discussed where a party fails to satisfy contractual pre-arbitration requirements. As anticipated in the introduction of this chapter, that happens when the parties stipulate a sequence of amicable or cooperative (rather than confrontational) methods of dispute resolution[54] before commencing arbitration. For example, parties commonly agree to a cooling-off period in their dispute resolution clauses. When a dispute arises, they should negotiate to amicably settle it during that period before submitting it to the arbitrators' decision. Similarly, dispute resolution clauses may require the parties to submit their controversies to mediation or conciliation prior to arbitration.

The English High Court decision in *PAO v. Ukraine* illustrates the conceptual distinction between 'admissibility' and 'jurisdiction' issues. In that decision, Justice Butcher explained that jurisdictional disputes are concerned with the *existence* or not of adjudicative power and its limits. Conversely, admissibility challenges deal with the *exercise* of that adjudicative power:

> Issues of jurisdiction go to the existence or otherwise of a tribunal's power to adjudge the merits of a dispute; issues of admissibility go to whether the tribunal will exercise that power in relation to the claims submitted to it.[55]

A successful jurisdictional objection interrupts the proceedings because it deprives the arbitrators of the authority to decide on the admissibility and merits of the claim. Meanwhile, a successful objection to the admissibility of a claim requires the tribunal to dismiss the claim (or perhaps stay or postpone the proceedings) because it affects the arbitrators' opportunity and timing to decide the dispute, not its investiture.[56]

Thus, the distinction between jurisdictional and non-jurisdictional questions is not solely a matter of optics. Identifying on which side of the conundrum the issue falls is possible and significant.

53. *See, e.g., BTN and others v. BTP and others,* [2020] SGCA 105, Singapore Court of Appeals, 20 October 2020, paras 64, 71: '... the doctrine of *res judicata* falls within the concept of admissibility of claim: it takes aim at the claim, and not at the defect of the improper forum'. *See also,* Gretta L. Walters, *Fitting a Square Peg into a Round Hole: Do Res Judicata Challenges in International Arbitration Constitute Jurisdictional or Admissibility Problems?,* 29(6) *Journal of International Arbitration* (2012), p. 675 DOI: 10.54648/joia2012041, where the author concludes that, 'neither logical, practical, nor policy reasons can justify treating res judicata objections as issues that affect the jurisdiction of an arbitral tribunal'.
54. Klaus Peter Berger, *Law and Practice of Escalation Clauses,* 22(1) *Arbitration International* (2006), p. 2 DOI: 10.1093/arbitration/22.1.1.
55. *PAO Tatneft v. Ukraine,* [2018] EWHC 1797 (Comm), England and Wales High Court (Commercial Court) Decisions, 13 July 2018 para. 97. Similarly, *see, Republic of Sierra Leone v. SL Mining Ltd,* [2021] EWHC 286 (Comm), England and Wales High Court (Commercial Court) Decisions, 15 February 2021, para. 18.
56. James Crawford, *Brownlie's Principles of Public International Law,* 9th ed. (Oxford University Press, 2019), p. 667.

[C] The Jurisdiction-Admissibility Distinction Matters

The immediate effect of a decision on inadmissibility (of claims) and one on lack of jurisdiction (of a tribunal) is similar. In both cases, the arbitration cannot continue. Yet, the correct conceptualisation of an issue as jurisdictional (or not) matters in terms of the allocation of competence to decide the issue. Before the arbitrators have decided on them, a court seized of action covered by an arbitration agreement could hear and answer jurisdictional questions.[57] But, it should not assess and settle objections related to the admissibility of the claims. Arbitrators should decide those matters, with a final and binding effect on the parties.

The correct conceptualisation of an issue as jurisdictional (or not) also matters regarding the standard of court review after arbitrators have preliminarily decided on that issue.[58] Generally, jurisdictional decisions are reviewable, while admissibility decisions are not. Arbitral decisions assuming jurisdiction may be extensively reviewed and invalidated by a competent court.[59] Conversely, arbitral findings on the admissibility of a claim are considered substantive matters and, therefore, not reviewable.[60]

Admittedly, some courts may conceptualise a legal point as procedural and others as substantive in character.[61] Consider, for example, the situation where a party in court proceedings raises a statutory time-bar defence to resist the referral to arbitration. The court may generally approach controversies involving statutes of limitations as substantive matters and, thus, governed by the law applicable to the merits.[62] But courts in a different jurisdiction might treat statute of limitations questions as procedural matters,[63] governed by the law of the forum.[64]

---

57. Articles 8(1) of the Model Law and II(3) of the New York Convention. The controversies lie on the extent (prima facie or full) of the court's determination of the jurisdictional dispute.
58. Bermann, *The Role of National Courts* (*supra* n. 3) pp. 450-451.
59. *See*, Arts 16(3) and 34(2)(a)(i) of the Model Law.
60. Park, *The Arbitrator's Jurisdiction* (*supra* n. 21) pp. 81-83. *See also*, Jan Paulsson, 'Jurisdiction and Admissibility', in *Global Reflections on International Law, Commerce and Dispute Resolution: Liber Amicorum in Honour of Robert Briner*, ed. Gerald Aksen and Robert Briner (ICC Publishing, 2005), p. 601.
61. *See, e.g.*, Saar A. Pauker, Substance and Procedure in International Arbitration, 36(1) *Arbitration International* (2020), pp. 8-12 DOI: 10.1093/arbint/aiaa005.
62. CIArb, 'Jurisdictional Challenges', para. 6 of the Preamble and Art. 3.
63. Gary B. Born, *International Commercial Arbitration*, 3rd ed., vol. 2 (Kluwer Law International, 2021), '[i]n some (particularly U.S.) jurisdictions, statutes of limitations have been regarded as "procedural" ... . In contrast, civil law states generally regard statutes of limitations as "substantive"', (at §19.03[G][2]). *See, e.g.*, the decision in *Chain Sales MKTG., INC. v. Roach*, NY Slip Op 51946, Supreme Court, Suffolk County (US), 10 December 2019, where the court held that determining if a claim is time-barred is a threshold issue that the court must decide, whilst whether a demand for arbitration was properly served is for an arbitrator to decide. Similarly, the decisions of the Indian Supreme Court in *Noharlal Verma v. Disst. Coop.Central Bank Limited*, (2008) 14 SCC (para. 27) and *Kamlesh Babu v. Lajpat Rai Sharma*, (2008) 12 SCC 577.
64. This is not necessarily the case for arbitral tribunals; Pauker, *Substance and Procedure*, (*supra* n. 61) p. 6 ('[i]n international arbitration, characterizing a legal issue or question (...) as procedural rather than as substantive, does not necessarily mean the lex arbitri (...) will apply to that question or issue'.). In this sense, *see, e.g.*, *Rual Trade Limited v. Roman Romanov, Vladimir Romanov and Ukio Banko Investicine Grupe UAB*, Swedish Court of Appeal, 24 February 2012.

This then triggers an antecedent choice-of-law enquiry. It requires the court to identify the law applicable to the given dispute, ascertain its content, and apply it to the facts of the case. There could be uncertainties on whether the law governing the merits refers to substantive matters only or procedural too (e.g., statute of limitations).[65] Therefore, whether an issue is characterised as procedural or substantive is relevant as it will impact on *who* should decide them (exclusively or concurrently) and the extent, if at all, of judicial scrutiny. This resonates with Bermann's distinction between 'gateway' and 'non-gateway' issues, according to which the former may be addressed by either a court or an arbitral tribunal, whichever is asked first, but non-gateway issues are uniquely for the arbitrators to decide in the first instance.[66]

The words of the arbitral tribunal in *Abaclat v. Argentine* illustrate the need to characterise these controversies properly. In its Decision on Jurisdiction and Admissibility, the arbitrators explained that:

> Although a lack of jurisdiction or admissibility may both lead to the same result of a tribunal having to refuse to hear the case, such refusal is of a fundamentally different nature and therefore carries different consequences:
>
> (i) While a lack of jurisdiction *stricto sensu* means that the claim cannot at all be brought in front of the body called upon, a lack of admissibility means that the claim was neither fit nor mature for judicial treatment.
> (ii) While a decision refusing a case based on a lack of arbitral jurisdiction is usually subject to review by another body, a decision refusing a case based on a lack of admissibility can usually not be subject to review by another body.
> (iii) Whereby a final refusal based on a lack of jurisdiction will prevent the parties from successfully re-submitting the same claim to the same body, a refusal based on admissibility will in principle not prevent the claimant from re-submitting its claim, provided it cures the previous flaw causing the inadmissibility.[67]

The explanations of the nature and effects of jurisdictional/admissibility matters in the context of investment and commercial arbitration are conceptually similar. For this reason, while the award in *Abaclat v. Argentine* was rendered in the context of an investment dispute, the passage quoted has been endorsed by arbitrators in commercial disputes.[68]

But the distinction between jurisdictional and admissibility issues is not always as clear as day and night; the distinctiveness blurs in the twilight zone.[69] Yet, as

65. *See, e.g.*, Jeffrey Waincymer, *Procedure and Evidence in International Arbitration* (Kluwer Law International, 2012), p. 989 ('The general presumption is that a choice of law deals with substantive and not procedural matters. Nevertheless, problems of classification will at times give rise to uncertainty ... where different legal families have different views on characterisation.').
66. Bermann, *The 'Gateway' Problem* (*supra* n. 1) p. 8.
67. *Abaclat and others (Case formerly known as Giovanna A Beccara and Others) (Claimants) and The Argentine Republic (Respondent), Decision on Jurisdiction and Admissibility,* ICSID Case No. ARB/07/5, 4 August 2011, para. 247.
68. *See, e.g., Final Award in ICC Case 19581*, August 2014.
69. I borrow the 'twilight zone' metaphor from the award in *Methanex Corporation v. the United States of America,* Partial Award (Preliminary Award on Jurisdiction and Admissibility),

Paulsson put it, '...only a fool would argue that the existence of a twilight zone is proof that day and night do not exist'.[70]

[D] The Twilight Zone Between Jurisdiction and Admissibility

A question that frequently lands in the twilight zone between admissibility and jurisdiction is the failure to comply with pre-arbitration requirements in a multi-tiered (or escalation) dispute resolution clause.[71] As mentioned above, if the pre-arbitration step is understood as jurisdictional, the parties' agreement would be viewed as granting arbitrators adjudicatory authority only after it has been complied with.[72] It would constitute a condition precedent to the parties' consent to arbitrate.[73] Thus, the precondition would amount to 'an element of "acceptance" of the agreement to arbitrate, such that the offer cannot be accepted until that condition is fulfilled'.[74]

If, instead, the failure to comply with the pre-arbitration requirements is understood as an admissibility matter, the parties may only assert substantive disputes after the conditions have been satisfied. However, the authority of the arbitrators is not contested. The United States Supreme Court decision in the *BG v. Argentina*[75] arbitration is an opposite example. It addressed the jurisdictional/non-jurisdictional debate related to pre-arbitration requirements. The Supreme Court dealt with this issue by answering the question: who - court or arbitrator - bears primary responsibility for interpreting and applying the local litigation requirement to an underlying controversy?

A substantive dispute had arisen under the Bilateral Investment Treaty (BIT) between Argentina and the United States, and it was decided in arbitration under the UNCITRAL Rules in Washington DC.[76] Though this was an investor-State arbitration, its analytical value applies to commercial arbitrations too. In part, because the Supreme Court stated that '[a]s a general matter, a treaty is a contract, though between

UNCITRAL, 7 August 2002 para. 139, where the tribunal used it to acknowledge that 'it is perhaps not easy to define the exact dividing line [between jurisdiction and admissibility], just as it is not easy in twilight to see the divide between night and day.'

70. Paulsson, *Jurisdiction* (*supra* n. 60) p. 601.
71. In Sweden, e.g., authors have concluded that '[i]t is uncertain under Swedish law what the consequences are of commencing an arbitration in disregard of any previous tiers'; Anders Relden et al., 'The Arbitration Agreement', in *International Arbitration in Sweden: A Practitioner's Guide*, ed. Annette Magnusson et al. (Kluwer Law International, 2021), p. 101.
72. For example, if the contract provides that 'no arbitration shall take place unless X'.
73. Conversely, in *BG Group v. Argentina*, the US Supreme Court understood that even if characterised as a condition precedent, a pre-arbitration requirement should be treated as a procedural one, the breach of which does not have jurisdictional consequences. *BG Group Plc v. the Republic of Argentina*, 572 U.S. 25 (2014), 134 S.Ct. 1198, Supreme Court of the United States, 5 March 2014, pp. 1207, 1209.
74. Bermann, *The Role of National Courts* (*supra* n. 3) p. 451.
75. *BG Group Plc v. the Republic of Argentina*, 572 U.S. 25 (2014), 134 S.Ct. 1198.
76. Since the seat of the arbitration was Washington DC, the *lex arbitri* was the Federal Arbitration Act, which is not based on the UNCITRAL Model Law.

nations. Its interpretation normally is, like a contract's interpretation, a matter of determining the parties' intent.'[77]

The decision of the Supreme Court highlights two crucial points for the characterisation quest. One is the essential role of the parties' intention at the time of the conclusion of the arbitration agreement. The other is the Court's conclusion that pre-arbitration procedural conditions are (generally) non-jurisdictional requirements. They fall within the power of arbitrators to decide, subject to deferential curial review, if any.[78]

Invoking Article 8 of the BIT, BG Group commenced arbitration against Argentina. Whilst denying the substantive claims, Argentina disputed the tribunal's jurisdiction and the admissibility of the claims. Amongst other grounds, Argentina argued that BG Group initiated arbitration without first litigating its claims in Argentina's courts, as the arbitration agreement required. The agreement provided that recourse to arbitration was possible after the parties had litigated the matter for eighteen months at the investment's host State courts (i.e., Argentina), (i) without receiving a final decision, or (ii) where the parties were still in dispute even after the court decision.[79]

In finding that the claims were admissible, the arbitral tribunal concluded that BG had an obligation to litigate in Argentina before bringing its claims to arbitration. However, the State's conduct had waived, or excused, BG Group's failure to comply with the local litigation requirement. The tribunal found that Argentina's legislation had 'hindered' recourse 'to the domestic judiciary'.[80] Therefore, it would have been absurd and unreasonable for BG Group to have complied with the pre-arbitration requirement.[81]

Argentina challenged the award before the US courts. Although the District Court confirmed the award, the Court of Appeals vacated it. It treated the matter as a jurisdictional one and, thus, it reviewed de novo the existence of arbitral authority. The Court of Appeals emphasised that it was bound to identify and enforce the parties'

---

77. *BG Group Plc v. the Republic of Argentina*, 572 U.S. 25 (2014), 134 S.Ct. 1198, p. 1208. This is not a new doctrine. The US Supreme Court's jurisprudence has long predicated that treaty interpretation differs from statutory interpretation because treaties are contracts, not acts of legislation. *See*, in general, Curtis J. Mahoney, Treaties as Contracts: Textualism, Contract Theory, and the Interpretation of Treaties, 116 *Yale Law Journal* (2007) DOI: 10.2307/20455741. For a comprehensive description of the evolution of treaty interpretation in the U.S., *see*, Evan Criddle, The Vienna Convention on the Law of Treaties in US Treaty Interpretation, 44 *Vanderbilt Journal of International Law* (2003).
78. The Supreme Court found support for this approach in earlier decisions, in which it had held, for example, that '... "procedural" questions which grow out of the dispute and bear on its final disposition" are presumptively not for the judge, but for an arbitrator, to decide'. *Howsam v. Dean Witter Reynolds, Inc*, 537 U.S. 79 (2002), Supreme Court of the United States, 10 December 2002, p. 84.
79. Article 8(1)(2) of the Argentina-UK BIT.
80. In response to a financial crisis, Argentina passed emergency measures and stayed all court proceedings that challenged them, including the ones that BG Group alleged had affected its rights under the relevant BIT.
81. *BG Group Plc. v. the Republic of Argentina*, UNCITRAL, Final Award, UNCITRAL, 24 December 2007, paras 146-147. On the merits, the arbitral tribunal awarded BG Group over USD 185 million in compensation for Argentina's breaches of its treaty obligations. *Ibid.*, para. 467(464).

intent, and, in doing so, it noted that the parties had desired, and the arbitration agreement *explicitly* required, judicial proceedings prior to arbitration.[82]

The Court also noted that BG Group had not disputed its ability to commence a lawsuit in Argentina. Instead, it had argued that the requirement was meaningless as no court could ever decide such complex disputes in eighteen months.[83] Therefore, the appellate court found that BG Group was not excused from complying with the pre-arbitration requirement. Given the failure to abide by the pre-arbitration jurisdictional[84] requirement, the arbitral tribunal lacked the authority to decide the substantive dispute. Further, it reiterated that the parties' intention controls whether a court or an arbitrator should answer the jurisdictional question.[85] It also recalled that the default position was that the authority to answer those questions rested on the court unless there was 'clear and unmistakable' evidence that the parties had agreed otherwise.[86] Consequently, the Court of Appeals found that it was a matter for courts to decide de novo (without deference to the arbitrator's decision).

Subsequently, the Supreme Court granted BG Group's petition for *certiorari*, disagreed with the Court of Appeals, and reversed its decision. It characterised the litigation requirement as a purely procedural condition precedent to arbitration rather than a precondition on the parties' consent to arbitrate.[87] In the Supreme Court's view, the litigation requirement 'determines *when* the contractual duty to arbitrate arises, not *whether* there is a contractual duty to arbitrate at all.'[88] Hence, to the question 'who -court or arbitrator - bears primary responsibility for interpreting and applying the local litigation requirement to an underlying controversy?', the Supreme Court answered that the matter was for the arbitrators to decide, and courts must review their decisions with deference.

The *Sierra Leone v. SL Mining*[89] case before an English court also dealt with the nature of pre-arbitration requirements in a commercial setting. The dispute resolution clause between the parties provided for a three-month cooling-off period. Failure to amicably settle disputes within that period entitled the parties to submit the dispute to an ICC tribunal.

The case reached the English High Court as a recourse against the arbitral award. The arbitrators had found that they enjoyed jurisdiction and that the claims were admissible despite the claimant 'prematurely' resorting to arbitration. In declining to

82. *The Republic of Argentina v. BG Group Plc*, 665 F.3d 1363, Court of Appeals, Dist. of Columbia Circuit, pp. 1372-1373. The court also noted that the BIT provided 'a prime example of a situation where the "parties would likely have expected a court" to decide the jurisdictional issue.'
83. *See BG Group v. Argentina*, UNCITRAL, Final Award, para. 142.
84. Different from *procedural* requirements concerning the arbitral process itself, and, therefore, reviewable de novo.
85. *The Republic of Argentina v. BG Group Plc*, 665 F.3d 1363, p. 1369.
86. The US Supreme Court case law established this rule; *see, e.g., AT&T Technologies, Inc. v. Communications Workers*, 475 U.S. 643 and *First Options of Chicago, Inc. v. Kaplan*, 514 U.S. 938.
87. *BG Group Plc v. the Republic of Argentina*, 572 U.S. 25 (2014), 134 S.Ct. 1198, pp. 1207, 1209.
88. '[A] claims-processing rule that governs when the arbitration may begin, but not whether it may occur (...).' *Ibid.*, p. 1207.
89. *Republic of Sierra Leone v. SL Mining Ltd*, [2021] EWHC 286 (Comm).

set aside the award, the court explained that where the question relates to whether a claim could be brought to arbitration (i.e., whether arbitration is the proper forum), the issue is typically one of jurisdiction and is subject to judicial review. However, if the point relates to whether a claim should not yet (or at all) be heard by the arbitrators, the issue is typically one of admissibility, and the tribunal decision is final.[90]

An earlier English decision had treated an agreed (four-week) negotiation period as a jurisdictional matter. That is, as a condition precedent to be satisfied before the arbitrators would have *legal authority* (jurisdiction) to hear and determine the dispute.[91]

In Switzerland, compliance with a mandatory mediation agreement appears to qualify as an issue of jurisdiction (*ratione temporis*), in the understanding that jurisdiction is transferred from state courts to arbitration only once such mediation has been conducted.[92] This exemplifies how thorny and unsettled characterisation might be, even within a legal system.

Similarly, the Singapore Court of Appeals understood a contractual pre-arbitration requirement as a jurisdictional matter. It concluded that the required steps 'were conditions precedent to any reference to arbitration' and stressed that the arbitration agreement itself referred to 'disputes...which cannot be settled by mediation...'.[93] In the Court's view, the arbitration agreement could not be invoked because its conditions precedent had not been fulfilled. Therefore, the Court held that the arbitrators had wrongly assumed jurisdiction.[94] Similar circumstances arose a few years later in *Swissbourgh v. Lesotho,* but Menon CJ took the opposite approach. He clarified that the failure to exhaust local remedies was a matter that went towards the *admissibility* of the claim, not the tribunal's jurisdiction.[95]

Interestingly, in *X. Ltd v. Y. S.p.A,* the Swiss Federal Supreme Court eschewed the characterisation debate altogether and opted for a pragmatic solution when deciding the consequence of a party's failure to comply with a mandatory pre-arbitration conciliation. Although the Court set aside the arbitrators' award that had assumed jurisdiction, it stayed the arbitral proceedings. It also kept the same arbitral panel in

90. *Ibid.*, para. 18.
91. *Emirates Trading Agency Llc v. Prime Mineral Exports Private Ltd,* [2014] EWHC 2104 (Comm), England and Wales High Court (Commercial Court) Decisions, 1 July 2014, para. 73. However, it is fair to mention that the court did not engage in a conceptual debate to distinguish jurisdictional and non-jurisdictional issues. Perhaps that discussion was unnecessary for the judge concluded that '[t]he arbitrators have jurisdiction to decide the dispute (...) because the condition precedent to arbitration (...) was satisfied.'
92. *See* Marco Stacher, Jurisdiction and Admissibility under Swiss Arbitration Law–the Relevance of the Distinction and a New Hope, 38(1) *ASA Bulletin* (2020), pp. 55, 59 (commenting on the decision of the Swiss Federal Supreme Court in DFT 142 III 296). The Court adopted the same characterisation (jurisdiction, rather than admissibility) with respect to time limits to initiate arbitration -DFT 4P.284/1994 DOI: 10.54648/asab2020005.
93. *International Research Corp PLC v. Lufthansa Systems Asia Pacific Pte Ltd and another,* [2013] SGCA 55, [2013] 1 SLR 973, Singapore Court of Appeal, 18 October 2013, para. 54.
94. *Ibid.*, para. 63.
95. *Swissbourgh Diamond Mines (Pty) Ltd v. the Kingdom of Lesotho,* [2018] SGCA 81, para. 206.

place until the required conciliation process was conducted. Lastly, the Court left it for the arbitrators to determine the timeframe for the arbitration to resume.[96]

Arbitral tribunals have also wrestled with this characterisation issue. The *ICC* Cases 16083[97] and 16262[98] are illustrative. In the former, the respondent had argued that the claimant's failure to comply with *amicable negotiations* and submit its claims to a Dispute Adjudication Board before commencing arbitration affected the arbitrators' jurisdiction rather than the admissibility of the claims. But the arbitral tribunal disagreed with the respondent's characterisation. It found no evidence that the parties' consent to arbitration was contingent on compliance with the various agreed pre-arbitral procedures'.[99] Nor that the parties would have preferred to submit their disputes to state courts if one party failed to comply with the pre-arbitration requirements. The tribunal concluded that the contractual preconditions, if applicable, were not a condition precedent to jurisdiction but a condition precedent to the admissibility of the claims.

In *ICC* Case 16262, the tribunal limited its analysis to the way the parties had characterised and argued the issue. It noted that the contract provided for all disputes to be first referred to a Dispute Adjudication Board and found that the reference to such a Board was a 'condition precedent to arbitration'. Since that condition had not been satisfied, the arbitral tribunal found that it lacked *jurisdiction*. In its decision, the tribunal explicitly indicated that the respondents had not pursued a separate argument that, if the tribunal had jurisdiction, the claimant's claim was nevertheless inadmissible.[100]

These examples are representative of the recurring characterisation debate regarding jurisdictional and non-jurisdictional disputes. Case law also evidences that characterising an issue as jurisdictional or otherwise is not a box-ticking exercise. It depends on the agreement of the parties in each case.[101]

[E] The Distinguishing Factor Between Jurisdictional and Admissibility Issues

This chapter does not claim to hold the key to an across-the-board distinction between jurisdictional and admissibility issues. However, it does cast light on some pivotal

96. *X.__ Ltd v. Y.__ S.p.A*, 4A_628/2015, Switzerland Federal Supreme Court, 16 March 2016.
97. *Interim Award in ICC Case 16083*, July 2010.
98. *Partial Award in ICC Case 16262*, May 2010. For an analysis on the 'jurisdiction or admissibility' approaches taken by arbitrators in construction disputes, *see*, José Ricardo Feris et al., Jurisdictional Issues in Construction Arbitration, *ICC Dispute Resolution Bulletin 2017*, no. 4 (2017).
99. *ICC Case 16083*, para. 65(b).
100. *ICC Case 16262*. For an analysis on the 'jurisdiction or admissibility' approaches taken by arbitrators in construction disputes, *see*, Feris et al., *Jurisdictional Issues* (*supra* n. 98).
101. In Rau's view, '... everything always reduces itself ultimately to "agreement" – and since the allocation of power responds to the choice of the appropriate default rule, it is hard to see the objection to allowing the parties to vary the assumed baseline presumption by contract.' Alan Scott Rau et al., BG Group and Conditions to Arbitral Jurisdiction, 43 *Pepperdine Law Review* (2015), p. 128.

factors. Admittedly, resolving jurisdictional challenges involves an interpretative examination of the parties' intentions and the wording of their contract.[102] Therefore, identifying and determining the parties' intentions serve as 'the touchstone and the lodestar'[103] in the characterisation quest.

In interpreting the parties' intention, the decision-maker can presume that the parties viewed the pre-arbitration conditions as procedural steps in their agreed dispute resolution process.[104] Consequently, it is natural that those steps are placed on the admissibility (not jurisdictional) side of the dividing line[105] and that arbitrators (not judges) are empowered to interpret the pre-arbitration requirements.[106] Dispelling the parties' presumptive intention would require clear reasons and evidence that the procedural steps were conditions precedent to consent to arbitrate. In that situation, courts would also be entitled to review and interpret the requirements.

The lodestar may take the form of a question and enquiry whether the objecting party aims at the arbitrators or the claim. Paulsson, for example, approaches that question with a result-driven test based on the reason behind a (potentially) successful challenge. If the outcome of the challenge translates into the impossibility of bringing the claim to the forum seized, then the dispute could be characterised as a jurisdictional one.[107] The dispute hinges on the 'investiture of the arbitral tribunal as such'.[108] Where, instead, the reason for the successful challenge is that the claim should not (yet or at all) be heard, then the dispute could be characterised as one on admissibility.[109]

With different words but similar content, the Singapore Court of Appeal talks about a 'tribunal versus claim' test to distinguish whether an issue focuses on jurisdiction or admissibility:

> [T]he 'tribunal versus claim' test underpinned by a consent-based analysis should apply for purposes of distinguishing whether an issue goes towards jurisdiction or admissibility. The 'tribunal versus claim' test asks whether the objection is targeted at the tribunal (in the sense that the claim should not be arbitrated due to a defect in or omission to consent to arbitration), or at the claim (in that the claim itself is defective and should not be raised at all).[110]

---

102. Born, *International Commercial Arbitration* (*supra* n. 22) pp. 999-1000.
103. Park, *The Arbitrator's Jurisdiction* (*supra* n. 21) p. 80.
104. *C v. D*, [2022] HKCA 729, Hong Kong Court of Appeal, 7 June 2022, para. 57.
105. This is the approach that Born and others prefer. *See*, Born, *International Commercial Arbitration* (*supra* n. 22) p. 1000. Also, Alex Mills, *Party Autonomy in Private International Law* (Cambridge University Press, 2018), pp. 282-283.
106. Born, *International Commercial Arbitration* (*supra* n. 22) p. 1001. *BG Group Plc v. the Republic of Argentina*, 572 U.S. 25 (2014), 134 S.Ct. 1198, p. 1212: '... evidence that shows the parties had an intent contrary to our ordinary presumptions about who should decide threshold issues related to arbitration.'
107. Paulsson, *Jurisdiction* (*supra* n. 60) pp. 614-616. Hwang and Lim put it in similar terms: 'the ... question which the tribunal [or a court] should be asking itself is whether or not the objection, if factually proven, would impinge upon the consent of the objecting party to the arbitration, so as to amount to a jurisdictional objection.' Hwang et al., *The Chimera of Admissibility in International Arbitration* (*supra* n. 49) pp. 287-288.
108. Paulsson, *Jurisdiction* (*supra* n. 60) p. 617.
109. *Ibid.*
110. *BBA v. BAZ*, [2020] 2 SLR 453, paras 76-77.

More recently, the Hong Kong Court of Appeal confirmed the 'tribunal versus claims' test, cementing the (generally accepted) understanding that the pre-arbitration requirements in 'escalation clauses' involve issues of admissibility of the claim(s) rather than arbitral jurisdiction.[111]

If we were to set a timeline or rule of priority for the intention-finding exercise, the admissibility-related enquiry would generally take place after the tribunal's jurisdiction has been established.[112] It is by a positive finding of jurisdiction[113] that arbitrators can assess the parties' substantive arguments on the admissibility of the claims. That includes whether a condition precedent to arbitration exists and whether it was fulfilled.[114]

§11.05 CONCLUSION

The correct characterisation of jurisdictional and admissibility disputes is crucial. It determines the preliminary allocation of decision-maker powers and the post-decision extent of court review.

As an attribute of arbitral tribunals, jurisdiction is synonymous with the legal authority to settle substantive disputes. Jurisdictional disputes, therefore, revolve around the existence, validity, and scope of that authority. Issues of admissibility, for their part, question the opportunity for a tribunal to exercise its (existent) authority.

Ingenious lawyering (or ignorance rather than design) may blur the distinction between an issue of jurisdiction and admissibility. Given the contractual nature of arbitration, the touchstone and the lodestar rest on the parties' intention. After all, party agreement is the doorway to arbitration. Their consent is foundational, as it creates an authority that did not exist: the arbitrators' authority to hear and settle the parties' substantive disputes. It is also dimensional because it shapes the jurisdictional contours. To delimit the extent of power, it first needs to exist.

It is no surprise then that the decisive task in the characterisation exercise is to establish whether the parties intended to arbitrate their substantive disputes, and the intended nature of their pre-arbitration agreements.

111. *C v. D*, [2022] HKCA 729, 7 June 2022.
112. Yas Banaiftemi, The Impact of Corruption on 'Gateway Issues' of Arbitrability, Jurisdiction, Admissibility and Procedural Issues, 13 *D. Baizeau, RH Kreindler, Addressing Issues of Corruption in Commercial and Investment Arbitration: Dossiers of the ICC Institute of World Business Law* (2015) para. 17: 'Admissibility is ... decided after a tribunal has affirmed its jurisdiction, whereas objections to jurisdiction strike at the logically prior ability of a tribunal to give rulings as to the admissibility or merits of a claim.'
113. Admittedly, arbitrators render jurisdictional decisions only (as a rule) where a party challenges them. Therefore, a decision on admissibility of a claim(s) does not always require a decision on jurisdiction.
114. CIArb, 'Jurisdictional Challenges', Art. 3. Paulsson, *Jurisdiction* (*supra* n. 60) pp. 607-608.

CHAPTER 12

The (Swedish) Doctrine of Assertion: And the Scope of the Arbitration Agreement

Monica Seifert

§12.01 INTRODUCTION

The scope of the arbitration agreement is central to the arbitral jurisdiction. It concerns the issue of the subject matter ambit (*ratione materiae*) of a binding arbitration agreement. The scope of the arbitration agreement is considered a question of interpretation that is to be determined according to the civil law rules and principles on contract interpretation.[1] In that sense, the arbitration agreement is an expression of the common intention of the parties to submit to arbitration instead of litigation; it is an exercise of party autonomy, by means of which the parties waive the right of access to court. Another significant factor concerns the identity of the matter in dispute. Arbitral jurisdiction requires that the actual dispute constitutes a type of dispute covered by the scope. This implies that it is necessary to establish what the matter in dispute concerns. Under Swedish law, the civil procedural law principle denoted '*påståendedoktrinen*' (the doctrine of assertion) is considered applicable when identifying the matter in dispute significant to the competence of the arbitral tribunal.[2]

1. *See, e.g.*, NJA 2019 p. 171 (Belgor); Stefan Lindskog, *Skiljeförfarande, En kommentar* (3rd ed. Norstedts Juridik 2020), 119, 194; Finn Madsen, *Commercial Arbitration in Sweden* (5th ed. Jure Förlag 2020), 52; Thorsten Cars, *Lagen om skiljeförfarande, En kommentar* (2nd ed. Faktas Digitala Bibliotek 2000), 37.
2. Lars Heuman, *Skiljemannarätt* (Norstedts Juridik 1999), 76 et seq., and in *Vilken beviskravsbetydelse har separabilitetsprincipen, påståendedoktrinen och anknytningsdoktrinen för bedömningen av behörighetsfrågor inom skiljedomsrätten?*, JT 2009-10, 335, *Undantag från påståendedoktrinen och regeln att en skiljeklausul endast avser avtalet*, JT 2017-18, 899; Lindskog, *supra* n. 1, at 195 et seq.; Patrik Schöldström, *Påståendedoktrinen och skiljeförfarande*, JT 2008-09, 138, and in *Kärandens påstående som grund för domstols behörighet, Till minnet av Södra Roslags tingsrätt* (Jure, 2007), 172 et seq.; NJA 2008 p. 406 (Petrobart).

This chapter seeks to capture the implications of the doctrine of assertion in relation to the scope of the arbitration agreement. The question that arises is whether an application of the doctrine of assertion implies that the dispute is identified in a way which implements the scope of the arbitration agreement – and it comes to a head where the parties agree that there are various binding contracts between them, but disagree on which of the contracts the matter in dispute concerns. A further question is whether the rather recent case NJA 2019 p. 171[3] is of importance in this context. The chapter will also briefly look at how the arbitral jurisdiction factor concerning the identity of the matter in dispute is dealt with in the legal systems of Switzerland and England,[4] and finally, whether and how the question is governed by the UNCITRAL Model Law on International Commercial Arbitration[5] (the Model Law).

§12.02 THE ARBITRAL JURISDICTION FACTOR CONCERNING THE IDENTITY OF THE MATTER IN DISPUTE

The starting point should be that the procedural law rules and principles applicable when identifying the matter in dispute significant to arbitral jurisdiction contribute, as far as possible, to the realisation of the scope of the arbitration agreement. In other words, that the applicable procedural law rules and principles result in the matter being identified in a way which does not permit a compromise with the intention of the parties – as expressed in the arbitration agreement – as to the type of disputes that are to be submitted to arbitration.

In the context of identifying the matter in dispute significant to arbitral jurisdiction, the English scholar Joseph stated in 2005 that '[t]here is surprisingly little discussion of this in the English authorities'.[6] However, more recently, in *Mozambique v. Credit Suisse International,*[7] Lady Justice Carr DBE said:

> I also accept that there is a two-stage test (although the considerations that arise may overlap and it may be convenient to consider the questions together): first to identify the matter and secondly to decide if that matter is one that the parties have agreed can only be arbitrated.

3. Also referred to by the Supreme Court as Belgor, Högsta domstolen, *Döpta rättsfall från Högsta domstolen*, www.domstol.se (2022-08-04).
4. English law means the law in England and Wales.
5. UNCITRAL Model Law on International Commercial Arbitration 1985: with amendments as adopted in 2006, Official Records of the General Assembly, Fortieth Session, Supplement No. 17 (A/40/17), annex 1 and Sixty-first Session, Supplement No. 17 (A/61/17), Annex 1.
6. David Joseph, *Jurisdiction and Arbitration Agreements and their Enforcement* (2nd ed. Sweet & Maxwell 2005), 285.
7. *Mozambique v. Credit Suisse International* [2021] EWCA Civ 329. *See also Premier Cruises Ltd v. DLA Piper Rus Ltd and DLA Piper UK LLP* [2021] EWHC 151 (Comm); *Melford Capital Partners (Holdings) LLP and others v. Frederick John Wingfield Digby* [2021] EWHC 872 (Ch); *Sodawiczny v. Ruhan* [2018] EWHC 1908 [Comm].

In Sweden, the doctrine of assertion applicable when identifying the matter in dispute has been intensely discussed in legal doctrine over a long period of time and in recent decades also referred to in case law.[8]

[A] Identifying the Matter in Dispute Significant to Questions of Jurisdiction

When the arbitral tribunal, on the basis of section 2 paragraph 1 of the Swedish Arbitration Act,[9] containing the principle of the competence-competence, is deciding whether a particular dispute falls under the arbitration agreement, the actual dispute per se requires an analysis in order to identify the matter in dispute.[10] The arbitral tribunal has to determine whether the actual dispute constitutes such a type of dispute as the parties have agreed to submit to arbitration. Identifying the matter in dispute, significant to arbitral jurisdiction, implies establishing whether it concerns the contract containing the arbitration agreement or another contract/matter covered by the scope of the arbitration agreement. In this chapter, the contract containing the arbitration agreement will be referred to as the 'host contract' where applicable.

The above may be compared to situations where the courts are determining whether proceedings have been initiated in the correct forum. Also then, it is often necessary to identify what matter the dispute concerns.[11] Identifying the matter in dispute here implies determining whether the circumstances founding the jurisdiction of the court are at hand. What is decisive is whether the dispute concerns a matter

8. *See, e.g.*, Lars Welamson, *Anm av Bolding*: Skiljedom, SvJT 1964 pp. 278 et seq.; Heuman, *supra* n. 2, at 76 et seq., and in *Vilken beviskravsbetydelse har separabilitetsprincipen, påståendedoktrinen och anknytningsdoktrinen för bedömningen av behörighetsfrågor inom skiljedomsrätten?*, JT 2009-10, 335, *Bevisbördan för skiljeavtal och tolkningsresonemang som grund för skiljebundenhet*, JT 2011-12, 652 et seq, *supra* n. 2, JT 2017-18, 899 et seq.; Lindskog, *supra* n. 1, at 195 et seq.; Schöldström, *supra* n. 2, JT 2008-09, 138, *Till Minne av Södra Roslags tingsrätt*, 172 et seq., and in *Skiljeklausuler och utomobligatoriska anspråk*, JT 2017-18, 719 et seq.; Finn Madsen, *Påståendedoktrin eller anknytningsdoktrin, Efter vilka principer ska en domstol eller skiljenämnd ta ställning till verkan av en skiljeklausul i ljuset av nyare rättspraxis?*, SvJT 2013 pp. 734 et seq., and in *The Swedish 'Belgor' case and the scope and applicability of arbitral agreements*, Dispute resolution in business law, ACLU (Lund University 2020) 79 et seq.; NJA 2008 p. 406 (Petrobart); NJA 2012 p. 183 (Concorp); NJA 2017 p. 226 (*Avräkningsfallet).*
9. *Lag* (1999:116) *om skiljeförfarande.*
10. Section 2 of the Swedish Arbitration Act is worded:

> (para. 1) The arbitrators may rule on their own jurisdiction to decide the dispute.
>
> (para. 2) If the arbitrators have rendered a decision finding that they have jurisdiction to adjudicate the dispute, any party that disagrees with the decision may request the Court of Appeal to review the decision. Such a request shall be brought within thirty days from when the party was notified of the decision. The arbitrators may continue the arbitration pending the court's determination.
>
> (para. 3) The provisions of Sections 34 and 36 apply in an action to challenge an arbitration award that includes a decision on jurisdiction. (Translated in *The Swedish Arbitration Act (Lag (1999:116) om skiljeförfarande)*, Swedish Ministry of Justice, Ds 1999:22, revised and updated by Joel Dahlquist on behalf of the Arbitration Institute of the Stockholm Chamber of Commerce).

11. *See, e.g.*, Lennart Pålsson, *Dubbelrelevanta rättsfakta vid prövning av domstols behörighet*, SvJT 1999 pp. 316 et seq.

governed by the relevant rule of jurisdiction.[12] One example is the *forum solutionis contractus* rule in Article 7(1) of the Recast Brussels Regulation, according to which it is decisive whether the matter in dispute concerns a contract.[13] A further, and similar, example is the domestic *forum contractus* rule contained in Chapter 10 section 4 of the Swedish Code of Judicial Procedure.[14]

Identifying the matter in dispute significant to arbitral jurisdiction raises questions of fact and questions of law. The first question that arises is whether the contract in question exists. Significant in that respect is, in the main, whether facts ultimate to the formation of contracts are present.[15] The second question is whether the circumstances in dispute pertain to the contract. The first question consequently regards the consideration of the relevant facts. The second question involves a legal consideration of these facts.

As to litigation, the main rule is that a party shall prove the circumstances relevant to the jurisdiction of a court that is called upon.[16] For instance, where proceedings are initiated in accordance with the *forum contractus* rule contained in Chapter 10 section 4 of the Swedish Code of Judicial Procedure, the claimant would have to prove the facts relevant to the existence of the contract alleged as basis to the jurisdiction.[17] This implies that the claimant has to prove the facts relevant when identifying the matter in dispute significant to the jurisdiction.

Considering the main rule in court proceedings, the starting point should be that the claimant has the burden of proving that the arbitral tribunal is competent. This

---

12. *See, e.g.*, Pålsson, *ibid.*
13. *See* Alexander Layton, Hugh Mercer, *European Civil Practice*, Vol. I (2nd ed. Thomson/Sweet & Maxwell 2004), 410. Art. 7(1) of the Regulation (EU) No. 1215/2012 of the European Parliament and of the Council of 12 December 2012 on jurisdiction and the recognition and enforcement of judgments in civil and commercial matters, *OJ L 351, 20.12.2012, p. 1-32*, is worded:

    > A person domiciled in a Member State may be sued in another Member State:
    > (1) (a) in matters relating to a contract, in the courts for the place of performance of the obligation in question;
    > (b) for the purpose of this provision and unless otherwise agreed, the place of performance of the obligation in question shall be:
    > – in the case of the sale of goods, the place in a Member State where, under the contract, the goods were delivered or should have been delivered,
    > – in the case of the provision of services, the place in a Member State where, under the contract, the services were provided or should have been provided;
    > (c) if point (b) does not apply then point (a) applies[.]

14. *Rättegångsbalk* (1942:740). Chapter 10 section 4 of the Swedish Code of Judicial Procedure is worded:

    > A person with no known residence within the Realm who has entered into an obligation or otherwise incurred a debt in the Realm may be sued in a dispute concerning the same at the place where the obligation was created or the debt incurred.

    (Translated in *The Swedish Code of Judicial Procedure (Rättegångsbalk (1942:740))*, Swedish Ministry of Justice, Ds 1998:65, updated 2015-04-02, www.regeringen.se, 2022-02-14, 11.45)
15. *See, e.g.*, NJA 2005 p. 586.
16. *See* NJA 2005 p. 586; Pålsson, *supra* n. 10, at 315 et seq.
17. Pålsson, *ibid.*

would then mean that the claimant has the burden of proof as regards all facts ultimate to the competence of the arbitral tribunal. Both facts relevant to the identity of the matter in dispute and facts relevant to the arbitration agreement may be considered to constitute facts ultimate to the arbitral tribunal's competence. In legal doctrine, the arguments concerning the burden of proof in arbitration primarily involve the arbitration agreement. The burden of proof in this regard is considered to lie with the claimant.[18] Yet, the arguments outlined above suggest that the claimant has the burden of proving the facts relevant to the identity of the matter in dispute, in the same way as the facts relevant to the arbitration agreement.

[B] The Meaning of the Doctrine of Assertion

The doctrine of assertion is a civil procedural law principle applicable when the courts determine questions of procedural impediments. It means that such determinations are based on the claimant's assertion regarding the claimed (substantive) right. The claimant does not have to prove the facts that are asserted.[19] Thus, the doctrine of assertion concerns the assessment of facts relevant to questions of procedural impediments.[20] It also applies to questions of jurisdiction.[21] For instance, when determining the jurisdiction where an action for the fulfilment of a contract obligation is initiated, and the defendant contests that a contract has been concluded.[22] When the jurisdiction of the court is being determined, applying the doctrine means that the mere assertion of the facts constituting the cause of action of the claim in question is decisive.[23]

Yet, the doctrine of assertion also comprises legal issues.[24] This means that it applies to questions of law significant to court jurisdiction. In this respect, the relevant legal issues have different characteristics. Decisive in that respect is the applicable jurisdiction rule. Applying the doctrine of assertion to the relevant legal issues when identifying the matter in dispute significant to court jurisdiction implies that no legal examination is made but that a party's legal assertions are sufficient.

Central to the meaning of the doctrine of assertion is the *rationes* behind it. The reasons for the doctrine include various aspects, all of which emanate from the importance of separating questions of procedural requirements from questions of the

---

18. Bolding, p. 55; Lindskog, *supra* n. 1, at 99 footnote 356.
19. Lars Heuman, Peter Westberg, *Argumentationsformer inom processrätten* (2nd ed. Juristförlaget Stockholm 1995), 31; Per Olof Ekelöf, Henrik Edelstam, Lars Heuman, *Rättegång IV* (7th edn Norstedts Juridik 2009), 80.
20. Ekelöf/Edelstam/Heuman, *ibid.*
21. As to international jurisdiction: NJA 2005 p. 586; NJA 2009 p. 519; NJA 2012 p. 483; Pålsson, *supra* n. 10, at 315 et seq., 319 et seq. As to questions of internal jurisdiction; Pålsson, *supra* n. 10, at 319; Schöldström, *supra* n. 2, *Till Minnet av Södra Roslags tingsrätt*, 173, and JT 2008-09, 140.
22. *See* NJA 2005 p. 586.
23. *See, e.g.*, Pålsson, *supra* n. 10, at 316 et seq.; Schöldström, *supra* n. 2, JT 2008-09, 140.
24. *See, e.g.*, NJA 1973 p. 1 (I-III); NJA 1973 p. 527; NJA 1976 p. 422; NJA 2004 p. 743; Heuman, *supra* n. 7, JT 2009-10, 349 et seq., *supra* n. 2, JT 2017-18, 899 et seq.; Schöldström, *supra* n. 2, *Till Minne av Södra Roslags tingsrätt*, 172. *See also* the dissenting opinion of the Supreme Court Judge Asp in NJA 2017 p. 577 (*Fjällägenheten*).

merits of a dispute.[25] According to both the case law and legal doctrine, policy reasons and procedural economy objectives suggest avoiding the court having to consider the merits of a dispute in order to determine its competence.[26] A requirement that a party shall prove the facts that are relevant when identifying a matter in dispute significant to the jurisdiction may result in a complex procedure before the addressed court as to a matter which the court (or another forum) may have to decide on later when trying the merits of the dispute.[27] Such matters should only be examined once, namely when the court determines the merits of the dispute. The fact that the determination of the jurisdiction can normally be challenged adds a further ingredient to the complexity.[28] Moreover, it is argued that it should be avoided that the determination of the jurisdiction anticipates the examination of the merits.[29] Another, particularly underlined *rationale* is to enable the attaining of binding judgments on the merits with res iudicata effect and to avoid dismissals of cases without such effect.[30] The opposite is considered to imply a substantial disadvantage for the defendant.[31]

As follows from the *ratio* of the doctrine of assertion, the doctrine deals with situations involving doubly relevant ultimate facts.[32] Similarly, it applies to legal issues which are doubly relevant.[33] Legal doctrine defines doubly relevant ultimate facts as facts to which two legal consequences are connected: one procedural and one substantive.[34] Doubly relevant ultimate facts constitute a general phenomenon in procedural law. Such facts may occur in connection with most procedural requirements. Inherent in the double relevance, in the context of jurisdiction, is that the fact simultaneously constitutes a prerequisite both to the jurisdiction and to the substantive matter. This means that the facts simultaneously constitute facts ultimate to the legal consequence provided for in the relevant rule of jurisdiction and to the legal consequence provided for in the relevant substantive legal rule. The result is that doubly relevant ultimate facts simultaneously constitute both facts ultimate to the competence and ultimate facts.

25. Heuman/Westberg, *supra* n. 18, at 31. It is further argued that the doctrine of assertion provides a solution in line with the general tendency to limit the number of questions determined in proceedings for procedural impediments. Pålsson, *supra* n. 10, at 319; Per Henrik Lindblom, *Processhinder: om skillnaden mellan formell och materiell rätt i civilprocessen, särskilt vid bristande talerätt* (Norstedts Förlag 1974), 257, *Miljöprocess: om domstolarnas roll, forum, kumulation, intresseavvägning, officialprövning, taleformer, talerätt, åberopsrätt, bevisning, förenklad skadeståndsberäkning och rättskraft vid civilprocessuell domstolstalan i miljömål D 1* (Iustus Förlag 2001), 42.
26. Pålsson, *supra* n. 10, at 326; NJA 2005 p. 586.
27. NJA 2005 p. 586.
28. *Ibid.*
29. Heuman/Westberg, *supra* n. 18, at 31.
30. Pålsson, *supra* n. 10, at 326 et seq.
31. *Ibid.*
32. *See* Per Olof Ekelöf, *Rättegång II* (8th ed. Norstedts Juridik 1996), 18, 107; Pålsson, *supra* n. 10, at 329; Per Olof Ekelöf, Henrik Edelstam, Mikael Pauli, *Rättegång II* (9th ed. Norstedts Juridik 2015), 11; Ekelöf/Edelstam/Heuman, *supra* n. 18, at 80; Schöldström, *supra* n. 2, JT 2008-09, 140; NJA 2005 p. 586.
33. *See, e.g.*, NJA 1973 p. 1 (I-III); NJA 1973 p. 527; NJA 1976 p. 422; NJA 2004 p. 743.
34. *See, e.g.*, Heuman, *supra* n. 7, JT 2009-10, 336.

The phenomenon of doubly relevant ultimate facts may occur in situations where jurisdiction is based on a *forum contractus* rule. For instance, if the claimant initiates court proceedings and claims delivery of goods on the basis of a sale and purchase contract, the existence of the contract is relevant both to the merits of the dispute and to the question of jurisdiction. The existence of the contract determines whether the defendant is under an obligation to deliver the goods and whether the claimant has initiated proceedings in the correct forum.[35]

A conceivable consequence of applying the doctrine of assertion may be that when a court examines the merits of the dispute at a later stage, the court may have to reject the claim despite that there, in fact, exist reasons to dismiss the action.[36] That may occur where the court bases the determination of the jurisdiction on the mere assertion of the relevant facts - because they are doubly relevant - but, later, when determining the merits of the dispute, examines the facts and concludes that they do not exist.

The doctrine of assertion contains a requirement implying that the assertion of facts ultimate to the competence which are doubly relevant is decisive only if it is not obviously unfounded.[37] This means that the court may base the determination of the jurisdiction on a party's assertion of doubly relevant ultimate facts - unless the assertion appears to be obviously unfounded.[38] The requirement may be considered to reveal the actual meaning of the alleviation of the standard of proof granted by the doctrine of assertion when the court identifies the matter in dispute significant to its jurisdiction. Of the party's burden of proof remains a requirement that doubly relevant ultimate facts are presented with a certain degree of plausibility and that ultimate facts of single relevance must be proven.

The doctrine of assertion does not seem to involve the requirement in respect of legal assertions.[39] This means that an intellectually awkward plausibility assessment of the question of law - which the requirement would result in - would be avoided.

Several legal systems contain principles corresponding to the Swedish doctrine of assertion. For instance, Swiss law contains a similar procedural law principle applicable, *inter alia,* when a court identifies a matter in dispute significant to its jurisdiction.[40] In the same way as the doctrine of assertion, the Swiss principle implies that a

35. *See, e.g.*, Pålsson, *supra* n. 10, at 319.
36. *See, e.g.*, NJA 2005 p. 586; Ekelöf/Edelstam/Pauli, *supra* n. 31, at 22; Schöldström, *supra* n. 2, JT 2008-09, 140.
37. *See* NJA 2005 p. 586; NJA 2009 p. 519; NJA 2012 p. 483; Schöldström, *supra* n. 2, *Till Minnet av Södra Roslags tingsrätt*, 172 et seq., and JT 2008-09, 140 et seq.
38. *See* Schöldström, *supra* n. 2, Södra Roslags tingsrätt, 172 et seq.
39. Cases where the doctrine of assertion has been applied to legal issues significant to questions of jurisdiction do not mention the requirement. *See, e.g.*, NJA 1973 p. 1 (I-III); NJA 1973 p. 527; NJA 1976 p. 422; NJA 2004 p. 743. Moreover, it may be noted that a separate opinion of the judge in NJA 1973 p. 1 (I), and referred to in both NJA 1973 p. 1 (II) and (III), may be understood to mean that the requirement should not apply to legal assertions.
40. Max Guldener, *Schweizerisches Zivilprozessrecht* (3rd ed. Schulthess Polygraphischer Verlag 1979), 106; Samuel Baumgartner, Annette Dolge, Alexander Markus, Karl Spühler, *Schweizerisches Zivilprozessrecht - und Grundzüge des internationalen Zivilprozessrechts* (10th ed. Stämpfli Verlag 2018),74; BGE 137 III 32; BGE 122 III 249; BGE 119 II 66; BGer 25.11.2020, 4A 440/2020.

party does not have to prove the facts relevant in that regard, but the party's corresponding assertion is sufficient.[41] In addition, the reasons for the Swiss principle emanate from the importance of separating questions of procedural requirements from questions of the merits of a dispute.[42] Moreover, the Swiss Federal Tribunal explicitly states that the very essence of the principle is to enable attaining binding judgments on the merits with res iudicata effect.[43]

The Swiss procedural law principle is denoted '*Grundsatz der Zulässigkeitsprüfung nach dem Klageinhalt*' (the principle of examination of admissibility according to the content of the action).[44] It applies both when the courts determine questions of substantive-matter jurisdiction as well as questions of territorial jurisdiction.[45] In a Swiss doctoral thesis from 2010, Hoffmann-Nowotny argues that Swiss law in fact involves two different principles. One of them is the principle mentioned. The other is denoted '*Theorie der doppelrelvanten Tatsache*' (the theory of doubly relevant facts). He is of the opinion that both principles lead to the same result and could be considered essentially identical.[46] However, after *inter alia* analysing BGE 122 III 249, Hoffmann-Nowotny concludes that this case suggests a shift from the former principle to the theory of doubly relevant facts.[47]

However, the more recent case BGE 137 III 32 appears to establish that the principle of examination of admissibility, according to the content of the action, constitutes an overall procedural law principle which concerns both the existence of the relevant facts and their legal qualification. In the former respect, the Swiss Federal Tribunal stated that an assertion of doubly relevant facts is sufficient.[48] Thus, the case may be understood to refer to both principles and to suggest that the theory of doubly relevant facts constitutes a part of the principle of examination of admissibility according to the content of the action. BGE 137 III 32 indicates that no comprehensive examination of questions of law significant to court jurisdiction is required. For instance, where the nature of a legal relationship is decisive to the jurisdiction, it is sufficient that the court investigates whether it may reasonably be inferred, based on the alleged facts, that such a legal relationship exists.

41. Guldener, *supra* n. 40, at 106; Baumgartner/Dolge/Markus/Spühler, *supra* n. 40, at 74; BGE 137 III 32; BGE 3 I 626 at 633; BGE 119 II 66; BGE 122 III 249; BGer 25.11.2020, 4A 440/2020; BGer 25.09.2006, 4P 104/2006. Urs H. Hoffmann-Nowotny, *Doppelrelevante Tatsachen in Zivilprozess und Schiedsverfahren* (Dike Verlag 2010), 64, 106 et seq.
42. BGE 119 II 68; BGE 122 III 252.; *see also* Guldener, *supra* n. 40, at 106; Hoffmann-Nowotny, *ibid.*, at 125 et seq.; Baumgartner/Dolge/Markus/Spühler, *supra* n. 40, at 74 et seq.
43. BGE 141 III 294; BGer 25.11.2020, 4A 440/2020; BGer 10.12.2019, 4A 484/2018; BGer 22.09.2015, 4A 93/2015.
44. BGE 137 III 32; BGE 122 III 249; BGE 119 II 68.
45. Guldener, *supra* n. 40, at 106; Baumgartner/Dolge/Markus/Spühler, *supra* n. 40, at 74; BGE 141 III 294; BGE 137 III 32; BGE 136 III 486; BGE 135 V 373; BGE 131 III 153; BGE 128 III p. 50.
46. Hoffmann-Nowotny, *supra* n. 41, at 64 et seq., 71 et seq., 84, 87, pp. 115 et seq., 366.
47. Hoffmann-Nowotny, *supra* n. 41, at 114.
48. *See also* BGer 25.09.2006, 4P 104/2006; Baumgartner/Dolge/Markus/Spühler, *supra* n. 40, at 74; Oskar Vogel, *Besprechung von BGE 122 III 249,* ZBJV 132 (1996), 766. The German words used in this context are 'doppelrelevante Tatsachen'. In legal doctrine the notion is sometimes translated as 'doubly pertinent facts' or 'facts of double pertinence'. *See, e.g.*, Poudret/Besson, *infra* n. 54, at 389.

It may be noted that the Swiss procedural law principle emanates from German law.[49] The corresponding German procedural law principle – which always seems to have been denoted as the 'theory of doubly relevant facts' – also deals with situations involving doubly relevant ultimate facts. Already in 1900, it was considered to follow from the German principle that when a court was determining its jurisdiction, the claimant never had to prove the existence of the obligation or contract in dispute. The opposite was considered to apply with regard to an agreement on the place of performance.[50] The latter does not constitute a doubly relevant ultimate fact.

The Swiss theory of doubly relevant facts seems to involve a requirement that the facts are presented with certain plausibility. More specifically, it is considered sufficient that the doubly relevant ultimate facts – when identifying the matter in dispute – are presented with a certain degree of plausibility.[51]

[C] The Doctrine of Assertion and Arbitration

In Swedish legal doctrine, the doctrine of assertion is considered applicable in arbitration.[52] In NJA 2008 p. 406,[53] the Supreme Court explicitly held that it is an established general principle under Swedish law that the arbitral tribunal when it rules on its competence, on the basis of section 2 of the Swedish Arbitration Act, shall apply the doctrine of assertion. The *Petrobart* case concerned arbitration based on statutory law and the legal qualification of the facts in question. The Supreme Court's reasoning, however, suggests that the case is relevant also to commercial arbitration.

As concerns Swiss law, it follows clearly from both legal doctrine and case law that the theory of doubly relevant facts is not applicable in arbitration.[54] The reason for

49. Baumgartner/Dolge/Markus/Spühler, *supra* n. 40, at 74.
50. Paul Mayer, *Zur Lehre vom Gerichtsstande des Erfüllungsortes*, Zeitschrift für deutschen Zivilprozeß Bd 14 (1890), 250; Julius Petersen, *Ueber den Beweis der Thatsachen welche die Zuständigkeit des Gerichts begründen*, (Gruchot) Beiträge zur Erläuterung des Deutschen Rechts 37 (1893), 11, 17 et seq.
51. Berger/Kellerhals, *infra* n. 54, at 120 et seq.; BGE 135 V 373; BGE 131 III 153; BGE 128 III p. 50.
52. Heuman, *supra* n. 2, at 76 et seq, *supra* n. 2, JT 2017-18, 899 et seq.; Lindskog, *supra* n. 1, at 195 et seq.
53. Also referred to by the Supreme Court as Petrobart. Högsta domstolen, *supra* n. 3.
54. Hoffmann-Nowotny, *supra* n. 41, at 95 et seq.; Maurice Courvoisier, Nadja Jaisli Kull, in *Basler Kommentar, Internationales Privatrecht* (4th ed. Helbing Lichtenhahn Verlag 2021), Art 186 N 120; Bernhard Berger, Franz Kellerhals, *International and Domestic Arbitration in Switzerland* (3rd ed. Stämpfli Publishers 2015), 120 et seq.; Jean-Francois Poudret, Sebastian Besson, *Comparative Law of International Arbitration* (2nd edn Sweet & Maxwell 2007), 389; BGE 128 III 50; BGE 121 III 495; BGer 19.01.2006, 4P 298/2005; BGer 09.03.2005, 4P 226/2004. In BGer 07.09.2006, 4P 114/2006, however, the opposite was held. Here, the Swiss Federal Tribunal referred to four cases, all involving the theory of doubly relevant facts, but none of these concerned arbitration. It can also be noted that the case did not concern the question of identifying the matter in dispute, but rather the matter of jurisdiction *ratione temporis* in an investment dispute. The question at hand was whether the facts constituting the cause of action of the claim were within the jurisdiction *ratione temporis* of the tribunal. From the case, however, it follows that the alleged facts were not in dispute, and hence did not have to be proven. That means that the question of whether or not to apply the theory of doubly relevant facts did in fact not arise. Subsequently, the Swiss Federal Tribunal analysed the cause of action and concluded that the opinion of the defendant regarding the basis of the claim was incorrect.

the legal position is that it shall not be possible to force a party to submit to arbitration where there is no binding arbitration agreement as to the raised claim.[55] The reason is clearly framed in Swiss case law and consistently approved and welcomed by legal doctrine.[56]

As stated above, the application of the doctrine of assertion in arbitration has been extensively debated in Swedish legal doctrine. However, the reason against an application identified in Swiss law is not specifically addressed. Nor is the question of why the doctrine of assertion is considered applicable in arbitration justified or developed in any detail. In the latter regard, it may, therefore, be assumed that the *rationes* of the doctrine of assertion captured above – emanating from the importance of separating questions of procedural requirements from questions of the merits of a dispute – have been decisive.

[D] Discussion

As stated above, the question of identifying the matter in dispute significant to arbitral jurisdiction raises questions of fact and questions of law. As indicated at the outset of this chapter, identifying the matter in dispute in a way which does not permit a compromise with the intention of the parties as expressed in the arbitration agreement, comes to a head where the parties agree that there are various binding contracts between them, but disagree on which of the contracts the matter in dispute concerns. This situation entails that the question of fact – the existence of the contract in question – is not always the most crucial issue when identifying the matter in dispute; instead the crucial point is the relevant question of law. In other words, whether the circumstances in dispute pertain to the host contract or a contract covered by the invoked arbitration agreement.

As to the question of fact, a result of the doctrine of assertion being considered applicable in arbitration would be that an alleviation of the standard of proof is granted when the arbitral tribunal identifies the matter in dispute significant to its competence. Thus, of the party's burden of proof remains a requirement that doubly relevant ultimate facts are presented with a certain degree of plausibility and that ultimate facts of single relevance must be proven. An application of the doctrine of assertion means that an assertion that the contract in question exists is decisive. The arbitral tribunal shall base the identification of the matter in dispute on such an assertion.

Applying the doctrine of assertion to questions of law means that the arbitral tribunal shall base the identification of the matter in dispute, significant to its competence, on the claimant's assertion that the circumstances in dispute pertain to the host contract or a contract covered by the invoked arbitration agreement. Where the parties agree that there are various binding contracts between them but disagree on

55. BGE 128 III p. 50; BGE 121 III 495; BGer 19.01.2006, 4P 298/2005; BGer 09.03.2005, 4P 226/2004.
56. BGE 128 III p. 50; BGE 121 III 495; BGer 19.01.2006, 4P 298/2005; BGer 09.03.2005, 4P 226/2004; Poudret/Besson, *supra* n. 54, at 389; Berger/Kellerhals, *supra* n. 54, at 120.

which of the contracts the matter in dispute concerns, a mere assertion in that regard is sufficient.

How is the question of identifying the matter in dispute significant to arbitral jurisdiction dealt with in the legal systems of Switzerland and England introduced above? As according to Swiss law, the theory of doubly relevant facts is not applicable in arbitration, all facts relevant when identifying the matter in dispute have to be proven.[57] That is, the claimant has to prove that the alleged contract exists. No alleviation of the standard of proof is consequently accorded in that regard. That also applies where the existence of the contract is doubly relevant.[58] This means that the arbitral tribunal when identifying the matter in dispute has to examine all relevant facts with a full power of review.[59] Also, under English law, all facts relevant to the competence shall be examined by the arbitral tribunal with a full power of review.[60]

Under Swiss law, the arbitral tribunal shall examine all questions of law relevant to the jurisdiction.[61] The relevant questions shall be examined comprehensively.[62] The Swiss Federal Tribunal has explicitly held that if the arbitral tribunal fails to do so, the award can be set aside according to section 190(2)(b) of the Swiss Federal Statute on Private International Law (PILA).[63,64] English law mainly corresponds to Swiss law.[65] This means that, in order to identify the matter in dispute, the arbitral tribunal shall examine whether the circumstances in dispute pertain to the host contract or the other

57. BGE 128 III 50; BGE 121 III 495; BGE 19.01.2006, 4P 298/2005; BGer 09.03.2005, 4P 226/2004. *See also* Poudret/Besson, *supra* n. 54, at 389.
58. *See* Poudret/Besson, *supra* n. 54, at 389.
59. BGE 128 III 50; BGE 121 III 495; BGE 19.01.2006, 4P 298/2005; BGer 09.03.2005, 4P 226/2004. *See also* Poudret/Besson, *supra* n. 54, at 389; Courvoisier/Jaisli Kull, *supra* n. 54, Art. 186 N 120; Berger/Kellerhals, *supra* n. 54, at 246, 249 et seq.
60. *See AOOT Kalmneft v. Glencore International and Berkeley* [2002] 1 Lloyd's Rep. 128.
61. Courvoisier/Jaisli Kull, *supra* n. 54, Art. 186 N 120; Berger/Kellerhals, *supra* n. 54, at 249.
62. Courvoisier/Jaisli Kull, *supra* n. 54, Art. 186 N 120; Berger/Kellerhals, *supra* n. 54, at 249, 257. *See also* BGer 27.10.2021, 4A 461/2021; BGer 07.05.2021, 4A 27/2021.
63. *Bundesgesetz über das Internationale Privatrecht*, SR 291.
64. BGer 09.03.2005, 4P 226/2004. Section 190 of PILA is worded:

    (1) The award is final from the time when it is communicated.
    (2) An arbitral award may be set aside only:
        (a) where the sole member of the arbitral tribunal was improperly appointed or the arbitral tribunal improperly constituted;
        (b) where the arbitral tribunal wrongly accepted or denied juris- diction;
        (c) where the arbitral tribunal ruled beyond the claims submitted to it, or failed to decide one of the claims;
        (d) where the principle of equal treatment of the parties or their right to be heard in an adversary procedure were violated;
        (e) where the award is incompatible with public policy.
    (3) As regards preliminary awards, setting aside proceedings may only be initiated on the grounds of the above paragraphs 2 (a) and 2 (b); the time-limit runs from the communication of the award.
    (4) The deadline for filing the appeal amounts to 30 days from the award being communicated. (Translated in *Federal Act on Private International Law (Bundesgesetz über das Internationale Privatrecht, SR 291)*, Fedlex, The publication platform for federal law (Status as of 1 July 2022)).

65. *See* David Joseph, *Jurisdiction and Arbitration Agreements and their Enforcement* (3rd ed. Sweet & Maxwell 2015), 146.

contract comprehensively. Thus, the arbitral tribunal shall examine the questions of law that are relevant when identifying the matter in dispute with a full power of review.

The arbitral tribunal's examination of the question of whether the dispute concerns the host contract or a contract covered by the invoked arbitration agreement with a full power of review conceivably contributes significantly to the realisation of the scope of the arbitration agreement. At the same time, however, the examination may imply that the arbitral tribunal takes a stance regarding parts of the substantive matter. That the arbitral tribunal has to consider the merits of a dispute in order to determine its competence results in several disadvantages from a procedural law and procedural economy perspective. Even if the parties agree that there are various binding contracts between them, the question of law relevant when identifying the matter in dispute may require complex considerations as to a matter which the arbitral tribunal, or another forum, may have to examine finally when determining the merits of the dispute. In addition, the determination of the jurisdiction may normally be challenged. Taking a position on the substantive matter further implies that the determination of the jurisdiction anticipates the examination of the merits. Yet, the anticipation would, in many cases, depending on the substance of the claim, be limited to parts of the substantive matter.

An application of the Swedish doctrine of assertion in the situation where the parties agree that there are various binding contracts between them but disagree on which of the contracts the matter in dispute concerns means that a party's assertion in the relevant respect is sufficient for jurisdiction. If the assertion is not correct, an application of the doctrine may imply that a party is, in effect, forced into arbitration. The arbitral tribunal will consider that it has competence concerning a contract not containing or covered by the invoked arbitration agreement. Indeed, that would not be in line with the intention of the parties - as expressed in the arbitration agreement - regarding what disputes are to be submitted to arbitration. In fact, the matter in dispute is not covered by the scope of the arbitration agreement. This means that there is no ground for arbitral jurisdiction regarding the claim in question. Ultimately, it could thus be called into question whether an application of the doctrine of assertion in arbitration complies with the right of access to court.

To the extent the identity of the matter in dispute is conclusive to the jurisdiction, an application of the doctrine of assertion with the described possible outcome conceivably means that the arbitral tribunal will consider itself competent in more cases compared to Swiss and English law. This in turn can be assumed to result in more cases of rejecting awards. The res iudicata effect then implies an advantage for the respondent from a legal certainty perspective. A full power of review according to Swiss and English law conceivably means that the arbitral tribunal, to a greater extent, will dismiss the case after examining the relevant questions of law within the frames of the jurisdiction proceedings.

§12.03 THE *BELGOR* CASE

Is the rather recent *Belgor* case of importance to the arbitral jurisdiction factor concerning the identity of the matter in dispute? The *Belgor* case pertains to the arbitral jurisdiction factor concerning the scope of the arbitration agreement, in respect of which it suggests a liberal approach.[66] Moreover, *Belgor* may be understood as providing authority for a one-forum presumption. Here, a statement made by the Supreme Court may be understood to mean that the arbitration agreement, like other contracts, in case of doubt, can be assumed to aim at a reasonable solution, implying a one-forum solution (in arbitration). In the *Belgor* case, the scope of the arbitration agreement was extended to disputes concerning other contracts.

In addition, however, *Belgor* seems to have introduced a new principle of procedural law. The principle applies when the arbitral tribunal's determination of its competence is challenged, and it entails a presumption that the examination, including both questions of law and questions of fact, is correct.

The Supreme Court made a statement in the legal points of departure concerning the significance of the arbitral tribunal's examination of the competence in relation to the court's assessment in setting aside proceedings and reasoned as follows.

> When a court in setting aside proceedings shall revise the arbitral tribunal's determination on the jurisdiction, it should be taken into account that the arbitral tribunal is normally best positioned to examine its jurisdiction. This suggests that the starting point for the court's determination should be that the arbitral tribunal's interpretation and evaluation of evidence is correct. With those starting points, it shall, in the setting aside proceedings, be examined whether the challenging party has established that the arbitral tribunal has made an incorrect assessment of the scope of the arbitration agreement. As to the former, the Supreme Court referred to NJA 2003 p. 379.[67]

The statement by the Supreme Court may be understood to mean that since the arbitral tribunal is normally best positioned to examine its jurisdiction, it should be presumed that its examination of the jurisdiction, including both questions of law and questions of fact, is correct.[68] On that basis, the court's examination should be limited to the question of whether the challenging party has established that the arbitral tribunal's examination was incorrect.

The Supreme Court's statement pertains to two issues. The first pertains to the court's review as such of the arbitral tribunal's assessment of the competence, and thus the examination which the court shall make in the setting aside proceedings. Upon a challenge in accordance with section 34 or 36 of the Swedish Arbitration Act, the Court

66. Concerning the question whether a liberal or restrictive approach applies to the assessment of the scope of an arbitration agreement, the Swedish legal position is less clear and less consistent compared to other legal systems. Before *Belgor*, the Swedish approach has changed from rather extensive to more restrictive.
67. Also referred to by the Supreme Court as *Fruits et Légumes*. Högsta domstolen, *supra* n. 3.
68. *See also* Lars Heuman, *Har det skett en omsvängning eller omläggning av praxis från restriktiv till extensiv tillämpning av skiljeavtal?*, SvJT 2019 p. 546; Lindskog, *supra* n. 1, at 306 et seq., 932 footnote 3676.

of Appeal, and if leave to appeal is granted, the Supreme Court, in principle, examines both questions of fact and law relevant to the jurisdiction.[69] This means, *inter alia,* that applicable rules on burden and standard of proof shall be considered.[70] As to the standard of review, a review for error may be considered inherent in the Swedish legal system.[71] The second issue, to which the Supreme Court's statement pertains, is related to the grounds for setting aside an award. Significant in that respect is the non-statutory principle, according to which a challenging party shall prove that there are grounds for setting aside an award.[72] In other words, that the arbitral tribunal has, in some way, committed an irregularity in the relevant respects. This issue consequently relates to the respects in which the arbitral tribunal's determination is incorrect and to the burden of proof in that regard. It is an issue distinct from, but connected to, the first issue. The common denominator is the error/irregularity.

From the Supreme Court's statement, understood in the way described above, it seems to follow that the court's review for error of the arbitral tribunal's assessment of the competence is replaced by a presumption that the examination, including both questions of law and questions of fact, is correct.[73] After the legal points of departure, the Supreme Court first described the arbitral tribunal's assessment of its competence. Thereafter, the Supreme Court merely concluded that Belgor had not established that the arbitral tribunal's assessment was incorrect. These considerations may thus be understood to imply that the arbitral tribunal's assessment was presumed to be correct and that Belgor's arguments did not rebut the presumption.

The presumption that the arbitral tribunal's examination of the jurisdiction is correct, as such, probably has no effect on the arbitral jurisdiction factor concerning the identity of the matter in dispute. However, the presumption may conceivably amplify the importance of a party's assertion that the matter in dispute concerns the host contract or another contract/matter covered by the scope of the arbitration agreement.[74] In that sense, the presumption interacts with the doctrine of assertion. This would in turn increase the risk, in the way described above, of the arbitral jurisdiction being based on an assertion which is in fact not correct. And thus, the arbitral tribunal is considered competent concerning a contract not containing or covered by the invoked arbitration agreement. Thus, the interaction would conceivably contribute to

69. Lars Welamson, *Rättegång VI* (3rd edn Norstedts Juridik 1994), 149; Per Olof Ekelöf, Henrik Edelstam, *Rättsmedlen,* (12th ed. Iustus Förlag 2008), 149 et seq. *See also* Heuman, *supra* n. 8, JT 2009-10, 349 et seq.

70. *See* Per Olof Bolding, *Skiljedom, Studier i rättspraxis beträffande svensk skiljedoms giltighet och verkställbarhet* (P A Norstedt & Söners Förlag 1962), 64 et seq.; Heuman, *supra* n. 3, at 591 et seq, and *supra* n. 8, JT 2009-10, 336; Lindskog, *supra* n. 2, at 99 footnote 356, 343 footnote 1388, 932 footnote 3676, 1251 footnote 4906. As to the corresponding review in enforcement proceedings, *see* Lindskog, *supra* n. 2, at 99 footnote 356, 1251 footnote 4906, 1271 footnote 4965.

71. *See* Ekelöf/Edelstam, *supra* n. 69, at 11 et seq., 15 et seq. As to challenge proceedings under Section 36 of the Swedish Arbitration Act, *see, e.g.*, Heuman, *supra* n. 3, at 535 et seq.

72. Heuman, *supra* n. 3, at 591, and *supra* n. 8, JT 2011-12, 662.

73. *See also* Madsen, *supra* n. 8, Dispute Resolution in Business Law, 94.

74. Likewise, the presumption may be assumed to amplify the presumption in favour of a one-forum solution introduced in the Belgor case. *See also* Heuman, *supra* n. 68, at 546 et seq.

a compromise with the intention of the parties as expressed in the arbitration agreement regarding what disputes are to be submitted to arbitration.

§12.04 THE MODEL LAW AND IDENTIFYING THE MATTER IN DISPUTE

During the preparation of the Swedish Arbitration Act, it was decided not to adopt the Model Law (as a model) but to consider its provisions in all relevant parts.[75] This justifies the question of whether and how the arbitral jurisdiction factor concerning the identity of the matter in dispute is governed by the Model Law.

Article 16 of the Model Law contains the principle of competence-competence, providing that the arbitral tribunal may rule on its own jurisdiction. However, the question of how to identify the matter in dispute is a procedural law issue not governed by the Model Law. Procedural law is fundamental to arbitration, particularly to the question of arbitral jurisdiction.[76] In principle, procedural law is national, which then leads to the legal system of the seat of arbitration.[77] That is a consequence of the concept of *lex arbitri*.[78]

The purpose of the Model Law is closely connected to party autonomy.[79] According to Fortese, the goal of the Model Law is to facilitate the resolution of disputes by encouraging and safeguarding party autonomy in international trade.[80] In line with that, Fortese refers to 'the arbitrators' overarching duty to enforce the parties' agreement and ensure efficiency'.[81]

An application of the doctrine of assertion, with the possible outcome that the arbitral tribunal bases its competence on an assertion which is in fact not correct, implying a deviation from the intention of the parties – as expressed in the arbitration agreement – regarding what disputes that are to be submitted to arbitration, cannot be considered to be in line with the principle of party autonomy. And thus not with the Model Law.

75. Government Bill 1998/99:35, p. 47; Heuman, *supra* n. 2, at 44.
76. *See, e.g.*, Howard Holtzmann, Joseph Neuhaus, *A Guide to the UNCITRAL Model Law on International Commercial Arbitration, Legislative History and Commentary* (Kluwer Law and Taxation Publishers 1994), 6 et seq.; European Parliament, Directorate General for internal Policies, Policy Department C: Citizens' Rights and Constitutional Affairs, Legal Instruments and Practice of Arbitration in the EU – Study, 2014, pp. 21 et seq.
77. *See* Holtzmann & Neuhaus, *ibid.*, at 6 et seq.
78. Emmanuel Gaillard, *Legal Theory of International Arbitration* (Martinus Nijhoff Publishers 2010), 20; European Parliament, Directorate General for Internal Policies, Legal Instruments and Practice of Arbitration in the EU, *supra* n. 76, at 21. Here, the concept of *lex arbitri* refers to the arbitral tribunal's equivalent of the national judges' *lex fori*. The concept thus establishes an exclusive correlation between a specific arbitration and a single national legal system and its procedural law. Gaillard, *ibid.*, at 20; European Parliament, Directorate General for Internal Policies, Legal Instruments and Practice of Arbitration in the EU, *supra* n. 76, at 21.
79. *See* General Assembly Resolution 40/72, Model Law on International Commercial Arbitration of the United Nations Commission on International Trade Law, 40 GAOR Supp No. 53, A/40/53, p. 308 (adopted 11 December 1985).
80. Fabricio Fortese, Early Determination of Arbitral Jurisdiction, Balancing efficacy, efficiency, and legitimacy of arbitration (Universitetsservice US-AB, Stockholm, 2022), 247 et seq.
81. Fortese, *ibid.*, at 231 et seq.

§12.05 CONCLUSION

An application of the Swedish doctrine of assertion when identifying the matter in dispute significant to the competence of the arbitral tribunal conceivably contributes to implementing the scope of the arbitration agreement to a lesser extent than legal systems providing for a full power of review. The Swedish approach may even result in a situation whereby a party is forced into arbitration. Implications of the doctrine of assertation may simultaneously jeopardise party autonomy and be in conflict with the right of access to court.

The *Belgor* case seems to have introduced a presumption applicable when the arbitral tribunal's determination of its competence is challenged, implying that the tribunal's examination is correct. The presumption may conceivably interact with the doctrine of assertion in a way which would permit a compromise with the intention of the parties as expressed in the arbitration agreement regarding what disputes are to be submitted to arbitration.

The question of identifying the matter in dispute significant to the competence of the arbitral tribunal is a procedural law issue not governed by the Model Law. It may be discussed whether an application of the Swedish doctrine of assertion can be considered to be in line with the Model Law, to which the principle of party autonomy is essential.

CHAPTER 13

The *Belgor* Case Four Years On: Under What Circumstances May a Decision to Restrict a Party's Right to Present Its Case Be Deemed Unjustifiable?

*Hanna Larsson**

§13.01 INTRODUCTION

An important part of an arbitral tribunal's management of the arbitration is to move the proceedings forward by issuing procedural decisions. These types of decisions often involve balancing the need for efficiency in the proceedings against a party's right to present its case.

In the *Belgor* case,[1] the Swedish Supreme Court stated that an arbitral tribunal's decision to deny a party's request for an extension of time does not constitute a procedural irregularity unless the decision is *unjustifiable* (my italics).[2]

The Supreme Court did not explain the precise meaning of the term "unjustifiable," and the concept has not appeared in later Supreme Court precedent. In the absence of such precedent, this chapter examines how the term "unjustifiable" has been applied in proceedings before the Svea Court of Appeal concerning the setting aside of an arbitral award under the first paragraph of section 34(7) of the Swedish Arbitration Act (the "Act") due to alleged procedural irregularities.[3]

---

* The author is grateful to juris doktor h.c. advokat Finn Madsen for his valuable comments on the chapter.

1. Swedish Supreme Court Case No. NJA 2019 p. 171.
2. An English translation of the *Belgor* case can be found on the SCC Arbitration Portal: https://www.arbitration.sccinstitute.com/Swedish-Arbitration-Portal/start/.
3. According to the first paragraph of section 34(7) of the Act, an arbitral award shall be wholly or partially set aside upon the request of a party if, without fault of the party, an irregularity occurred in the course of the proceedings which probably influenced the outcome of the case.

The purpose of this chapter is to answer the following questions:

(1) What is the *scope* of the term "unjustifiable"? Is the term relevant for the assessment of procedural decisions other than an arbitral tribunal's decision to deny a request for an extension of time?
(2) What is the *meaning* of the term "unjustifiable"? What circumstances are relevant to the interpretation of the term?

This chapter does not discuss the requirement set forth in section 34(7) of the Act that, in order for the award to be set aside, the challenging party must demonstrate that the procedural irregularity probably influenced the outcome of the case, although it should be noted that this is a key requirement that the challenging party needs to satisfy.

§13.02 THE *BELGOR* CASE

[A] Circumstances of the Case

The Belarus company Joint Stock Company Belgorkhimprom (Belgor) and the Turkish company Koca Inşaat Sanayi Ihracat Anonim Şirketi (Koca) had entered into a construction contract. Following Belgor's cancellation of the contract, Koca initiated arbitral proceedings. Belgor disputed Koca's claim and filed a counterclaim. The arbitral tribunal rejected Belgor's claim and ordered Belgor to pay compensation to Koca.

Following Belgor's challenge of the award, it was partially set aside by the Svea Court of Appeal. Belgor appealed to the Supreme Court, seeking that the award be set aside in full. Belgor submitted several grounds for its request, including that the dispute was not covered by a valid arbitration agreement. The legal ground for the challenge of relevance to this essay was Belgor's argument that Belgor had been denied the right to present its case.

Belgor argued that the arbitral tribunal's decision to deny Belgor's request for an extension of time to submit an expert report constituted a procedural irregularity and that the award should be set aside on the basis of the first paragraph of section 34(7) of the Act. Belgor also argued that a procedural irregularity had occurred when the arbitral tribunal had denied Belgor's request that the tribunal appoint an independent expert. According to Belgor, the Arbitral Tribunal's decisions deprived Belgor of the opportunity to prove defects in Koca's work. Belgor stated that the procedural irregularity was not caused by Belgor and that it had influenced the outcome of the case.

The Supreme Court stated:

> 39. Within the framework of the management of the case, the arbitral tribunal must give the parties the opportunity to present and argue their respective cases to the extent necessary (Section 24, first paragraph of the Act and the SCC Arbitration Rules 2010, Article 19.2). In an arbitration under the SCC Arbitration Rules, the

arbitral tribunal is entitled to conduct the arbitration in any manner it considers appropriate. A provisional timetable must be established. The arbitral tribunal has mandate to decide, amongst other things, when written statements are to be submitted, including any other documents the parties wish to rely upon. The tribunal and the parties should act in accordance with the adopted provisional timetable. The tribunal may grant a party an extension of time unless the extension is considered inappropriate. In that assessment, it should be taken into account at what stage of the proceedings the decision is made, the effect that the extension may have on the other party, and any other relevant circumstances (*see* Arts. 19 and 23-25 of the SCC Arbitration Rules).

> 40. The arbitral tribunal is best placed to consider the reasons presented by the parties, and to assess whether a request for an extension should be granted or denied. As a starting point, the decision of the arbitral tribunal should be upheld, unless the decision appears unjustifiable. In this assessment, case law concerning article V 1 (b) of the New York Convention is of relevance (*see* Supreme Court Case No. NJA 2018 p. 291, "Robot Grader," para. 15).
>
> 41. A second prerequisite for the setting aside of an award due to a decision concerning a time extension, is that the challenging party did not cause its own predicament. For the award to be set aside, the challenging party must demonstrate that, due to circumstances beyond his control that he was not obligated to have foreseen, he was prevented from presenting his case in time. Furthermore, the party must demonstrate that alternative ways of presenting the case did not exist.
>
> 42. A rejection of a party's request that the arbitral tribunal appoint its own expert cannot constitute a procedural irregularity, unless otherwise provided by the arbitration agreement.

In paragraphs 44-45 of the judgment, the Supreme Court took into account that the arbitral tribunal had rejected Belgor's request since an extension would have resulted in a postponement of the final hearing. Furthermore, the Supreme Court noted that the arbitral tribunal, in its decision, had stated that it would be possible for Belgor to submit a supplement to the expert report at a later stage. The Supreme Court noted that the expert report was primarily of relevance to Belgor's counterclaim. Therefore, it was possible for Belgor to withdraw the counterclaim and initiate new arbitration proceedings at a later stage. In paragraph 47, the Supreme Court found that Belgor had not demonstrated that the arbitral tribunal's decision was unjustifiable.

[B] The *Belgor* Case in the Swedish Jurisprudential Debate

Belgor has given rise to much debate in Sweden. As to the scope and the meaning of the term "unjustifiable," the following statements are of particular interest.

Based on the above-cited paragraphs 40-41 of the Supreme Court's judgment, Patrick Schöldström states that the term "unjustifiable" sets a very high bar. He does not object to this since the arbitral tribunal's case management, more often than not, consists of balancing more or less incompatible considerations, sometimes under time pressure. Schöldström questions whether an equally high bar can or should apply not only to issues regarding a party's right to a time extension but also to other procedural decisions or even the handling of the case in general. According to Schöldström, paragraph 41 of the Supreme Court's judgment seems to imply that the tribunal's decision should first of all be tested against the requirement contained in section 24 of the Act; the arbitrators "shall give the parties the opportunity to present their case to the extent necessary." If that requirement has not been met, the tribunal's decision must be regarded as unjustifiable.[4]

Stefan Lindskog states that the "unjustifiable" requirement applied by the Supreme Court appears to be quite onerous but that the requirement, nevertheless, can be justified when the party, despite a denial of its request for a time extension, has certain leeway. Consequently, the level of tolerance should depend on the effect of the tribunal's decision. Whether the tribunal has provided reasoning for its decision should also be of importance. If the arbitration panel has not adequately presented the grounds for its position, the scope for a challenge of the award should be greater than when the panel has done so.[5]

Oscar Gentele argues, in line with *Belgor*, that the arbitrators are in the best position to assess whether new material should be accepted or rejected, considering the reasons given by the parties. Consequently, if a decision to reject or allow new material is to be reviewed based on a motion to set aside the award, the court should not perform a de novo review of the decision, thus acting as if it were considering the question for the first time. Instead, the court must grant significant deference to the arbitrators' decision. An award must, as a starting point, be affirmed unless the court finds that the decision to allow or reject new material was unjustifiable. Oscar Gentele notes that the Supreme Court did not explain in *Belgor* when a procedural ruling is unjustifiable. He refers to US court rulings, which have applied an abuse of discretion standard to arbitrators' procedural rulings in annulment actions. This standard would involve reviewing whether the decision-maker has made a clear error of judgment or has applied an incorrect legal standard.[6]

§13.03 JUDGMENTS FROM THE SVEA COURT OF APPEAL, 2019-2022

I have identified three decisions of the Svea Court of Appeal where the term "unjustifiable" has been applied with reference to *Belgor* since 2019.[7] In all three cases, the challenging party invoked the first paragraph of section 34(7) of the Act and argued that a procedural error had been made since the challenging party was not afforded a right to present its case. In two of the cases, the challenging party also argued that the parties had not been treated equally. The cases are presented chronologically below.

4. *See* Patrick Schöldström, Juridisk Tidskrift 2019/20, 249.
5. *See* Stefan Lindskog, *Skiljeförfarande—en kommentar*, JUNO v 3, re section 34 p. 7 of the Act, para. 5.2.1.
6. *See* Oscar Gentele, Stockholm Arbitration Yearbook 2019, 155.
7. The review includes Svea Court of Appeal judgments rendered from March 20, 2019 until March 13, 2023.

[A] The *BDO* Case

Svea Court of Appeal judgment dated June 10, 2021, in Case No. T 13364-19, *Hans L v. The Partners of BDO* (the "Partners")

This case concerned the question of whether new information invoked by a party at a late stage of proceedings should have given rise to a reopening of the proceedings in order to give the challenging party the opportunity to comment on the new information. Both parties to the arbitration were Swedish. The facts of the case were, briefly, the following.

The Partners requested that the award be set aside in its entirety due to procedural error. The arbitration agreement included a reference to the Rules for Expedited Arbitration of the Stockholm Chamber of Commerce's Arbitration Institute.

The Partners claimed that the arbitrator had allowed Hans L to invoke, in his closing statement, a new factual ground in support of his case. Even if Hans L's statement should not be regarded as a new factual ground, it constituted, according to the Partners, an "addition" according to Article 31 of the SCC Rules for Expedited Arbitration.[8] By deciding to deny the Partners' motion to disregard Hans L's statement or, alternatively, that the proceedings be reopened, the arbitrator had deprived the Partners of their right to respond to Hans L' statement. The Partners should have been given the opportunity to comment on the statement regardless of whether the statement was merely a comment on the Partners' evidence.

Hans L opposed the Partners' motion, stating, in short, that no new facts were presented during his closing remarks. The purpose of Hans L's statement was merely to point out flaws in the evidence relied upon by the Partners. The proceedings were closed at the final hearing after the parties' closing statements. There was no ambiguity as to whether the proceedings were closed, nor were there sufficient reasons for reopening the proceedings.

The Svea Court of Appeal stated that the arbitrator, taking into account the SCC rules and the parties' instructions, may handle the arbitration in the manner the arbitrator deems appropriate. The arbitration should always be managed in an impartial, efficient and expeditious manner which, taking into account the expedited nature of the procedure, should give the parties equal opportunity to present their case to a reasonable extent. Pursuant to Article 41 of the SCC Rules, the arbitrator should declare that the proceedings are closed when the arbitrator is satisfied that the parties have had a reasonable opportunity to present their cases. Thereafter, before a final award has been made, the arbitrator may only reopen the proceedings on his own initiative or at the request of a party in exceptional circumstances.

8. According to Art. 31 of the SCC Rules for Expedited Arbitration, a party may, at any time prior to the close of proceedings, amend or supplement its claim, counterclaim, defense or set-off provided its case, as amended or supplemented, is still comprised by the arbitration agreement, unless the Arbitrator considers it inappropriate to allow such amendment or supplement having regard to the delay in making it, the prejudice to the other party or any other relevant circumstances.

The Svea Court of Appeal noted that, according to section 24 of the Act, a party's right to present its case includes the right to be given the opportunity to respond to the other party's statements. A party is entitled to present its case only to the extent necessary, and the party should not be allowed to delay the proceedings. The arbitrator must determine a time for the closing of the proceedings, after which time no new material may be brought into the proceedings. This can be done by ordering the parties to complete their case in writing. When a final hearing has been held, the proceedings should generally be considered to have ended after the hearing.[9]

The Svea Court of Appeal stated that the requirement that the parties be granted an opportunity to present their case is a fundamental aspect of the rule of law. A decision depriving a party of this opportunity may constitute a procedural error, which may result in the award being set aside. With reference to *Belgor*, the Svea Court of Appeal noted that the arbitral tribunal is best placed to assess, in light of the parties' arguments, whether a request for an extension of time should be granted or denied and that the starting point is that the arbitral tribunal's decision should be affirmed unless it appears unjustifiable.

The Court of Appeal found that the arbitration proceedings, according to Article 41 of the SCC Rules, had been closed at the end of the hearing and that the parties had understood this. The Court of Appeal then carried out a thorough analysis of the arbitrator's decision to deny the Partners' motion to either disregard Hans L's statement or to reopen the case and give the Partners the opportunity to comment on Hans L's remarks.

The Svea Court of Appeal held that the arbitrator, in his decision, had stated that the remarks made by Hans L during his closing statement were comments on the Partners' evidence and not a change of the factual grounds for his position in the case. According to the Court of Appeal, the arbitrator's decision did not deprive the Partners of their right to present their case to the extent necessary. The arbitrator's decision not to resume the proceedings did not, therefore, constitute a procedural error.

[B] The *Transgaz* Case

Svea Court of Appeal judgment dated October 8, 2021, in Case No. T 8181-19, *GTB Transgaz Belarus ("Transgaz") v. Energoprojekt Oprema a.d. Beograd ("EPO")*

The parties to the arbitration were from Belarus and Serbia. The facts of the case were, in brief, the following.

The parties had entered into a construction contract. Transgaz terminated the contract, invoking an alleged delay by EPO as a cause for the termination. EPO initiated

9. The Svea Court of Appeal referred to the legislative history of the Act (Govt. Bill 1998/99:35, 226) and to Lindskog, *Skiljeförfarande*, re section 24 of the Act, point 4.1.6. Stefan Lindskog's commentary to the Act concerns mainly Swedish domestic arbitrations. The commentary is, nonetheless, often quoted by the Svea Court of Appeal in challenge proceedings concerning both domestic and international arbitrations.

arbitration, and Transgaz filed a counterclaim. In the arbitral award, EPO's claim was upheld, but the arbitral tribunal held that Transgaz's termination was unfounded.

In its motion to set aside the award, Transgaz argued that the arbitral tribunal's decision to grant EPO an extension of time to argue its claim constituted a deviation from the agreed timetable in Procedural Order no 1. The decision had created unequal conditions for the parties to present their respective cases.

EPO opposed Transgaz's motion, arguing that the arbitral tribunal's decision had been correct and in accordance with Article 23 of the SCC Arbitration Rules, the Act, and Procedural Order no 1. The EPO argued that the arbitral tribunal was best placed to make decisions on procedural matters.

The Court of Appeal held that an arbitral tribunal may adapt the management of the proceedings to the nature of the dispute and to the parties' instructions. However, the requirements of the rule of law must be complied with, and the parties must be granted an adequate opportunity to present their cases. As a consequence, the parties must be treated impartially, and the proceedings must be transparent and reasonably foreseeable for the parties. With reference to *Belgor*, the Court of Appeal stated that the arbitral tribunal's decision must be upheld unless it is unjustifiable.

The Court of Appeal stated that when a motion to set aside an award concerns a procedural decision, the Court's assessment of the decision should primarily focus on how the arbitral tribunal reached its decision rather than on the substance of the decision. This means, according to the Court of Appeal, that if the arbitral tribunal properly reported the reasons for its decision, the decision should normally be upheld. However, if, for example, the arbitral tribunal did not provide reasoning for its decision and the decision concerns an issue that was essential for a party's ability to present its case, the Court should assess the issue at hand and decide on the issue in the arbitral tribunal's stead. In such a situation, the Court may conclude that a procedural error has been made.[10]

In its examination of the arbitral tribunal's decision, the Court of Appeal found that the arbitral tribunal had given Transgaz the opportunity, during the hearing, to make a separate statement in response to the written statement submitted by EPO and that Transgaz had, in fact, availed itself of this opportunity. Transgaz had also been given the opportunity to respond to the submission in writing after the hearing. In light of this, the Court of Appeal found that Transgaz had been given an adequate opportunity to present its case and that the parties had been treated equally. The arbitral tribunal's decision was not unjustifiable, and no procedural error had been committed.

[C] The *ICA* Case

Svea Court of Appeal judgment dated June 30, 2022, in Case No. T 7158-20, *ICA Sverige AB ("ICA") v. Bergsala SDA AB ("Bergsala")*

10. The Svea Court of Appeal referred to Stefan Lindskog, *Skiljeförfarande—En kommentar*, JUNO version 3, re section 34 of the Act, para. 5.1.3.

The main issue in this case was whether the challenging party's right to present its case was unduly restricted when the arbitral tribunal, over the challenging party's objection, decided that the hearing should be held virtually and not physically. Both parties to the arbitration were Swedish. The relevant facts of the case were, in brief, the following.

ICA and Bergsala had entered into a master agreement, according to which Bergsala would sell products to ICA and/or other companies within the ICA group. In 2018, a dispute arose between the parties regarding the purchase of products. On May 13, 2019, Bergsala initiated arbitration against ICA. ICA filed a counterclaim. The arbitral award was issued on June 11, 2020. ICA was ordered to pay the amount sought by Bergsala. ICA was awarded only a small part of its counterclaim.

ICA requested that the arbitral award be annulled in accordance with section 33 of the Act.[11] ICA requested, alternatively, that the award be set aside in accordance with section 34 of the Act.

ICA's grounds for the request for an annulment were that the award was manifestly incompatible with the foundations of the Swedish legal system. ICA argued that the arbitral tribunal had refused to grant ICA an oral hearing, that the virtual hearing did not guarantee the equal treatment of the parties, and that the principle of party autonomy had been infringed since the arbitral tribunal's decision to conduct a virtual hearing had placed Bergsala in a better position in the arbitration than ICA. Alternatively, ICA argued that the award should be set aside as the arbitral tribunal's decision to conduct a virtual hearing violated ICA's right to an oral hearing under section 24 of the Act and the right to a hearing under Article 32 of the SCC Arbitration Rules. These rules required, according to ICA, that the hearing be physical. In addition, ICA argued that independent of its right to an oral hearing, its right to due process had been violated by the arbitral tribunal's decision. ICA argued that the travel restrictions during the COVID-19 pandemic had resulted in ICA not being able to meet with its witnesses and legal representatives. This meant, according to ICA, that the case could not be prepared satisfactorily and that it could not be presented in a manner consistent with due process. Furthermore, ICA argued that the credibility of the witnesses in the dispute was of particular importance and that the virtual hearing did not allow for an adequate witness hearing.

Bergsala objected to ICA's requests and argued that the timetable had been agreed jointly by the parties. Furthermore, Bergsala had already been forced to accept a postponement of the proceedings since ICA had not presented its final claims until March 2020. Bergsala argued that a physical hearing could have been carried out in a safe way with both parties present despite the COVID-19 pandemic and that the arbitral tribunal's decision to cancel the physical hearing was a result of ICA's refusal to participate.

The Court of Appeal noted that the term "oral hearing" is not defined in section 24 of the Act. Furthermore, the Court of Appeal noted that section 24 of the Act should,

11. According to section 33 p. 2 of the Act, an award is null and void if the award, or the manner in which the award was made, is manifestly incompatible with the basic principles of the Swedish legal system.

according to the legislative history of the Act, be interpreted based on the Swedish Code of Civil Procedure in Swedish domestic arbitration and in accordance with the right to a fair trial under Article 6 of the European Convention on Human Rights.

The Court of Appeal stated that if the parties are unable to agree, the question of when a hearing should take place and what form it should take falls within the arbitral tribunal's discretionary authority.

Furthermore, the Court of Appeal stated that according to Chapter 5, section 10 of the Swedish Code of Civil Procedure, a hearing may, under certain circumstances, be held even though the court, the parties and the witnesses are not physically present. The Court of Appeal held that the right to a physical hearing under the Swedish Code of Civil Procedure is not absolute. Consequently, section 24 of the Act and the SCC Arbitration Rules do not rule out a virtual hearing. The Court of Appeal stated that unless the parties have agreed otherwise, it falls within the arbitral tribunal's discretionary authority to decide whether the hearing should be held virtually, notwithstanding that one of the parties has objected to the hearing being conducted in that manner.

Furthermore, the Court of Appeal stated that, when deciding whether a virtual hearing should be held despite the objection of one of the parties, the arbitral tribunal must decide whether a virtual hearing is *appropriate* in the circumstances of the case. In this assessment, according to section 24 of the Act, the arbitral tribunal must balance the parties' rights to present their case against the requirement that the dispute be handled impartially, expediently and quickly under section 21 of the Act. The technology used during the hearing must enable sufficiently good communication. The Court of Appeal referred to *Belgor* and stated that the arbitral tribunal's decision must not, from an overall point of view, appear unjustifiable.

As to the circumstances of the case, the Court of Appeal found that the arbitral proceedings had been pending for a year at the time of the arbitral tribunal's decision. Furthermore, at the time of the decision, it was unclear how long the pandemic would continue. There was, consequently, a strong interest for the arbitration to not be further delayed. The Court of Appeal found that the technical conditions during the hearing had been acceptable. Furthermore, the arbitral tribunal had given the parties an opportunity to take part in a physical hearing in May and June. ICA had stated, due to the pandemic and due to health issues affecting ICA's legal counsel, that it was unable to participate in the physical hearing and sought a postponement until August. The reasons given by ICA did not constitute an obstacle to the hearing. For that reason, according to the Court of Appeal, ICA had not been deprived of its right to a hearing.

The Court of Appeal concluded that, from an overall point of view, the proceedings had been conducted in accordance with due process and that the parties had been given an opportunity to present their cases. The arbitral proceedings had been handled impartially, expediently and quickly. No procedural error had been committed, and there were no grounds to set aside the award.

§13.04 ANALYSIS

In the following section, the questions posed in the introduction will be analyzed in light of the Svea Court of Appeal's judgments.

[A] What Is the Scope of the Term "Unjustifiable"?

One of the purposes of this chapter is to examine whether the term "unjustifiable" is relevant to the assessment of whether procedural decisions other than an arbitral tribunal's decision to deny a motion for an extension of time may constitute a procedural error under the first paragraph of section 34(7) of the Act.

The review of the Court of Appeal cases suggests that the court has held that the term "unjustifiable" has a broader scope than what directly follows from *Belgor* and that the term is also relevant for assessing procedural decisions other than a denial of a motion for an extension of time. Is the term relevant for the assessment of all procedural decisions?

The enquiry that presented proposals for the revisions of the Act that entered into force on March 1, 2019, proposed an amendment of the provision concerning challenge due to procedural error, to the effect that only gross errors by the tribunal should result in the award being set aside.[12] However, that proposal was not included in the revised Act. In the *travaux préparatoires* to the revised Act, it was stated that the proposed amendment would impede the possibilities of setting aside the award when a procedural error has influenced the outcome of the case and that such a provision would be difficult to justify.[13]

According to the Supreme Court in *Belgor,* the decision of the arbitral tribunal should hold unless the decision is deemed unjustifiable. The Supreme Court did not clarify whether this means that only gross errors committed by a tribunal are challengeable. In light of the aforementioned statement in the *travaux préparatoires*, namely that all errors affecting the outcome are challengeable, it can be surmised that an unjustifiable error can cause the award to be set aside only in cases where the challenged decision is of a *discretionary* nature.[14] In other words, it may be concluded that the criterion "unjustifiable" only applies to procedural decisions which require that an assessment or a balancing of the parties' respective interests is made by the arbitral tribunal. Other errors, which are not the result of an erroneous assessment by the arbitral tribunal, may result in the award being set aside regardless of whether the decision may be deemed unjustifiable, provided the decision has affected the outcome of the case.

A common factor between *Belgor* and the Court of Appeal judgments is that the court's assessments of whether the arbitral tribunals' procedural decisions were unjustifiable concerned solely decisions that in some way limited the challenging

12. SOU 2015:37, 132.
13. Govt. Bill 2017/18:257, 50.
14. *See* Finn Madsen, *The Challenges of the Arbitral Awards in the Gas Sales and Gas Transit Arbitrations in Stockholm, Sweden*, Juridisk Tidskrift 2019/20, at 944.

party's right to an equal opportunity to present its case. In addition to *Belgor*, the term unjustifiable has been applied as part of the assessment of the following issues:

- Whether an arbitrator's decision to refuse the challenging party's request to reopen the case in order to give the challenging party an opportunity to comment on a statement made by the counterparty during the final remarks constituted a procedural error under the first paragraph of section 34(7) of the Act.[15]
- Whether the challenging party's right to present its case was unduly restricted due to the arbitral tribunal's decision to grant the opposing party an extension of time, which led to new facts being relied upon at a late stage of the proceedings.[16]
- Whether the arbitral tribunal's decision to hold a virtual hearing over the challenging party's objection constituted a restriction of the challenging party's right to present its case, which was contrary to the second paragraph of section 33 or the first paragraph of section 34(7) of the Act.[17]

In conclusion, the scope of the term unjustifiable is wider than what can be deduced from the Belgor case. However, it may also be concluded that the applicability of the term is limited to errors resulting from an erroneous assessment or a balancing of the parties' interests made by the arbitral tribunal.

[B] What Does the Term "Unjustifiable" Mean? What Circumstances Are Relevant to the Interpretation of the Term?

[1] The Belgor *Case*

The term "unjustifiable" was introduced by the Supreme Court in paragraph 40 of the *Belgor* case. The Supreme Court stated that precedents concerning Article V(1)(b) of the New York Convention are of relevance in the assessment of whether an arbitral tribunal's decision should be deemed to be unjustifiable.[18] The Supreme Court specifically referred to (paragraph 40) the *Robot Grader* case,[19] paragraphs 15-17:

15. Svea Court of Appeal judgment dated June 10, 2021 in Case No. T 13364-19, *Hans L v. The Partners of BDO.*
16. Svea Court of Appeal judgment dated October 8, 2021 in Case No. T 8181-19, *GTB Transgaz Belarus v. Energoprojekt Oprema a.d. Beograd.*
17. Svea Court of Appeal judgment dated June 30, 2022 in Case No. T 7158-20, ICA *Sverige AB v. Bergsala SDA AB.*
18. Article V.1 of the New York Convention reads: Recognition and enforcement of the award may be refused, at the request of the party against whom it is invoked, only if that party furnishes to the competent authority where the recognition and enforcement is sought, proof that: [...] (b) The party against whom the award is invoked was not given proper notice of the appointment of the arbitrator or of the arbitration proceedings or was otherwise unable to present his case.
19. *Robot Grader* (Swedish Supreme Court Case No. NJA 2018 p. 291) concerns the enforcement of a foreign arbitral award. The facts were, in brief, as follows: Belaya ptitsa requested arbitration in May 2015 against Robot Grader. On July 6, 2015, ICAC ordered Robot Grader to appoint an arbitrator within fifteen days and to submit a written response within thirty days. Robot Grader

15. Recognition and enforcement of an arbitral award may be refused if fundamental aspects of due process in international arbitration have been disregarded. The parties must be afforded a fair hearing before the arbitral tribunal ("due process of law").

16. Due process includes the equal treatment of the parties, the transparency of the proceedings and the proceedings being reasonably foreseeable to the parties. It is a fundamental requirement that the parties be given an opportunity to present their cases. This requirement is set out in the Model Law: "each party shall be given a full opportunity of presenting his case" (Article 18, UNCITRAL Model Law on International Commercial Arbitration, 1985) and in the UNCITRAL Arbitration Rules: "a reasonable opportunity of presenting its case" (Article 17, UNCITRAL Arbitration Rules, as revised in 2010). According to the Swedish Arbitration Act (Section 24, first paragraph), the parties must be given the right to present their cases to the extent necessary. This requires that a party is given the time and opportunity to present its case. The meaning of this requirement depends, to a great extent, on the circumstances of the case (*see*, for instance, UNCITRAL 2012 Digest of Case Law on the Model Law on International Commercial Arbitration, p. 97).

17. A party who claims that it was unable to present its case, bears the burden of proving this. Furthermore, the party must demonstrate that it has participated in the arbitration in good faith (cf. Article 25 of the Model Law, cf. also Section 24, third paragraph of the Swedish Arbitration Act).

It may be concluded from the reference in *Belgor* to Article V(1)(b) of the New York Convention that the meaning of the term "unjustifiable" is closely linked to the parties' right to due process.[20] In *Robot Grader*, the Supreme Court stated that due process includes, in addition to the equal treatment of the parties, that the arbitral proceedings are transparent and reasonably foreseeable to the parties and that the parties are given sufficient time and opportunity to present their cases. Furthermore, it may be concluded from the Supreme Court's references in *Robot Grader* to the UNCITRAL Model Law and to the UNCITRAL Arbitration Rules that international

---

appointed an arbitrator but did not submit a response. On September 23, 2015, the arbitration panel summoned the parties to a hearing to be held on November 19, 2015. Robot Grader was requested to submit a response by November 1 at the latest. Robot Grader did not submit any response. The parties then announced their joint intention to settle. After the hearing was postponed a number of times, the parties informed the arbitral tribunal, during a hearing, that they were unable to reach a settlement. Belaya ptitsa requested that the arbitral tribunal immediately issue an award, while Robot Grader requested that the hearing be postponed in order to prepare a reply. The arbitral tribunal rejected Robot Grader's request. The tribunal stated that Robot Grader had had enough time to prepare its case and emphasized, in particular, that the company had not filed a reply. In an award issued on March 25, 2016, Robot Grader was ordered to pay compensation to Belaya ptitsa. Robot Grader opposed Belaya ptitsa's enforcement of the award. The Supreme Court found that Robot Grader had had reason to assume that the dispute would not be tried on the merits due to the ongoing settlement discussions. The Supreme Court found that the conditions had changed by the time Belaya ptitsa requested that the arbitral tribunal issue an award. The arbitral tribunal should, therefore, have given Robot Grader reasonable time to prepare a response and to submit evidence. The Supreme Court held that the arbitral tribunal had disregarded fundamental aspects of due process in international arbitration, which had led to Robot Grader having been deprived of its right to present its case. For these reasons, the award was not recognized or enforceable in Sweden.

20. *See* van den Berg, *The New York Convention of 1958*, Kluwer Law 1981, 296.

sources are of relevance in the assessment of whether, in a specific case, due process has been observed.

The following circumstances appear to have been of relevance in the Supreme Court's determination of whether the arbitral tribunal's decision to deny an extension of time was unjustifiable:[21] (i) Belgor had previously, at one occasion, been granted a time extension; (ii) the date for the final hearing had been decided jointly by the parties; (iii) Belgor's request for a further time extension was denied in order to avoid a postponement of the hearing; (iv) it was possible for Belgor to submit a supplement to the expert report at a later stage; and (v) the expert report was primarily of relevance to Belgor's counterclaim, which (if withdrawn) would not be covered by the *res judicata* of the award.

[2] The Svea Court of Appeal Judgments

In the *BDO* case, the Court of Appeal considered the arbitrator's decision to deny the challenging party's request to reopen the proceedings in order to allow the challenging party to comment on a statement given by the counterparty during the final remarks. It is clear from the Court of Appeal's judgment that the Court carried out a thorough analysis of the arbitrator's decision. According to the arbitrator, the remarks given during the closing statement constituted arguments in relation to the evidence relied upon by the challenging party. It is possible that the arbitrator concluded that it would not have had any impact on the outcome of the case if the challenging party had been given the opportunity to comment on the remarks. The Court of Appeal concluded that the circumstances did not justify a reopening of the proceedings. A determining factor in the Court of Appeal's conclusion appears to be that the statement made by Hans L during his final remarks did not include ultimate facts (Sw. "*rättsfakta*"). The Court of Appeal did not carry out any de novo assessment, instead basing its decision on the arbitrator's conclusion concerning the nature of Hans L's statement.

In the *Transgaz* case, the Court of Appeal stated that, when assessing whether an award should be set aside due to a procedural error by the arbitral tribunal, the Court's assessment of the case should, as a rule, focus on the arbitral tribunal's method and examine how the arbitral tribunal arrived at its decision rather than on the content of the decision. In the *Transgaz* case, one of the questions before the Court of Appeal was whether Transgaz's right to present its case had been unduly restricted and whether the principle of equal treatment had been disregarded when the arbitral tribunal granted the opposing party the right to submit a written statement at a late stage of the proceedings. The Court of Appeal noted that the arbitral tribunal had given Transgaz the opportunity, during the final hearing, to respond to the written statement and that Transgaz had, in fact, taken the opportunity to comment on it during the hearing. Furthermore, Transgaz had been given an opportunity to submit comments to the statement in writing after the conclusion of the final hearing.

21. Supreme Court Case No. NJA 2019 section 171 (*Belgor*), paras. 43-45.

In the *ICA* case, the Court of Appeal stated that an arbitral tribunal's decision to deny a party a physical hearing must be appropriate and that the arbitral tribunal should balance the party's right to present its case against the need for speed and efficiency in the proceedings. From an overall point of view, the arbitral tribunal's decision must not appear unjustifiable. The Court of Appeal specifically stated that the technology used during the hearing must enable sufficient communication. The practical consequence of the Court of Appeal's statement may be that the arbitral tribunal, prior to the hearing, must ensure that the tribunal's and the parties' technical equipment are in working order and that the parties have equal access to the necessary technical equipment.

In the ICA Case, the following circumstances appear to have been of relevance to the Court of Appeal's decision: (1) the timetable was approved by both parties; (2) the decision not to participate in the physical hearing was taken by ICA and the parties were not denied the right to participate in a hearing when ICA announced its intention, due to the COVID-19 pandemic, not to participate in the *physical* hearing; (3) the tribunal decided that both parties should participate in a virtual hearing; (4) at the time of the tribunal's decision, it was uncertain how long the pandemic would continue; (5) the circumstances invoked by ICA, in its request for a postponement of the physical hearing, did not constitute sufficient reason to conclude that there was an obstacle to the hearing; (6) the technical conditions during the hearing were acceptable; and (7) ICA's opportunity to present its evidence was not affected by the arbitral tribunal's decision.

[C] Summary

It is a common factor in *Belgor* and the three Court of Appeal cases that the courts reviewed the arbitral tribunals' method and the way the tribunals had arrived at their decisions. A second common factor in the four cases is that the courts assumed that arbitral tribunals are best placed to assess the circumstances of relevance to the procedural decision. The courts did not carry out any de novo examination of the issues at hand. It is possible that a de novo examination would have been carried out if the Courts had found that the arbitral tribunals' methods were not acceptable.[22]

As a second step, the courts examined the effect of the arbitral tribunal's decision on the challenging party's ability to present its case. The Court of Appeal took into account that the arbitral tribunals had taken measures to ensure that the restriction on the challenging party's right to present its case was as limited as possible. For example, in the *Transgaz* case, the Court of Appeal noted that the challenging party was given an

22. Cf. Stefan Lindskog, *Skiljeförfarande—en kommentar*, JUNO v 3 re the first paragraph of section 34(7), para. 5.1.3. According to Lindskog, if the arbitral tribunal's decision is unfounded and it concerns an issue that is essential for the parties right to present their claims, the court should make its own assessment of what decision the arbitral tribunal ought to have reached. Should the court come to a conclusion different than that of the arbitral tribunal, it may be assumed that a procedural error has been made. The arbitral tribunal's failure to provide reasoning for its decision may result in the tribunal's decision being deemed "unjustifiable."

opportunity to respond to the written statement, which the opposing party was permitted to submit at a late stage of the proceedings. In the *ICA* case, the Court of Appeal found that the challenging party's presentation of its evidence was not affected by the hearing being held virtually.

In all four cases, the courts balanced one party's right to present its case against the risk of delay in the proceedings. It may be of importance that the extent of the delay is difficult to foresee at the time of the arbitral tribunal's decision. For instance, in the *ICA* case, it was uncertain, at the time of the tribunal's decision, how long the COVID-19 pandemic would continue.

The *Belgor* case involved an international arbitration. In *Belgor*, the Supreme Court stated that the New York Convention and, by way of the *Robot Grader* case, Article 18 of the UNCITRAL Model Law and the UNCITRAL Arbitration Rules, are of relevance to the assessment of whether a decision by an arbitral tribunal should be deemed unjustifiable. Despite the numerous references to international sources, it may be argued that the term "unjustifiable" has the same scope and meaning in Swedish domestic arbitration as in international arbitration, as the Svea Court of Appeal has considered *Belgor* to be of relevance also in two Swedish domestic arbitrations.[23]

In conclusion, in their assessments of whether the arbitral tribunal's procedural decision may be deemed unjustifiable, the courts appear to have taken into account the following circumstances.

- Whether the reasons for the arbitral tribunal's decision were clearly recorded, well elaborated and reasoned.
- Whether the parties jointly agreed on a timetable for the proceedings.
- To what extent the challenging party's right to present its case was affected by the tribunal's decision.
- Whether the tribunal took measures to ensure that the restriction on the challenging party's right to present its case was as limited as possible.
- Whether an extensive delay would have occurred unless the challenging party's right to present its case was restricted.
- Whether the circumstances that caused a restriction on the challenging party's right to present its case were within the control of the challenging party.

§13.05 CONCLUDING REMARKS

In the concluding section, I will discuss whether the meaning of the term "unjustifiable" in relation to a party's right to present its case can be further specified.

According to the first paragraph of section 24 of the Act, the parties must be afforded the right to present their cases to the extent *necessary*. This entails a

23. Cf. Lindskog, *Skiljeförfarande—en kommentar*, JUNO v 3, re section 34 p. 7, para. 5.2.1. Stefan Lindskog states that the reference to the New York Convention is of limited relevance to Swedish domestic arbitrations.

limitation.[24] However, if a procedural decision made by an arbitral tribunal is clearly motivated by a wish to avoid an extensive delay, can it still be deemed unjustifiable? Is there a core aspect of a party's right to present its case that cannot be limited regardless of the consequences for the timeliness and efficiency of the arbitral proceedings?

According to Matti S. Kurkela och Santtu Turunen, a party's right to present its case, as expressed in Article 18 of the UNCITRAL Model Law,[25] includes the following elements:

(1) the right to receive all information contained in submissions and due notice of the initiation of the proceedings;
(2) full and simultaneous access with other parties and the panel to all communications, pleadings, arguments and testimony;
(3) the right to be present at all physical hearings and at hearings via the Internet or by means of teleconferencing or video conferencing;
(4) full access to all written documents, evidence and reports submitted in the proceedings by the parties, witnesses, experts, or third parties without undue delay;
(5) the right to submit claims and argue in support of them, to raise material and procedural defenses and objections, and to bring new claims and raise new defenses;
(6) the right to submit relevant documentary evidence in either defense or support of claims;
(7) the right to cross-examine witnesses and experts and other parties testifying in the proceedings (including reasonable time to prepare);
(8) the right to comment on any and all statements, comments, and communications, and reasonable time to elaborate on an answer to any of them;
(9) the right to introduce further evidence and testimony as may be necessary to fully elucidate and defend the party's position should new facts emerge or new claims be made;
(10) adequate notice of the closing of the proceedings must be given in ample time to allow the parties to fully develop their pleadings and exhaust their testimony.[26]

The requirement of equality and full opportunity to participate is perhaps the most fundamental role of due process and *ordre public*.[27] The right to be informed of

24. *See* Finn Madsen, *Commercial Arbitration in Sweden*, 5th ed., Jure Förlag, 2020, 270.
25. According to Art. 18 of the UNCITRAL Model Law, a party shall be awarded a full opportunity of presenting its case. The SCC Rules states that the parties shall be awarded an equal and reasonable opportunity whereas the first paragraph of section 24 of the Act affords the parties an opportunity to present their respective cases to the extent necessary. Finn Madsen states: "There is probably no material difference between the varying formulations as the opportunity to be heard is impliedly limited by considerations of reasonableness and fairness." Commercial Arbitration in Sweden, 5th edition, Jure Förlag, 2020, 269.
26. *See* Kurkela and Turunen, *Due Process in International Commercial Arbitration*, 2nd ed. 2010, Oxford University Press, 187-189.
27. *See ibid.*, 189.

the fact that arbitral proceedings have been initiated and the right to be given a reasonable time to respond constitute the core of a party's right to present its case.[28] The equal right to access all written documentation and evidence submitted in the arbitration and the right to be present at all hearings stems from the communication principle, which is a fundamental element of a party's right to present its case.[29] It is difficult to imagine a situation where timeliness and efficiency in the proceedings would justify a restriction of the communication principle, particularly in light of access to modern technology.[30] I therefore respectfully submit that a procedural decision restricting the rights listed in points 1-4 and 10 above may be considered unjustifiable and result in the arbitral award being set aside, regardless of any delay that may ensue.[31]

However, timeliness is one of the criteria of a fair trial, and the tribunal must control the proceedings to guarantee it. As mentioned above, a party's right under the first paragraph of section 24 of the Act to present its case is not unlimited. I believe that the elements listed in points 5-9 above may be restricted by an arbitral tribunal in the interest of timeliness and efficiency. An important part of the arbitral tribunal's task is, therefore, preferably jointly with the parties and at the early stages of the proceedings, to set a time limit for the closing of the proceedings. In order to limit the risk that the parties' right to present their cases will be affected by the deadline, sufficient advance notice of the deadline and its legal consequences should be given. The tribunal may also reserve the right to extend the deadline if the circumstances so warrant. Furthermore, the deadline should not make it impossible to establish the originally alleged relevant facts unless sufficient opportunity has been given to the parties to bring evidence and they have failed to do so for no sound reason.[32]

A party's right to present its case is diversified and complex. The conflict between a party's right to present its case and the timeliness of the proceedings is one of the most difficult problems in the arbitral tribunal's case management. It follows from *Belgor* and the Court of Appeal cases reviewed above that an arbitral tribunal, in order to ensure, to the extent possible, that the award will be final and binding, should ask itself two questions when faced with a situation where a party's right to present its case may need to be restricted for the sake of timeliness and efficiency. First, the arbitral tribunal should consider what aspect of that right the procedural decision would affect.

28. Cf. Swedish Supreme Court Case NJA 2010 p. 219.
29. Section 24 second paragraph of the Act.
30. *See* Lars Heuman, *Skiljemannarätt*, 1st ed., 1999, Norstedts Juridik, 650.
31. A party who, despite having received proper notification, refuses to participate in the arbitration is of course a different matter. According to the third paragraph of section 24(3) of the Act, if a party has been afforded an opportunity to present its case but has failed to avail itself of this opportunity without valid reason, the arbitrators may determine the dispute based on the material presented to them. Furthermore, a party should not be permitted to disrupt the efficient conduct of the proceedings by calling for a meeting at a late stage. According to the preparatory works, the arbitrators should be able to request that the parties call for an oral hearing within a particular period of time, failing which they will be deemed to have impliedly waived such right; *see* Govt. Bill 1998/99:35, 227.
32. *See* Kurkela and Turunen, *Due Process in International Commercial Arbitration*, 2nd ed., 2010, Oxford University Press, 195.

Second, if the arbitral tribunal finds that a restriction of the party's right is justified, the arbitral tribunal should ensure that the restriction is as limited as possible and that the arbitral tribunal thoroughly records the reasoning underlying its decision.

CHAPTER 14

Preserving Evidence in Arbitration Proceedings: From a Swedish and Norwegian Perspective

Knud Jacob Knudsen & Olof Olsson

§14.01 INTRODUCTION

The outcome of the majority of commercial disputes depends on the evidence presented during the proceedings. Consequently, access to evidence is a crucial aspect of almost every dispute. This includes preserving evidence which may be at risk of deteriorating or being lost. This chapter discusses the possibility of requesting court assistance to secure evidence prior to the commencement of arbitration proceedings – an opportunity that may have been overlooked in the past.

Requesting assistance from courts to preserve evidence prior to filing suit is regulated in many jurisdictions and is fairly uncontroversial with respect to court litigation. However, the matter is not clearly regulated with regard to arbitration proceedings. This has caused uncertainty as to whether it is possible for parties to request such assistance from the courts.

The purpose of this chapter is to examine whether parties who are bound by an arbitration agreement may request assistance from the general courts to secure evidence prior to the initiation of the arbitration. The chapter examines the issue under both Swedish and Norwegian law. The reason for the comparative perspective is that the relevant legislation is very similar in Sweden and Norway. However, legal scholars have approached the issue differently in the two countries, and this provides for an interesting comparison. The comparative aspect is also compelling because the issue has been a subject of dispute in some fairly recent lower court decisions in Norway. In Sweden, on the other hand, the relevant court decisions are from the Supreme Court, but the rulings are quite old.

Both Norwegian and Swedish law allow parties to secure evidence prior to the initiation of a legal action before the regular civil courts. This is regulated in Chapter 28 of the Norwegian Dispute Act (NDA) and Chapter 41 of the Swedish Code of Judicial Procedure (SCJP).

However, neither the Norwegian Arbitration Act (NAA) nor the Swedish Arbitration Act (SAA) contain any express rules on preserving evidence and do not refer to the rules in the NDA Chapter 28 or the SCJP Chapter 41, respectively. The UNCITRAL Model Law on International Commercial Arbitration (the 'Model Law'), by which both arbitration acts are influenced, also lacks rules on the securing of evidence.[1]

Accordingly, the question is whether the rules on securing evidence in the NDA and SCJP may be applied to disputes that are to be settled by arbitration.[2]

The fundamental background for the question is that the considerations which justify the provisions in Chapter 28 of the NDA and Chapter 41 of the SCJP are equally relevant in arbitration. This includes the primary purpose of the rules which is to promote substantively correct decisions by ensuring that the facts of the case are as clear and well-established as possible. The alternative to securing evidence would be that the case is decided without the specific evidence being presented to the tribunal or the quality of the evidence being significantly reduced. It could also be argued that the need to be able to secure evidence is even more important in arbitration since it in practice is a one-instance dispute resolution procedure.[3] In addition, a large share of arbitration cases are decided on the facts.[4]

Another key purpose of the provisions is to provide a party with the opportunity to evaluate the strength of its case before any proceedings are initiated.[5] This consideration also applies when the parties have agreed to have their disputes settled through arbitration.

Section §14.02 provides a general overview of the provisions concerning the preservation of evidence under the NDA and the SCJP. Section §14.03 is the core part of the chapter, where we analyze the legal authorities in Norway and Sweden. In §14.04, we summarize our conclusions and provide some final comments.

1. That fact that the NAA is based on the Model Law is evident from NOU 2001:33 pp. 49-50 and Ot. prp. no. 27 p. 25. In Sweden the legislator used the Model Law as a road map when drafting the SAA and noted that having a similar design as the Model Law was of substantive value in itself, government bill. 1998/99:35 pp. 43-46.
2. There are additional legal issues that must be considered if the seat of arbitration is outside Norway or Sweden respectively. These issues are not examined further in this chapter.
3. Neither of the NAA nor the SAA allow for arbitral awards to be appealed to the courts or be set aside due to an incorrect assessment of the merits, *see* the SAA section 34 and the NAA section 43.
4. Per M. Ristvedt og Sven Eriksrud, 'Bevistilgang i voldgift', *Tidsskrift for forretningsjus* 2015, pp. 275-330 (Ristvedt and Eriksrud), and Nigel Blackaby et al., *Redfern and Hunter on International Arbitration* (6th ed.) point 6.75 og 6.76 (Blackaby).
5. NOU 2001:32 pp. 987-988, Ot. prp. no. 51 (2004-2005) p. 470, and NJA II 1943 p. 515.

§14.02 OVERVIEW OF THE LEGAL PROVISIONS

The following section provides a brief overview of the Norwegian and Swedish rules on the securing of evidence as a foundation for the analysis of the question of application of the rules in arbitration.

The main provisions of the NDA have the following wording:[6]

> Section 28-1. Securing evidence
>
> Evidence may be secured outside of legal proceedings by judicial examination of parties and witnesses and by providing access to and inspecting real evidence.
>
> Section 28-2. Conditions for securing evidence
>
> Evidence may be secured if it can be of significance in a dispute to which the applicant may become a party or intervener, and there is either a clear risk that the evidence will be lost or considerably weakened, or there are other reasons why it is particularly important to obtain access to the evidence before legal proceedings are instigated.[7]

The corresponding provisions in the SCJP read as follows:

> Section 41-1. Preservation of evidence for the future
>
> If there is a risk that evidence concerning a circumstance of importance to a person's legal rights may be lost or difficult to obtain and no trial concerning the rights is pending, a district court may take and preserve for the future evidence in the form of witness examination, expert opinion, view, or written evidence. However, evidence may not be taken pursuant to this chapter for the purpose of investigating an offence.

The provisions are most commonly invoked to enable the examination of witnesses or to obtain access to physical evidence, such as relevant documents which are in the possession of the opposing party. It should be noted that the NDA allows for parties to be examined, while this is not allowed under the SCJP.

A prerequisite for a petition to be granted is that there is a risk that the evidence will be lost, considerably weakened or difficult to obtain. The SCJP does not allow for the securing of evidence for other reasons. The NDA, on the other hand, also encompasses other reasons of particular importance.

Under the NDA, the petition to preserve evidence shall as a main rule be filed at the court where the case could have been brought, *see* section 28-3(1). The SCJP allows the applicant to choose which district court it wishes to submit its petition. However, witnesses and experts are only required to appear before the district court where they reside, *see* sections 41-2 and 41-3.[8]

6. The wording referred to in this chapter is based on the official translations of the acts that are available. The NDA refers to the 'securing' of evidence, while the SCJP uses the term to 'preserve' evidence. These terms are used as synonyms throughout the chapter.
7. The full text of the NDA is accessible in Norwegian and English at www.lovdata.no.
8. Fitger, *Rättegångsbalken* (JUNO 21 March 2023), commentary to section 41-2.

Under the NDA, the person to whom the petition is directly addressed and the person towards whom any ensuing action is likely to be directed shall be identified as opposing parties, *see* section 28-3(2). If possible, the opposing party shall be notified before the securing of evidence is initiated, but the securing of evidence may be carried out immediately without notification if prompt action is necessary, *see* section 28-3(3).

Under the SCJP, the general rule is that the person against whom proceedings may be instigated is only to be summoned to a hearing if there are specific reasons for this, *see* section 41-3.

The provisions concerning the taking of evidence outside of a main hearing apply *mutatis mutandis* under both acts; *see* the NDA section 28-4 and the SCJP section 41-3.

§14.03 SECURING OF EVIDENCE BEFORE ARBITRATION PROCEEDINGS ARE INITIATED

[A] Starting Point

As indicated in the introduction, the main question is whether the rules on securing of evidence in the NDA and SCJP can be applied to disputes that are to be settled by arbitration, or if the fact that the parties have agreed to arbitration also means that they have agreed to waive the possibility of invoking the rules on preserving evidence outside court proceedings. This question will be examined first from a Norwegian perspective and then from a Swedish perspective.

[B] The Norwegian Perspective

[1] Section 28-2 of the NDA

The natural starting point is the wording of Chapter 28 of the NDA. According to section 28-2, evidence may be secured 'if it can be of significance in a dispute'. The use of the general term 'dispute' strongly suggests that the rules are not only limited to disputes before the courts but also may apply to disputes that are to be resolved by arbitration. In other words, a natural interpretation of the wording of the NDA is that the rules on securing of evidence can be invoked by parties in advance of arbitration proceedings.[9]

The fact that the provisions concerning the securing of evidence are found in the NDA, which applies to cases before the courts and which generally does not apply to arbitration, may, give reason to question the application of the rules in cases where the parties have agreed to arbitration. However, such an interpretation would entail a restrictive understanding of the wording of section 28-2 by introducing an additional

9. Schei et al. *Tvisteloven, kommentarutgave,* comments to section 28-1 point 1.3, write that the wording of section 28-1 strongly suggests that it will be possible to secure evidence under Chapter 28 before arbitration proceedings are commenced.

requirement that the evidence specifically can be of significance in a court case rather than in a dispute in general.

The next question is whether or not the provisions in the NAA limit the parties' rights to invoke the rules on preserving evidence in the NDA.

[2] Section 6 and Section 8 of the NAA

As a clear general rule, an agreement to arbitrate implies that the parties waive the right to have disputes heard by the ordinary courts. Accordingly, the NAA section 6 (1) provides that the courts have jurisdiction to hear or decide disputes that are subject to arbitration only where the law so provides:

> The courts have jurisdiction over the deliberation and resolution of disputes subject to arbitration only to the extent provided by this Act.

According to the wording, the provision requires a legal basis in the NAA for the ordinary courts to render decisions in disputes where the parties have agreed to arbitrate.[10] In international jurisprudence, it is held that the wording of the corresponding provision in the Model Law Article 5 entails that the courts' involvement is limited 'strictly to such matters as are specifically provided in the Law'. However, it is presumed that the Model Law Article 5 does not completely rule out that the courts may have jurisdiction in arbitration cases with regard to issues that are not expressly regulated in the Model Law. As a result, it is not entirely clear how strictly the requirement for a legal basis is to be interpreted.[11]

As mentioned above, the NAA does not contain any explicit provisions allowing the courts to render decisions on the securing of evidence. By comparison, section 8 states that the courts may make an order for provisional security even if a dispute is subject to arbitration:

> The courts may make an order for provisional security pursuant to chapters 32 to 34 of the Act relating to the resolution of disputes even if a dispute is subject to arbitration.

The fact that the NAA contains an express provision on the authority of the courts to order provisional security (interim measures) but no corresponding provision on the securing of evidence suggests that securing of evidence is not available in arbitration proceedings. It could be argued that the NAA would contain provisions concerning the preserving of evidence outside court proceedings if the legislator intended this form of action to be available in disputes where arbitration has been agreed.

However, there is no basis for drawing firm conclusions on this point. The question is not mentioned in the preparatory works. Furthermore, the reason that the NAA section 8 expressly regulates provisional security is that the Model Law has a

10. The provision corresponds to the Model Law Art. 5.
11. Bantekas et al., *UNCITRAL Model Law on International* Commercial *Arbitration – A Commentary* (2020), p. 84 (Bantekas).

corresponding provision on this in Article 9.[12] In connection with the work on the NAA, it was established that it should correspond as closely as possible to the content and system of the Model Law, and the preparatory works underline that section 8 is based on the parallel provision in the Model Law.[13]

Further to this, it should be considered that the Model Law Article 9 does not clearly indicate which interim measures the courts can grant. However, it has been held that the courts can grant the same interim measures as an arbitral tribunal can decide under the Model Law Article 17.[14] Pursuant to Article 17 (2)(d), an arbitral tribunal can order a party to 'preserve evidence that may be relevant and material to the resolution of the dispute'. This indicates quite clearly that the courts can decide to preserve evidence under the Model Law, and that the NAA should be interpreted accordingly.

It may also be questioned whether the wording of section 6 (1) of the NAA – 'disputes subject to arbitration' – must be interpreted as referring to the substantive issues and not procedural issues such as the securing of evidence. The connection with section 7 (1) supports such an interpretation. According to the latter provision, the courts shall dismiss 'a lawsuit that is the subject of arbitration' if a party so requests no later than in his first submission on the 'substance of the dispute'. This can be understood to mean that the court's obligation to dismiss relates to actions concerning the merits of a case; *see* further in §14.03[B][4] below.

[3] Section 6 (2) and (3) of the NAA

Section 6 (2) of the NAA regulates which court is competent when the courts have jurisdiction under the act. The last sentence of the provision appears to presume that the courts may make decisions to secure evidence even if a dispute is subject to arbitration:

> Securing of evidence may also take place before a different court.

The preparatory works do not contain any further discussion of the provision but mention as an example that evidence may be secured at the court where the witness who is to give evidence lives.[15]

The wording of section 6 (2) does not expressly refer to Chapter 28 of the NDA, but it is natural to interpret the word 'securing of evidence' as a reference to these rules. Section 6(3) stipulates that the rules in the NDA apply to the court's involvement in the case unless otherwise stated in the NAA. Furthermore, only Chapter 28 uses the term securing of evidence.

12. The provision reads as follows: 'It is not incompatible with an arbitration agreement for a party to request, before or during arbitral proceedings, from a court an interim measure of protection and for a court to grant such measure.'
13. NOU 2001:33 pp. 49-50 and 92, and Ot. prp. no. 27 (2003-2004) pp. 25 and 90.
14. Bantekas p. 160.
15. NOU 2001:33 p. 85 and Ot. prp. no. 27 (2003-2004) p. 89.

[4] Section 7 of the NAA

Section 7 (1) of the NAA provides that the courts shall dismiss a legal action that is subject to arbitration if a party so requests no later than in his first submission on the merits of the dispute.

The court's duty to dismiss refers to 'a lawsuit that is the subject of arbitration'. The text does not specify what is meant by 'a lawsuit', and this is not commented on in the preparatory works. However, it is natural to understand the term to mean a case before the courts concerning a legal claim; *see* the NDA section 1-3 (1).

Further, a lawsuit is normally understood as a claim for a judicial determination with regard to the substance of a matter but may also concern procedural claims, such as an action to set aside an arbitral award as invalid under Chapter 9 of the NAA.[16]

The term lawsuit is thus not entirely unambiguous, but as used in section 7 of the NAA, it must be understood to refer to the merits of the case, *see* section 7(1), which provides that a party must request dismissal 'no later than in his first submission on the merits of the dispute'. This is in accordance with section 8 of the Model Law, which stipulates that the courts shall dismiss the case if a party so requests 'not later than when submitting his first statement of the substance of the dispute'.[17] In international jurisprudence concerning the Model Law, it is held that Article 8 does not apply to petitions to preserve evidence.[18]

Furthermore, it is linguistically not natural to characterize a petition to preserve evidence outside court proceedings as a lawsuit and a request to secure evidence will not relate to the merits of the case.[19] Consequently, the provision in section 7 does not seem to imply an obligation for the courts to dismiss applications to secure evidence.

This conclusion must have a bearing on the interpretation of the provision in section 6 (1) concerning the court's jurisdiction. There appears to be a clear connection between sections 6 and 7 whereby the courts according to section 7 shall dismiss cases which they do not have jurisdiction to hear pursuant to section 6 (if a party so requests no later than in his first submission on the merits of the dispute).

When section 7 is also read in conjunction with section 6(2), which seems to presume that the courts may hear requests for the securing of evidence, this further supports the view that a party may request evidence to be secured under Chapter 28 of the NDA, even if the parties have agreed that disputes are to be resolved by arbitration.

16. Schei et al., commentary on section 1-3 of the NDA, point 1.2.
17. The Model Law Article 8 and its preparatory works are discussed in more detail by Borgar Høgetveit Berg, 'Voldgiftslova § 7. Særlig om fristen for å krevje søksmål för domstolane avvist på grund av voldgift', in Borgar Høgetveit Berg and Ola Ø. Nisja (ed.), *Avtalt prosess*, Universitetsforlaget 2015, pp. 29-31.
18. Bantekas pp. 141: 'Pre-actions, such as those that seek to obtain documentary evidence, are generally viewed as not falling within the scope of article 8 [...].'
19. Woxholth, p. 160, writes that section 7 cannot be used as a barrier to the securing of evidence, and that it is not linguistically natural to refer to a request for the securing of evidence as a 'lawsuit' within the meaning of the provision.

[5] *The Arbitration Agreement*

Both sections 6 and 7 of the NAA refer to disputes and actions that are 'subject to arbitration'. The question is whether the specific arbitration agreement may have an impact on the right to request the securing of evidence and whether the parties' agreement may constitute a waiver of the possibility to preserve evidence through the courts.

It is common for arbitration clauses to state that all disputes between the parties relating to the agreement in question are to be settled by arbitration. Furthermore, there may be a dispute between the parties not only concerning the substance of the case, but also about access to evidence, such as relevant documents. In other words, the question is whether an arbitration agreement must be interpreted to entail that not only the merits of the case, but also all procedural issues, must be settled by arbitration.

Section 2 of the NAA establishes that the provisions of the act may be derogated from by agreement to the extent provided for in the individual section. Thus, if the parties wish to deviate from the act by agreement, this must have statutory authority in the individual provision of the act. No such statutory authority appears in sections 6, 7 or 8, which regulate the relationship with the ordinary courts. Consequently, these provisions cannot be derogated from the parties' arbitration agreement.[20]

The limitations on the right to derogate from the rules of the NAA also apply when the parties agree that the dispute shall be resolved according to the rules of an arbitration institute. The main arbitration institute in Norway is the Oslo Chamber of Commerce Institute for Arbitration and Alternative Dispute Resolution (OCC).[21] The rules for arbitration institutions in Norway must stay within the framework of the NAA and can thus only deviate from the declaratory rules of the act. Accordingly, the OCC rules Article 2 states that the rules are supplemented by the provisions of the NAA.[22]

The fact that the parties cannot deviate from sections 6, 7 and 8 in the arbitration agreement must imply that disputes on procedural issues relating to the jurisdiction of the courts must be determined by an interpretation of the provisions of the NAA, regardless of the parties' agreement or the rules of the OCC. Accordingly, the individual arbitration agreement cannot expand nor restrict any right to secure evidence under the NAA. Thus, when sections 6 and 7 refer to disputes or actions 'subject to arbitration', this must as a starting point clearly refer to the substantive issues, not procedural matters such as the issue of securing of evidence.

20. *See* Høgetveit Berg et al., *Voldgiftsloven, kommentarutgave*, p. 101, which points out that since section 6 is mandatory, the parties cannot in principle assign more tasks to the court than what is stipulated in the Act.
21. The Nordic Offshore & Maritime Arbitration Association (NOMA) should also be mentioned, though it is not a traditional arbitration institution.
22. Rules of The Arbitration and Dispute Resolution Institute of the Oslo Chamber of Commerce.

[6] The Preparatory Works

The question of whether evidence may be preserved outside of legal proceedings when the parties have agreed to arbitration is not directly addressed in the preparatory works of the NAA or the NDA.

However, in the preparatory works to the NDA, it is emphasized that the rules on the taking of evidence in court proceedings in Chapter 27 of the NDA are also applicable to arbitration.[23] This will be the case where the arbitral tribunal requests assistance from the courts pursuant to section 30 of the NAA, which provides that 'the arbitral tribunal or a party with the consent of the arbitral tribunal may ask the court to take testimony from parties and witnesses and take other evidence'. The preparatory works do not provide a similar clarification with regard to the application of Chapter 28 of the NDA to arbitration.

[7] Case Law

There are no Supreme Court decisions concerning the securing of evidence in connection with arbitration. However, there are some lower court decisions which may have argumentative value and which illustrate the questions of interpretation raised by the NAA.[24]

The question of securing of evidence when the parties have agreed to arbitration first came up in a case before the Bergen District Court (TBERG-2011-13681). The case involved a party's request for documents from a limited liability company in connection with a dispute concerning additional remuneration under a share purchase agreement. The reason for the request was that the party needed the documentation in order to determine whether she was entitled to additional remuneration.

The court based its decision on sections 6 and 7 of the NAA, and the determining factor was whether the request for the securing of evidence was 'a lawsuit that is the subject of arbitration'. The court found that it was not natural to consider the request for the securing of evidence as a 'lawsuit'. On this basis, the District Court concluded that the petition to preserve evidence fell outside the scope of section 7 of the NAA.

The District Court further held that the fact that section 8 of the NAA contains a separate provision giving the court jurisdiction to order interim measures and that there is no express provision concerning the securing of evidence was not sufficient to substantiate that the District Court could not order evidence to be preserved.

In addition, the District Court stressed that compelling substantive considerations supported the court's finding.

The decision by the Bergen District Court was appealed to the Gulating Court of Appeals (LG-2011-92858), which found that the arbitration agreement implied that evidence could not be secured pursuant to Chapter 28 of the NDA.

---

23. NOU 2001: 32 pp. 983 and 987.
24. The significance of lower court practice as a source of law is discussed by, among others, Jens Edvin A. Skoghøy, *Rett og rettsanvendelse*, Universitetsforlaget, 2018 p. 215.

The Court of Appeals based its decision on section 7 of the NAA and held that the question was whether the request for production of the documents was a dispute that was 'subject to arbitration'.

The Court of Appeals found that there undoubtedly was a dispute between the parties as to which documents the company was obligated to produce. The court interpreted the arbitration clause in the share purchase agreement to also cover disputes concerning the production of documents and that it was not decisive that the dispute involved a procedural issue.

Furthermore, the Court of Appeals emphasized that section 6 of the NAA states that the courts may only decide disputes which are subject to arbitration where there is a statutory basis in the NAA. In that respect, the court pointed out that section 8 of the NAA only applies to provisional security, such as arrest and interim measures and does not include the securing of evidence under Chapter 28.

Both lower-court decisions contain flaws in their argument. The ruling from Bergen District Court did not discuss the wording of section 6 (1) and whether the court's ability to order the securing of evidence requires statutory authority in the NAA. Furthermore, it is a weak point in the reasoning of the Court of Appeals that it did not address section 6 (2) which presumes that the courts may hear cases concerning the securing of evidence. In addition, it is a flaw in the court's reasoning that when interpreting the arbitration clause, it did not discuss the fact that sections 6 and 7 cannot be derogated from by agreement between the parties, *see* §14.03[B][5] above. The court should also have discussed whether the petition to secure evidence constituted a lawsuit that the court had jurisdiction to dismiss under section 7.

In conclusion, little emphasis can be placed on the decisions from the lower courts when determining how to interpret the provisions of the NAA.

[8] Jurisprudence

In jurisprudence, there appears to be – with one exception – consensus that a party can request the securing of evidence when the dispute is subject to arbitration.[25] For instance, Woxholth provides the following opinion:

> A petition for securing of evidence prior to a possible dispute must be considered to fall outside the scope of the NAA section 7. This provision cannot be used to prevent the securing of evidence. Linguistically it is not natural to describe a petition for securing of evidence as a 'lawsuit' in the context of the provision, and good, substantive reasons [...] support the view that securing of evidence can be carried out in these cases.

25. *See* Woxholth, *Voldgift*, p. 160, Ristvedt and Eriksrud point 5, Schei et al., *Tvisteloven, kommentarutgave*, comment to section 28-1 item 1.3, and Amund Bjøranger Tørum, '"Best practice" i norsk og nordisk voldgift og NOMAs Guidelines', *Tidsskrift for forretningsjus*, 2018 (Tørum 2) p. 122, footnote 47.

Only Hjort takes the view that it is not possible to secure evidence outside court proceedings when arbitration has been agreed.[26] In her opinion, it is difficult to arrive at a different conclusion than the one reached by the Gulating Court of Appeals in LG-2011-92858. We do not agree with this. As pointed out, there are multiple weak points in the court's reasoning and several clear indications in the NAA that securing of evidence outside court proceedings may be requested even when the parties have agreed to arbitration.

Hjort does, however, state that she finds it puzzling that the act allows the courts to order interim measures pursuant to section 8 of the NAA but does not provide a similar statutory basis for the securing of evidence. In Hjort's opinion, there is reason to question whether this is a well-considered distinction.

The fact that a majority of legal scholars believe that the NAA must be interpreted to allow the securing of evidence is significant but is clearly not a decisive argument.

[9] Considerations Based on the Objects and Interests of the Legislation

It is equally important in arbitration proceedings as in cases before the ordinary courts to give the parties the opportunity to secure evidence that may be lost or substantially impaired, or to allow a party to have access to evidence in order to assess its legal position before initiating proceedings.

As indicated in the introduction, it could also be argued that it is even more important that a party can obtain access to evidence when disputes are subject to arbitration. This reason is that arbitral awards are final, even though it in theory is possible for the parties to agree that an arbitral award may be appealed to another arbitral tribunal.[27] Further, it is not possible to re-open arbitration proceedings, for instance, due to new information or factual errors in the decision; *see* by comparison the NDA section 31-4(a). In addition, an arbitral award cannot be declared invalid due to errors in the court's assessment of evidence, *see* the NAA section 43. It is, therefore, particularly important to ensure that the facts in arbitration proceedings are as accurate and complete as possible.

In accordance with this, the legal scholars who have examined the issue all agree that there *should be* a right to secure evidence under Chapter 28 of the NDA, even if the parties have agreed to arbitration. A right to secure evidence is also well in line with the arbitral tribunal's and the parties' right to request the courts to record evidence or to order the production of evidence pursuant to the NAA section 30.[28]

Tørum points out that if the conditions in section 28-2 are not interpreted strictly, this could open up a form of discovery, which is time-consuming and costly and not in

26. Maria Astrup Hjort, *Tilgang til bevis i sivile saker: Særlig om digitale bevis*, Universitetsforlaget 2016, p. 247.
27. Woxholth, p. 50 and Høgetveit Berget al. p. 315 and section 464 (2) of the former Civil Procedure Act. An arbitral award cannot be appealed to the ordinary courts for a substantive review, but can only be set aside as invalid, *see* section 42 of the NAA.
28. *See also* Schei et al., commentary on section 28-1, point 1.3.

accordance with the Nordic tradition in arbitration cases.[29] We agree that this may be a counterargument, but as the conditions are worded and interpreted, there is, in our view, little risk that the possibility of securing evidence will allow for a form of discovery. The requirement for securing of evidence pursuant to section 28-2 is that it is 'particularly important' to gain access to the evidence before proceedings are instigated. Furthermore, it is specified in the preparatory works that this indicates a strict standard.[30]

[10] Conclusion

As apparent from the discussion above, the wording of the NAA is not entirely clear. There is no decisive case law and little guidance in the preparatory works.

With such a lack of clarity in authoritative legal sources, decisive weight should in our opinion be given to the substantive considerations that undeniably support the view that it should be possible to secure evidence under Chapter 28 of the NDA also when the parties have agreed to arbitration.

[C] The Swedish Perspective

[1] Chapter 41 of the SCJP

Similar to the discussion above regarding Norwegian law, the natural starting point for the analysis under Swedish law is Chapter 41 in the SCJP.

As mentioned, section 41-1 provides that a person may apply to have evidence preserved by a court if there is a risk that the evidence may be lost or difficult to obtain and the evidence concerns a circumstance of importance to a person's legal rights. The provision requires that the dispute is not already subject to a trial. An arbitration is in this regard considered equivalent to trial, i.e., a court shall reject a party's application if the issue is subject to an initiated arbitration.[31]

The wording of the provision does not stipulate any requirement that the evidence is to be used in future court proceedings. The preparatory works state that Chapter 41 primarily relates to evidence that may be submitted to litigation before general courts; however, this distinction is not made in relation to arbitration but to proceedings before administrative courts.[32]

From a systematic perspective, one may question if the fact that the provisions of Chapter 41 are found in the SCJP instead of the SAA means that the provisions do not

29. Tørum 2018, p. 122, footnote 47.
30. NOU 2001:32 p. 988 and Ot. prp. no. 51 (2004-2005) p. 470.
31. The alternative would allow a party of an arbitration to circumvent the requirement that parties must otherwise obtain the consent of the arbitral tribunal in order for evidence to be examined in court, *see* Justitieombudsmannens Ämbetsberättelse 1953, pp. 61-62.
32. NJA II 1943 p. 516. In the motives, the legislator indicated that the provisions of Chapter 41 may be applied in cases where special provisions of administrative law permit preservation of evidence.

cover disputes which are to be decided through arbitration. The preparatory works do not indicate that the legislator made any association between Chapter 41 and arbitration. This could imply that granting the preservation of evidence would be in conflict with the legislator's intention. However, in light of the fact that the statutory text does not require the relevant right to be tried in general court, the argument is rather weak and should in our opinion not be decisive. Such an interpretation would in fact suggest that an additional requirement is read into section 41-1, namely that the evidence must be used before a general court.

Consequently, it is reasonable to conclude that section 41-1 of the SCJP does not constitute any obstacle to securing evidence for a possible arbitration procedure. In the following, we will discuss whether other provisions or considerations may entail a different conclusion.

[2] Chapter 10, Section 17a of the SCJP and Section 4 of the SAA

Chapter 10, section 17a of the SCJP, regulating the jurisdiction of the courts, states that the SAA contains special provisions on barring proceedings in courts. According to section 4 of the SAA, a court may not, against a party's objection, try an issue which is to be examined by arbitrators. The provision contains an exemption for interim measures, which may be decided by the courts without prejudice to the arbitration agreement. This applies irrespective of whether the arbitration is ongoing or has not yet been instigated:

> A court may not, over an objection of a party, rule on an issue which, pursuant to an arbitration agreement, shall be decided by arbitrators.
>
> [...] During the pendency of a dispute before arbitrators or prior thereto, a court may, irrespective of the arbitration agreement, issue such decisions in respect of interim measures as the court has jurisdiction to issue.[33]

Thus, section 10-17a of the SCJP and section 4 of the SAA prevents a court from examining issues which are to be examined by an arbitral tribunal.

As will be discussed in §14.03[C][3] below, an arbitral tribunal has exclusive jurisdiction to decide whether evidence should be examined before a court when an arbitration has been initiated. There is no provision in the SAA that allows a tribunal to decide on the preservation of evidence prior to a dispute. This follows from the fact that the tribunal does not exist until the arbitration has been initiated. Consequently, the wording of section 4 of the SAA and section 10-17a of the SCJP does not prevent courts from preserving evidence.

It should be noted that the courts' jurisdiction to decide on interim measures, before and during the arbitration, is expressed in section 4 of the SAA. This could support the argument that there is no legal basis for deciding on preserving of evidence prior to arbitration, as there is no similar exemption. However, there is no clear support in the preparatory works that this was a deliberate position of the legislator. Another

33. Section 4 of the SAA.

interpretation is that the regulation of interim measures is an issue that is often raised in proceedings. It was therefore warranted for the legislator to include an explicit regulation of the issue. As stated in §14.03[B][2] above regarding the NAA, the existence of the stipulation in the Model Law is presumably one of the reasons for including such a provision in the SAA. The Swedish preparatory works refer in particular to the existence of a similar provision in the Model Law. Accordingly, the argument that the omission of provisions concerning the preserving of evidence was a deliberate position from the legislator is weak.[34]

[3] Sections 25 and 26 of the SAA

According to section 25 of the SAA, it is the arbitral tribunal that decides whether to admit or dismiss evidence:

> The parties shall supply the evidence. However, the arbitrators may appoint experts, unless both parties are opposed thereto.
>
> The arbitrators may refuse to admit evidence presented if it is manifestly irrelevant to the dispute or if such refusal is justified having regard to the time at which the evidence is invoked.
>
> [...]

Section 26 of the SAA states that evidence may be admitted before a court provided that the arbitral tribunal has given its permission:

> If a party wishes a witness or an expert to testify under oath, or a party to be examined under truth affirmation, the party may, after obtaining the consent of the arbitrators, submit an application to such effect to the District Court. The aforementioned shall apply if a party wishes that a party or other person be ordered to produce as evidence a document or an object. If the arbitrators consider that the measure is justified having regard to the evidence in the case, they shall approve the request. If the measure may lawfully be taken, the District Court shall grant the application.

As indicated in the wording, the court shall reject the request if a party to an arbitration files a request for the taking of evidence without the permission of the tribunal. The court shall not make any assessment of its own of the admissibility of the evidence.[35]

Consequently, the provisions give arbitral tribunals exclusive authority to decide on evidence, including the taking of evidence in court, at least during the arbitration proceedings. The provisions do not make any references to the preservation of evidence under Chapter 41 of the SCJP. However, allowing the preservation of evidence with the assistance of a court would constitute a deviation from the principle that a tribunal has exclusive authority to decide on evidence. Legal scholars have

34. Government bill 1998/99:35 pp. 71 ff.
35. Government bill 1998/99:35, p. 226 f.

therefore argued that the provisions prevent the preservation of evidence as it could constitute a circumvention of the arbitral tribunal's exclusive jurisdiction.[36]

However, it should be noted that section 25 of the SAA provides that it is the parties who are responsible for the evidence and that the arbitral tribunal's ability to dismiss evidence is limited to situations where the evidence is clearly irrelevant or where it is justified from a time perspective. This is further emphasized in the preparatory works:

> According to the committee, the parties' right to control the evidence should not extend so far that the arbitrators are forced to take up evidence that is irrelevant to the dispute. The committee further states that there also must exist a restriction against a party - perhaps for the purpose of procrastination - invoking new evidence at a late stage of the proceedings. The Government shares the Committee's assessment and proposes that a provision with this effect is included in the Act.[37]

The exclusive jurisdiction of the arbitral tribunal to decide on evidence in arbitration is thus only warranted for the purpose of ensuring that the arbitration proceeds efficiently and expeditiously. The implication of this is discussed in §14.03[C][7] below.

[4] Preparatory Works

The preparatory works of the SCJP and the SAA do not address the issue of securing evidence for future arbitration proceedings. There is no indication that the legislator has considered the issue. This calls for some caution when it comes to drawing far-reaching conclusions from the exact wording of the statutory text. For example, it may be questionable to interpret sections 4, 25 and 26 of the SAA *e contrario* to exclude the preservation of evidence for a future arbitration.

[5] Case Law

The question of whether it is possible to secure evidence prior to an arbitration has not been settled in Swedish case law. However, there are two judgments from the Swedish Supreme Court concerning the Former Swedish Arbitration Act (FSAA) which contain relevant statements.[38]

In the Swedish Supreme Court case no. NJA 1971 p. 521, a constructor and an association had agreed to build a terraced house for a buyer. Under the agreement, certain costs for the house were to correspond to the association's own cost price. The obligations of the association were later transferred to a housing association. The

36. *See* section §14.03[C][6] below.
37. Government bill 1998/99:35, p. 114.
38. The FSAA also required the approval of the arbitral tribunal in order for evidence to be admitted in court, *see* section 15 of the FSAA. The provision required that the examination of evidence was necessary. An arbitration agreement also barred court proceedings under the previous act, *see* Hassler, *Skiljeförfarande*, p. 20 f, and Lindskog, *Skiljeförfarande*, 3rd ed., p. 333.

agreement contained an arbitration clause. After some time, the buyer questioned whether the costs corresponded to the association's cost price and therefore applied to the district court to order the housing association to present certain documentation. The housing association contested the application, partly on the grounds that there was no danger of the documentation being destroyed. The district court granted the buyer's request, an assessment which the court of appeal upheld after the housing association had appealed the decision.

Supreme Court reversed the lower courts' decisions and rejected the application as it found that the buyer had not substantiated any risk concerning the destruction or deterioration of the documents.

What is interesting in this decision is that none of the three courts expressed any hesitation as to whether the arbitration clause could affect the right to preserve evidence. The Supreme Court's reasoning also shows that the court took note of the existence of the arbitration agreement:

> Nor has any particular circumstance been presented of such a nature which entail the existence of a risk that the documents in question will be destroyed or lost; or that [the Buyer's] ability to produce them as evidence in court proceedings or arbitration will otherwise be denied or impaired.[39]

In light of the fact that the Supreme Court rejected the request, it is unclear if the Supreme Court's decision includes a position on whether the arbitration clause could have constituted an obstacle to the preservation of evidence. The Supreme Court's reference to a possible future court proceeding, despite the existence of the arbitration clause, may be interpreted to mean that the court chose not to assess whether the arbitration clause constituted an obstacle per se. However, the Supreme Court's statement is a stronger argument in support of permitting the preservation of evidence with regards to a future arbitration, rather than the opposite, as the court referred to it as a possible and perhaps relevant proceeding in the future.

In the Supreme Court case no. NJA 1994 p. 683, a company requested the district court to allow the examination of two of its employees. The company had received indications that it would be evaluated for a tax surcharge. The employees were to be questioned about their contacts with the tax authorities to preserve their statements for future administrative proceedings. Thus, the case did not concern a future arbitration but the question of whether Chapter 41 of the SCJP could be applied for future administrative proceedings. The Supreme Court concluded that this was not possible, but it granted the application as the company had amended its request before the Supreme Court by including that the company was also considering a civil action for damages due to the issue. The Supreme Court stated that:

> It is true that the wording of chapter 41, section 1 of the [SCJP] cannot be regarded as precluding the preservation of evidence in order to safeguard the individual's rights in a context other than a trial before a general court. However, as previously indicated, such a broad application of the law is not consistent with the structure of [SCJP] and the general formulation of the rules of evidence in the [SCJP]. In

39. NJA 1971 p. 521.

> view of the fact that the administrative courts are to be regarded as equal to the general courts, the outset should also be that the provisions regulating the administrative courts are exhaustive within their field and are not supplemented by the provisions of the [SCJP] [...], unless otherwise stated.[40]

The reasoning of the Supreme Court corresponds to the considerations presented above in §14.03[C][1], i.e., that a systematic approach may perhaps prevent the application of Chapter 41 with regard to arbitration. It should, however, be noted that there is reason to distinguish arbitration proceedings from administrative proceedings, as arbitration is a substitute for litigation in general court.[41] Accordingly, the Supreme Court's decision does not address the relevant question for the article as it targets administrative proceedings instead of civil proceedings. One of the justices, who disagreed with the reasoning of the judgment, commented on the issue of securing evidence prior to arbitration.

> The prerequisite stated in chapter 41, section 1 of [SCJP] for the taking of evidence for future security that the evidence must relate to a circumstance that is of significance to someone's right does not include any requirement that the legal claim must necessarily be relevant in a future trial before a general court. It is also clear from the preparatory works to the provisions of the chapter that these are indeed primarily aimed at evidence that may be invoked in such a trial, but that they are also intended to be mainly applicable when the taking of evidence is required, for example, for an administrative procedure (NJA II 1943, p. 516). According to the generally accepted opinion, the taking of evidence for future security is also considered to be possible in general civil court with regard to circumstances covered by an arbitration agreement, provided that arbitration proceedings have not been initiated (*see*, *inter alia*, Lars Heuman in Juridisk Tidskrift 1989/90, p. 234).[42]

As evident from the quote, the dissenting judge expressed a positive view on the issue that there is an accepted opinion that evidence may be secured prior to an arbitration. His position is not contradicted by the majority's argumentation but is based, among other things, on statements from Professor Heuman. Heuman's statements are further discussed in the section below.

Consequently, there are no direct statements from case law that close the door to allowing the securing of evidence prior to arbitration. On the contrary, it is more logical to interpret the judgments as the door has been left open, even if the statements have been made *obiter dictum* and in a dissenting opinion. That being said, the reasoning of the majority in NJA 1994 p. 683 could be invoked as a reason why the systematic of the SCJP speaks against such an application. However, arbitration proceedings and civil cases in general courts generally have greater similarities with each other compared to administrative proceedings, especially when it comes to evidence. This speaks in

40. NJA 1994 p. 683.
41. It may be noted that the legislator expressed an ambition that the SAA should be independent of the rules of the SCJP, *see* government bill 1998/99:35, p. 46. However, this has not prevented the Supreme Court from often being inspired by the provisions of the SCJP if the SAA has not provided an answer to a question.
42. Justice Munck's dissenting opinion in the Swedish Supreme Court Case No. NJA 1994 p. 683.

favour of applying Chapter 41 prior to an arbitration, even if it is not permissible with regard to administrative proceedings.

[6] *Jurisprudence*

The topic of this article has not received much attention in Swedish jurisprudence. However, there are mainly three publications that deal with the issue.

In the article referred to by the dissenting justice in NJA 1994 p. 683, Heuman stated that a party may request the preservation of evidence before the court, provided that the arbitration has not yet been initiated. If the proceedings have commenced, the court shall reject the request. Heuman refers partly to the fact that an ongoing arbitration proceeding prevents the taking of evidence under section 41-1 of the SCJP and partly to the fact that the taking of evidence during the arbitration circumvents the FSAA requirement for the arbitral tribunal's permission to examine the evidence before the court.[43]

Later, Heuman appears to have changed his position. In a subsequent publication, written after the entry into force of the SAA, Heuman states that the provisions on the preservation of evidence are not applicable prior to arbitration proceedings because a party would then be able to circumvent the requirement of the arbitrators' permission for the taking of evidence in court.[44] Heuman does not elaborate on his apparent change of position. Even if the statement itself is clear, the lack of reasoning raises the question of whether Heuman actually meant to refer to the situation where a party attempts to conduct an evidentiary hearing pursuant to Chapter 41 SCJP during the course of an arbitration. Indeed, Heuman refers to a legal source which refers exactly to that situation. This would then be in line with his position in the previous publication.[45]

Lindskog questions Heuman's position that the arbitration agreement would prevent the securing of evidence:

> It has been argued that an arbitration agreement is an obstacle for preservation of evidence. However, it is doubtful whether this is the case.
>
> The fact that a district court should not approve an application for securing of evidence when an arbitration proceeding is in progress follows from the fact that it would constitute a circumvention of the provisions on the taking of evidence before a court set out in section 25. However, this argument has less bearing in the case of the taking of evidence for preservation in accordance with the provisions of chapter 41 of the [SCJP]. It is doubtful whether the mere interest in taking evidence is sufficient to allow a party the right to initiate arbitration proceedings. The requirement of the arbitral tribunal's authorisation in section 25 can hardly justifiably be invoked as a reason against a party's right to apply directly to a court;

43. Heuman, *Editionsföreläggande i civilprocesser och arbetstvister Del II*, Juridisk Tidskrift 1989/90, p. 233. In the article Heuman refers to section 15 of the FSAA, corresponding to section 26 of the SAA.
44. Heuman, *Skiljemannarätt*, p. 349.
45. Heuman only reference is to Justitieombudsmannens Ämbetsberättelse 1953, p. 61, which concern the situation where an arbitration is already initiated.

the purpose of this requirement should be limited to enabling an ongoing proceeding to be enforced efficiently and with legal certainty. The conclusion therefore seems to be that the arbitration agreement does not constitute an obstacle for taking of evidence by way of preservation.[46]

[7] Considerations Based on the Objects and Interests of the Legislation

As stated in the introduction and in the discussion of §14.03[B][8] above on Norwegian law, there are significant interests that support the conclusion to allow parties to secure evidence prior to arbitration.

Arguably, the procedure in arbitration calls for a greater interest in collecting evidence prior to the initiation of proceedings compared to court cases, as arbitration proceedings are characterized by the parties agreeing on a timetable early on in the proceedings and the fact that the procedure is often more front-loaded than in court cases.

Even though the SCJP requires that there is a risk that the evidence will be destroyed or impaired, the preparatory works state that the securing of evidence may help a party determine its evidentiary position before any legal steps are taken. Thereby, a party may avoid proceedings where the evidence to support its claim is insufficient.[47]

Given that there is no clear answer in the wording of the law, the preparatory works, or case law and that the legal scholars have not managed to close the door on the securing of evidence prior to arbitration, the assessment must be determined by balancing of purposes of the alternatives.

The main reason for not allowing the securing of evidence is that the arbitral tribunal shall have exclusive jurisdiction to rule on the admissibility of evidence. This jurisdiction is based on the tribunal's interest in conducting the arbitration in an expeditious and practical manner.[48] These interests are in fact not affected by allowing the preservation of evidence prior to the commencement of arbitration proceedings. As the arbitration has not been initiated, the taking of evidence cannot affect the conduct of the arbitration. Should the evidence turn out to be irrelevant once the arbitration has commenced, the arbitral tribunal may still reject it pursuant to section 25 of the SAA. Arguably, securing evidence prior to the arbitration could mean that the arbitration proceeds more efficiently as some evidence is already secured prior to the proceedings.

It could be argued that the commencement of an evidentiary hearing may disturb the opposing party by requiring the opposing party to present evidence and shift focus from preparing the arbitration. This is, however, a consideration of lesser concern as it is still required that the applicant must demonstrate an actual risk of destruction or

46. Lindskog, *Skiljeförfarande*, 3rd ed., p. 352.
47. NJA II 1943 p. 515. It may be noted that the rule should not be applied to enable searching for evidence. The main purpose of the rule is to allow a party to protect evidence that the party knows exists.
48. *See* §14.03[C][2]-§14.03[C][3].

deterioration of the evidence.[49] The fact that the applicant must also reimburse the opposing party for its costs pursuant to Chapter 41-4 of the SCJP may also act as a deterrent against petitions which lack sufficient merit. Lastly, it is not possible to hold examinations of the counterparty to the arbitration, which is justified precisely to avoid abuse.[50]

In our opinion, on the whole, the balance of purposes in allowing the preservation of evidence in arbitration outweighs the negative aspects.

[D] Conclusion

Similar to the situation under the Norwegian law, the legal authorities fail to provide an unambiguous answer to the question raised in this chapter. However, none of the legal sources appear to prohibit the securing of evidence prior to an arbitration. If anything, we would argue that the legal sources lean towards allowing it. We would also contend that this is further supported by the fact that the considerations which form the basis of the provision in SCJP section 41-1 strongly support this conclusion.

§14.04 SUMMARY AND CONCLUSION

The provisions in the respective acts in Sweden and Norway are very similar, not least the arbitration acts, which are both inspired by the Model Law. However, even though the legislation is comparable, the approach to the issue concerning the securing of evidence is quite dissimilar, and emphasis is placed on different arguments.

For instance, in Sweden, the strongest argument against allowing the securing of evidence prior to an arbitration case being commenced is, at least in jurisprudence, the arbitral tribunal's exclusive authority to decide on the evidence pursuant to the SAA sections 25 and 26. The NAA contains corresponding provisions, but these have not been accentuated by any courts or legal scholars when examining the issue of preserving evidence.

In our view, the different approach taken in each country demonstrates the value of a comparative analysis. It displays that the quality of the assessment of a legal issue can be improved by examining how the question has been analyzed in another country with comparable rules.

The conclusion with regard to the issue of securing of evidence is the same both in Norway and Sweden. Despite some uncertainty in the wording in each country's legislation, the acts in both countries should be interpreted to allow for evidence to be secured prior to the commencement of arbitration proceedings.

The lack of clarity is in our view unnecessary. There appears to be a broad consensus that an opportunity to secure evidence is just as important in arbitration proceedings as in cases before the ordinary courts. This is strongly supported by

49. In addition to the wording of the legal provisions, this was emphasised by the Supreme Court in NJA 1971 p. 521.
50. *See* Fitger et al., *Rättegångsbalken* (12 December 2022, JUNO), commentary to Chapter 41 §1.

substantive considerations and, in Sweden, also by the statements from the Supreme Court. In our opinion, both the SAA and NAA could benefit from being amended by including a provision expressly stating that the courts have the power to secure evidence prior to the commencement of arbitration proceedings in the same manner as section 8 of the NAA and section 4 of the SAA states that the courts may order interim measures.[51]

Such clarification may help to ensure that evidence is preserved where this is essential. From a broader perspective, this may contribute to the facts in arbitration cases being clearer, thereby ensuring more materially correct arbitral awards.

51. Legislation could also solve practical issues regarding preserving of evidence. For example, in Sweden an examination of a witness is generally recorded by video. Preferably, the recording could be used as evidence before the tribunal. However, the general rule is that a video recording may not be handed out by the court without the witness consent (43-4 of the Swedish Public Access to Information and Secrecy Act). A party has an unconditional right to see the recording, for example at the court, but not an unconditional right to receive a copy of the recoding (Swedish Supreme Court case No. NJA 2008 p. 883), and a party may always receive copy of a sound recording. It is probable that a party may receive a video recording by referring to overriding provisions in the Information and Secrecy Act, such as section 10-2, but it would be favourable if the right was clearly acknowledged by the legislator.

CHAPTER 15

What Is the Difference Between a Judge and an Arbitrator?

Emilia Lundberg & Fanny Gleiss Wilborg

§15.01 INTRODUCTION

Is the role of an arbitrator the same as the role of a judge? The short answer is "no, not at all." Although both arbitrators and judges administer justice, being an arbitrator is not like being a judge in a court of law. Even though arbitrators are sometimes described to non-lawyers as "private judges," this description can be misleading because there are, in fact, big differences between the tasks carried out by arbitrators and those effectuated by judges. However, despite these differences, the questions put before a court in a civil matter and an arbitral tribunal are often the same, and therefore comparing the two makes sense.

Comparisons between arbitration and civil litigation are often undertaken from the perspective of the parties or parties' counsel. In this chapter, by contrast, we will explore the issue from the decisionmaker's perspective. Having experience as both state judges and arbitrators, we have observed the differences between the roles first-hand. Some of the differences are necessary, some are beneficial, but others may be unnecessary and arguably detrimental to the administration of justice. It is our hope that by highlighting varying perspectives, disparities, and alternatives, our reflections can catalyze improved arbitral processes.

§15.02 SWEDEN'S STATE COURT JUDGES: POWERS & DUTIES

As our readers likely know, an arbitration is rooted in an agreement, whereas a court proceeding is rooted in law. This fundamental difference is crucial, but in what ways? For the purposes of this chapter, we will focus solely on Swedish civil law cases where the parties were free to choose either a state court or an arbitral tribunal for their dispute. We will begin by laying a foundation regarding the powers and duties of judges and arbitrators.

In Sweden, the judiciary's power is primarily derived from and governed by the Instrument of Government (*Sw. Regeringsformen*), which is the country's constitution, and the Code of Judicial Procedure (*Sw. Rättegångsbalken*). The Instrument of Government establishes the principle of the separation of powers, including the independence of the judiciary from other branches of government. It also sets out the general principles of justice, such as the right to a fair and public trial. The Code of Judicial Procedure details the rules that judges must follow in the administration of justice. It sets out rules for conducting trials, the presentation of evidence, the role of judges and other court officials, and the rights and obligations of parties involved in legal proceedings.

Judges in Sweden are appointed by the government, are almost never replaced, and perform their duties without risk of personal liability. Still, judges are required to follow relevant laws and regulations, as well as case law and legal precedent established by higher courts, and a judge's decision is subject to review by appellate courts. A Swedish judge in a court of general jurisdiction handles a wide array of cases, both criminal and civil cases, and while judges are experts at court procedure and managing a courtroom, it is unusual for a judge to specialize in any particular area of the law.

In Sweden, judges are required to take an oath of office before assuming their duties. The oath is set out in Chapter 5 section 7 of the Swedish Instrument of Government and reads as follows:

> I swear to exercise my office with loyalty, impartiality, and in accordance with the law and regulations, to the best of my ability and understanding. I shall protect the fundamental values and rights upon which the Swedish Constitution is founded, including the rule of law, human rights, democracy and gender equality.

The purpose of the oath is to emphasize the importance of upholding the law and the principles of justice and to ensure that judges remain independent and impartial in the performance of their duties.

§15.03 ARBITRATORS: POWERS & DUTIES

Disputes that are subject to arbitration clauses necessitate the existence of arbitral tribunals. Unlike a court, to which an application may be made at almost any time, an arbitral tribunal must be created before it can exercise any jurisdiction over the dispute and the parties.[1] Each arbitrator on a tribunal is a neutral third party appointed to resolve a dispute between two or more parties outside of court. In contrast to judges, most arbitrators are attorneys with limited experience managing a hearing or drafting an award, and they are often hand-picked because of their expertise in a certain legal

1. The absence of a standing body of arbitrators can be disadvantageous when there is a "pre-arbitral" phase that requires time-sensitive decisions. Most arbitral institutions have processes to accommodate emergency arbitrations, but even in these situations, an arbitrator must first be appointed.

field. Furthermore, under general contract law, an arbitrator can be held liable for damages if a party suffers a loss due to an arbitrator's negligence.[2]

The powers of an arbitrator acting under the Swedish Arbitration Act or under the rules of the SCC Arbitration Institute (Stockholm Chamber of Commerce (SCC)) vary depending on the specific arbitration agreement. Any power that an arbitrator has originates from the parties and their agreement.[3] The origin of powers differentiates an arbitrator's work from that of a sitting judge in ways that permeate every step of the proceedings.

One other key difference between the role of an arbitrator and that of a judge is the issue of compensation. Unlike a judge whose salary is paid by the state, an arbitral tribunal must secure payment of its fees and expenses from the parties. Even though an arbitral tribunal does not need to concern itself with payment issues when an arbitration is being administrated by an established institution, the arbitral tribunal still must keep track of events that may require a deposit of additional funds.

§15.04 CONFIDENCE AND INDEPENDENCE

[A] Confidence and Independence: Parties' Perspective

One of the most appealing features of arbitration compared to litigation is that parties get an opportunity to choose at least one arbitrator. Unsurprisingly, the parties choose arbitrators who instill confidence. When appointing an arbitrator, the party can ensure that the tribunal includes someone with relevant expertise and skills, or even with a known opinion on disputed legal issues. By contrast, if parties take the case to court instead, they cannot choose the judge. Pursuant to Chapter 11 section 3 of the Instrument of Government, only the court itself can decide how cases shall be allocated among the judges. Chapter 4 section 11a of the Code of Judicial Procedure further ensures that cases are distributed in a neutral way since it clarifies that the court must have rules in place that clarify how a case is assigned to a specific judge.

In theory, decisions should be the same regardless of which judge is assigned to a case. However, in practice, outcomes vary significantly. For example, in the court where one of us served, a hearing was held before three judges. At the end of the oral hearing, circumstances necessitated a re-hearing before a new set of judges. The new set of three judges conducted the re-hearing, deliberated, and reached a judgment. A few weeks later, one of the judges from the first hearing expressed that he had been surprised when reading the judgment since he had been almost certain that he and his two co-judges would have reached the opposite decision.

2. The SCC rules include a general exclusion of liability for arbitrators. By contrast, in an ad hoc arbitration it is common that the parties agree to exclude arbitrator liability.
3. An arbitrator's power is, of course, also governed by law. In fact, the powers, duties and jurisdiction of an arbitral tribunal arise from a complex mixture of the will of the parties, the law governing the arbitration agreement, the law of the place of arbitration, and the law of the place where recognition or enforcement of the award may be sought.

As noted above, being able to choose arbitrators is a powerful tool since different arbitrators also often reach entirely divergent conclusions. To illustrate anecdotally, in two arbitration cases, the tribunals drafted two versions of the award, reaching two completely opposite outcomes. In both instances, the arbitral tribunal deliberated and agreed on an outcome, of which one of the co-arbitrators was strongly in favor. The draft award was circulated among the arbitrators and, subsequently, another co-arbitrator requested continuing deliberations. After the continued deliberations, all the arbitrators came to different conclusions, and a new award was drafted, reaching the opposite judgment. The commonality between these two disputes is that they were both decided on law rather than evidence. Looking back at the two versions of the final awards, both versions in both disputes could be defended.

Nevertheless, although parties can choose their own arbitrator in an arbitration, in our experience, it is still difficult (if not impossible) to predict how the arbitrator will decide a specific case.[4] Every decision is made case-by-case based on the myriad circumstances unique to each dispute. An arbitrator (or a judge) is independent and free to change her mind on legal issues. But perhaps 100% certainty is not necessary; rather, if parties have confidence in the person deciding the case, it is easier to accept the award, whatever it may be.

[B] Confidence and Independence: Decisionmaker's Perspective

Having established that outcomes are influenced by who decides a case and that it is easier to feel confident in the decisionmaker (and the decision) if you have chosen her, we must consider how/if decisionmakers themselves are affected by whether they were selected by the parties.

According to the principle of the courts' independence expressed in Chapter 11 section 2 of the Swedish Instrument of Government, no authority, not even the Parliament, may decide how a court should act. This rule has been construed to cover not only the courts' independence from the outside world but also the individual judge's independence internally in relation to the other judges, including the head of court. In essence, when deciding a case, a judge in a civil court must not be controlled by colleagues, any of the parties, or the head of the court.

Naturally, parties expect that it should not matter if their dispute is tried in court or before an arbitral tribunal. Either way, both independence and confidence are expected from the judge/arbitrator. An arbitrator should not be connected to a party to the case at issue, so, in theory, the judges and arbitrators should be similarly positioned. But, again, the parties provide the arbitrator with billable hours and ultimately pay the arbitrator's fees. As such, one can imagine that a selected member of the arbitral tribunal considers the arguments brought forward by the party who

4. Even if you are allowed to ask a presumptive arbitrator questions before appointing her, the possible questions are limited and can only be focused on availability, conflict or experience in general terms.

appointed her more closely than a state court judge would have done. However, it must be pointed out that in our experience, this can in fact be a good thing.

As mentioned above, since payment is not a consideration among judges, the courts may be the recipients of higher perceived confidence. However, there are other factors that influence the work performed by the judges that do not adversely impact an arbitral tribunal. For example, there is an informal (and sometimes formal) hierarchy among state court judges that may influence how they work together. In Sweden, a constant evaluation process between judges is part of the career path. The judges often know each other and have worked together on many different cases. When reaching a decision, hierarchy and professional dynamics among the judges can have positive impacts but also undermine independence.

§15.05 TRANSPARENCY AND CONFIDENTIALITY

Transparency is a procedural concept that denotes openness, accessibility to information, clarity, and reliability of the judicial process. For example, one aspect of transparency is civil litigation being open to the public.

In arbitration, transparency more often refers to the parties involved. In general, arbitration is considered to be a private and confidential process where the parties can agree to keep the proceedings and the outcome confidential.[5] The hearings are not open to the public. However, there are situations where transparency in arbitration is important, such as in cases where the public has a significant interest in the outcome of the arbitration, or where transparency can contribute to the fairness and legitimacy of the arbitration process. Though transparency and confidentiality may appear to be two opposing concepts, that is not entirely true.

The rule of thumb in arbitration is transparency between the parties and the tribunal. The tribunal cannot communicate with only one party. All evidence, documents, etc., must be visible and open to all participants. These transparency safeguards ensure that both parties are treated equally. For example, arbitrators avoid even making a telephone call to only one party regarding administrative matters without informing the other party about the conversation. Thus, emails to everyone or phone/video conferences involving all participants are the preferred forms of contact in an arbitration.

In a Swedish state court, a judge can contact one party's counsel without the other party's counsel being made aware of it. There is no requirement for a party to be privy to all communication between the court and the other party. The possibility for the judge to communicate with only one side can sometimes be a strength and an advantage for the judge as compared to the arbitrator. Once in a dispute, the parties and counsel often lack confidence in one another, and even simple matters of a practical nature tend to cause lengthy disputes. Communicating with only one party allows the judge to expedite cases that would otherwise be mired in argument.

5. Although the idea of transparency was once unfamiliar in international arbitration, recent regulations have popularized the concept.

The access to procedural precedents in civil court matters is, of course, also an advantage for judges compared to arbitrators. However, this advantage should not be overstated. Since procedural lapses in arbitration can be grounds for a challenge of an arbitral award under the Swedish Arbitration Act, the Swedish courts have clarified how arbitrators must deal with procedural matters in an arbitration.[6]

§15.06 WRITTEN SUBMISSIONS

The conduct of an arbitration may require the arbitral tribunal to undertake a considerable amount of administrative work. In a court, there is an existing administrative structure to handle logistics, such as structuring evidence or making sure that submissions are filed on time. There are templates for all sorts of written communication and IT systems that are designed to facilitate the management of a case. An arbitrator might have some templates of her own, but certainly no comparably sophisticated system. Objectively, an arbitrator must perform far more administrative work than a judge.

One thing that creates administrative work is written submissions. Written submissions play a crucial role in litigation and arbitration, as they allow the parties to present their arguments, evidence, and legal authorities to the judges or arbitrators in a clear and concise manner. Despite the importance of the submissions, a judge might not be involved in that process at all. It is not unusual for a judge to get involved in a case just before the main hearing. The judges' comparatively late arrival to the dispute is a huge difference when compared to the arbitral process. In an arbitration, the arbitrators study the submissions closely when they have been filed.

A timetable for, *inter alia,* submissions is always established as a first step when an arbitration is referred to an arbitral tribunal. The timetable outlines the key milestones and deadlines for the various stages of the arbitration. It is surprising that a timetable is not always established initially in a civil court, as it is an important component of the process that helps to ensure that the proceeding is conducted efficiently, fairly, and in a timely manner.

§15.07 THE PRELIMINARY MEETING

One main difference between an arbitration and a civil proceeding is the preliminary meeting, which plays a key role in a civil proceeding, but only a subordinate role (if any) in an arbitration. At the preliminary meeting in a civil court, the judge aims to clarify the parties' positions and, almost more importantly, help the parties reach a settlement. The state court judge must, under law, try to settle the dispute. Since all participants are aware of this requirement, the preliminary meeting serves as an opportunity for the parties to settle. This rarely happens in an arbitration. For obvious

6. *See, e.g.*, NJA 2019 p. 171.

reasons, an arbitrator must not get involved in the parties' settlement negotiations unless the parties instruct an arbitrator to do so.[7]

Another thing that differs is how the judge approaches the case at the preliminary meeting. The judge is often very active and asks a lot of questions, many more than is usually the case for an arbitrator in an arbitration. Also, it is common that an arbitration lacks a preliminary meeting. If there is a preliminary meeting, it is often focused only on practical matters and not matters of substance. In our experience, almost all arbitration proceedings benefit from a preliminary meeting. Instead of increasing the time and money spent, our conclusion is that a preliminary meeting actually reduces the time and money spent on arbitration. A preliminary meeting makes the proceeding run more smoothly and reduces the instances of misunderstandings among the parties and tribunals.

Whilst arbitrators would benefit from following the courts' example and regularly summon parties to a preliminary meeting, the judges could learn from the arbitrators and provide the parties with an agenda before the meeting. An agenda should list the issues that the judge plans to go through at the meeting, but also a list of questions on the substance of the dispute if the judge plans to ask such questions at the meeting. Otherwise, counsel stands no chance of preparing properly, and the meeting may not be as productive as it could have been.

Regarding the judge's task to clarify the parties' positions on the merits at the preliminary meeting, it could be argued that the counsel's performance level is generally higher in an arbitration, and therefore, the need for clarification is reduced. But even if that is sometimes true, that explanation is too simple. A judge tends to openly dissect the dispute, compared to the arbitrator's more cautious approach. This divergence in method is also expected by the parties. They do not expect an arbitrator to ask a plethora of questions on substance or reveal ambiguities in the parties' written submissions. However, being a bit provocative, one could also argue that the arbitrator does not want to reveal anything to the parties beforehand and, therefore, stays silent up until the award is rendered. For arbitrators, being perceived as neutral is paramount. Neutrality is, of course, commendable, but if the arbitrator does not sort out the case, the arbitrator risks being unclear or missing key points in the future award.

§15.08 THE FINAL HEARING

[A] The Right to a Hearing

A party's right to a hearing is fundamental and laid out in Article 6 of the Convention for the Protection of Human Rights and Fundamental Freedoms. For court cases, this right is included in the Code of Judicial Procedure: as a default rule, a case shall be

7. We must mention Article 26 under the DIS Rules stating: "Unless any party objects thereto, the arbitral tribunal shall at every stage of the arbitration, seek to encourage an amicable settlement of the dispute or of individual disputed issues." From a Swedish perspective, it is an interesting but unfamiliar thought that the arbitrator should at every stage of the arbitration seek to encourage a settlement.

decided on after a final hearing (with some listed exceptions). In arbitration, a hearing shall be held if requested by a party or if the arbitral tribunal deems it appropriate. In the mainstream of commercial arbitration, it is unusual to conclude proceedings without at least a brief hearing.

Given this assumption, one might ask: are there any differences between a court case and an arbitration with respect to (i) whether a hearing shall be held; and (ii) how the hearing itself is conducted—and do any such differences have any effect on the decision-making?

[B] When Can a Case Be Judged Without a Hearing?

In an arbitration where party autonomy is crucial, and the arbitrator's power is derived from the parties and their agreement, an arbitral tribunal would seldom initiate a final hearing if the parties have agreed that the dispute can be tried without a hearing. By contrast, it is not certain that a state court would always accept the parties' instruction to decide a case without a hearing. If there is no consent between the parties, and one party requests a hearing, a hearing will most certainly be held—regardless of whether requested in an arbitration or a court proceeding.

Another area of comparison between courts and arbitral tribunals has to do with whether an online hearing should be regarded as a hearing (in the context of a party's right to a fair trial or hearing)[8]. In general, the state court has vast possibilities to conduct online hearings or to examine parties or witnesses remotely. This is also the default position in the court of appeal where, as provided for in the Code of Judicial Procedure, witnesses are not called again; instead, the video recordings from the district court are played. A hearing held remotely or in a "mixed mode" (remotely to some extent, for example, witness examinations held online) in a civil court case would probably be considered "a hearing."

Recently, the traditional divide between acceptance of online hearings in courts and rejection of online hearings in arbitration has shrunk significantly, and online hearings and remote examinations are now common in arbitration as well. Before the COVID-19 pandemic, the general opinion of the arbitration community was that remote witness examinations were of less value as evidence. Fortuitously, with a greater understanding of the digital tools, and perhaps with a glance at court proceedings, the common position today is that a hearing held remotely gives as good a basis for decision-making as a "live" hearing. Also, the prevailing view is that an online hearing would also be regarded as "a hearing" in an arbitration. In the case of the *Svea Court of Appeal,*[9] the court held that an online hearing against one party's will was not a procedural error that could give reason to set aside the final award.

8. Stefan Lindskog, Virtuella slutförhandlingar i skiljeförfaranden mot parts bestridande, SvJT 2021 s. 293, Lars Edlund, Om virtuell förhandling—en replik, SvJT 2021 s. 401, Kristoffer Löf, Remembrance of Things Past—a reply to Stefan Lindskog's argument that only a traditional hearing is a hearing in arbitration, SvJT 2021 s. 407.
9. Svea Court of Appeal, Final Award dated June 30, 2022 in case T 7158-20.

Having said that, both arbitral tribunals and courts prefer to conduct hearings remotely only with the consent of both parties. Some arbitral tribunals may be more reluctant than courts to proceed with an online hearing without the consent of both parties. But does this reluctance undermine the tribunals' ability to assess the case? We would say it does not.

[C] Are There Any Differences in the Conduct of the Hearing That Influence the Decision-Making?

The Code of Judicial Procedure has historically been built on certain principles, specifically the principle of oral proceedings and the principle of immediateness. Both principles have been modified to some extent, but, as a primary matter, following the principle of immediateness, a party must present its case and its evidence orally, and it should be done at the final hearing (and only there). The final award is based on what has been brought forward at the hearing. Opening statements and closing arguments should therefore be conducted in full orally before the judges of the court at the final hearing; examinations of witnesses are conducted by examination-in-chief, cross-examination, and a redirect examination. Witness statements rarely occur. Post-hearing briefs are not admitted, not even on costs.

This judicial focus on oral argument is extremely disparate from the arbitral approach, especially in international arbitration, where more emphasis is placed on written statements and expert opinions and where skeletal arguments and post-hearing briefs are often used. An arbitral tribunal relies more on written material, and the final hearings are generally shorter than in a court case.

These preferences reflect different traditions. A state court judge, who is trained to deal with the principle of oral proceedings and the principle of immediateness, is accustomed to listening to and absorbing extensive oral pleadings. An arbitrator, however, especially an international arbitrator, is trained to absorb lengthy written documents before and after the hearing. The expert opinions and witness statements must be thoroughly reviewed before the hearing, especially if there is only a cross-examination at the hearing—or no examination at all. Arbitrators are used to evaluating witness statements and considering post-hearing briefs in their decision-making process. Court judges are not.

But what are the ramifications of these two different preferences? For a party in a court case, acknowledgment of these preferences could inform a strategic approach when proposing that witness statements should be used or when the party wishes to refer to documents without comments. Using the methods of an arbitration in a court case might mean taking the risk that the court does not absorb the facts in the way that one hopes. However, a party who intends to bring oral evidence or argument into an arbitration should consider the risk that the arbitral tribunal has a shorter attention span than a court and therefore truncates the available time. In that scenario, the party's counsel should be prepared to summarize on the spot, which could affect the argument's overall efficacy.

[D] The Organization of the Hearings

There are several administrative arrangements that must be made before and during a hearing, arrangements that the state court judge does not take any part in. The task of organizing hearings (the responsibility of the sole- or the presiding arbitrator) should, however, not be underestimated, and this is a great difference between the roles of a judge and an arbitrator. A suitable hearing room must be provided, with break-out rooms for the representatives of the parties; there should be technical arrangements regarding recording and remotely held examinations, document sharing, etc., and practical arrangements regarding lunch and other facilities must be made. Many arbitrators arrange pre-hearing conferences to facilitate and arrange the hearings. Parties and their counsel should bear in mind that the organization of hearings is a workload put on the chair of the arbitral tribunal. The court judge has the luxury of focusing only on the dispute.

§15.09 THE FINAL AWARD AND THE MAKING OF THE FINAL AWARD

The Code of Judicial Procedure contains regulations regarding the court's final award, the formal criteria (it must be dated and undersigned, etc.) and requirements regarding the merits. There are also rules on the deliberation process. Additionally, there are working methods that have been developed over a long period of time for the decision-making process. There are certain traditions and habits at every court, as at any workplace. The judges know each other, and they work together on a daily basis. As noted above, some courts have developed templates and standard documents for drafting awards, and they have IT and operational support to facilitate the drafting.

In arbitration, there are certain rules regarding the formal criteria of the final award. But that's almost it. An arbitral tribunal is constituted for each dispute alone, and the arbitrators may not know each other. A tribunal may grapple with differences in culture and divergent approaches to the deliberation, the decision-making process, the drafting of the award, and the definition of best practices.

[A] The Rules and the Law

The Arbitration Act states that a final award should be made in writing and should be signed by the arbitrators and that an award shall also include the date of the award and the seat of the arbitration. The SCC Arbitration Rules contain the same requirements as the formalities of an award. The Arbitration Act also states that the dispute shall be ruled by the law or set of rules that the parties have agreed on. In a similar vein, the SCC Arbitration Rules state that the award shall state the reasons upon which the award is based (Article 42).

Neither the Arbitration Act nor the SCC Arbitration Rules contain further regulations on the content of the award. An award can however be set aside if, among other reasons, the arbitral tribunal has exceeded its mandate, and this is likely to have affected the outcome of the case. There are no regulations regarding the deliberation process.

The Code of Judicial Procedure stipulates more detailed requirements regarding the content. Namely, the Code states that if there has been a final hearing, the judgment must be based on what has been put forward at the main hearing (Chapter 17 section 2, the principle of oral proceedings and the principle of immediateness). The Code (Chapter 17 section 7) also dictates that an award must contain: (i) the name of the court, (ii) the date and seat for rendering the award, (iii) the decision, (iv) the claims and objections of the parties and the facts that the claims and objections are based on, and (v) the basis for the award including the court's conclusions on the arguments and evidence presented in the case. The Code of Judicial Procedure also contains regulations regarding when and how the court shall deliberate after the final hearing.

The Code of Judicial Procedure (Chapter 16), the SCC Arbitration Rules, and the Arbitration Act all contain rules providing that a decision shall be made by a majority vote and rules regarding the next steps if a majority fails to be achieved. There is a specific order to the voting process in a court (voting question-by-question, and the youngest judge shall be the first to vote) that is not stipulated in arbitration. The rules when failing a majority also differ. The differences in voting requirements and processes can, of course, affect the outcome of the decision.

[B] The Decision-Making Process: The Deliberation

As alluded to above, in addition to the "hard" rules governing how courts deliberate, there are also "soft factors" that influence the process. Do these soft factors impact decision-making?

In our experience, the deliberations start as soon as the final hearing has ended, in litigation as well as in arbitration. At the very least, fundamental issues are then identified and discussed. In a Swedish court, the first opinion is usually given by the youngest judge. This matter is not regulated for arbitrations, and there is no obvious best practice. Furthermore, the chair in a Swedish court will usually not make the first draft of the judgment. In an arbitration, by contrast, the chair will usually make the first draft of the award.

The deliberation process is influenced by several circumstances. If the judges/arbitrators know each other well, the discussion can be constructive, open, and ego-free. However, an overly familiar dynamic could lead to a failure to thoroughly debate the issues at hand. Further, the deliberation process in a court, where the youngest lawyer speaks first, can result in issues being well explained since that person is at the beginning of his or her career and is motivated to do a good job. However, this can inhibit an open discussion if the young lawyer feels reluctant to be an opponent to an elder colleague who will evaluate him. Similar conditions can, of course, exist among arbitrators. Clearly, all those matters can affect the discussion, but it is not feasible to draw any general conclusions.

Some argue that arbitral tribunals are "freer" in their deliberation and decision-making processes and that arbitrators tend to let fairness and justness influence the decisions to a larger extent than a state court would. It is also a common opinion that courts are more "formal" and that their attachment to a certain order for decision-making leads to square and close-minded judgments. While we understand these arguments, we posit that the differences in approach may be best explained by the fact that court judges are trained in a special working method and that arbitrators more often act as counsel. As such, arbitrators are used to other types of problem-solving and dispute resolution. The differences might not be material but are, of course, reflected in the judgment and in the wording of the final award.

[C] The Content of the Award

As cited above, the Code of Judicial Procedure (Chapter 17 section 7) contains detailed requirements regarding the content of the award and in which order the questions shall be considered. Does the lack of such regulation in arbitration make the decision-making process or the award rendered in an arbitration different from that of the courts?

In our experience, there are differences between awards rendered by a court and awards rendered in an arbitration. However, the dissimilarity is not wholly explained by the differences between the law and the rules but instead by the working methods and differences in experience between judges and arbitrators. The judges are trained in a method that originated from the Code of Judicial Procedure and developed over a long time. Young court lawyers have been supervised by senior colleagues and have been influenced by them regarding the structure, the order in which the issues are tried, and the language. This training is clearly evident in decisions and awards rendered by courts—the structure of the award and the reasoning are laid out in a certain way, regardless of which court or from what judge it is rendered. If a Swedish arbitral award is written by an arbitrator who serves or has served as a court judge, one can expect the award to be written in the same way as an award rendered by a court.

However, if the arbitral tribunal consists of arbitrators not trained in court, the award may be written in another manner. Arbitrators who mainly act as counsel are accustomed to writing in another way. Submissions from a party address the issues from other perspectives, use different word choices, and handle the presentation of evidence in an argumentative manner. This approach can be seen in any award written by an arbitrator with vast experience in acting as counsel. For example, the facts that the parties' claims are based on (*Sw. rättsfakta/grunderna*) are summarized in another way (if at all summarized), and the evaluation of evidence might not be highlighted as clearly as in an award rendered by a court. The structure and the order in which the issues are judged may also differ.

Since arbitrators tend to be more used to handling written documents, witness statements and opinions,[10] one might see differences in this respect in relying on and evaluating the written documents.

10. *See* above §15.08[C] regarding the hearing.

An award rendered in an arbitration also contains an introduction setting out a number of facts relating to the arbitration (identification of the arbitration agreement, a description of the dispute, specific procedural agreements of the parties and rulings of the arbitral tribunal). This section has no counterpart in a final award rendered by a court. An award rendered by an arbitral tribunal also contains the reasoning behind its determination of costs for arbitration. Obviously, there is no need for this section in an award rendered by a court.

[D] "To Write for the Court of Appeal"

In certain instances, a court will dismiss a claim on the very first ground, or alternatively, a court will grant a claim on the first ground, even though the claimant relied on several grounds. For example, hypothetically, if a claim is dismissed since it is time-barred, is it then necessary to try the questions of breach of the agreement, the right to damages, and the amount of such damages? A court would most definitely try the other issues, even if the outcome remained the same. The reason for this is the principle of the court hierarchy. If a district court does not try all the issues, and the court of appeal rules the opposite (the claim is not time-barred), the claims regarding breach of the agreement and damages would be dealt with only in one instance—in conflict with the court hierarchy. The case could then be remanded to the district court for a full trial.

When we sit as arbitrators, we most often try the dispute in full, even if the outcome is not affected. It probably has partly to do with our experiences as court judges, but it could also be due to our understanding of the assignment we have been given by the parties. A party must feel that it has been heard and understood, and its willingness to accept a dismissal is greater if the party sees that all grounds have been tried. In arbitration, one does not "write for the court of appeal" but may "write for the losing party." Needless to say, costs remain an important consideration. A losing party is likely unwilling to pay to read unnecessarily lengthy reasoning on all grounds for dismissal. The reasoning in those sections should be written carefully and concisely.

As it is not a requirement, arbitrators who have not served in a state court may rule differently and may not try the dispute in full if it is not necessary. This approach may be in deference to cost considerations and/or if the described scope of work and assignment is narrower.

[E] Challenge of the Award

If a district court judge writes an award with the court of appeal in mind, an arbitrator does so with the risk of challenging the award in mind. This risk affects award writing in a way that has no obvious counterpart in a court proceeding. Due to the risk of challenge, a final award in an arbitration contains considerations of procedural decisions and reasoning related to issues such as the tribunal's impartiality and giving each party an equal and reasonable opportunity to present its case.

In a court proceeding, the court is obliged to produce recitals, clarifying the parties' claims and positions. Recitals are not always produced and circulated in an arbitration. Therefore, the arbitral tribunal must verify the claims, positions, and the assignment from the parties before rendering the award. This additional step may also be reflected in the award in unique ways as compared to an award rendered by a court.

[F] The Party-Appointed Arbitrators

In this context, it is interesting to review the position of the party-nominated arbitrator. In a court dispute, the court has no connection at all with the parties and cannot be claimed to be under any influence. In an arbitration, each arbitrator, however, appointed, is under the duty to act impartially and to decide on the issues in a fair and unbiased manner. Nevertheless, questions commonly arise regarding whether an arbitrator tends to rule in favor of the party who has appointed them. In our opinion, while a preferential tendency may exist– it is not a tendency to rule in favor. Rather, it is an ambition to thoroughly analyze the facts and claims/objections brought forward by the party who has appointed you. A party-nominated arbitrator might ensure that the arbitral tribunal properly understands the case being advanced by that party. This ensures that all circumstances are considered and improves the quality of the judgment. In our opinion, a tendency for arbitrators to rule in favor of the party who has appointed them is exceedingly rare.

[G] Dissenting Opinions

Are dissenting opinions more common in court than in arbitration? To our knowledge, yes. In a court, dissenting opinions are not a big issue. Most of the court judges (handling a vast number of cases) have, on occasion, dealt with a dissenting opinion. The threshold is higher in an arbitration, and an arbitrator is generally more reluctant to hold a dissenting opinion. The arbitration community frequently discusses whether or not dissenting opinions should even be permitted. An arbitral tribunal renders an award that cannot be appealed, and this may be a reason why tribunals strive to decide unanimously.

§15.10 CONCLUSION

To summarize, there are differences between being a judge in a state court and an arbitrator, but the similarities are greater than the differences. The most striking difference is that a court judge has a substantial duty to try to settle the case, whereas an arbitrator must not get involved in the parties' settlement negotiations. What can we learn by reflecting upon this difference? Would it be prudent for a court judge to de-emphasize settlement? Would it be in the parties' best interest if the arbitrator initiated settlement negotiations?

In our view, judges have a tendency to be overeager to settle a dispute, an eagerness that can reduce the trust in the judge. A court judge who is responsive and respectful of the parties' willingness to settle can be particularly well-equipped to assist the parties in arriving at a settlement. Settlement benefits the parties by increasing efficacy and decreasing costs. Those benefits apply in arbitration as well, but most arbitrators hesitate to assist in any settlement negotiations. Alternative approaches do exist; however, for example, according to the rules of the German Arbitration Institute ("DIS"), the arbitral tribunal shall, at every stage of the arbitration, seek to encourage an amicable settlement of the dispute or individual disputed issues (section 26, 2018 DIS Arbitration Rules). Also, Annex 3 of the DIS Arbitration Rules states, as a measure for increasing procedural efficiency, that the arbitrator can provide the parties with a preliminary non-binding assessment of factual or legal issues in the arbitration, provided all the parties consent. As commercial arbitration becomes more time-consuming and more costly, perhaps arbitrators should have the duty to encourage an amicable settlement.

It is also interesting to, on the one hand, reflect upon the motivation of an international arbitral tribunal to shorten the oral phase of the proceedings as far as practicable and, on the other hand, the principles of oral proceedings and the principle of immediacy that influence the hearing in a state court. There is a tendency in Swedish arbitration to rely more and more on documents and witness statements. However, at the same time, witnesses are often called regardless of the witness statements and are subject to examination-in-chief, followed by cross-examination and re-direct-examination. Sometimes, the examination-in-chief is merely a "warm-up" and shorter than a standard examination-in-chief. In Swedish courts, there is a tendency to rely more on documents (but not yet on witness statements), and parties more often refer to documents quite briefly. It is not certain that this mixture of methods of undertaking the hearing and taking evidence is an effective compromise.

The purpose of this chapter was to encourage further reflection on how best practices are exercised in commercial court proceedings and arbitration. We hope that by highlighting varying perspectives, disparities, and alternatives, our reflections have sparked additional thoughts and discussion regarding the optimization of arbitral processes.

CHAPTER 16

When Enough Is Enough: The Arbitral Tribunal's Power to Stay or Terminate Proceedings due to Party Non-compliance with Procedural Obligations

Sven Lange & Felipe Volio Soley[*]

Parties to arbitration often 'cry foul' and complain about alleged procedural violations by the opposing side. If there is a breach, tribunals may usually choose from a range of potential mechanisms to enforce compliance. In limited cases, this may include the stay or termination of the arbitration. This chapter will analyse both situations in which arbitration laws and arbitration rules expressly provide for the stay and termination of proceedings in reaction to a procedural breach, as well as situations in which such a measure is deemed possible even without an express rule to this effect. In this regard, a particular focus of the chapter will be on the consequences related to the failure by a claimant to provide security for costs.

§16.01 INTRODUCTION

Parties have a great number of procedural obligations – starting with the obligation to pay the advance on costs and including, e.g., the obligation to produce documents if ordered and, potentially,[1] to keep the arbitration confidential. Parties often comply

* The authors would like to thank David Cambridge, Stephan Walter and Jan Homann for their support in the preparation of this chapter. All opinions expressed in this chapter are the authors' own and do not necessarily reflect the opinions of their firm or their clients.

1. Cf. with regard to the existence or not of confidentiality obligations in arbitration Gary Born, *International Commercial Arbitration* § 20.02-20.04 (3rd ed. Kluwer Law International 2021); *Redfern and Hunter on International Arbitration*, paras 2.183 et seq. (Nigel Blackaby, Constantine Partasides, et al. eds, 7th ed. Oxford Univ. Press 2023); Michael Hwang & Katie Chung, *Defining*

with all of their procedural obligations. However, in many cases, one party alleges that the other party failed to comply with its obligations. And sometimes, things might get even more heated, and both parties accuse each other of breaching their respective obligations.

In case a party breaches its procedural obligations, the tribunal may react in different ways, depending on the obligation and on the breach in question. Generally, the applicable rules provide for a range of proportionate reactions, including the allocation of additional costs to the non-complying party, the drawing of adverse inferences and the issuance of interim orders forcing compliance. In the case of other breaches, the tribunal might, however, want to consider more drastic measures such as the stay and eventual termination of the arbitration. This has been discussed in particular in relation to failures by a claimant to provide security for costs despite a respective order by the tribunal. Arguably, such steps should only be taken in exceptional circumstances, given that a termination essentially means that the claimant's claims will not be heard. That said, there are certain situations in which 'enough is enough' and a stay or termination may be appropriate.

This chapter will first explore in §16.02 the express rules in arbitration laws and arbitration rules allowing a tribunal to stay or terminate proceedings due to party non-compliance with procedural obligations. Section §16.03 will analyse to which extent a tribunal may stay or terminate proceedings in reaction to party non-compliance, even in the absence of express language in the applicable arbitration laws and arbitration rules. To this end, the analysis will focus on the failure by a claimant to provide security for costs but will also look at further potential cases. Section §16.04 will assess the critical question of whether the termination of proceedings results in a rejection of the claimant's claims with prejudice and, concomitantly, the form of the tribunal's decision on termination. Section §16.05 will provide guidance on how the tribunal should exercise its discretion to stay or terminate proceedings in case it has such discretion. Thereafter, §16.06 will assess a further and separate potential argument for the termination of arbitration in case of party non-compliance with procedural obligations – namely, the idea that the non-compliance constitutes a breach of the arbitration agreement allowing the termination of the arbitration agreement. Finally, §16.07 will provide a brief conclusion.

§16.02 EXPRESS PROVISIONS ON THE STAY OR TERMINATION OF PROCEEDINGS DUE TO PARTY NON-COMPLIANCE WITH PROCEDURAL OBLIGATIONS

Arbitration laws and arbitration rules typically provide for the stay or termination of proceedings in case of specific types of party non-compliance with procedural obligations. For a start, the parties' failure to pay the advance on costs will lead to a stay and

the Indefinable: Practical Problems of Confidentiality in Arbitration, 26 J. Intl Arb. 609, 628 et seq. (2009) DOI: 10.54648/joia2009034; Serge Lazareff, *Confidentiality and Arbitration: Theoretical and Philosophical Reflections*, ICC ICArb. Bull. Special Supplement: Confidentiality in Arbitration: Commentaries on Rules, Statutes, Case Law and Practice 81, 85 et seq. (2009).

eventually a termination of the arbitration (*see* §16.02[A]). Moreover, a claimant's default may also be a reason for a tribunal to terminate the arbitration (*see* §16.02[B]). Finally, an increasing number of arbitration rules expressly regulate the stay and termination of proceedings in case a claimant fails to provide security for costs despite a respective order from the tribunal (*see* §16.02[C]).

[A] Failure to Pay the Advance on Costs

Arbitration rules typically oblige parties to pay an advance on costs, consisting of the fees and expenses of the tribunal and, in the case of institutional arbitration, the administrative fees of the institution.[2] Principally, the advance needs to be paid at the beginning of the proceedings, but further advance payments may be requested over the course of the arbitration if the initial deposit proves insufficient.[3] In all instances, the aim is that payment of the costs of the arbitration is ensured and that neither the tribunal nor the institution needs to pursue claims against a party to obtain payment for services rendered.[4]

Parties are usually required to pay the advance in equal shares.[5] In practice, parties, however, do not always comply with this obligation. For instance, respondents that raise a jurisdictional objection occasionally refuse to pay the advance on costs, arguing that they are not bound to the arbitration agreement and the arbitration rules, and are thus not obliged to pay the advance.[6] Moreover, claimants occasionally also fail to pay advances.

Arbitration rules typically provide that if a party is unable or unwilling to pay its share of the advance on costs, the other party may pay the defaulting party's share.[7] In case neither party makes the outstanding advance payments despite respective requests, arbitration rules most commonly provide that the proceedings may first be

2. Arif Hyder Ali et al., *The International Arbitration Rulebook: A Guide to Arbitral Regimes* 458 (Kluwer Law International 2019); ICC Rules (2021), Art. 37; SIAC Rules (2016), Rule 34; LCIA Rules (2020), Art. 24; HKIAC Rules (2018), Art. 41; SCC Rules (2023), Art. 51; UNCITRAL Rules (2010), Art. 43.
3. Cf. ICC Rules (2021), Art. 37.5; LCIA Rules (2020), Art. 24.1; HKIAC Rules (2018), Art. 41.3; Swiss Arbitration Rules (2021), Art. 41.3; SIAC Rules (2016), Rule 34.4.
4. Cf. Michael Bühler & Marco Stacher, *Chapter 18, Part IV: Costs in International Arbitration*, in *Arbitration in Switzerland: The Practitioner's Guide*, para. 17 (Manuel Arroyo ed., 2nd ed. Kluwer Law International 2018); Reinmar Wolff, *Chapter 18, Part XII: Rights and Duties of Arbitrators*, in *Arbitration in Switzerland: The Practitioner's Guide*, para. 28 (Manuel Arroyo ed., 2nd ed. Kluwer Law International 2018).
5. ICC Rules (2021), Art. 37.2; HKIAC Rules (2018), Art. 41.1; SIAC Rules (2016), Rule 34.2; Swiss Arbitration Rules (2021), Art. 41.1.
6. Cf. Venus V. Wong & Alfred Siwy, *The Arbitrator and the Arbitration Procedure, Recalcitrant Parties and the Tribunal's Power to Order Cost Advance Payments*, 8 Austrian Y.B. Int'l Arb 201 (2014).
7. Cf. ICC Rules (2021), Art. 37.5; LCIA Rules (2020), Art. 24.6; HKIAC Rules (2018), Art. 41.5; ICDR Rules (2021), Art. 39.4; DIS Arbitration Rules (2018), Art. 35.4; SIAC Rules (2016), Rule 34.5; Swiss Arbitration Rules (2021), Art. 41.4.

stayed and eventually terminated.[8] This only makes sense. Having the payment to the arbitrators and the institution secured by way of an advance payment is a key requirement for an arbitration to take place. Without the advance, neither the arbitrators nor the institution can reasonably be required to progress their work. Accordingly, if the advance is not paid, the arbitration should first be stayed so that the parties have another opportunity to pay in the funds without the tribunal and the institution performing further work in the interim. And if the parties still fail to pay, the arbitration should be terminated. Incidentally, this is no feature exclusive to arbitration. In many jurisdictions, court proceedings will also not advance in case of non-payment of an advance on costs.[9]

The question of who makes the decision to stay or terminate is answered differently by different arbitration rules. Some rules give this responsibility to the institution,[10] sometimes requiring that the institution consult with the tribunal.[11] Other rules provide for the tribunal to make the decision (at least once it has been constituted).[12] The Stockholm Chamber of Commerce (SCC) falls into the latter category, but only since the 2023 version of the SCC Rules;[13] previously, the SCC Rules gave the respective responsibility to the SCC Board.[14] Yet other rules provide for a mixture of the two approaches, meaning, e.g., that the decision to stay is reserved for the tribunal and the decision to terminate lies with the institution.[15] Curiously, under the 2020 version of the LCIA Rules, both the London Court of International Arbitration (LCIA) and the tribunal may separately decide to treat a claim or counterclaim as withdrawn.[16]

The different approaches as to competence for staying and terminating the arbitration reflect that the advance typically secures payment of the costs of both the institution and the tribunal. As such, both the institution and the tribunal have an interest in having a say on the matter. Thus, it is perhaps unsurprising that different arbitration rules provide for different solutions. Irrespective thereof, the above clearly demonstrates that it is generally recognised that an arbitration should be stayed and eventually terminated if the advance on costs is not paid.

---

8. Cf. SIAC Rules (2016), Rule 34.6; LCIA Rules (2020), Art. 24.5 and 24.8; Swiss Arbitration Rules (2021), Art. 41.4; HKIAC Rules (2018), Art. 41.4; ICC Rules (2021), Art. 37.6; ICDR Rules (2021), Art. 39(5); ICSID Administrative and Financial Regulations (2022), Regulation 16(2); UNCITRAL Rules (2010), Art. 43(4).
9. Cf. only German Court Fees Law (*Gerichtskostengesetz*), section 12(1); Swiss Code of Civil Procedure (*Zivilprozessordnung*), Art. 101(3).
10. Cf. ICSID Administrative and Financial Regulations (2022), Regulation 16(2).
11. Cf. ICC Rules (2021), Art. 37.6; SIAC Rules (2016), Rule 34.6.
12. Cf. Swiss Arbitration Rules (2021), Art. 41.4; HKIAC Rules (2018), Art. 41.4; ICDR Rules (2021), Art. 39(5).
13. SCC Rules (2023), Art. 51.5.
14. SCC Rules (2017), Art. 51.5.
15. Cf. DIS Arbitration Rules (2018), Arts 35.5 and 42.5. Cf. also SIAC Rules (2016), Rule 34.6, which addresses both the suspension of the proceedings by the tribunal as well as the suspension of the administration of the case by the institution.
16. LCIA Rules (2020), Art. 24.8. Cf. further Rémy Gerbay, *Chapter 21: Costs and Advance Payment for Costs*, in *Arbitrating under the 2020 LCIA Rules: A User's Guide* para. 53 (Maxi Scherer et al. eds, Kluwer Law International 2021).

[B] Default by the Claimant

When parties agree to arbitration, they usually presume that, if a dispute arises, they will each actively participate in future arbitration proceedings.[17] In practice, this expectation is, however, not always met, resulting in a default proceeding.[18] In particular, parties may abstain from participating in an arbitration because of a lack of confidence or a lack of financial means to pay for legal fees.

For present purposes, the situation of a default by the claimant is of interest. While this will happen only rarely, such cases do exist, usually because the claimant runs out of funds in the course of the proceedings. If the claimant fails to file the statement of claim, arbitration laws and arbitration rules typically provide for the termination of the arbitration. For example, Article 25 lit. a of the UNCITRAL Model Law (2006) states that, unless otherwise agreed by the parties, the tribunal shall terminate the proceedings if the claimant fails to submit the statement of claim without showing sufficient cause.[19] Similar rules also exist in jurisdictions that have not as such adopted the Model Law,[20] as well as in various arbitration rules.[21] Typically, these rules do not provide for the discretion of the tribunal but instead use mandatory language requiring the termination of the proceedings (without first foreseeing a suspension period).

Conversely, in other cases of default by a claimant (such as failure to file submissions after the statement of claim or failure to appear at the hearing), arbitration laws and rules usually do not expressly provide for termination of the proceedings.[22] On the contrary, they often state that, in the case of such default, the tribunal may continue with the arbitration and render an award.[23] That said, arbitration laws and arbitration rules often contain general clauses on the termination of proceedings which may become relevant here. For example, Article 32(2) lit. c of the UNCITRAL Model Law (2006) provides that the tribunal shall issue an order for the termination of the proceedings if it finds that the continuation of the proceedings has become unnecessary

17. Chartered Institute of Arbitrators, Guidelines on Party Non-participation, Preamble, para. 1 (2015).
18. Cf. generally with regard to default proceedings Julio César Betancourt, *What Are the Arbitral Tribunal's Powers in Default Proceedings?* 36 J. Intl Arb. 485-502 (2019) DOI: 10.54648/joia2019024.
19. This rule has been adopted from the UNCITRAL Model Law e.g. in Germany (German Code of Civil Procedure, section 1048(1)), Austria (Austrian Code of Civil Procedure, section 600(1)) and Qatar (Qatari Law No. 2 of 2017 Promulgating the Civil and Commercial Arbitration Law, Art. 25(1)).
20. Cf. Dutch Code of Civil Procedure, section 1043a para. 1.
21. Cf. Swiss Arbitration Rules (2021), Art. 30.1; HKIAC Rules (2018), Art. 26.1; SIAC Rules (2016), Rule 20.8.
22. Cf. however section 41.3 of the English Arbitration Act (1996) as a rule that potentially allows a tribunal to dismiss a claim in case of any 'inordinate and inexcusable delay on the part of the claimant in pursuing his claim'.
23. Cf. UNCITRAL Model Law (2006), Art. 25 lit. c; Swedish Arbitration Act (1999), section 24(3); Swiss Arbitration Rules (2021), Art. 30.2; HKIAC Rules (2018), Art. 26.3; ICDR Rules (2021), Art. 29.2.

or impossible. Such rules naturally exist in Model Law jurisdictions[24] but have also been included in the arbitration laws of other jurisdictions.[25] Moreover, various arbitration rules contain similar provisions.[26]

Arguably, these rules may become relevant if a claimant defaults after the submission of the statement of claim and the respondent itself has no interest in an award, e.g., if it is clear that the claimant has abandoned the claims and will not resubmit them. In such a situation, the respondent may want to save costs and inform the tribunal that it does not seek an award. If that happens, and the claimant does not suddenly 'reappear' and insist on an award, the tribunal may arguably conclude that it is unnecessary to continue the proceedings and terminate the arbitration on this basis.[27] Conversely, if the respondent insists on an award, the continuation of proceedings is still necessary, and the tribunal cannot terminate proceedings. Instead, it must proceed to an award.

[C] Failure to Provide Security for Costs

A failure of a claimant to provide security for the costs of the respondent (so-called *cautio judicatum solvi*) may also give rise to a stay or termination of arbitral proceedings.

An order for security for costs is a specific type of interim measure.[28] In general terms, such an order requires a claimant to effectively guarantee the payment of a potential future costs award in favour of the respondent –[29] and thus seeks to provide the respondent with comfort that it will be 'made whole' in case it ultimately prevails in the arbitration. Typically, security will be provided in the form of a bank guarantee or by depositing funds with a trustee.[30] Deciding whether to issue an order for security for costs can be a complex endeavour, and the decision will typically depend on a variety of factors, including the claimant's financial ability to satisfy an adverse cost award (and the extent to which such ability has changed since the conclusion of the

---

24. German Code of Civil Procedure, section 1056(2) no. 3; Costa Rican Law 8937 on International Commercial Arbitration, Art. 32(2) lit. c; Qatari Law No. 2 of 2017 Promulgating the Civil and Commercial Arbitration Law, Art. 31(9) lit. c.
25. Cf. Moroccan Code of Civil Procedure, Art. 327-19(3); Portuguese Arbitration Act, Art. 44(2) lit. c.
26. HKIAC Rules (2018), Art. 37.2 lit. b; Swiss Arbitration Rules (2021), Art. 36.2; UNCITRAL Rules (2010), Art. 36.2; KLRCA Arbitration Rules (2017), Art. 36(2).
27. Cf. *Münchener Kommentar zur ZPO* § 1048 ZPO, para. 16 (6th ed. C.H. Beck 2022) (Germany); Beck'scher Online Kommentar § 1048 ZPO, para. 9.1 (47th ed C.H. Beck 2022) (Germany).
28. Julian D.M. Lew, Loukas A. Mistelis & Stefan M. Kröll, *Comparative International Commercial Arbitration* paras 23-52 to 23-54 (Kluwer Law International 2003); *Unnamed ICC Case,* Procedural Order No. 3, 2015, 2 ICC Disp. Res. Bull. 109, para. 24 (2020); *ABC AG v. Mr. X,* Procedural Order of 27 November 2002, 23 ASA Bulletin 108, para. 4.1 (2005).Cf. also VIAC Arbitration Rules (2021), Art. 33(6).
29. Pierre A. Karrer & Marcus Desax, *Security for Costs in International Arbitration: Why, When, and What If ...*, in *Law of International Business and Dispute Settlement in the 21st Century: Liber Amicorum Karl-Heinz Böckstiegel* 339, 340 (Robert Briner et al. eds., 2001); Noah Rubins, *In God We Trust All Others Pay Cash,* 11 ARIA 307, 311 (2000).
30. Cf. Chartered Institute of Arbitrators, Guidelines on Applications for Security for Costs, Commentary on Art. 5, para. 3(a) (2016).

arbitration agreement),[31] the prospects of success of the claims,[32] and fairness considerations.[33] Critically, an order for security for costs may hinder a claimant's access to justice.[34] Accordingly, security for costs should only be ordered in rare circumstances,[35] although according to an article published in last year's edition of this yearbook: '[s]ecurity for costs should remain the exception, but not a unicorn.'[36]

Security for costs is a feature known in the litigation systems of many jurisdictions.[37] Conversely, most arbitration laws and arbitration rules do not expressly address the issue of security for costs. That said, some do address it - and there has been a growing trend in recent years to explicitly regulate the issue, including the issue of the stay or termination of the arbitration in case of a party's failure to provide security.

English law has had a leading role in the development of arbitral practice on the issue of security for costs.[38] Thus, it is unsurprising that the English Arbitration Act (1996) contains a provision on security for costs, expressly allowing the tribunal to dismiss claims in case of a failure to provide security for costs.[39] Similarly, the Hong Kong Arbitration Ordinance provides for the stay or dismissal of claims in case security for costs is not provided.[40] In arbitration rules, provisions regulating security for costs,

31. Chartered Institute of Arbitrators, Guidelines on Applications for Security for Costs, Art. 3 (2016); Marco Stacher, *Swiss Rules of International Arbitration: Commentary* Art. 41, para. 26 (Tobias Zuberbühler et al. eds, 2nd ed. Juris Publishing 2013); *Unnamed ICC Case*, Procedural Order No. 3, 2015, in: 2 ICC Disp. Res. Bull. 109, para. 36 (2020); *ICC Case No. 12542/EC*, 19 December 2003, 23 ASA Bulletin 685 para. 43 (2005).
32. Chartered Institute of Arbitrators, Guidelines on Applications for Security for Costs, Art. 2 (2016).
33. Chartered Institute of Arbitrators, Guidelines on Applications for Security for Costs, Art. 4 (2016).
34. Cf. *Fouchard Gaillard Goldman on International Commercial Arbitration* 687 (Emmanuel Gaillard & John Savage eds, Kluwer Law International 1999); Simon Bachmann, *The Impact of Third-Party Funding on Security for Costs Requests in International Arbitration Proceedings in Switzerland*, 38 ASA Bull. 842, 849 (2020).
35. *Unnamed ICC Case*, Procedural Order No. 3, 2015, 2 ICC Disp. Res. Bull. 109, paras 29-30 (2020); *ICC Case No. 13620*, Procedural Order of May 2006, ICC ICArb. Bull. Special Supplement: Procedural Decisions in ICC Arbitration 65, para. 2.5 (2014); *ABC AG v. Mr. X*, Procedural Order of 27 November 2002, 23 ASA Bull. 108, para. 4.1 (2005); Julian D.M. Lew, Loukas A. Mistelis & Stefan M. Kröll, *Comparative International Commercial Arbitration* para. 23-54 (Kluwer Law International 2003).
36. Jan Heiner Nedden & Inga Witte, *Chapter 4: The Exception in Theory, a Unicorn in Practice? Revisiting Security for Costs from a Practitioner's Perspective*, 4 Stockholm Arbitration Yearbook 39, 40 (Kluwer Law International 2022).
37. Jeffrey Waincymer, *Procedure and Evidence in Arbitration* 643 (Kluwer Law International 2012); Weixia Gu, *Security for Costs in International Commercial Arbitration*, 22 J. Intl Arb. 167, 168 (2005) DOI: 10.54648/joia2005012. Cf. for specific references to Indian, English and Swiss law Parties Not Indicated, Procedural Order No. 4, 2009, 28 ASA Bull. 59, paras 161-168 (2010).
38. Weixia Gu, *Security for Costs in International Commercial Arbitration*, 22 J. Intl Arb. 167, 173 (2005) DOI: 10.54648/joia2005012.
39. English Arbitration Act (1996), section 41.6 ('If a claimant fails to comply with a peremptory order of the tribunal to provide security for costs, the tribunal may make an award dismissing his claim.').
40. Hong Kong Arbitration Ordinance (2011), section 56(4): 'An arbitral tribunal may make an award dismissing a claim or stay a claim if it has made an order under subsection (1)(a) but the order has not been complied with within the period specified under subsection (3)(a) or extended under subsection (3)(b).'

including the stay or termination of the arbitration, are contained, e.g., in the LCIA Rules (2020),[41] the SCC Rules (2023),[42] the VIAC Arbitration Rules (2021),[43] and the ICSID Arbitration Rules (2022).[44]

That said, there are still various arbitration rules that do not expressly regulate security for costs at all[45] or that – while mentioning the possibility of an order for security for costs – do not expressly empower the tribunal to stay or terminate the arbitration in case security is not provided.[46] How to handle non-compliance with a security for costs order in case there are no express rules will be addressed immediately below.[47]

§16.03 THE STAY OR TERMINATION OF PROCEEDINGS DUE TO PARTY NON-COMPLIANCE WITH PROCEDURAL OBLIGATIONS IN THE ABSENCE OF EXPRESS RULES

In certain situations, a stay and eventual termination of the arbitration may also be possible in the absence of express rules. In that regard, the most important case to be discussed is, again, non-compliance with an order for security for costs (*see* §16.03[A]). However, there may also be further cases in which a stay and eventual termination may be possible (*see* §16.03[B]).

[A] Failure to Provide Security for Costs

As explained above, the issue of security for costs is being increasingly regulated in arbitration laws and arbitration rules. However, in the clear majority of cases, neither the *lex arbitri* nor the agreed arbitration rules address security for costs. Even in such cases, it is however recognised that a tribunal has the power to order a claimant to provide security for costs, based on the tribunal's power to issue interim measures.[48]

41. LCIA Arbitration Rules (2020), Art. 25.2 ('In the event that a claiming, counterclaiming or cross-claiming party does not comply with any order to provide security, the Arbitral Tribunal may stay that party's claims, counterclaims or cross-claims or dismiss them by an award.').
42. SCC Arbitration Rules (2023), Art. 38(3) ('If a party fails to comply with an order to provide security for costs, the Arbitral Tribunal may stay or terminate the proceedings in whole or in part.').
43. VIAC Arbitration Rules (2021), Art. 33(7) ('If a party fails to comply with an order by the arbitral tribunal for security for costs, the arbitral tribunal may, upon request, suspend in whole or in part, or terminate the proceedings (Article 34 paragraph 2.4).').
44. ICSID Arbitration Rules (2022), Art. 53(6) ('If a party fails to comply with an order to provide security for costs, the Tribunal may suspend the proceeding. If the proceeding is suspended for more than 90 days, the Tribunal may, after consulting with the parties, order the discontinuance of the proceeding.').
45. Cf. ICC Rules (2021); UNCITRAL Rules (2010); Swiss Rules (2021); DIS Rules (2018); KLRCA Arbitration Rules (2017).
46. Cf. HKIAC Rules (2018), Art. 24; SIAC Rules (2016), Rule 27 lit. j.
47. *See* §16.03[A].
48. Jan Heiner Nedden & Inga Witte, *Chapter 4: The Exception in Theory, a Unicorn in Practice? Revisiting Security for Costs from a Practitioner's Perspective*, 4 Stockholm Arbitration Yearbook,

This naturally raises the question: What happens if the claimant fails to provide security?

The traditional way of enforcing an interim measure – turning to the courts for assistance –[49] does not seem helpful in such circumstances. If a respondent seeks security for costs, it does so because it expects that the claimant will not be able to meet an adverse cost award.[50] If the respondent were forced to turn to the courts to enforce a security for costs order, it would need to incur further costs for such enforcement proceedings, always facing the high risk that such costs would not be reimbursed either. From a practical point of view, it would thus make much more sense to understand compliance with a security for costs order as a prerequisite for the proceedings to continue.[51] Under this approach, the claimant is practically forced to provide security if it wants to proceed with its claims, and the respondent is protected against incurring non-secured costs.[52] Accordingly, in domestic litigation, failure to provide security for costs typically leads to the dismissal of the claim.[53]

However, one may well wonder whether, in the absence of an express rule, such an approach is admissible in arbitration. After all, the tribunal is generally under a duty to render an (enforceable) award,[54] and it is questionable whether the tribunal can forego this obligation simply on the basis that it would be more practical to do so in order to give effect to a security for costs order.

In analysing this question, one should differentiate between a stay of proceedings on the one hand and their termination on the other. Insofar as the former is concerned, tribunals may, as part of their general power to conduct the proceedings,[55] order the

---

39-40 (Kluwer Law International 2022); Weixia Gu, *Security for Costs in International Commercial Arbitration*, 22 J. Intl Ar. 167, 184 (2005) DOI: 10.54648/joia2005012. Cf. further United Nations Commission on International Trade Law, Report of the 47th Session of the Working Group on Arbitration and Conciliation: doc. A/CN.9/641, para. 48. Some have also suggested that it may be the tribunal's general procedural powers that allow it to issue security for costs orders, cf. Pierre A. Karrer & Marcus Desax, *Security for Costs in International Arbitration: Why, When, and What If ...*, in *Law of International Business and Dispute Settlement in the 21st Century: Liber Amicorum Karl-Heinz Böckstiegel* 339, 344 (Robert Briner et al. eds, 2001).

49. Cf. UNCITRAL Model Law (2006), Art. 17H.
50. Cf. Jonas von Goeler, *Third-Party Funding in International Arbitration and its Impact on Procedure* 333 (Kluwer Law International, 2016); Weixia Gu, *Security for Costs in International Commercial Arbitration*, 22 J. Intl Arb. 167, 168 (2005) DOI: 10.54648/joia2005012.
51. Cf. Noah Rubins, *In God We Trust, All Others Pay Cash: Security for Costs in International Commercial Arbitration*, 11 ARIA 307, 366 (2000); Alan Redfern & Sam O'Leary, *Why It Is Time for International Arbitration to Embrace Security For Costs*, 32 Arb. Intl 397, 412-413 (2016) DOI: 10.1093/arbint/aiw030.
52. Alan Redfern & Sam O'Leary, *Why It Is Time For International Arbitration to Embrace Security For Costs*, 32 Arb. Intl 397, 413 (2016) DOI: 10.1093/arbint/aiw030.
53. Cf. Swiss Code of Civil Procedure, Art. 101(3); German Code of Civil Procedure, section 113; Austrian Code of Civil Procedure, section 60(3).
54. Günther J. Horvath, *The Duty of the Tribunal to Render an Enforceable Award*, 18(2) J. Intl Arb. 135 (2001) DOI: 10.54648/317806. Cf. also Gary Born, *International Commercial Arbitration* § 13.03[A] (3rd ed. Kluwer Law International 2021).
55. Cf. UNCITRAL Rules (2010), Art. 17.1; LCIA Rules (2020), Art. 14.1 and 14.2; SCC Rules (2023), Art. 23.1; Swiss Arbitration Rules (2021), Art. 19.1; German Code of Civil Procedure, section 1042(4); Qatari Law No. 2 of 2017 Promulgating the Civil and Commercial Arbitration Law, Art. 19(2).

stay of the proceedings after having weighed both parties' interests.[56] When engaging in such an evaluation, the respondent's interest in not incurring further non-secured costs may well outweigh the claimant's interest in a continuation of proceedings.[57]

The situation is however different when it comes to the termination of proceedings. As explained above,[58] arbitration laws and arbitration rules address a variety of situations in which proceedings may or must be terminated – but failure to provide security for costs is often not included as a ground for termination. Moreover, there is also no general open-ended ground for termination which would cover a failure to provide security for costs. In particular, the continuation of proceedings does not become unnecessary or impossible within the meaning of Article 32(2) lit. c of the UNCITRAL Model Law (2006) (or similar rules) just because security has not been provided.

Nonetheless, there seems to be a general consensus that, even in the absence of an express rule, the tribunal may ultimately terminate proceedings in case of a failure to provide security for costs.[59] In this respect, the reasoning of the International Centre for Settlement of Investment Disputes (ICSID) annulment committee in the case of *RSM v. Saint Lucia*[60] is illustrative. This reasoning was given at a time when the 2006 version of the ICSID Arbitration Rules applied. This version of the ICSID Arbitration Rules did not expressly regulate security for costs.

According to the *RSM* annulment committee, the decision to discontinue proceedings for lack of security for costs is a logical consequence of an earlier decision to stay the proceedings. Thus, in the view of the committee, the power to discontinue proceedings derives from the tribunal's general power to conduct the proceedings.[61] In other words, if it is clear that a stay will never be lifted because the claimant cannot provide security, there is no alternative but to eventually terminate the proceedings. Otherwise, the case would remain in suspension indefinitely which would be contrary to the tribunal's function to manage proceedings in a fair manner.[62]

---

56. Cf. Joachim Knoll, *Chapter 2, Part II: Commentary on Chapter 12 PILS*, in *Arbitration in Switzerland – The Practitioner's Guide*, Art. 182, para. 61 (Manuel Arroyo ed., 2nd ed. Kluwer Law International 2018); Swiss Federal Tribunal, Case No. 4P.64/2004/kra, 2 June 2004, para. 3.2.
57. Cf. with regard to the tribunal's exercise of its discretion to stay proceedings below §16.05.
58. *See* §16.02.
59. Cf. *Unnamed Case*, Procedural Order No. 4, 2009, 28 ASA Bull. 59 (2010); Bernhard Berger & Franz Kellerhals, *International and Domestic Arbitration in Switzerland* para. 1605 (Stämpfli Verlag 2015) (Switzerland); Micha Bühler & Marco Stacher, *Chapter 18, Part IV: Costs in International Arbitration*, in *Arbitration in Switzerland: The Practitioner's Guide* para. 60 (Manuel Arroyo ed., 2nd ed. Kluwer Law International 2018) (Switzerland); Marco Stacher *Swiss Rules of International Arbitration: Commentary* Art. 41, para. 29 (Tobias Zuberbühler et al. eds, 2nd ed. Juris Publishing 2013) (Switzerland); Karl Pörnbacher & Sophie Thiel, *Kostensicherheit in Schiedsverfahren*, 8 SchiedsVZ 14, 15 (2010) (Germany).
60. *RSM Production Corporation v. Saint Lucia*, ICSID Case No. ARB/12/10, Decision on Annulment, 29 April 2019.
61. *RSM Production Corporation v. Saint Lucia*, ICSID Case No. ARB/12/10, Decision on Annulment, 29 April 2019, paras 189-191, with reference to the tribunal's general power to conduct proceedings in ICSID Convention, Art. 44 sentence 2.
62. *RSM Production Corporation v. Saint Lucia*, ICSID Case No. ARB/12/10, Decision on Annulment, 29 April 2019, paras 190-191.

This reasoning is convincing – and can arguably be applied outside the ICSID context as well. Arbitration rules[63] and arbitration laws[64] typically grant the tribunal a general power to conduct proceedings, including the power to stay proceedings. By extension, tribunals also have the power to terminate proceedings where it would otherwise impose a never-ending series of stays.

[B] Other Cases Allowing for Stay or Termination of the Proceedings?

In the course of their research, the authors have not encountered other cases in which it has been argued that the breach of a procedural obligation results in the tribunal having the unwritten procedural power to stay and eventually terminate the arbitration. This is perhaps unsurprising, given the tribunal's principal duty to render a substantive decision, and considering further that the tribunal may typically address party non-compliance in other ways. For example, if a claimant submits evidence belatedly and in contradiction to the procedural calendar established by the tribunal, the tribunal may potentially strike such evidence from the record –[65] or at least take the claimant's conduct into account when rendering its cost decision.[66] Conversely, no one seems to argue that, instead, the tribunal should punish the claimant even further by terminating the arbitration.

As such, something more than a mere breach of procedural obligations is needed to assume that the tribunal may stay or terminate the arbitration. Considering the situations described above in which arbitration laws, arbitration rules or arbitral practice allow for stay and termination, the breach of the procedural obligation must have one of two effects. As a first option, the breach must make it practically impossible to continue with the arbitration. This is the case if the advance on costs is not fully paid in because the tribunal cannot be required to work without payment of its fees being secured.

As a second option, the breach must be one of the claimant, and it must be the case that the respondent cannot reasonably be required to pursue other means to remedy such breach. This is the case if no statement of claim is filed, as the respondent cannot reasonably be required to seek to force the claimant to submit a statement of claim, e.g., by asking for a respective order from the tribunal. Otherwise, the respondent would essentially be forced to work against its own interests. Further, this is also the case if the claimant fails to provide security for costs. Given that a security order is an interim measure, the respondent could theoretically turn to the courts to

63. ICC Rules (2021), Art. 19; SIAC Rules (2016), Rule 19.1; LCIA Rules (2020), Art. 14.2; Swiss Arbitration Rules (2021), Art. 19.1; HKIAC (2018), Art. 13.1; DIS Rules (2018), Art. 21.3.
64. UNCITRAL Model Law (2006), Art. 19(2); Belgian Judicial Code, Art. 1700(2); German Code of Civil Procedure, section 1042(4); English Arbitration Act (1996), section 34.1; French Code of Civil Procedure, Art. 1509(2); Costa Rican Law 8937 on International Commercial Arbitration, Art. 19(2).
65. Cf. Jeffrey Waincymer, *Procedure and Evidence in Arbitration* 822-824 (Kluwer Law International 2012).
66. Cf. ICC Rules (2021), Art. 38(5); LCIA Rules (2020), Art. 28.4; Swiss Arbitration Rules (2021), Art. 40; DIS Arbitration Rules (2018), Art. 33.3.

have it enforced. However, as explained above, this cannot be reasonably required of the respondent, as it would mean that the respondent would have to incur further unsecured costs in domestic enforcement proceedings.

In light of these considerations, not many cases come to mind in which an arbitration should potentially be stayed and eventually terminated in response to a procedural violation. However, the authors could conceive of one possible scenario, namely the failure by a claimant to disclose the identity of a third-party funder. Under an increasing number of arbitration rules, parties are required to disclose the existence and identity of third-party funders.[67] Moreover, even in the absence of such rules, tribunals have ordered claimants to disclose the identity of third-party funders.[68] The idea is to provide arbitrators with all the information needed to allow them to disclose any relationship with third-party funders so as to make sure that there are no unknown circumstances which could potentially give rise to a conflict of interest.[69] Ultimately, the goal is to preserve the integrity of the proceedings.

Assuming that, in a given case, it was clear that the claimant is using a third-party funder, but it refuses to disclose the funder's identity, it could be argued that the tribunal should stay and eventually terminate the arbitration. While the tribunal could theoretically issue a disclosure order in the form of an interim measure, which the respondent could then take to the courts for enforcement (e.g., through the imposition of penalty payments), this can arguably not be reasonably required of the respondent. Essentially, the respondent would have to do the claimant's work and thus advance the claimant's position, which would be fundamentally unfair. Moreover, in case the arbitration was to continue without the disclosure, there would be a real risk to the integrity of the proceedings, as an unwillingness to disclose the funder could by itself indicate that there may be a conflict.

Admittedly, this constellation will be rather rare, and it will require very clear indications that the claimant is indeed using a third-party funder before a tribunal could even consider staying or terminating the arbitration. It remains to be seen whether such a case will ever arise.

67. ICC Rules (2021), Art. 11(7); ICSID Arbitration Rules (2022), Rule 14; VIAC Arbitration Rules (2021), Art. 13a; HKIAC Rules (2018), Art. 44.
68. *Muhammet Çap & Sehil Inşaat Endustri ve Ticaret Ltd. Sti. v. Turkmenistan*, ICSID Case No. ARB/12/6, Procedural Order No. 3, 12 June 2015, para. 13; *South American Silver Limited v. Plurinational State of Bolivia*, PCA Case No. 2013-15, Procedural Order No. 10, 11 January 2016, para. 85 lit. b; *Bacilio Amorrortu v. Republic of Peru*, PCA Case No. 2020-11, Procedural Order No. 2 dated 19 October 2020, para. 12. Cf. also SIAC Investment Rules, Rule 24 lit. l, which expressly allows the tribunal to order the disclosure of the existence and identity of third-party funders.
69. Marlena Harutyunyan, *The Revised ICSID Rules: A Further Step Towards Transparency and Efficiency*, 40(3) ASA Bull. 529, 531 (2022) DOI: 10.54648/asab2022045; *Muhammet Çap & Sehil Inşaat Endustri ve Ticaret Ltd. Sti. v. Turkmenistan*, ICSID Case No. ARB/12/6, Procedural Order No. 3, 12 June 2015, para. 9; Jonas von Goeler, *Third-Party Funding in International Arbitration and its Impact on Procedure* 276 et seq. (Kluwer Law International, 2016). Cf. also ICC Rules (2021), Art. 11(7), which expressly alludes to this purpose.

§16.04 THE TRIBUNAL'S POWER TO TERMINATE PROCEEDINGS WITH PREJUDICE AND THE FORM OF THE TRIBUNAL'S DECISION

If a tribunal considers terminating proceedings, it will also have to consider the effect of such a decision on the claimant's claims. Specifically, the tribunal will need to decide whether to simply terminate the proceedings without making any substantive determination on the claimant's claims or to dismiss the claimant's claims with prejudice. This decision will have a profound impact. If the proceedings are simply terminated, the claimant may reintroduce its claims in a new arbitration. This may lead the respondent to complain about not having obtained a final dismissal of claims and of facing the risk of an abusive repeat introduction of claims.[70] Conversely, if the claims are dismissed with prejudice, the claimant will no longer be able to pursue them. This may also be problematic, in particular, if the claimant was merely facing a procedural obstacle, such as a lack of funds to provide security for costs. Such an obstacle may be temporary, but in the case of a dismissal with prejudice, the claimant would never again be able to pursue its claims, even if the obstacle later falls away.[71]

Accordingly, the effect of the tribunal's decision will be of huge practical importance for the parties. In addition, it will also have an impact on the form of the tribunal's termination decision, i.e., whether the tribunal issues an award or an order. In the following, the effect of the termination and the form of the termination decision will be analysed for the particular situations addressed above.

[A] Failure to Pay the Advance on Costs

In case of a failure to pay the advance on costs, the termination of proceedings will not entail dismissal of the claimant's claims with prejudice. Indeed, some institutional rules state expressly that the claims may be reintroduced in subsequent proceedings.[72] But even if this is not stated expressly in the applicable arbitration rules, it is generally accepted to be the case.[73] And indeed, this only makes sense: The advance on costs must be deemed a prerequisite for the tribunal to make any substantive decisions. Thus, the tribunal cannot substantively dismiss claims without full payment of the advance on costs.

70. Cf. Weixia Gu, *Security for Costs in International Commercial Arbitration*, 22 J. Intl Arb. 167, 200 (2005) DOI: 10.54648/joia2005012.
71. Cf. Karl Pörnbacher & Sophie Thiel, *Kostensicherheit in Schiedsverfahren*, 8 SchiedsVZ 14, 15 (2010).
72. LCIA Rules (2020), Art. 24.8; ICC Rules (2021), Art. 37.6; SIAC Rules (2016), Rule 34.6 lit. b; ICDR Rules (2021), Art. 39.3.
73. Cf. Thomas Rohner & Michael Lazopoulos, *Respondent's Refusal to Pay its Share of the Advance on Costs*, 29 ASA Bull. 549 (2011) DOI: 10.54648/asab2011063; Jan Paulsson & Georgios Petrochilos, *UNCITRAL Arbitration Rules* section IV, Art. 43 [Deposit of costs], para. 11 (Kluwer Law International 2017). Cf. further Jakob Ragnwaldh, Fredrik Andersson & Celeste E. Salinas Quero, *A Guide to the SCC Arbitration Rules* 161 (Kluwer Law International 2019) (with regard to the SCC Rules); Tobias Zuberbühler, *Chapter 3, Part II: Commentary on the Swiss Rules* in *Arbitration in Switzerland: The Practitioner's Guide* Art. 41, para. 18 (Manuel Arroyo ed., 2nd ed. Kluwer Law International 2018) (with regard to the Swiss Rules).

Of course, there may be situations where this may have undesired consequences. In particular, if an arbitration has progressed substantially, but one party is unable or unwilling to pay its share of a late increase of the advance on costs, there is a real risk that the efforts made in the arbitration up to that point will be for naught. Here, the only chance to achieve a substantive decision will be for the other party to pay both parties' shares of the increased advance – a possibility which is usually expressly foreseen in arbitration rules.[74] Subsequently, the case will progress normally to an award.

Insofar as the form of the termination decision is concerned, much will depend on the applicable arbitration rules. As mentioned above,[75] a considerable number of arbitration rules provide for a termination decision by the arbitral institution. If it is, however, for the tribunal to terminate the proceedings, the decision to terminate will usually be taken in an order and not in an award.[76] This accords with the nature of such a decision as a without-prejudice decision. Contrary to awards, orders do not contain a definitive decision on a substantive issue in dispute (but rather merely address procedural issues).[77] As such, an order is generally the appropriate form for a decision to terminate without prejudice.

[B] Default of the Claimant

In case of a default by the claimant leading to a termination of the arbitration, the claimant's claims will usually also not be dismissed with prejudice. Arbitration laws and arbitration rules generally provide that, in case of a failure by the claimant to submit the statement of claim, the tribunal shall issue an order for the termination of the arbitration.[78] In light of what was said immediately above about the nature of orders, the termination thus cannot entail a substantive decision. Accordingly, if the claimant fails to submit the statement of claim, its claims are generally not dismissed with prejudice.[79]

In case of a default by the claimant subsequent to the filing of the statement of claim, and as explained above,[80] it may be possible to terminate the arbitration on the basis that the continuation of the proceedings has become unnecessary. Here too, the decision is typically rendered via an order,[81] meaning that the termination cannot entail a substantive decision. Thus, the claimant's claims can again not be deemed to be

74. ICC Rules (2021), Art. 37.5; LCIA Rules (2020), Art. 24.6; HKIAC Rules (2018), Art. 41.5; ICDR Rules (2021), Art. 39.4.
75. *See* §16.02[A].
76. Cf. Swiss Arbitration Rules (2021), Art. 41.4; HKIAC Rules (2018), Art. 41.4; ICDR Rules (2021), Art. 39.5; UNCITRAL Rules (2010), Art. 43.4.
77. Gary Born, *International Commercial Arbitration* § 22.02[B][3] (3rd ed. Kluwer Law International 2021); *Redfern and Hunter on International Arbitration*, para. 9.08 (Nigel Blackaby et al. eds, 7th ed. Oxford Univ. Press 2023).
78. Cf. UNCITRAL Rules (2010), Art. 30(1) lit. a; German Code of Civil Procedure, section 1056(2) No. 1 lit. a; SIAC Rules (2016), Rule 20.8.
79. Cf. Chartered Institute of Arbitrators, Guidelines on Party Non-Participation, Commentary on Art. 2, para. (b) (2015).
80. *See* §16.02[B].
81. UNCITRAL Model Law (2006), Art. 32(2) lit. c.

dismissed with prejudice. However, everything will – as usual – depend on the specific legal framework, and the result may well be different if there are any specific provisions regulating the legal consequences of a default in a different manner.[82]

[C] Failure to Provide Security for Costs

A failure to provide security for costs may raise complex questions when it comes to deciding whether the claimant's claims are to be dismissed with prejudice or not. In that vein, one needs to again differentiate between cases in which the termination of the arbitration due to a failure to provide security is expressly regulated and cases in which an express rule is missing.

[1] Express Rules on the Termination of Proceedings

As mentioned above,[83] some arbitration laws expressly regulate the termination of proceedings in response to a failure to provide security for costs. In particular, both the English Arbitration Act (1996) and the Hong Kong Arbitration Ordinance contain express provisions allowing arbitrators to 'make an award dismissing' the claimant's claims.[84] The reference to an award and to the claimant's claims being dismissed is generally understood to mean that the claimant's claims are being dismissed with prejudice.[85] Under both provisions, such an award may, however, only be rendered if the tribunal has set a time limit within which security must be provided.[86] In the case of the English Arbitration Act (1996), the tribunal must set such time limit in a separate 'peremptory order' issued after the claimant has failed to provide security in response to the initial order.[87] In the case of the Hong Kong Arbitration Ordinance, the time limit must be contained in the initial order for security for costs.[88]

Similarly, the LCIA Rules (2020) also allow the tribunal to dismiss the claimant's claims 'by an award'.[89] In light of the reference to an 'award' and considering the rules of the English Arbitration Act (1996), which certainly inspired the LCIA, this too must

82. Such as e.g. English Arbitration Act 1996, section 41.3.
83. *See* §16.02[C].
84. English Arbitration Act (1996), section 41.6 ('If a claimant fails to comply with a peremptory order of the tribunal to provide security for costs, the tribunal may make an award dismissing his claim.'); Hong Kong Arbitration Ordinance (2011), section 56(4) ('An arbitral tribunal may make an award dismissing a claim or stay a claim if it has made an order under subsection (1)(a) but the order has not been complied with within the period specified under subsection (3)(a) or extended under subsection (3)(b).').
85. *Swallowfalls Limited v. Monaco Yachting & Technologies S.A.M. and another* [2015] EWHC 2013 (Comm); SCC Case No. 2020/f, Final Award, 7 April 2021, XLVI ICCA Y.B. Comm. Arb. 163, paras 77-85 (2021).
86. English Arbitration Act (1996), sections 41.5 and 41.6; Hong Kong Arbitration Ordinance (2011), section 56(4).
87. English Arbitration Act (1996), section 41.5.
88. Hong Kong Arbitration Ordinance (2011), section 56(3)(a).
89. LCIA Arbitration Rules (2020), Art. 25.2 ('In the event that a claiming, counterclaiming or cross-claiming party does not comply with any order to provide security, the Arbitral Tribunal may stay that party's claims, counterclaims or cross-claims or dismiss them by an award.').

be understood to mean that the dismissal of the claims is with prejudice. The situation is, however, somewhat different for the SCC Rules (2023) which provide more flexibility.[90] Pursuant to the SCC Rules (2023), '[a]ny decision to stay or to terminate the proceedings in whole or in part shall take the form of an order or an award.'[91] Commentators have noted that this rule allows the tribunal to take into account the circumstances of the case, including the *lex arbitri*, when deciding whether to issue an order or an award.[92] In line with this logic, a sole arbitrator in a recent arbitration seated in London and conducted under the SCC Expedited Rules (2017) relied entirely on the provisions of the English Arbitration Act (1996) (and their interpretation by English courts) to justify the dismissal of the claimant's claims with prejudice,[93] without invoking the power to decide on the termination in the form of an award stemming from the SCC Expedited Rules.[94]

Finally, something else applies under the VIAC Arbitration Rules (2021) and the ICSID Arbitration Rules (2022). The VIAC Arbitration Rules (2021) expressly state that if a party fails to comply with an order for security for costs, the tribunal terminates the proceedings by way of an order.[95] As explained above, this entails that the claims are not dismissed with prejudice. Moreover, under the ICSID Arbitration Rules (2022), the tribunal 'may [...] order the discontinuance of the proceeding' if a party fails to comply with an order to provide security. The fact that there is an express rule on the termination of proceedings which, however, only allows an 'order', speaks of the purely procedural act of 'discontinuance', and does not refer to the dismissal of claims also seems to indicate that, under the ICSID Arbitration Rules (2022), tribunals are not authorised to dismiss claims with prejudice.[96] It will, however, be interesting to see how tribunals and annulment committees will interpret this provision.

[2] No Express Rules on the Termination of Proceedings

As explained above,[97] the vast majority of arbitration laws and arbitration rules do not expressly regulate the termination of proceedings in case the claimant fails to provide security. Nonetheless, and as explained, it is generally recognised that, even without an

90. SCC Rules (2023), Art. 38(3).
91. SCC Rules (2023), Art. 38(4).
92. Jakob Ragnwaldh, Fredrik Andersson &Celeste E. Salinas Quero, *A Guide to the SCC Arbitration Rules* 123 (Kluwer Law International 2019).
93. SCC Case No. 2020/f, Final Award, 7 April 2021, XLVI ICCA Y.B. Comm. Arb. 163, paras 77-85 (2021).
94. The respective provisions in the SCC Expedited Rules (2017) are the same as in the SCC Rules (2023), cf. SCC Expedited Rules (2017), Art. 39(3) and (4).
95. VIAC Arbitration Rules (2021), Art. 34(2.4).
96. Cf. Chiann Bao, *Case Comment, RSM v Saint Lucia: With Prejudice – The Unlikely Death Knell*, 35 ICSID Review 48-49 (2020), who voices doubts as to the tribunal's power to dismiss claims with prejudice under the rule. Cf. further *RSM Production Corporation v. Saint Lucia*, ICSID Case No. ARB/12/10, Decision on Annulment, 29 April 2019, para. 198, which notes the lack of a reference to discontinuance with prejudice in the new rule.
97. *See* §16.03[A].

express rule, tribunals may terminate proceedings for lack of security.[98] However, it is much less clear whether this power extends to a dismissal with prejudice. Insofar it could be argued, on the one hand, that it must be possible to dismiss claims with prejudice. Otherwise, the claimant could reintroduce its claims and potentially harass the respondent with repeat proceedings.[99] On the other hand, a dismissal with prejudice has a devastating impact on the claimant. Effectively, the claimant loses its claim without having had a chance to fully present its case and without the tribunal having properly considered the merits. This would be particularly unfair if the claimant faced actual difficulties in providing security which it overcomes after the dismissal with prejudice. Potentially, this could create the risk of a denial of justice.[100]

As a starting point, it is indeed doubtful whether it is possible to dismiss claims with prejudice for failure to provide security for costs in the absence of an express provision to this effect. As explained above,[101] the source of the tribunal's power to terminate proceedings is not self-evident but is best understood as stemming from the tribunal's general power to conduct the proceedings. However, that power only entitles the tribunal to decisions on the procedure, not on substance. Accordingly, it would seem to be a stretch to argue that a tribunal may dismiss claims with prejudice in the absence of an express rule to that effect.

This also seems to be the prevailing view[102] and was in particular argued by the ICSID annulment committee in the case of *RSM v. Saint Lucia.*[103] In this case, the tribunal (in an unpublished award) dismissed the claimant's claims due to a failure to provide security.[104] Although the tribunal failed to clarify in the operative part of the award that the dismissal was with prejudice, both parties understood this to be the case based on the tribunal's reasoning.[105] Subsequently, the annulment committee was

98. *See* above §16.03[A].
99. Cf. Pierre A. Karrer & Marcus Desax, *Security for Costs in International Arbitration: Why, When, and What If ...*, in *Law of International Business and Dispute Settlement in the 21st Century: Liber Amicorum Karl-Heinz Böckstiegel* 339, 352 (Robert Briner et al. eds, 2001); Weixia Gu, *Security for Costs in International Commercial Arbitration*, 22 J. Int. Arb. 167, 200 (2005) DOI: 10.54648/joia2005012.
100. Cf. *RSM Production Corporation v. Saint Lucia*, ICSID Case No. ARB/12/10, Decision on Annulment, 29 April 2019, para. 198.
101. *See* §16.03[A].
102. Jan Heiner Nedden & Inga Witte, *Chapter 4: The Exception in Theory, a Unicorn in Practice? Revisiting Security for Costs from a Practitioner's Perspective*, 4 Stockholm Arbitration Yearbook, 39, 50 (Kluwer Law International 2022); Jean-François Poudret & Sebastien Besson, *Comparative Law on International Arbitration* para. 593 (Sweet & Maxwell 2007); Bernhard Berger & Franz Kellerhals, *International and Domestic Arbitration in Switzerland* para. 1605 (Stämpfli Verlag 2015) (Switzerland); Micha Bühler & Marco Stacher, *Chapter 18, Part IV: Costs in International Arbitration*, in *Arbitration in Switzerland: The Practitioner's Guide*, para. 60 (Manuel Arroyo ed., 2nd ed. Kluwer Law International 2018) (Switzerland); Marco Stacher *Swiss Rules of International Arbitration: Commentary* Art. 41, para. 29 (Tobias Zuberbühler et al. eds., 2nd ed. Juris Publishing 2013) (Switzerland).
103. *RSM Production Corporation v. Saint Lucia*, ICSID Case No. ARB/12/10, Decision on Annulment, 29 April 2019, paras 193 et seq.
104. *RSM Production Corporation v. Saint Lucia*, ICSID Case No. ARB/12/10, Decision on Annulment, 29 April 2019, paras 13-25.
105. *RSM Production Corporation v. Saint Lucia*, ICSID Case No. ARB/12/10, Decision on Annulment, 29 April 2019, paras 193-195.

tasked, *inter alia,* with assessing whether the tribunal committed a manifest excess of power within the meaning of Article 52(1)(b) of the ICSID Convention. It found that while the dismissal as such was covered by the tribunal's general power to conduct proceedings,[106] the dismissal with prejudice was not. According to the annulment committee, that is because a dismissal with prejudice is no longer a procedural but rather a substantive decision.[107] On this basis, the annulment committee partially annulled the award insofar as it provided for the dismissal of claims to be with prejudice.[108]

Incidentally, a similar conclusion in favour of the set aside of an award could also be drawn in a non-ICSID context. In particular, if a claim is dismissed with prejudice on the basis that the claimant failed to provide security for costs, and there is no express provision allowing for such a decision, it could be argued that the claimant was unable to present its case (Article V(1)(b) of the New York Convention), that there was a violation of the arbitral procedure (Article V(1)(d) of the New York Convention) or that the claimant's right to be heard was violated (procedural *ordre public,* Article V(2)(b) of the New York Convention).[109]

Understandably, some might find this result unsatisfactory, as it might mean that a claimant repeatedly reintroduces claims. However, these concerns do not justify a tribunal overstepping its powers. Rather, these concerns should motivate lawmakers and rule drafters to expressly provide for the possibility of a dismissal with prejudice in future reforms of arbitration laws and arbitration rules.

§16.05 THE EXERCISE OF THE TRIBUNAL'S DISCRETION TO STAY OR TERMINATE PROCEEDINGS

If a tribunal has the power to terminate proceedings in a given situation, this does not necessarily mean that it should do so or that it should do so immediately. Generally, the tribunal will first stay proceedings before eventually opting for termination.[110] Moreover, before both a decision to stay and a decision to terminate, the tribunal will need to weigh all circumstances to make sure that its decision does not violate its duties and the parties' corresponding rights.

106. *RSM Production Corporation v. Saint Lucia,* ICSID Case No. ARB/12/10, Decision on Annulment, 29 April 2019, paras. 189-191, with reference to the tribunal's general power to conduct proceedings in ICSID Convention, Art. 44 sentence 2.
107. *RSM Production Corporation v. Saint Lucia,* ICSID Case No. ARB/12/10, Decision on Annulment, 29 April 2019, paras 196-201.
108. *RSM Production Corporation v. Saint Lucia,* ICSID Case No. ARB/12/10, Decision on Annulment, 29 April 2019, paras 200-201.
109. Cf. more generally with regard to grounds for non-recognition in the context of security for costs Noah Rubins, *In God We Trust, All Others Pay Cash: Security for Costs in International Commercial Arbitration,* 11 ARIA 307, 321 (2000); Weixia Gu, *Security for Costs in International Commercial Arbitration,* 22 J. Int. Arb. 167, 192 (2005) DOI: 10.54648/joia2005012.
110. Cf. Gerold Zeiler & Lisa Beisteiner, *VIAC Rules of Arbitration 2018,* in *Handbook VIAC Rules of Arbitration and Mediation: A Practitioner's Guide* 238 (Vienna International Arbitral Centre of the Austrian Federal Economic Chamber ed., 2nd ed. Verlag WKÖ Service 2019); Brooks William Daly, Evgeniya Goriatcheva & Hugh Meighen, *A Guide to the PCA Arbitration Rules* para. 6.110 (Oxford Univ. Press 2016).

As a starting point, the claimant is entitled to a decision on the merits being rendered within a reasonable time, i.e., without undue delay.[111] To this effect, arbitration rules variously provide that the tribunal has to conduct the proceedings efficiently.[112] Thus, in case of doubt, the tribunal should generally continue with the proceedings (rather than stay or terminate them) in order to avoid a delay or denial of justice.[113] At the same time, in case of a breach of procedural obligations, as described above, considerable arguments weigh against continuing with the proceedings. In particular, if the advance is not fully paid, the tribunal runs the risk of doing work without receiving payment in the end. Equally, if security is not provided, the respondent runs the risk of incurring costs for further work in the proceedings without a respective cost claim being secured.

Once there is a breach of a procedural obligation, and to ensure the parties' right to be heard, the tribunal should always seek to ascertain the reasons for the failure to comply with the obligation and the likely time it will take to remedy such failure.[114] If the non-complying party provides a credible explanation and credibly indicates that the failure will be remedied within a reasonable time period, it may not even be necessary to stay the proceedings at all. Conversely, if the explanation given is insufficient or if the time indicated for remedying the failure appears unreasonably long, the tribunal should opt for a stay.

Once the arbitration is stayed, the position of the complying party is secured in that it does not need to incur (major) costs for further procedural steps until the procedural breach is remedied. For example, in the case of security for costs, this means that a respondent will not need to incur (major) further costs until it can be sure that it can make good on a potential claim for such costs based on the security.[115] As such, once the arbitration is stayed, there is no overwhelming urgency to move on to termination. However, as explained by the annulment committee in the *RSM* case, it would be unfair to keep proceedings in limbo forever.[116] In particular, even a suspended arbitration causes some costs, such as for the submission of arguments on how long the stay should continue and for reporting the status of the arbitration to a

111. *RSM Production Corporation v. Saint Lucia*, ICSID Case No. ARB/12/10, Decision on Annulment, 29 April 2019, para. 191; Pierre Heitzmann, *Chapter 31: Arbitration and Criminal Liability for Competition Law Violations in Europe*, in *EU and US Antitrust Arbitration: A Handbook for Practitioners*, para. 31-054 (Gordon Blanke & Phillip Landolt eds., Kluwer Law International 2011).
112. ICC Rules (2021), Art. 22.1; LCIA Rules (2020), Art. 14.1.ii; SCAI Rules (2021), Art. 19.1; HKIAC (2018), Art.s 13.1, 13.5; DIS Rules (2018), Art. 27.1.
113. Cf. Swiss Federal Tribunal, Case No. 4P.64/2004, 2 June 2004, para. 3.2; Joachim Knoll, *Chapter 2, Part II: Commentary on Chapter 12 PILS*, in *Arbitration in Switzerland: The Practitioner's Guide*, Art. 182, para. 61 (Manuel Arroyo ed., Kluwer Law International 2013). Cf. also Luka Groselj, *Stay of Arbitration Proceedings – Some Examples from Arbitral Practice*, 36 ASA Bull. 560, 576 (2018) DOI: 10.54648/asab2018054.
114. Cf. Jakob Ragnwaldh, Fredrik Andersson & Celeste E. Salinas Quero, *A Guide to the SCC Arbitration Rules* 114 (Kluwer Law International 2019); Michael J. Moser & Chiann Bao, *A Guide to the HKIAC Arbitration Rules* para. 9.227 (2nd ed. Oxford Univ. Press 2022).
115. Cf. *LCIA Case No. 132551*, Procedural Order No. 4 dated 2014, 36 ASA Bull. 664, para. 27 (2018) DOI: 10.54648/asab2018067.
116. *RSM Production Corporation v. Saint Lucia*, ICSID Case No. ARB/12/10, Decision on Annulment, 29 April 2019, para. 191.

party's auditors. Moreover, merely having to account for a claim in the company books may have a real economic impact, as potential litigation exposure is reflected in stock prices.[117]

Against this background, the authors consider that it is good practice for a tribunal to clearly indicate for how long it intends to stay proceedings in the stay order. In doing so, the tribunal may wish to clarify that if the breach is not remedied within such period, it will terminate the arbitration unless there are extraordinary circumstances justifying a continued stay of proceedings. During the stay period and before terminating the arbitration, the tribunal should allow the parties to comment on the likelihood and likely timing of the non-complying party eventually remedying the breach. If called upon, the tribunal should balance the impact that the continued pending of the arbitration will have on the complying party and the impact a termination would have on the non-complying party. If the tribunal considers that there are no exceptional circumstances that warrant prolonging the stay, it should terminate the proceedings. Arguably, the tribunal should exercise additional restraint if the claimant's claims would be dismissed with prejudice, given the greater ramifications of such a decision.[118]

Notably, in some cases, the tribunal might even 'make a U-turn' and decide to modify the original order with which one of the parties is not complying. For example, if the tribunal ordered the claimant to provide security in the form of a guarantee by a bank from certain countries, but the claimant is only able to obtain a guarantee from a bank based in another country (and that guarantee is still deemed acceptable to the respondent), the tribunal might adapt the initial security for costs order and set a new time limit for compliance. Moreover, in some cases, it might even be appropriate to revoke the original security for costs order altogether. In *Unionmatex v. Turkmenistan*, for instance, the tribunal was unanimously convinced that the claimant had seriously and diligently tried but failed to procure security for costs.[119] In addition, the inability to post security resulted from the fact that the claimant had been placed in insolvency proceedings, allegedly due to the wrongful conduct of the respondent.[120] Against this background, the tribunal rescinded its initial security for costs order, finding that maintaining the order would 'deny the claimant the opportunity to proceed to the merits' and would result in 'a denial of access to justice'.[121]

117. Cf. Gregory A. Horowitz, *A Further Comment on the Complexities of Market Evidence in Valuation Litigation*, 68 Bus. Law 1071, 1077 (2013).
118. Cf. in this regard Jan Heiner Nedden & Inga Witte, *Chapter 4: The Exception in Theory, a Unicorn in Practice? Revisiting Security for Costs from a Practitioner's Perspective*, 4 Stockholm Arbitration Yearbook, 39, 50 (Kluwer Law International 2022).
119. *Dirk Herzig as Insolvency Administrator over the assets of Unionmatex Industrieanlagen GmbH v. Turkmenistan, ICSID Case No. ARB/18/35*, Decision and Procedural Order No. 5, 9 June 2020, para. 21.
120. *Dirk Herzig as Insolvency Administrator over the assets of Unionmatex Industrieanlagen GmbH v. Turkmenistan, ICSID Case No. ARB/18/35*, Decision and Procedural Order No. 5, 9 June 2020, para. 22.
121. *Dirk Herzig as Insolvency Administrator over the assets of Unionmatex Industrieanlagen GmbH v. Turkmenistan, ICSID Case No. ARB/18/35*, Decision and Procedural Order No. 5, 9 June 2020, para. 22.

§16.06 TERMINATION OF THE ARBITRATION AGREEMENT IN REACTION TO PARTY NON-COMPLIANCE WITH PROCEDURAL OBLIGATIONS?

Notwithstanding the above, there may be an alternative argument to justify the termination of proceedings in case of party non-compliance with procedural obligations, namely that the compliant party has a right to terminate the arbitration agreement. Assuming the arbitration agreement is validly terminated, the tribunal would have to terminate the proceedings with an award declaring that it has no jurisdiction.

[A] Background

Generally, the arbitration agreement is subject to the same rules on contract formation and validity that apply to contracts in general[122] (with the caveat that an arbitration clause in a contract is treated as a separate contract under the doctrine of separability).[123] Thus, it is also generally recognised that an arbitration agreement can be terminated in accordance with the principles laid out in general contract law.[124] As such, a breach of the agreed arbitral procedure by one party could potentially give rise to a termination of the arbitration agreement by the other party.[125] The same potentially applies to a breach of a procedural order issued by the tribunal. That is because a breach of a procedural order can also be deemed a breach of the arbitration

122. Gary Born, *International Commercial Arbitration* § 5.04[A][3] and § 5.06[A][3] (3rd ed. Kluwer Law International 2021). Cf. further *Circuit City Stores v. Adams*, 279 F.3d 889, 892 (9th Cir. 2002); Christoph Müller, *Chapter 2, Part II: Commentary on Chapter 12 PILS*, in *Arbitration in Switzerland: The Practitioner's Guide*, Art. 178 PILS, para. 35 (Manuel Arroyo ed., 2nd ed. Kluwer Law International 2018) (Switzerland); *Zivilprozessordnung* § 1029 ZPO, para. 3 (Hans-Joachim Musielak & Wolfgang Voit eds, 19th ed. Verlag Franz Vahlen 2022) (Germany).
123. UNCITRAL Model Law (2006), Art. 16(1); Art. 178(3) PILS (Switzerland); Dutch Code of Civil Procedure, Art. 1053. Cf. further *Redfern and Hunter on International Arbitration*, paras 2.107 et seq. (Nigel Blackaby et al. eds., 7th ed., Oxford Univ. Press 2023).
124. Gary Born, International Commercial Arbitration § 5.06[D][6] (3rd ed. Kluwer Law International 2021); Daniel Girsberger & Nathalie Voser, *International Arbitration: Comparative and Swiss Perspectives*, para. 528 (4th ed. Schulthess Juristische Medien AG 2021); Lars Heuman, *Arbitration Law of Sweden: Practice and Procedure*, 125 et seq. (Juris Publishing 2003) (Sweden); *Münchener Kommentar zur ZPO* § 1029 ZPO, paras 153 et seq. (6th ed. C. H. Beck 2022) (Germany); *Zivilprozessordnung* § 1029 ZPO, para. 3 (Hans-Joachim Musielak & Wolfgang Voit eds, 19th ed. Verlag Franz Vahlen 2022).
125. Gary Born, *International Commercial Arbitration* § 5.06[D][6][b][iii] (3rd ed. Kluwer Law International 2021) (with further references to domestic law); Higher Regional Court of Munich, 10 SchiedsVZ 96, 99 (2012); Lars Heuman, *Arbitration Law of Sweden: Practice and Procedure* 125 et seq. (Juris Publishing 2003) (Sweden); Anders Relden & Jacob Frank, *International Arbitration in Sweden: A Practitioner's Guide* Chapter 4, para. 122 (Annette Magnusson et al. eds., 2nd ed. Kluwer Law International) (Sweden); *Münchener Kommentar zur ZPO* § 1029 ZPO, paras 156 (6th ed. C. H. Beck 2022) (Germany); Thomas Granier, *Unilateral Termination of an Arbitration Agreement by a Party after the Arbitration Has Commenced*, 45 Revista Brasileira de Arbitragem 108, 114 et seq. (2015) (Germany).

agreement. After all, by agreeing to arbitration, the parties generally also agree to abide by the tribunal's procedural orders.[126]

[B] Limited Scope for the Termination of the Arbitration Agreement

Whether the compliant party may indeed terminate the arbitration agreement in reaction to the other party's non-compliance will depend on the facts of the case and on the law applicable to the arbitration agreement.[127] It would go beyond the limitations of this chapter to conduct a comparative law study on how specific national contract laws regulate the potential termination of an arbitration agreement in case of non-compliance with procedural obligations. However, it would seem fair to say that, generally, the termination of the arbitration agreement should only be possible in very serious and exceptional cases.[128]

Typically, the general idea behind a termination in case of a breach of procedural obligations is that, due to the breach by the non-complying party, the complying party can no longer be reasonably required to abide by the arbitration agreement. However, that will only rarely be the case because arbitration rules and arbitration laws contain a wide variety of mechanisms to address party non-compliance. For example, and as mentioned above, the delayed submission of evidence may be addressed by striking such evidence from the record[129] or by taking the breach into account at the cost stage.[130] Moreover, and as explained above, the failure by a claimant to submit the statement of claim may allow the tribunal to terminate the arbitration by way of a

126. Cf. ICC Rules 2021, Art. 22(5); Swiss Arbitration Rules (2021), Art. 16.1; Guy Pendell & Juliette Huard-Bourgois, *Chapter 17: Rights and Duties of the Parties and Counsel*, in *Arbitration in England, with Chapters on Scotland and Ireland*, para. 17-50 (Julian D.M. Lew et al. eds, Kluwer Law International 2013); Nadia Smahi, *Due Process under the Swiss Rules of International Arbitration*, 38 ASA Bull. 930, 941 (2020) DOI: 10.54648/asab2020149.
127. The question of the law applicable to the arbitration agreement is an evergreen that has gained renewed attention with the 2020 decision of the UK Supreme Court in *Enka v. Chubb*. For a helpful overview of the current state of play in England and Sweden, cf. James Hope, Lisa Johansson, *What Is the Governing Law of the Arbitration Agreement? A Comparison Between the English and Swedish Approaches*, 3 Stockholm Arbitration Yearbook, 296 (Kluwer Law International 2022).
128. Gary Born, *International Commercial Arbitration* § 5.06[D][6][b][iii] (3rd ed. Kluwer Law International 2021); Daniel Girsberger & Nathalie Voser, *International Arbitration: Comparative and Swiss Perspectives*, para. 528 (4th ed. Schulthess Juristische Medien AG 2021); *Bulgarian Foreign Trade Bank Ltd. v. A.I. Trade Finance Inc.*, XXIVa Y.B. Comm. Arb. 321, para. 8 (Svea Court of Appeal, 1999) (Sweden); Lars Heuman, *Arbitration Law of Sweden: Practice and Procedure* 126 (Juris Publishing 2003) (Sweden); *Münchener Kommentar zur ZPO* § 1029 ZPO, paras. 154 (6th ed. C. H. Beck 2022) (Germany). Cf. also Thomas Granier, *Unilateral Termination of an Arbitration Agreement by a Party After the Arbitration has Commenced*, 45 Revista Brasileira de Arbitragem 108, 115 (2015) DOI: 10.54648/rba2015005.
129. Cf. Waincymer, *Procedure and Evidence in Arbitration* 822-824 (Kluwer Law International 2012).
130. Cf. ICC Rules (2021), Art. 38(5); SCC Rules (2023), Art. 49(6); LCIA Rules (2020), Art. 28(4); ICSID Arbitration Rules (2022), Rule 52(1) lit. b; Swiss Rules (2021), Art. 40; DIS Rules (2018), Art. 33.3.

termination order.[131] In light of such mechanisms, the complying party will generally not be allowed to terminate the arbitration agreement.[132]

Arguably, this even applies where the available mechanisms do not fully remedy a breach of procedural obligations. For example, if a party breaches a document production order by a tribunal, the tribunal will typically only be able to react by drawing adverse inferences.[133] However, the tribunal may not always be able to draw meaningful adverse inferences, given that it has been argued that an adverse reference requires that the tribunal be presented with separate prima facie evidence supporting the inference sought.[134] Against this background, the available mechanisms could arguably be deemed insufficient to react to the breach of the procedural obligation. Nonetheless, even in such a situation, the complying party should generally not be allowed to terminate the arbitration agreement. That is because, by agreeing to arbitration under a given set of rules, the parties must be deemed to have accepted that the mechanisms provided to address breaches of procedural obligations may sometimes be imperfect.

Against this background, a termination of the arbitration agreement should generally only be considered if (i) there is a breach of procedural obligations with a serious impact on the complying party; and (ii) the applicable rules do not allow to remedy this breach at all, or the available redress is entirely insufficient.

[C] Consequences of the Termination of the Arbitration Agreement

In case of a valid termination of the arbitration agreement, the tribunal no longer has jurisdiction to decide on the merits of the case. Accordingly, the tribunal has to issue an award declining jurisdiction, and it is impeded from rendering a decision on the merits. Thus, in this scenario, the claimant's claims are not dismissed on the merits and with prejudice. Rather, the claimant will still be able to pursue its claims in the future, just not before the incumbent tribunal.

A termination of the arbitration agreement also entails that the parties cannot initiate any new arbitration proceedings and that they instead have to turn to the courts to resolve their existing dispute or any future disputes. This may be a rather undesirable consequence for the complying party, as it may be satisfied with arbitration as

131. *See* §16.02[B] and §16.04[B].
132. Cf. Gary Born, *International Commercial Arbitration* § 5.06[D][6][b][iii] (3rd ed. Kluwer Law International 2021); Higher Regional Court of Munich, 10 SchiedsVZ 96, 100 (2012); Lars Heuman, *Arbitration Law of Sweden: Practice and Procedure* 125 et seq. (Juris Publishing 2003) (Sweden); Thomas Granier, *Unilateral Termination of an Arbitration Agreement by a Party After the Arbitration has Commenced*, 45 Revista Brasileira de Arbitragem 108, 115 (2015) DOI: 10.54648/rba2015005.
133. Cf. generally IBA Rules (2020), Art. 9.6 and 9.7; Jeffrey Waincymer, *Procedure and Evidence in Arbitration* 880-881 (Kluwer Law Intl 2012).
134. Cf. Jeremy K. Sharpe, *Drawing Adverse Inferences from the Non-production of Evidence*, 22 Arb. Intl 549, 550 (2006) DOI: 10.1093/arbitration/22.4.549; Markus Benzing, *Das Beweisrecht vor internationalen Gerichten und Schiedsgerichten in zwischenstaatlichen Streitigkeiten* 333 et seq. (Springer 2010).

such and may simply want the particular breach by the non-complying party addressed. Against this background, *Born* argues that, in most cases, termination should only be allowed with respect to the pending arbitration in which the breach has occurred and not with respect to the arbitration agreement in general (and thus with respect to future disputes).[135] Whether an arbitration agreement can indeed be 'split up' and only partially terminated in this sense will, however, depend on the law applicable to the arbitration agreement.

[D] The *Bulbank v. AIT* Case

In this context, it is worth revisiting a landmark Swedish case regarding the termination of an arbitration agreement due to an alleged breach of the duty of confidentiality. The case of *Bulbank v. AIT* stems from an arbitration initiated in 1996 under the Arbitration Rules of the United Nations Economic Commission for Europe and seated in Stockholm.[136] In the applicable contract and arbitration agreement, the parties had not provided for an express confidentiality obligation, and the Swedish Arbitration Act also did not expressly provide for the confidentiality of the arbitration.[137] During the course of the arbitration, the claimant AIT released a partial award rendered by the tribunal to an arbitration publication.[138] In response, the respondent Bulbank alleged that this constituted a fundamental breach of confidentiality and, thus, of the arbitration agreement, allowing Bulbank to declare the arbitration agreement avoided.[139] The tribunal, however, rejected the argument and subsequently rendered a final award in 1997.[140]

The respondent challenged the award, arguing that it had validly avoided the arbitration agreement.[141] In the first instance, the City Court of Stockholm accepted the argument. It concluded that, unless otherwise agreed by the parties, a confidentiality regime applied in arbitration proceedings under Swedish law, even in the absence of an express provision to this effect. It then held that the claimant had fundamentally

135. Gary Born, *International Commercial Arbitration* § 5.06[D][6][b][iii] (3rd ed. Kluwer Law International 2021).
136. *Bulgarian Foreign Trade Bank Ltd. v. A.I. Trade Finance Inc.*, XXIVa Y.B. Comm. Arb. 321 (Svea Court of Appeal, 1999). Cf. for background and a detailed overview of the arbitral and subsequent court proceedings Mark F. Rosenberg, *Chronicles of the Bullbank Case – The Rest of the Story*, 19 J. Intl Arb. 1 (2002) DOI: 10.54648/394171.
137. *Bulgarian Foreign Trade Bank Ltd. v. A.I. Trade Finance Inc.*, XXVI Y.B. Comm. Arb. 291, paras 4-5 (Swedish Supreme Court, 2001).
138. *Bulgarian Foreign Trade Bank Ltd. v. A.I. Trade Finance Inc.*, XXIVa Y.B. Comm. Arb. 321-322 (Svea Court of Appeal, 1999).
139. *Bulgarian Foreign Trade Bank Ltd. v. A.I. Trade Finance Inc.*, XXIVa Y.B. Comm. Arb. 321-323 (Svea Court of Appeal, 1999).
140. *Bulgarian Foreign Trade Bank Ltd. v. A.I. Trade Finance Inc.*, XXIVa Y.B. Comm. Arb. 321, 322 (Svea Court of Appeal, 1999).
141. *Bulgarian Foreign Trade Bank Ltd. v. A.I. Trade Finance Inc.*, XXIVa Y.B. Comm. Arb. 321, 322 (Svea Court of Appeal, 1999).

breached the arbitration agreement by breaching confidentiality and that this constituted valid grounds for the respondent to avoid the contract.[142]

The Svea Court of Appeal, however, reversed the City Court's decision.[143] It concluded that there was no general confidentiality obligation and that no implied agreement on confidentiality could be assumed.[144] However, it held that the passing on of information from the arbitration could breach a duty of loyalty, depending on the sensitivity of the information and the reasons for its publication, the extent to which the other party suffers damage by the publication, and the intention behind the publication.[145] Interestingly, the court expressly referred to another mechanism to address the breach of such duties, namely a claim for compensation, and argued that, in light of this remedy, the scope for avoidance of the arbitration agreement due to a fundamental breach was very limited.[146] On this basis, the Svea Court of Appeal concluded that there had been no fundamental breach which would have allowed the respondent to avoid the arbitration agreement.[147]

Finally, the Swedish Supreme Court held that a party in arbitration proceedings cannot be bound by a duty of confidentiality unless it concluded a separate agreement to this effect.[148] On this basis, the court held that there was no breach and that, accordingly, the respondent did not have grounds for avoiding the arbitration agreement.[149] As a result, the award survived the respondent's challenge.[150]

Although the Swedish Supreme Court ultimately did not weigh in on the question of the precise requirements for the termination of an arbitration agreement, the *Bulbank* case is quite illustrative. In particular, the Svea Court of Appeal's reasoning confirms that the scope for avoiding the arbitration agreement should be limited, in particular, because there are other remedies to address breaches of confidentiality (or, under the court's approach, breaches of the duty of loyalty). In this regard, the court had not even considered that tribunals may also order interim measures prohibiting the dissemination of confidential information.[151] Furthermore, and irrespective thereof, one may well wonder whether the termination of the arbitration agreement can be an

142. *Bulgarian Foreign Trade Bank Ltd. v. A.I. Trade Finance Inc.*, XXIVa Y.B. Comm. Arb. 321, 322-323 (Svea Court of Appeal, 1999).
143. *Bulgarian Foreign Trade Bank Ltd. v. A.I. Trade Finance Inc.*, XXIVa Y.B. Comm. Arb. 321, 324-327 (Svea Court of Appeal, 1999).
144. *Bulgarian Foreign Trade Bank Ltd. v. A.I. Trade Finance Inc.*, XXIVa Y.B. Comm. Arb. 321, para. 7 (Svea Court of Appeal, 1999).
145. *Bulgarian Foreign Trade Bank Ltd. v. A.I. Trade Finance Inc.*, XXIVa Y.B. Comm. Arb. 321, para. 7 (Svea Court of Appeal, 1999).
146. *Bulgarian Foreign Trade Bank Ltd. v. A.I. Trade Finance Inc.*, XXIVa Y.B. Comm. Arb. 321, para. 8 (Svea Court of Appeal, 1999).
147. *Bulgarian Foreign Trade Bank Ltd. v. A.I. Trade Finance Inc.*, XXIVa Y.B. Comm. Arb. 321, para. 9 (Svea Court of Appeal, 1999).
148. *Bulgarian Foreign Trade Bank Ltd. v. A.I. Trade Finance Inc.*, XXVI Y.B. Comm. Arb. 291, para. 21 (Swedish Supreme Court, 2001).
149. *Bulgarian Foreign Trade Bank Ltd. v. A.I. Trade Finance Inc.*, XXVI Y.B. Comm. Arb. 291, para. 21 (Swedish Supreme Court, 2001).
150. *Bulgarian Foreign Trade Bank Ltd. v. A.I. Trade Finance Inc.*, XXVI Y.B. Comm. Arb. 291, para. 21 (Swedish Supreme Court, 2001).
151. Ileana M. Smeureanu, *Confidentiality in International Commercial Arbitration* 174-179 (Kluwer Law International 2011). Cf. however Michael Hwang & Katie Chung, *Defining the*

appropriate remedy for a breach of confidentiality in the first place. After all, the consequence of a valid termination of the arbitration agreement would be that the parties must have their dispute decided in litigation, and thus without any confidentiality arrangement.[152]

§16.07 CONCLUSION

As the above analysis has shown, tribunals are only entitled to stay or terminate an arbitration due to a procedural violation in narrow and specific circumstances. Arbitration laws and arbitration rules rarely provide for a stay or termination in response to procedural breaches. Moreover, the scope for a stay or termination based on the general procedural powers of the tribunal is very limited. At the same time, and according to the prevailing view, the tribunal should only dismiss the claimant's claims with prejudice in the rare case that this is expressly allowed by the applicable legal framework.

These limitations on staying and terminating proceedings because of procedural violations are unsurprising, as the tribunal is principally required to move the procedure ahead and render a substantive decision. On top of that, there are usually other means through which the tribunal can ensure compliance. However, if the tribunal is faced with a situation in which it may principally stay or terminate the arbitration, it should take great care not to violate the party's (usually the claimant's) procedural rights. As such, it should grant sufficient opportunities for the parties to comment and for the violation to be remedied.

Finally, depending on the facts and the law applicable to the arbitration agreement, it may also be possible to terminate the arbitration agreement because of a procedural violation. In this case, the tribunal will have to render an award declining jurisdiction. This should, however, only be possible in exceptional cases.

Indefinable: Practical Problems of Confidentiality in Arbitration, 26 J. Intl Arb. 609, 641 (2009) DOI: 10.54648/joia2009034, who doubt the usefulness of this remedy.

152. Cf. Michael Hwang & Katie Chung, *Defining the Indefinable: Practical Problems of Confidentiality in Arbitration*, 26(5) J. Intl Arb. 609, 641 (2009) DOI: 10.54648/joia2009034.

CHAPTER 17

Tactical Misuse of the GDPR in Arbitration: Is It an Actual Risk?

Nika Larkimo & Katja Hoppu[*]

§17.01 INTRODUCTION

The data protection landscape has evolved significantly in recent years, particularly following the entry into force of the European Union's General Data Protection Regulation (Regulation (EU) 2016/679, the 'GDPR') in May 2018. The GDPR's broad applicability has raised significant yet unanswered questions for international arbitration practitioners. Many articles have been written on the general applicability of the GDPR to arbitration proceedings. This chapter will, however, focus on a specific question: tactical misuse of the GDPR in arbitration. The chapter explores potential scenarios involving tactical misuse of data protection regulation in different stages of arbitration proceedings, and ways that the arbitral tribunal or the opposing party and its counsel may have to prevent such misconduct or react to it.

The chapter broadly defines tactical misuse as situations where a party to an arbitration invokes the GDPR with the aim of obtaining tactical benefit in the proceedings without legitimate grounds for doing so. Most often, such situations arise when a party invokes the GDPR to avoid disclosing unfavourable documents in arbitration. This chapter will focus on the GDPR. But that is not to belittle the relevance of any other pieces of data protection legislation, particularly local regulations applicable in each party, counsel, or arbitrator's home jurisdiction.

* The views expressed in this chapter are strictly those of the authors and should not be attributed in any way to Roschier, Attorneys Ltd.

This chapter is not the first to observe the possibility of misuse of data protection regulation in arbitration.[1] However, the topic is usually bypassed by mentioning that these situations should be handled on an ad hoc, case-by-case basis. While the authors of this chapter ultimately agree with this conclusion, the chapter will explore the possibility of providing general guidelines applicable in situations that arise from a party's use of data protection-related arguments for purely tactical purposes.

The first part of the chapter will set the scene by brushing up on some of the key concepts under the GDPR and their relevance in arbitration. The section will not seek to provide a comprehensive course on the GDPR, which is better left for data protection specialists but will focus on the essential concepts that impact the assessment of when tactical misuse of the GDPR is likely to be at hand.

The second part will seek to establish stages in arbitration that are most prone to tactical misuse of the GDPR and explore how likely such conduct really is in each of those.

The third part will examine ways to prevent or react to potential tactical misuse of data protection regulation. When it comes to the prevention of misuse, the chapter will seek to offer practical solutions for arbitrators and counsel by, among others, discussing what should be included in procedural orders regarding GDPR compliance in different stages of an arbitration. Further to the preventive actions, the chapter also explores possible reactions and solutions to problems that have already occurred.

The final section of the chapter will conclude the above topics and seek to identify some best practices that may help arbitrators and counsel to address potential misuse of the GDPR.

§17.02 KEY GDPR CONCEPTS AND THEIR APPLICATION TO ARBITRATION

[A] GDPR Definitions and Principles Relevant to Arbitration

The GDPR entered into force on 25 May 2018 in all EU Member States.[2] The aim of the regulation is to harmonize data privacy laws across Europe, including the protection of

1. *See, e.g.*, Komninos Komnios, *Legal Consequences for Non-compliance With the GDPR in International Arbitration*, in Stavros Brekoulakis (ed.), Arbitration: The International Journal of Arbitration, Mediation and Dispute Management, (© Kluwer Law International; Kluwer Law International 2022, Volume 88 Issue 4) s. 2.2; Rosenthal, David, *Complying with the General Data Protection Regulation (GDPR) in International Arbitration – Practical Guidance*, in ASA Bulletin, December 2019, Topic No. 5 Dealing with other Provisions of the GDPR, 2. Solution; Emily Hay, *Chapter 7: Data protection and international arbitration: never the twain shall meet?*, in Pietro Ortolani et al. (eds), International Arbitration and Technology (© 2022 Wolters Kluwer Nederland B.V., Nijmegen; Kluwer Law International 2022) p. 131.
2. The International Council for Commercial Arbitration (ICCA) and the International Bar Association (IBA) have published a joint roadmap to data protection in international arbitration, which provides useful explanations and descriptions of data protection issues in international arbitration. The document is widely referenced in this chapter, and we invite all arbitration practitioners to familiarize themselves with its content. *See* ICCA-IBA Joint Task Force on Data Protection in International Arbitration – Roadmap to data protection in international arbitration 2022. https:/

fundamental rights and freedoms of natural persons in respect of processing activities and to ensure the free flow of personal data between the Member States.[3]

Parties to an arbitration cannot deselect the application of the GDPR when the regulation is applicable in accordance with its material and territorial scope.[4]

The GDPR defines personal data as 'any information relating to an identified or identifiable natural person'.[5] The GDPR refers to such identified or identifiable natural persons as 'data subjects'. While legal persons are not considered data subjects under the GDPR,[6] it is important to note that any personal data disclosed in a business context is also protected by the GDPR.[7] The European Commission has provided a list of examples of what information is included in the scope of personal data under the GDPR.[8] For the purposes of an arbitration practitioner, the key is to understand that the definition of personal data under the GDPR is extremely broad.

The GDPR sets strict limitations on the processing of personal data. The regulation defines processing as 'any operation or set of operations which is performed on personal data or on sets of personal data, whether or not by automated means, such as collection, recording, organisation, structuring, storage, adaptation or alteration, retrieval, consultation, use, disclosure by transmission, dissemination or otherwise making available, alignment or combination, restriction, erasure or destruction'.[9] It follows that basically any kind of handling of personal data is covered by the GDPR's definition of processing.[10] This, combined with the broad definition of personal data, means that all arbitral activities involving data that either identifies or could identify an individual are likely to be covered by the GDPR.

The GDPR is applicable in 'the processing of personal data in the context of the activities of an establishment of a controller or a processor in the Union, regardless of

/cdn.arbitration-icca.org/s3fs-public/document/media_document/ICCA_Reports_No_7_ICCA-IBA_Joint_Task_Force_on_Data_Protection_in_International_Arbitration.pdf (accessed 4 April 2023).

3. Recital 3 of the GDPR.
4. *See, e.g.*, Komninos Komnios, *Legal Consequences for Non-compliance With the GDPR in International Arbitration*, in Stavros Brekoulakis (ed.), Arbitration: The International Journal of Arbitration, Mediation and Dispute Management, (© Kluwer Law International; Kluwer Law International 2022, Volume 88 Issue 4) p. 567.
5. The GDPR, Art. 4(1).
6. Recital 14 of the GDPR.
7. Roadmap to data protection in international arbitration (ICCA-IBA) 2022, p. 9; Kathleen Paisley, *It's All about the Data: The Impact of the EU General Data Protection Regulation on International Arbitration*, in Volume 41 Fordham International Law Journal 841 (2018), p. 863.
8. *See, What Is Personal Data?*, EUROPEAN COMMISSION https://commission.europa.eu/law/law-topic/data-protection/reform/what-personal-data_en (accessed 10 March 2023).
9. The GDPR, Art. 4(2).
10. *See, What constitutes data processing?*, EUROPEAN COMMISSION https://commission.europa.eu/law/law-topic/data-protection/reform/what-constitutes-data-processing_en (accessed 10 March 2023). *See also Paisley's* list of activities relating to documents containing personal arbitral data, which would likely be considered data processing in the meaning of the GDPR: Kathleen Paisley, *It's All about the Data: The Impact of the EU General Data Protection Regulation on International Arbitration*, in Volume 41 Fordham International Law Journal 841 (2018) pp. 864-865.

whether the processing takes place in the Union or not.'[11] In other words, when the controller or the processor of personal data is established in the EU, the GDPR cannot be avoided by moving the processing of personal data outside the EU. The GDPR also specifically prohibits the transfer of personal data to countries outside the European Economic Area[12] unless one of the prerequisites provided in Chapter 5 of the GDPR applies.[13]

The GDPR classifies actors who process personal data into data controllers and data processors.[14] In simple terms, the processor processes personal data on behalf of the controller, whereas the controller determines the purposes and means of the processing of personal data.[15] Unlike processors, controllers process personal data on their own authority and not based on instructions given to them by another actor and decide certain key elements of processing.[16] The distinction between these two concepts matters because the prerequisites for the processing of data by a controller and a processor are different.[17] Furthermore, the controller always retains the main responsibility for the processing and is primarily responsible for compliance and demonstrating compliance with the GDPR.[18] In an arbitration context, the parties and their legal counsel, members of the arbitral tribunal, and experts and witnesses are all likely to be deemed as data controllers.[19] The GDPR also establishes a concept of joint controllership, which means that several controllers jointly determine the purposes and means of data processing, and are jointly and severally liable for any violations.[20]

11. The GDPR, Art. 3(1); Recital 22 of the GDPR. Also, the GDPR, Art. 3(2) sets out that the regulation applies in the situations specified in the article to the processing of personal data of data subjects who are in the Union by a controller or processor not established in the Union. The regulation aims to ensure the protection of natural persons who are in the Union where the processing activities are related to offering goods or services to such data subjects irrespective of whether connected to a payment. *See* Recital 23 of the GDPR.
12. The GDPR, Art. 44.
13. Data transfer is allowed, e.g., where an adequate level of data protection is ensured, and where the controller or processor has provided appropriate safeguards, and on condition that enforceable data subject rights and effective legal remedies for data subjects are available. Transfer of personal data can also be based on an international agreement, 'such as such as a mutual legal assistance treaty, in force between the requesting third country and the Union or a Member State'. Also, the data subject's explicit consent to make the data transfer enables it. *See* the GDPR, Arts 45, 46 and 48 and Roadmap to data protection in international arbitration (ICCA-IBA) 2022, p. 99.
14. *See* the GDPR, Ch. 4 on controller and processor.
15. The GDPR, Art. 4(7) and (8).
16. The GDPR, Art. 28(1) and Recital 74 of the GDPR; European Data Protection Board Guidelines 07/2020 on the concepts of controller and processor in the GDPR, p. 3.
17. The GDPR, Ch. 4.
18. Roadmap to data protection in international arbitration (ICCA-IBA) 2022, p. 12.
19. Roadmap to data protection in international arbitration (ICCA-IBA) 2022, p. 12; Emily Hay, *Chapter 7: Data Protection and International Arbitration: Never the Twain Shall Meet?*, in Pietro Ortolani et al. (eds), International Arbitration and Technology (© 2022 Wolters Kluwer Nederland B.V., Nijmegen; Kluwer Law International 2022) pp. 104-105.
20. Article 4(7) of the GDPR. It has been argued that parties and their legal counsel as well as the members of the tribunal should be determined as 'joint controllers' in arbitration under the GDPR, Art. 26. Roadmap to data protection in international arbitration (ICCA-IBA) 2022 mentions that arbitral participants will generally be data controllers, and joint controllers under certain circumstances. Joint controllers have an obligation to determine and agree their respective responsibilities for compliance with the obligations under the GDPR in a transparent

The starting point of the GDPR is that any processing of personal data requires a legal basis.[21] The possible legal bases that may allow processing of personal data are listed in Article 6 of the GDPR. In the arbitration context, the legal basis most often relied on is legitimate interest.[22] The legitimate interest in arbitration is likely to stem from, for example, the administration of justice, ensuring that the parties' rights are respected, as well as the expeditious and fair resolution of claims under the applicable arbitration rules.[23] Legitimate interest can, however, be overridden by the interests or fundamental rights and freedoms of the data subject.[24] This means that a proportionality assessment of the data subjects' rights and freedoms should be performed even when a legitimate interest in the processing of personal data exists.[25] In other words, the interests, freedoms and rights of a data subject need to be balanced with the legitimate interests of a data processor.[26] The data subject's freely given, specific, informed and unambiguous consent for processing its personal data also constitutes a legal basis for processing.[27] However, as will be discussed in more detail in the next section, relying on data subjects' consent to process personal data in arbitration is not necessarily a workable solution.

Finally, before diving deeper into the core of this chapter, it is important to understand the basic principles for data processing that the GDPR relies on.[28] As noted by one author, the application of these principles has been subject to confusion and uncertainty among arbitration practitioners.[29]

Perhaps the most important principle in the context of tactical misuse of the GDPR is the principle of data minimization, according to which personal data should be processed only to the necessary extent. What is considered necessary is assessed in relation to the purpose of the processing of the data. Compliance with the principle also requires that the processed personal data is adequate and relevant.[30] The principles of fair, transparent, and lawful processing, as well as integrity and confidentiality, are also relevant in this context.[31] The first aims to ensure that personal data is processed

---

manner, as set out in the before mentioned article of the GDPR. *See, e.g.*, Emily Hay, *Chapter 7: Data Protection and International Arbitration: Never the Twain Shall Meet?*, in Pietro Ortolani et al. (eds), International Arbitration and Technology, (© 2022 Wolters Kluwer Nederland B.V., Nijmegen; Kluwer Law International 2022) pp. 105-106.

21. The GDPR, Art. 6.
22. The GDPR, Art. 6(1)(f). *See also* Annex 5 (Checklist: Legitimate Interest Assessment) of the Roadmap to data protection in international arbitration (ICCA-IBA) 2022.
23. Roadmap to data protection in international arbitration (ICCA-IBA) 2022, p. 89.
24. The GDPR, Art. 6(1)(f). *See also* Recital 4 of the GDPR.
25. Emily Hay, *Chapter 7: Data protection and International Arbitration: Never the Twain Shall Meet?*, in Pietro Ortolani et al. (eds), International Arbitration and Technology, (© 2022 Wolters Kluwer Nederland B.V., Nijmegen; Kluwer Law International 2022) p. 115.
26. Denis Kelleher Karen Murray, *EU Data Protection Law*, Bloomsbury Professional Ltd 2018, p. 177.
27. The GDPR, Arts 4(11) and 6(1)(f).
28. Recital 39 of the GDPR provides a summary of the most important principles for data processing.
29. Kathleen Paisley, *It's All About the Data: The Impact of the EU General Data Protection Regulation on International Arbitration*, in Volume 41 Fordham International Law Journal 841 (2018) pp. 846-847.
30. The GDPR, Art. 5(1)(c), Recital 39 of the GDPR.
31. The GDPR, Art. 5(1)(a) and 5(1)(f).

only in such ways that data subjects can reasonably expect and in a transparent manner. The second sets out that there should be appropriate security of the personal data in place, including protection against unauthorized or unlawful processing and against accidental loss, destruction, or damage, using appropriate technical or organizational measures.[32]

Finally, the principle of accountability requires the controller to demonstrate compliance with the GDPR.[33] Hence, it does not suffice to comply with the GDPR, but the controller must also be able to demonstrate its compliance with the GDPR to avoid responsibility for breaching the regulation. This becomes crucial in arbitration when assessing what data protection measures should be recorded and how.

[B] Application of GDPR Principles to Disclosure of Personal Data in Arbitration

As a result of digitalization and fast technological development, processing extensive volumes of personal data is inevitable in modern international arbitration.[34] Understanding when the GDPR prohibits processing of personal data is important for the parties and the arbitral tribunal who wish to avoid any breaches. It also draws the line between when the reliance on the GDPR is warranted as opposed to situations where a party is likely trying to use it to obtain tactical benefit.

However, the GDPR does not expressly state when a party can refuse to submit personal data in arbitration.[35] Assessing when the GDPR prohibits disclosure of personal data in arbitration, therefore, requires understanding its general functioning.

The GDPR is only applicable to information that contains personal data.[36] However, the fact that a document contains some personal data does not automatically mean that its use in arbitration is prohibited. Often, documents can be produced in arbitration once the parts containing personal data are anonymized or pseudonymized from the document.[37] As the definition of personal data is rather extensive, the definition of anonymized data, which cannot include any identifiers, has to be correspondingly narrow.[38] It is relevant that the data subject can no longer be

32. Roadmap to data protection in international arbitration (ICCA-IBA) 2022 provides a useful guide on general data protection principles that are relevant to arbitration, *see* section 4.1 of the article on Roadmap to data protection in international arbitration (ICCA-IBA) 2022.
33. The GDPR, Art. 5(2).
34. *See, e.g.*, Komninos Komnios, *Legal Consequences for Non-compliance With the GDPR in International Arbitration*, in Stavros Brekoulakis (ed.), Arbitration: The International Journal of Arbitration, Mediation and Dispute Management, (© Kluwer Law International; Kluwer Law International 2022, Volume 88 Issue 4) p. 566; Emily Hay, *Chapter 7: Data Protection and International Arbitration: Never the Twain Shall Meet?*, in Pietro Ortolani et al. (eds), International Arbitration and Technology (© 2022 Wolters Kluwer Nederland B.V., Nijmegen; Kluwer Law International 2022) p. 101.
35. The GDPR does not even mention the word 'arbitration'.
36. The GDPR, Art. 1(1).
37. *See* Recitals 26 and 28 of the GDPR.
38. Denis Kelleher, Karen Murray, *EU Data Protection Law*, Bloomsbury Professional Ltd 2018, p. 91.

identifiable from the anonymized data.[39] Pseudonymization of data, however, is defined in the GDPR as 'the processing of personal data in such a manner that the personal data can no longer be attributed to a specific data subject without the use of additional information, provided that such additional information is kept separately and is subject to technical and organizational measures to ensure that the personal data are not attributed to an identified or identifiable natural person.'[40] In other words, pseudonymized data is coded so that the data subject cannot be identified but in such a manner that the data can later be decoded if needed.[41] Importantly, pseudonymized data is within the scope of the GDPR, whereas anonymized data is not.[42]

As noted earlier, a party may be allowed to process personal data if there is legal basis to do so. The tricky part is, however, that legal basis should be assessed separately for each situation where personal data is processed. A legitimate interest to process data at a certain stage in arbitration does not give the controller or the processor free hands to process the data as they wish throughout the lifecycle of an arbitral proceeding.[43] As mentioned above, the key question to be asked when considering the disclosure of personal data is whether there is a legitimate interest in accordance with Article 6(1)(f) of the GDPR to do so. That legitimate interest is, however, to be balanced against the data subject's fundamental rights that can prevent the processing of personal data. The same was confirmed in the context of document production in court proceedings in the CJEU Case No. C-268/21 *Norra Stockholm Bygg AB v. Per Nycander AB*.[44] The CJEU emphasized the parties' right to effective judicial protection when assessing what kind of evidence the parties are allowed to submit in dispute proceedings based on the GDPR.[45] Furthermore, the ruling clarifies that Articles 5 and 6 of the GDPR:

> must be interpreted as meaning that, when assessing whether the production of a document containing personal data must be ordered, the national court is required to have regard to the interests of the data subjects concerned and to balance them according to the circumstances of each case, the type of proceeding at issue and

39. Denis Kelleher, Karen Murray, *EU Data Protection Law*, Bloomsbury Professional Ltd 2018, p. 93.
40. Article 4(5) of the GDPR. According to Recital 28 of the GDPR, pseudonymization of personal data can help the data processors and controllers to meet their data protection obligations.
41. Kathleen Paisley, *It's All about the Data: The Impact of the EU General Data Protection Regulation on International Arbitration*, in Volume 41 Fordham International Law Journal 841 (2018), p. 903. European Union Agency for Cybersecurity has published multiple guidelines for data pseudonymization. *See, e.g.*, ENISA Pseudonymization techniques and best practices, November 2019, and ENISA Data Pseudonymization: Advanced Techniques and Use Cases, January 2021.
42. Case No. C-268/21, *Norra Stockholm Bygg AB v. Per Nycander AB*, 2 March 2023, para. 57.
43. Emily Hay, *Chapter 7: Data protection and International Arbitration: Never the Twain Shall Meet?*, in Pietro Ortolani et al. (eds), International Arbitration and Technology (© 2022 Wolters Kluwer Nederland B.V., Nijmegen; Kluwer Law International 2022) p. 117.
44. In the mentioned case, the concerned personal data was originally collected and processed for tax purposes.
45. Case No. C-268/21, *Norra Stockholm Bygg AB v. Per Nycander AB*, 2 March 2023, para. 53.

duly taking into account the requirements arising from the principle of proportionality as well as, in particular, those resulting from the principle of data minimisation referred to in Article 5(1)(c) of that regulation.[46]

The starting point of the GDPR is that personal data can be processed only for the purpose for which the data has been collected.[47] It follows that, in principle, any data that is collected for a purpose other than arbitration should not be disclosed in the arbitration. Typically, the evidence processed by the parties and the personal data contained therein have not been created for the purposes of an arbitration.[48] Personal data is also often processed by arbitral participants who did not initially collect the personal data. In such cases, the possibility of processing the data for the purposes of arbitration should either be included in the original notice provided to the data subject or, alternatively, be compatible with the purposes of processing that have been identified in such notice.[49]

When assessing whether disclosure of personal data is allowed in arbitration, it is also worth keeping in mind that the disclosure of personal data should be relevant. The principle of data minimization in Article 5(1)(c) provides that unnecessary processing of personal data should be avoided.[50] Of course, in an arbitration context, information that is relevant for one party may not be equally important for the other. Especially in the context of document production, parties are often obliged to produce documents that are not relevant to making their points but rather the opposite. An objective assessment of the application of the data minimization principle accordingly seems warranted. It is also often hard to tell in advance what pieces of data become relevant in arbitration. Thus, assessing the scope of and ensuring compliance with the principle of data minimization is not a simple task.

Finally, as mentioned earlier, disclosure of personal data is allowed when the data subject has given its consent for the processing of its personal data. While arguably the clearest of the legal bases provided under Article 6 of the GDPR, the data subject's consent as a basis to process personal data in arbitration can be somewhat problematic to rely on. Issues may arise if the data subject withdraws its consent for the processing of its data at any stage of the arbitration.[51] It is included in the nature of valid consent that the data subjects must have an actual opportunity to withdraw their

46. Case No. C-268/21, *Norra Stockholm Bygg AB v. Per Nycander AB*, 2 March 2023, para. 59.
47. The GDPR, Art. 6(3) and 6(4).
48. Roadmap to data protection in international arbitration (ICCA-IBA) 2022, p. 24.
49. Roadmap to data protection in international arbitration (ICCA-IBA) 2022, p. 24. The points mentioned in this paragraph are included in the regulation of the GDPR mainly throughout the 'purpose limitation' that is set out in Art. 5(1)(b) of the GDPR.
50. *See also* Recital 39 of the GDPR.
51. Rosenthal, David, *Complying with the General Data Protection Regulation (GDPR) in International Arbitration – Practical Guidance*, in ASA Bulletin, December 2019, Topic No. 4 How Personal Data may be processed, 2. Solution; Emily Hay, *Chapter 7: Data Protection and International Arbitration: Never the Twain Shall Meet?*, in Pietro Ortolani et al. (eds), International Arbitration and Technology (© 2022 Wolters Kluwer Nederland B.V., Nijmegen; Kluwer Law International 2022) p. 114.

permission without suffering any penalty if they change their mind.[52] Also, it has been argued that consent is unlikely to be a sufficient basis for the processing of large volumes of documents containing personal data, which is commonplace in arbitration.[53] Finally, obtaining each data subject's separate consent is often impracticable in arbitration, which may comprise thousands of documents containing hundreds of data subjects' personal data. It follows that in arbitration, reliance on other legal bases for the processing of personal data is recommended, if possible, over the data subject's consent.[54]

§17.03 STAGES OF ARBITRATION PRONE TO TACTICAL MISUSE OF THE GDPR

A party to an arbitration has the right and the obligation to invoke the GDPR when processing of personal data is not allowed. A party may, however, also try to invoke the GDPR to gain tactical benefit, without having an actual obligation to do so.

It is fair to assume that in arbitration, most of the personal data is contained in evidence. It is widely accepted that the likelihood of a party invoking the GDPR increases in connection with the taking of evidence, especially in document production.[55]

A party may invoke the GDPR to object to a request for document production or to refuse to comply with an order to produce documents. As outlined in the previous section, in such scenarios, it is key to understand what the actual scope of the GDPR is and how it limits a party's possibility to disclose personal data.

In many instances, redacting personal data from the documents to be disclosed is required to fully comply with the GDPR. A question arises: when does the production become 'unreasonably burdensome' in the meaning of Article 9.2(c) of the IBA Rules, constituting a valid ground to object to a document production request? Unreasonable burden can take many forms, and it has been left to the arbitral tribunal's discretion to determine what kind of burden is considered unreasonable.[56] Eventually, it is for the arbitral tribunal to determine whether a party's objection on the ground of unreasonable burden based on the GDPR has a legitimate basis.

The scope of any redactions is also prone to create issues in arbitration. Parties' attempting to redact information unfavourable to their case on the basis of legal

---

52. *See* Working Document on a Common Interpretation of Art. 26(1) of Directive 95/46/EC of 24 October 1995 (Art. 29 Data Protection Working Party, 2093/05/EN WP 114, 2005), p. 11.
53. Kathleen Paisley, *It's All about the Data: The Impact of the EU General Data Protection Regulation on International Arbitration*, in Volume 41 Fordham International Law Journal 841 (2018), p. 887.
54. *See, e.g.*, Roadmap to data protection in international arbitration (ICCA-IBA) 2022, p. 43.
55. It has been stated that issues of data protection can arise in particular in document production. *See* 'Chapter 20: Data Protection and Cybersecurity', in Neil Kaplan, Chiann Bao, *So, Now You Are an Arbitrator: The Arbitrator's Toolkit* (© Kluwer Law International; Kluwer Law International 2022), p. 152.
56. The IBA Commentary on the Revised Text of the 2020 IBA Rules on the Taking of Evidence in International Arbitration (2020), p. 29.

privilege or commercial confidentiality is not uncommon in international arbitration. Similar objections can be made based on the GDPR.

An added complexity is that parties seldom refer to the GDPR as the only basis to object to a document production request but instead combine it with other reasons, such as privilege and commercial confidentiality.[57] To address concerns of confidentiality and trade secrets, parties may request that certain evidentiary documents be displayed only to the arbitral tribunal and legal counsel representing the parties. This may help resolve situations where there are reasons to believe that a party has invoked commercial confidentiality without having an actual basis to do so. The same is, however, unlikely to help in the context of a party invoking the GDPR. When the GDPR prohibits the disclosure of personal data, it is not possible to bypass such prohibition by disclosing the data to a smaller group.

Another part of taking evidence where the GDPR could be invoked is witness examination. Technically, a witness could try to refer to the GDPR to avoid having to answer a difficult question. However, this does not seem very likely, and we have not heard of such instances. It would require courage from a witness to do so. For a witness to invoke the GDPR also carries the risk of ultimately damaging the witness' credibility, as it may be perceived as a way to avoid having to answer difficult questions.

Another relevant aspect of compliance with the GDPR is its potential role in the recognition and enforcement of arbitral awards. The CJEU has ruled that arbitrators must apply the provisions of the EU law falling under the EU public policy.[58] Member State courts are obliged to verify the compliance of an arbitral award with mandatory EU law on their own motion.[59] The Advocate General in the ECJ Case No. C-681/13 aptly set out in his opinion that 'although every Member State is to determine the requirements of its own public policy, there is still within national public policy a core set of values, principles and fundamental rules of the European Union, with the same legislative content, that every Member State must take into account.'[60] A party could seek to set aside an award on the basis of a violation of public policy if it has reasons to believe that the GDPR has not been complied with in the proceedings and the award is contrary to the regulation of the GDPR.[61]

Whether breaches of the GDPR affect the validity of an arbitral award is a complex issue. GDPR breaches often concern persons who are not involved in the

57. *See, e.g.*, the IBA Rules on the Taking of Evidence in International Arbitration, Art. 9.2(b) and 9.2(e).
58. Case No. C-126/97, *Eco Swiss China Time Ltd. v. Benetton International NV*, CJEU, 1 June 1999, para. 37.
59. *See, e.g.*, Komninos Komnios, *Legal Consequences for Non-compliance with the GDPR in International Arbitration*, in Stavros Brekoulakis (ed.), Arbitration: The International Journal of Arbitration, Mediation and Dispute Management (© Kluwer Law International; Kluwer Law International 2022, Volume 88 Issue 4) p. 572.
60. Opinion of Advocate General Szpunar delivered on 3 March 2015. *Diageo Brands BV v. Simiramida*-04 EOOD, section 39.
61. Komninos Komnios, *Legal Consequences for Non-compliance with the GDPR in International Arbitration*, in Stavros Brekoulakis (ed.), Arbitration: The International Journal of Arbitration, Mediation and Dispute Management, (© Kluwer Law International; Kluwer Law International 2022, Volume 88 Issue 4) p. 578.

arbitration.[62] Setting aside an arbitral award that the data subject whom the breach concerns does not even have access to seems unlikely. However, interestingly, for the topic of this chapter, it has been suggested that a party to an arbitration could knowingly violate or have the arbitral tribunal violate the provisions of the GDPR to have the option to dispute the validity of the award after it has been rendered.[63] While the possibility for a party to rely on its own breach to have an arbitral award set aside sounds somewhat far-fetched, this cannot be excluded. This again highlights the importance for the arbitral tribunal to understand the applicable data protection regulations, which is likely to be the best protection against their misuse.

§17.04 PREVENTING AND REACTING TO TACTICAL MISUSE OF THE GDPR

[A] Data Protection Framework Provided in Institutional and Other Rules

The natural first place for arbitrators and parties to seek guidance when assessing procedural issues is the applicable institutional rules.

Arbitration institutes have taken different approaches to addressing data protection issues. To date, most institutional rules are completely silent on data protection. For example, the ICC (2021), HKIAC (2018), FAI (2020) and SCC (2023) rules do not even mention data protection. The ICC Note to Parties and Arbitral Tribunals on the Conduct of the Arbitration (2021), however, emphasizes the importance of data protection in international arbitration and establishes key principles to be followed when processing personal data under the GDPR. The Note further highlights that the parties and their representatives, as well as the arbitral tribunal, are obliged to ensure a reasonable level of data security in the arbitration.[64] The ICC has also provided a model for the data protection clause to be used in Procedural Order No. 1.[65]

Of the institutional rules reviewed for the preparation of this chapter, the only rules to expressly oblige the arbitral tribunal to consider data protection issues were the LCIA (2020) and the ICDR Rules. The ICDR Rules contain a recommendation to the

62. Komninos Komnios, *Legal Consequences for Non-compliance with the GDPR in International Arbitration*, in Stavros Brekoulakis (ed.), Arbitration: The International Journal of Arbitration, Mediation and Dispute Management, (© Kluwer Law International; Kluwer Law International 2022, Volume 88 Issue 4) p. 574.
63. Komninos Komnios, *Legal Consequences for Non-compliance with the GDPR in International Arbitration*, in Stavros Brekoulakis (ed.), Arbitration: The International Journal of Arbitration, Mediation and Dispute Management, (© Kluwer Law International; Kluwer Law International 2022, Volume 88 Issue 4) p. 574.
64. The ICC Note to Parties and Arbitral Tribunals on the Conduct of the Arbitration (2021), section E – Protection of Personal Data.
65. *See* ICC Model Data Protection Clause for Procedural Order 1, which is intended for arbitrators, to provide guidance in the drafting of data protection clause in Procedural Order one, where issues related to the GDPR are addressed, https://cdn.iccwbo.org/content/uploads/sites/3/2021/01/icc-model-po1-data-protection-english.pdf (accessed 4 April 2023).

arbitral tribunal to discuss data protection to provide for an appropriate level of security and compliance.[66]

Article 30A of the LCIA rules clarifies that '[a]ny processing of personal data by the LCIA is subject to applicable data protection legislation' and refers to the LCIA's data protection notice. The provision also requires the arbitral tribunal to, 'at an early stage of the arbitration', consult the parties as to the need of adopting 'any means to address the processing of personal data produced or exchanged in the arbitration in light of applicable data protection or equivalent legislation'. The LCIA or the arbitral tribunal may also issue binding directions to the parties addressing data protection.

The IBA rules on the Taking of Evidence in International Arbitration (2020) mention data protection issues. But they do not provide much guidance: the IBA Rules simply highlight that it is advised to consider 'treatment of any issues of cybersecurity and data protection' as part of the evidentiary issues.[67]

As such, it is fair to conclude that institutional rules and guidelines do not provide many tools for arbitrators or counsel to address the possibility of misuse of the GDPR. Accordingly, such tools need to be sought from other sources.

[B] Tools for Preventing Tactical Misuse of the GDPR

In the authors' view, the first step in preventing tactical misuse of GDPR in arbitration is making sure that all participants in an arbitration understand the basics of the GDPR and its implications. By way of a simple demonstration, it is harder for a party to argue that an entire, large category of documents cannot be disclosed due to the GDPR if the arbitral tribunal and the opposing side understand that the GDPR only prevents disclosure of personal data.

The second step is to document such understanding. As suggested in the ICCA-IBA Roadmap to data protection in international arbitration, a natural place for such documentation is Procedural Order No. 1 or a separate Data Protection Protocol.[68] Addressing the GDPR in a procedural order signals to the parties that the arbitrators are familiar with the GDPR and take its implications seriously.

The previous step raises an obvious question: what should be documented? The ICCA-IBA Roadmap to data protection in international arbitration lists eight data protection issues that should be recorded. The listed issues include, for instance, the legal basis for processing and data transfer, disclosure or production of documents, data security and data breach protocols.[69] In addition to the listed issues, the tribunal should clarify in Procedural Order No. 1 that it can draw adverse inferences from a

66. ICDR International Dispute Resolution Procedures Rules, Amended and Effective 1 March 2021, Art. 22(3) of the International Arbitration Rules.
67. The mention of data protection was added in the revised text of the 2020 rules. The IBA Commentary on the Revised Text of the 2020 IBA Rules on the Taking of Evidence in International Arbitration (2020), p. 6.
68. Roadmap to data protection in international arbitration (ICCA-IBA) 2022, p. 41. The Roadmap collectively refers to data protection rules set out in a procedural order, terms of reference or data protection protocol as 'Data Protection Directions'.
69. Roadmap to data protection in international arbitration (ICCA-IBA) 2022, p. 42.

party's failure to produce documents. The ICCA-IBA Roadmap provides sample language for inclusion in a procedural order where the rules of the GDPR are to be followed.[70]

As mentioned above in section 3, the likelihood of a party invoking the GDPR increases in connection with the taking of evidence, and especially document production. The ICCA-IBA Roadmap lists issues related thereto that should be addressed in a procedural order to avoid them being raised later on in the proceedings. Such issues include the following:

> (1) limiting disclosure/data minimisation (taking into account the IBA Rules where applicable); (2) redaction/pseudonymisation in light of the applicable data protection standard; (3) entering into confidentiality provisions/protective orders; and (4) entering into standard contractual clauses or another adequate safeguard for third-country data transfers so that additional safeguards are not required, or where that is not feasible, employing a derogation when possible.[71]

As noted in the ICCA-IBA Roadmap, addressing these issues at the beginning of the proceedings saves money and time.[72] It is fair to assume that the parties are more consensual when agreeing on the common ground rules in the procedural order than when facing actual problems in the arbitration. One should also keep in mind that the parties to an international arbitration sometimes need to comply with data protection regimes that differ from each other. Agreeing on related issues helps to ensure compliance with all applicable data protection laws in the arbitration.[73]

At the end of the day, the arbitral tribunal will need to decide on applying data protection measures on a case-by-case basis. Applying such measures will depend on many circumstances, for example, the type of processing being undertaken, the type of data, including the assessment of the damages that the disclosure may cause, and the security measures of the arbitral participants.[74]

While procedural orders are ultimately issued by arbitral tribunals, making sure that those address data protection issues is not only in the arbitral tribunal's interest. Counsel also have an interest in, and arguably bear a responsibility for, ensuring that the tribunal is oriented in making the arbitration as GDPR-compliant as possible. Thus, counsel should review the draft procedural order carefully with respect to data protection issues, propose necessary additions and flag any potential issues they find. In case data protection is not addressed by the arbitrators, it is for the parties' counsel to suggest that the required language be included. In case the parties disagree on data protection measures that should be implemented in the arbitration, it is highly recommended that the tribunal provides the parties with an opportunity to address

70. Roadmap to data protection in international arbitration (ICCA-IBA) 2022, p. 42, and Annex 7.
71. Roadmap to data protection in international arbitration (ICCA-IBA) 2022, p. 48.
72. Roadmap to data protection in international arbitration (ICCA-IBA) 2022, p. 48.
73. Emily Hay, *Chapter 7: Data Protection and International Arbitration: Never the Twain Shall Meet?*, in Pietro Ortolani et al. (eds), International Arbitration and Technology, (© 2022 Wolters Kluwer Nederland B.V., Nijmegen; Kluwer Law International 2022) p. 112.
74. Roadmap to data protection in international arbitration (ICCA-IBA) 2022, p. 50.

what measures they consider reasonable and proportionate in the arbitration before issuing a procedural order on such measures.[75]

While addressing data protection issues early on in the proceedings is perhaps likely to limit the possibilities of misuse of the GDPR or other data protection regulations, it will not entirely prevent such misuse. It is, therefore, worthwhile considering how a party or an arbitrator should react to any misuse of the regulation.

[C] Possible Reactions to Tactical Misuse of the GDPR in Arbitration

Sometimes, the arbitral tribunal or a party may have reasons to believe that the other party is hiding behind the GDPR without a legitimate reason. As noted earlier, the parties are most likely to wrongly invoke the GDPR in connection with document production. A party may object to a document production request or refuse to comply with a tribunal's document production order.

The opposing party has limited ways to act on its own in such situations and will often need to escalate its concerns to the arbitral tribunal. In many instances, the party that has requested the documents has a better understanding of the likely content of the documents being withheld than the arbitral tribunal, which may help that party to demonstrate why the GDPR is unlikely to apply. In such scenarios, it is in the party's interest to try to clarify why it is unlikely that the GDPR impacts the other party's possibility to disclose information.

From an arbitral tribunal's perspective, the most obvious tool in its toolbox when detecting possible improper reliance on the GDPR is to request a detailed reasoning for the withholding of information. At a minimum, the party should be able to indicate which articles and sections of the GDPR prevent the disclosure of information. The party's reasoning is likely to reveal whether there are valid grounds to withhold the information based on the GDPR or not.

Refusing to submit a whole document due to data protection restrictions is very rarely, if ever, justified.[76] Such behaviour should usually raise red flags. While most GDPR concerns can typically be dealt with by redactions, the necessity and scope of such redactions may also result in debate.

When it comes to assessing the scope of redactions, the arbitral tribunal is again typically relying on the reasoning of the redacting party. If the other party successfully challenges that reasoning or it otherwise fails to convince, the arbitral tribunal should have the power to ask the redacting party to revisit its redactions and resubmit the documents with fewer redactions.

Finally, if the methods above have proved inefficient, but the arbitral tribunal still has its suspicions over the redactions or refusal to produce documents, a reminder to the parties of the possibility of drawing adverse inferences might help.[77] As in similar situations, this is often considered as the last warning by the arbitral tribunal,

---

75. *See, e.g.*, American Arbitration Association, International Centre for Dispute Resolution, Best Practices Guide for Maintaining Cybersecurity and Privacy, p. 3.
76. Roadmap to data protection in international arbitration (ICCA-IBA) 2022, p. 50.
77. *See, e.g.*, the IBA Rules on the Taking of Evidence in International Arbitration, Art. 9(6) and 9(7).

signalling that it is not convinced, but any undesirable consequences can still be avoided. Even after such a reminder, the arbitral tribunal can still consider whether drawing adverse inferences in the situation at hand exists.

§17.05 CONCLUSIONS

The arbitral tribunal is put in a difficult position when having to decide whether a party has a legitimate basis to rely on the GDPR or not. On the one hand, the arbitral tribunal should not allow a party to use the GDPR to obtain tactical benefit by taking every GDPR-related argument at face value. On the other, the potential consequences of a GDPR breach could be serious[78] and even put the validity of the arbitral award at risk.

While the GDPR raises difficult questions, playing ostrich is certainly not the answer. Instead, the best way to prevent and react to potential misuse of the GDPR is to understand the basics of the GDPR. At the end of the day, while the material and territorial applicability of the GDPR is broad, there are only so many instances where a party can effectively invoke the GDPR in arbitration. Understanding the key principles and legal basis required for processing of personal data under the GDPR is often sufficient for assessing if a party has grounds to invoke it or if it is more likely that such invoking has been done to obtain tactical benefit. Arbitral tribunals have wide powers to probe further information on the grounds on which a party is relying on the GDPR and are encouraged to do so.

Finally, addressing data protection issues early on in any arbitral proceedings is key not only to ensure compliance but is also likely to reduce a party's willingness and possibilities to rely on data protection regulation later without an actual basis to do so.

78. Under Art. 83(5) of the GDPR, an infringement of a data subject's rights is subject to administrative fines of up to EUR 20,000,000, or in the case of an undertaking, up to 4 % of the total worldwide annual turnover of the preceding financial year, whichever is higher. Non-compliance with the GDPR may also result in civil liability of the data controller or processor. *See, e.g.*, Komninos Komnios, *Legal Consequences for Non-compliance with the GDPR in International Arbitration*, in Stavros Brekoulakis (ed.), Arbitration: The International Journal of Arbitration, Mediation and Dispute Management (© Kluwer Law International; Kluwer Law International 2022, Volume 88 Issue 4) p. 567.

CHAPTER 18

There Is Ordinary Situation and There Is Latvia's Situation

Inga Kačevska & Aleksandrs Fillers

§18.01 INTRODUCTION: HOW LATVIA REINVENTED THE ARBITRATION WHEEL

Latvia made its first attempt to introduce modern arbitration law in 1998 when the Chapter D "Arbitration" of the Civil Procedure Law[1] was adopted. This Chapter specifically dealt with arbitration. However, unlike regulatory frameworks in the two other Baltic states (Estonia and Lithuania[2]), it was not based on the UNCITRAL Model Law.[3] The Chapter D was extremely unsuccessful. While it was in force, Latvia had numerous arbitral institutions (there were more than 200), and many of them were vaguely structured "pocket arbitrations." As a result, Latvia suffered from an extremely low level of trust in arbitration.

There was a pressing need for a reform. Finally, the new Arbitration Law of Latvia was adopted on September 11, 2014, and entered into force on January 1, 2015.[4] The new law did not fully substitute the Chapter D. The Chapter D still contains rules on

1. Civil Procedure Law (October 14, 1998), Latvijas Vēstnesis, 326/330, November 3, 1998.
2. *See*: Status: UNCITRAL Model Law on International Commercial Arbitration (1985), with amendments as adopted in 2006. Available at https://uncitral.un.org/en/texts/arbitration/modellaw/commercial_arbitration/status (accessed April 11, 2023) and Vilija Vaitkute Pavan & Giedre Aukstuoliene, *National Report for Lithuania (2018 through 2020)*. Kluwerarbitration.com, p. 1.
3. UNCITRAL Model Law on International Commercial Arbitration (1985 with 2006 amendments), U.N. Doc. A/40/17, Annex I, 24 I.L.M. 1302 (1985).
4. Arbitration Law (January 11, 2015), Latvijas Vēstnesis, 194, October 1, 2014. Available in English: https://likumi.lv/ta/en/en/id/269189-arbitration-law (accessed April 11, 2023).

enforcement of institutional arbitral awards rendered in Latvia[5] (Articles 534-537). Notably, Article 536 of the Chapter D preserves the grounds that entitle courts to refuse to issue a writ of execution for enforcement of institutional arbitral awards. However, most other issues relevant to arbitration were transferred to the Arbitration Law.

One of the main objectives of Law was to bolster the trust in arbitration, i.e., to reduce the number of arbitral institutions and to fight with biased arbitrators and pocket arbitrations. Unfortunately, as explained below, similarly to the old regulation, the Law also suffers from numerous drawbacks, and the goal of the legislative act has not been reached. This is principally due to the fact that, just like its predecessor, it is not based on the Model Law. For example, the Model Law provisions on the court's role with respect to the constitution of the arbitral tribunal, the powers of the arbitral tribunal to order interim measures, and the setting aside procedure were not incorporated into the Law.

The aim of this chapter is to demonstrate how a reinvented arbitration wheel is not properly functioning in Latvia and, taking into consideration that the Law will be opened for new amendments in the nearest future, to make recommendations for improving the Law and, thus, facilitate the smooth operation of "the arbitration vehicle."

Before the discussion, it shall be noted: (1) that the Arbitration Law does not distinguish between domestic and international arbitration; (2) that Latvia is a party to the New York Convention on Recognition and Enforcement of Foreign Arbitral Awards[6] and the European Convention on International Commercial Arbitration.[7]

§18.02 ESTABLISHING AND RUNNING AN ARBITRAL INSTITUTION: DRIVING CAR WITH A SQUARE WHEEL?

The high number of registered arbitral institutions is the most distinctive feature of the Latvian arbitration.

Five years after the adoption of Chapter D of the Civil Procedure Law, in 2003, there were already eighty-six arbitral institutions, as there were no restrictive criteria for establishing an arbitral institution except a notification sent to the Ministry of Justice.[8] With amendments dated from May 10, 2004, the legislator established the Register of Arbitration Institutions under the Enterprise Register, and all arbitral institutions had to be registered in this new Register; in particular, they were obliged to submit their Rules to the Register. The aim of those amendments was to reduce the number of arbitral institutions; however, this was not reached; by December 2013,

5. Awards rendered in other states parties to the New York Convention are recognized and enforced pursuant to that Convention.
6. United Nations, Treaty Series, vol. 330, p. 3.
7. United Nations, Treaty Series, vol. 484, p. 349.
8. *See*: Ziedonis Ūdris & Inga Kačevska, *Arbitration in Latvia: Urgent Need for Statutory Reform*, 21(2) J. Int. Arbitr, 220 (2004) DOI: 10.54648/joia2004006.

already 214 arbitral institutions were registered.[9] Thus, the legislator once again decided in favor of grandiose changes; however, as explained below, the outcome generated counter-productive and undesirable results.

The legislator took a decision to delete the Chapter D from the Civil Procedure Law and draft a new separate law on arbitration. Initially, upon the advice of international and national experts, the draft Law was based on the UNCITRAL Model Law. Moreover, the first draft contained significant restrictions as to the establishment of an arbitral institution—it could only be established by a non-governmental organization (previously, limited liability companies and law firms could register the arbitration institutions) registered for at least three years, with a minimum of ten members, having a combined turnover above LVL 50 million (~ EUR 71 million).[10] Only two arbitral institutions would have satisfied those criteria. However, after three readings in the Parliament, all those requirements vanished, and the legislator simply copied the old legal framework, adding specificities that allegedly could help to fight against the "pocket arbitrations."

Current Arbitration Law provides that a permanent (institutional) arbitration court may be established by an association (the founder of the arbitration institution) registered with the Register of Enterprises with the purpose of operating the arbitration institution (Article 2). The founder of the arbitration institution shall ensure that the arbitration institution has separate premises suited for the operation, the personnel necessary for record-keeping and receiving visitors and the maintenance of a website. On the website, the arbitration institution shall publish the information on the name and address, the procedures and office hours for receiving visitors, the costs of arbitration proceedings and the account number to which payments for arbitration proceedings shall be transferred, the rules, a list containing a minimum of ten arbitrators, specifying their given names and surnames, contact information (address of the location, telephone number, e-mail address) (Article 4), etc.

The name of the arbitration institution may not coincide with the name of the already registered legal person in any of the registers maintained by the Register of Enterprises, and it may not include any misleading information regarding the purpose of operation, type and legal form of the institution. Nevertheless, numerous institutions remained registered notwithstanding their similar or even confusing names, for example, "Baltic Region Arbitration Court," "Baltic Regional Arbitration Court," "Baltic Trade Arbitration," "Arbitration of Law of European Nation," "Supreme Arbitration," Hanza International Arbitration Court," "Hanza Arbitration Court," "Independent Arbitration Court," "Latvian First Arbitration Court," "Latvian Arbitration Court," "The Arbitration Court of the Arbitration—Consultation Center," "The

9. Legal Instruments and Practice of Arbitration in the EU 2014, Directorate General for Internal Policies, Policy Department, Citizen's Right and Constitutional Affairs, p. 104. Available at https://www.europarl.europa.eu/RegData/etudes/STUD/2015/509988/IPOL_STU(2015)509988(ANN01)_EN.pdf (accessed April 11, 2023).

10. Draft Law on Arbitrations for the first reading in Parliament. Available in Latvian: https://titania.saeima.lv/LIVS11/saeimalivs11.nsf/0/A182DD228B4DAF6CC2257C4E003D7B1B?OpenDocument (accessed April 11, 2023).

Mediation Court of Arbitration," Riga International Arbitration Court," "Riga Arbitration Court," "Riga Judicial District Arbitration Court," etc.[11] As one can imagine, all these names create abundant grounds for legal disputes, in particular in cases where the parties have initiated parallel arbitration proceedings in different arbitrations.[12]

Unfortunately, due to this situation, there are a few possibilities to effectively interpret a pathological clause, i.e., to interpret it in a way that enables the clause to be in force because it may lead to multiple arbitral institutions with similar names. Now, in order to avoid disagreements about which exact arbitration institution is competent to settle the dispute—e.g., in cases where parties have misspelled the name of an arbitration institution—in practice, the parties indicate the registration number of the institution in their arbitration agreement.

In this context, it shall be noted that arbitration agreements are interpreted according to the general principles of contract interpretation, i.e., to the Civil Law adopted in 1937.[13] These rules on interpretation do not always correspond to recent developments and do not suit the specifics of arbitration agreements.

§18.03 ARBITRATION AGREEMENT: IS ELECTRONIC ENGINE OF THE DOMESTIC ARBITRATION ALWAYS EFFICIENT?

[A] The Form of Arbitration Agreement and Arbitrability

An arbitration agreement shall be entered into in written form; however, the Arbitration Law includes a new feature—such agreement, which has been entered into by means of electronic communication by the parties, shall be recorded with a safe electronic signature (Article 12). Authors have not heard about any cases or problems with this rule as in the domestic communications, the safe electronic signature is widely used; however, it is hard to predict how Latvian courts would treat international arbitration agreement concluded by means of electronic communication without safe electronic signature.

The Law is silent on whether an arbitration agreement is concluded if it is contained in an exchange of statements of claim and defense.

An arbitration agreement may be entered into by any natural person with the capacity to act, a legal person governed by private law, or a legal person governed by public law in the private law area (Article 11). However, *inter alia,* the arbitration institution is not competent to resolve disputes where at least one of the parties is a state or local government authority (Article 5(1)(2)). Thus, the governmental or municipal institutions cannot agree on dispute settlement in arbitration in Latvia.

11. Arbitration Court Register at the Enterprise Register in Latvian https://www.ur.gov.lv/lv/registre/organizaciju/skirejtiesa/skirejtiesu-saraksts/ (accessed April 11, 2023).
12. *See*: Ziedonis Ūdris & Inga Kačevska, *Observations on the Judgment by the Riga Regional Court rendered on 19 August 2004 in the Case CA-4208/20, 2004 (Forscan Timber Export AB v. Interwood.* 2 SIAR 193 (2006).
13. The Civil Law (September 1, 1992), Valdības Vēstnesis, 41, February 20, 1937. Available in English: https://likumi.lv/ta/en/en/id/225418-civil-law (accessed April 11, 2023). The law was reintroduced in 1992 when Latvia re-gained independence from USSR.

Nevertheless, the Supreme Court clarified that the concept of "governmental institution" does not extend to companies established by the state as they are deemed to be private law legal persons capable of concluding arbitration agreements.[14]

A prohibition for state and municipal institutions to agree on arbitration in Latvia has one specific exemption resulting from the ratified European Convention on International Commercial Arbitration. When Latvia ratified the Convention in 2003, it made a reservation pursuant to Article II(2) of the Convention, excluding the application of the Convention to arbitration agreements concluded by state and municipal institutions. However, in 2013, Latvia withdrew the reservation. Withdrawal of the reservation signifies that Latvia's state and municipal institutions are bound by agreement to arbitration in Latvia, provided they fall within the scope of the Convention.

[B] Challenge of Arbitration Agreement

The Arbitration Law provides that the arbitral tribunal shall decide on the jurisdiction of a civil legal dispute, including the validity of an arbitration agreement (Article 24(1)).[15] Referring to this provision, Latvian courts took the position that the validity of the arbitration agreement could not be contested before courts but only before tribunals. This solution was recognized as being incompatible with Satversme (The Constitution) by the Constitutional Court of the Republic of Latvia.[16] It found that the right to challenge the validity of an arbitration agreement cannot be vested exclusively to the arbitration tribunals.

In the case at hand, the applicant (respondent in the arbitration proceedings) submitted that the "Latvian Arbitration Court" rejected the respondent's request to recognize the forged arbitration agreement as being invalid, but the state court found that the claim regarding the validity of arbitration agreement fell outside the court's competence. In front of the Constitutional Court, the applicant argued that the competence-competence principle may not be understood in a way that would grant an arbitral tribunal an exclusive right to decide on the issue of the jurisdiction of arbitration. Moreover, in Latvia, there has not been a setting aside procedure yet;[17] thus, at a later stage, the respondent to the arbitration could not challenge the award.

The legislator had never introduced the court assistance in arbitration proceedings as it would create additional workload for courts; however, in the case cited above, the Constitutional Court stated that this argument per se could not serve as grounds for depriving a person substantially of his or her rights, i.e., the aim chosen by the legislator—decreasing the workload of the courts, thus speeding up other legal

14. Supreme Court's Senate, October 29, 2013, No. SPC-46/2013.
15. Previously: Art. 495(1) of the Civil Procedure Law.
16. *On Compliance of Section 495(1) of the Civil Procedure Law with the first sentence in Article 92 of the Satversme of the Republic of Latvia*, case No. 2014-09-01, November 28, 2014. Available in English at https://www.satv.tiesa.gov.lv/web/viewer.html?file=/wp-content/uploads/2014/03/2014-09-01_Spriedums_ENG.pdf#search=2014-09-01 (accessed April 11, 2023).
17. Despite the fact that Latvia is a party to the European Convention of International Commercial Arbitration providing for set aside procedure (Art. IX).

proceedings—may not threaten such fundamental rights of a person that he or she has not voluntarily waived.[18]

Notwithstanding the judgement of the Constitutional Court, the disputed provision of the Arbitration Law was left unchanged, and the Law still does not specify at which stage of proceedings the arbitration agreement can be challenged before the court and what is the time period for such challenge. Recently, this created an avalanche of claims submitted to courts requesting an acknowledgment of invalidity of arbitration agreements, thus trying to avoid arbitration. These claims are differently motivated, for example, it is claimed that the opposing party included an arbitration agreement in the contract by using its dominant position in the market, and this arbitration agreement did not comply with fair commercial practice,[19] an arbitration agreement provided that the dispute shall be settled by an arbitration institution chosen by the claimant (no specific name was mentioned),[20] the arbitration institution was liquidated,[21] a party had no knowledge of the language in which an arbitration agreement was drafted,[22] a party did not understand the meaning of an arbitration agreement due to mental health problems, etc.[23]

It also leads to situations where one party submits the statement of claim to an arbitration institution, but the other—a claim requesting to recognize the arbitration agreement invalid to the court. Typically, in such cases, arbitration proceedings are more rapid, and only after the award is rendered, the court recognizes an arbitration agreement invalid. Nonetheless, the award remains in force as there is no set aside procedure. This absurd situation is accepted by the Supreme Court's practice. In fact, in one case, the Supreme Court ruled that the courts have competence to review the validity of the arbitration clause both before the arbitral award is rendered and also once it is rendered.[24] In another case, the Supreme Court decided that even if the award was rendered two years prior and a writ of compulsory execution was already issued, the interested party could still challenge the validity of the arbitration agreement.[25]

This situation could be cured if Latvia introduced a rule similar to that embodied in Article 16(3) UNCITRAL Model Law, giving a certain period of time for the interested party to request the court to decide on the jurisdiction of the tribunal as well as Article 34 regarding recourse against award.

[C] Agreement on Ad Hoc Arbitration

The Arbitration Law is filled with unique and exotic features and has been rightly described as a failure that "contains serious anomalies that go against the core

18. *Ibid.*, para. 20.2.2.
19. Zemgale's District court, October 26, 2022, No. C73295922. The claim denied.
20. Riga City Pārdaugava's court, May 24, 2017, No. C31227616. The claim denied.
21. Riga District court February 4, 2019, No. C33587617. The claim satisfied. Riga City Ziemeļu court, May 18, 2017, No. 32370115. The claim satisfied.
22. Cēsis District Court, April 18, 2017, No. C30328215. The claim denied.
23. Riga City Court, May 8, 2017, No. C32244315. The claim satisfied.
24. Supreme Court's Senate September 25, 2019, No. C30474518.
25. Supreme Court's May 15, 2020 No. SPC-12/2020.

principles of arbitration."[26] One of these anomalies seems to be unmatched—the treatment of *ad hoc* arbitration. The treatment is not only unique for Western Democracies,[27] but it leaves parties who have—for some inexplicable reason—decided to agree on *ad hoc* arbitration with a Catch-22. They risk of ending up being stuck with a binding arbitration agreement and a non-enforceable award.

Currently, the Arbitration Law allows parties to agree either on institutional or *ad hoc* arbitration (Article 2(1)). However, both types of arbitration are treated differently, to say the least. The minor difference concerns provisional protection (measures). Article 139(2) of the Civil Procedure Law allows a party to request provisional protection (measures) before a national court prior to bringing an action before an arbitration tribunal, but only if the parties have agreed on institutional arbitration. The request will be rejected by the court if the parties have agreed on *ad hoc* arbitration. But this discriminatory treatment of *ad hoc* arbitration becomes trivial in comparison with the elephant in the room.

That elephant is the enforceability of *ad hoc* awards. It may be hard to believe, but the Latvian regulatory framework[28] grants forced enforceability only to institutional awards.[29] Pursuant to Article 58(1) of the Arbitration Law *ad hoc* awards are to be complied with voluntarily. Obviously, foreign *ad hoc* awards are still enforceable under the New York Convention.[30] Likewise, a local *ad hoc* is still enforceable abroad on the basis of the New York Convention on Recognition and Enforcement of Foreign Arbitral Awards.[31] However, a local *ad hoc* award is only worth in Latvia so much as the losing party is willing to comply with it. This puts the winning party between a rock and a hard place—a validly concluded arbitration agreement makes the recourse to a national court inadmissible, but the award creditor might be unable to enforce its

26. Toms Krūmiņš, *Arbitration in Latvia: A Cautionary Tale?*, 34 J. Int. Arbitr. 303, 310 (2017) DOI: 10.54648/joia2017016.
27. *Ad hoc* arbitration is not legal in China. *See* Giovanni Pisacane, Lea Murphy & Calvin Zhang, *Arbitration in China: Rules & Perspectives*, 8 (Springer, 2016). The enforceability of *ad hoc* awards is disputable in Taiwan. *See* Tifanny Huang & Amber Hsu, *Taiwan*, Baker & McKenzie International Arbitration Yearbook: 2010-2012, 119-120 (2011). *See also* Agris Repšs, *Nav pamata neizdot izpildrakstu ad hoc šķīrējtiesu spriedumiem* [There Is No Justification Not to Issue an Enforcing Order for Ad Hoc Arbitral Awards], 22(824) Jurista Vārds (2014).
28. Art. 58(2) of the Arbitration Law and Art. 534(1) of the Civil Procedure Law. These provisions make it clear that the writ of execution is granted to an institutional award.
29. Ģirts Lejiņš & Eva Kalnina, *National Report for Latvia (2018 through 2023)*, in ICCA International Handbook on Commercial Arbitration, 1-43, 37 (Lise Bosman ed., Kluwer Law International 2021); Toms Krūmiņš, *Arbitration in Latvia: A Cautionary Tale?*, 34 J. Int. Arbitr. 303, 304 (2017) DOI: 10.54648/joia2017016; Inga Kačevska & Kalvis Torgāns, *533.pants* [Art. 533], in Civilprocesa Likuma Komentāri: III daļa (61.-86.nodaļas) [Commentary to Civil Procedure Law: Part III (Sections 61-86), 142-144, 142-143 (Kalvis Torgāns ed., Tiesu Namu Aģentūra, 2014).
30. Agris Repšs, *Nav pamata neizdot izpildrakstu ad hoc šķīrējtiesu spriedumiem* [There Is No Justification Not to Issue an Enforcing Order for Ad Hoc Arbitral Awards], 22(824) Jurista Vārds (2014).
31. While Art. V(1)(e) of the New York Convention provides that recognition and enforcement of a foreign award may be refused if the award has not yet become binding on the parties, ad hoc awards are binding on the parties under the Arbitration Law, they simply lack the enforcement mechanism.

award.[32][33] Hence, it would be hard to rationalize the motives of parties who willingly (and knowingly) consent to *ad hoc* arbitration in Latvia.[34]

The logic behind this discriminatory regime seems hard to understand. The drafters of the Arbitration Law offered the following explanation: since the Latvian state does not determine criteria for the creation of *ad hoc* tribunals and arbitrators (e.g., no list of arbitrators), it cannot be responsible for enforcement of *ad hoc* awards![35] However, these motives behind the 2014 Arbitration Law resemble retrospective rationalization. This is due to the fact that originally, Chapter D of the Civil Procedure Law did not deprive *ad hoc* awards of enforceability. However, in 2005, the Latvian legislator amended the Chapter D, providing that enforceability is a privilege of institutional awards. In 2005, Latvia did not have a requirement for arbitration institutions to have mandatory lists of arbitrators. Making it impossible to understand what could justify the different treatment. To the best knowledge of the authors, it is, in fact, unknown what was the official justification of the decision to ill-treat *ad hoc* arbitration in 2005. Certainly, the justification used in 2014 could not have been relevant in 2005.

There is, however, a suggestion of what really happened in 2005. As one practitioner writes, the real reason behind the 2005 amendments was a lobby of arbitration institutions willing to get rid of a cheaper *ad hoc* procedure.[36] While the veracity of this explanation is hard to verify, it does sound at least plausible. And if true, it is a sad diagnosis of the mechanics behind Latvia's legislation.

---

32. Toms Krūmiņš, *Arbitration in Latvia: A Cautionary Tale?*, 34 J. Int. Arbitr. 303, 310 (2017) DOI: 10.54648/joia2017016; Maija Tipaine & Līga Fjodorova, *Arbitration in Latvia: Was a Restart a Failure?* (Kluwer Arbitration Blog 2016), https://cobalt.legal/uploads/news/2514/M_Tipaine_L_Fjodorova_Arbitration_in_Latvia_Was_a_Restart_a_Failure_Kluwer_Arbitration_Blog_25_01_2016.pdf (accessed 23 Ap. 2023).
33. According to some authors, the problem of non-enforceability has been overcome via arbitration institutions taking generic names, e.g., International Arbitration (*Starptautiskā šķīrējtiesa*) or Latvian Arbitration (*Latvijas šķīrējtiesa*). In their opinion, "The existence of permanent arbitral institutions with such names allows a party to submit an initially *ad hoc* arbitration dispute to arbitration organized by a permanent arbitral institution, which subsequently allows a party to request compulsory execution of the award before national courts." Ģirts Lejiņš & Eva Kalnina,*National Report for Latvia (2018 through 2023)*, in ICCA International Handbook on Commercial Arbitration, 1-43, 3 (Lise Bosman ed., Kluwer Law International 2021). *See also* Maija Tipaine & Līga Fjodorova, *Arbitration in Latvia: Was a Restart a Failure?* (Kluwer Arbitration Blog 2016), https://cobalt.legal/uploads/news/2514/M_Tipaine_L_Fjodorova_Arbitration_in_Latvia_Was_a_Restart_a_Failure_Kluwer_Arbitration_Blog_25_01_2016.pdf (accessed April 23, 2023). This approach remains risky. The award debtor could oppose the issuance of the writ of execution on the basis that the action was commenced in an inappropriate forum. At the end of the day, local courts will know that these are no *ad hoc* tribunals.
34. Unless they expect enforcement of an eventual arbitration award to take place entirely abroad.
35. *The Draft 2015 Arbitration Law, Preliminary impact assessment report (Explanatory report)*, https://titania.saeima.lv/LIVS11/SaeimaLIVS11.nsf/0/A182DD228B4DAF6CC2257C4E003D7B1B?OpenDocument#b (accessed April 23, 2023). *See also* Inga Kačevska & Kalvis Torgāns, *533.pants* [Art. 533], in Civilprocesa Likuma Komentāri: III daļa (61.-86.nodaļas) [Commentary to Civil Procedure Law: Part III (Sections 61-86), 142-144, 143 (Kalvis Torgāns ed., Tiesu Namu Aģentūra, 2014).
36. Ziedonis Ūdris, *Uzticību šķīrējtiesām var nodrošināt ar tiesas kontroli pār to nolēmumiem* [Trust in Arbitration Courts May Be Achieved with Court Control over Arbitral Awards], 22(824) Jurista Vārds (2014).

If true, then the discriminatory regime was preserved in 2014 for one of two reasons. One alternative—it was simply a case of path dependence when the drafters of the Arbitration Law simply preserved the existing law. Second alternative—the lobby was still there. In any case, even in 2014, the twisted arguments behind this regime were inconclusive at best. First, Articles 14 and 15 of the Arbitration Law that determine the requirements for a person to be able to serve as an arbitrator apply both to arbitrators in *ad hoc* and institutional arbitration. Thus, indeed, the only significant difference is that self-evidently *ad hoc* does not have mandatory lists of arbitrators, which is, first of all, a natural consequence of the absence of a permanent institution. And this is the difference that the authors of the 2014 Arbitration Law used to justify the discriminatory regime. A dubious argument, to say the least.

The argument becomes even weaker if we consider the facts. First, the drafters of the 2014 Arbitration Law note that there is no need to prohibit *ad hoc* arbitration as it exists in the Model Law. However, the authors of the Model Law would no doubt find it appalling to refuse forced enforcement for *ad hoc* awards. Were the drafters of the 2014 Arbitration Law actually trying to capture the philosophy behind the Model Law, they failed miserably. Second, if we were to continue the argument that the Latvian state cannot enforce awards by tribunals that are not established by the state and having mandatory lists of arbitrators, Latvia would have to denounce the New York Convention on Recognition and Enforcement of Foreign Arbitral Awards as it requires enforcement of foreign awards, rendered by tribunals that are not subject to the Latvian *lex arbitri* with all its extravagant requirements. Luckily, this fake reasoning has not been pushed to the limits.

The scholars have rightly criticized the lack of enforcement mechanism for *ad hoc* awards. Notably, in the words of Dr. T. Krūmiņš: "by not providing a mechanism for recognition and enforcement of domestic *ad hoc* arbitral awards, there might be a violation of Article 6(1) ECHR and Article 1 of Protocol No. 1 to the ECHR."[37] An urgent reform is necessary in order to align the status of *ad hoc* with that existing in other Western democracies.

[D] Transfer of an Arbitration Agreement

The Arbitration Law is extremely unbalanced in terms of its approaches to arbitration. On the one hand, if not for the decisions of the Constitutional Court, parties would not have been able to challenge the validity of arbitration agreements before courts. Moreover, the Arbitration Law still lacks a setting aside mechanism. The peculiarities would seem to indicate that the Latvian legislator has a very pro-arbitration mindset and unshakable trust in this method of dispute settlement. On the other hand, it has such characteristics that evidently undermine arbitration. For example, the Arbitration Law allows parties to evade the duty to comply with the arbitration agreement. The mechanism of evasion is assignment of a claim.

37. Toms Krūmiņš, *Arbitration and Human Rights*, 330 (Springer, 2020).

It is a truism that "in most jurisdictions, it is presumed that assignment of the underlying contract entails the assignment of the associated arbitration agreement."[38] Latvian court practice diverged from that opinion even prior to the adoption of the Arbitration Law.

Before 2015, arbitration in Latvia was governed by the Chapter D of the Civil Procedure Law that was silent about the effect of assignment on arbitration. However, national courts were facing a question: is the assignee bound by the arbitration agreement after the assignment? They based their answer on Article 1800 of the Latvian Civil Law that states that "if no other agreement has been made, the cession of the right to bring an action shall be considered to be the cession of the claim which is the subject-matter of the action; but only the right to claim shall be transferred to the cessionary (Article 1801), rather than the contractual relation giving rise to the rights." Following their interpretation of this provision, the assignee was not bound by the arbitration agreement since only the claim was transferred to the assignee.[39]

Historically, Article 1800 had nothing to do with arbitration. Rather, it is a twofold provision. Its first part reflects upon the practice of Roman law, where the actual assignment of a claim was not allowed, but the creditor would evade that prohibition by granting another person the right to bring legal action.[40] Article 1800, which, on the contrary, allows assignment, simply specifies that such rights to bring an action are to be treated as an actual assignment of the claim itself. The second part of the provision represents a more general principle that a person cannot exit from the contract unilaterally. Therefore, while the creditor could assign the claim, it could not "assign" the whole contract, thus freeing oneself of obligations under that contract.[41]

However, in the early 2000s, widespread understanding that Article 1800 prevented the transfer of an arbitration agreement was formed among courts. In 2015, that understanding was codified in the Arbitration Law. Currently, Article 13(4) of the Law provides that "If a claim is assigned, the right of claim shall pass to the assignee apart from the arbitration clause regarding the resolution of a civil legal dispute in an arbitration court as included in the agreement." As a result, two different acts provide that arbitration agreements do not follow the assigned claim: (1) the Latvian substantive civil law as interpreted by Latvian courts; and (2) the *lex arbitri* applicable if the arbitration takes place in Latvia.

Assignment is an often-useful escape route from unwanted arbitration. The interaction between succession and arbitration agreements is obviously way less relevant in practice. Nonetheless, the Supreme Court has likewise decided that the

38. Gary B. Born, *International Commercial Arbitration. Volume I: International Arbitration Agreements*, 1579 (3rd. ed., Wolter Kluwer, 2021).
39. Supreme Court's Senate May 12, 2004, No. SPC-28.
40. The analysis of Art. 1800 of the Latvian Civil Law in connection to arbitration agreements is discussed in a detailed manner, in: Aleksandrs Fillers, *Līgumiskās cesijas un šķīrējtiesas līguma mijiedarbība* [Interaction Between a Contractual Assignment and an Arbitration Agreement], 35(835) Jurista Vārds (2014).
41. *Ibid.*

consent to arbitrate is strictly personal and cannot be passed on to the heir even if the position of *de cujus* in the substantive contract is inherited by the heir.[42]

Overall, we can observe that in relation to assignment, the Latvian law is once again an outlier. The possibility of unilaterally escaping from arbitration might not be condemnable if the arbitration environment is so deficient. However, once the Latvian arbitration law and practice are significantly improved, assignment should not serve as an escape route to avoid arbitration. Or, to put it in other words, to simply break the promise to arbitrate the dispute by purposefully assigning claims to someone else.

§18.04 ARBITRATORS: NO SURPRISE WHO IS DRIVING YOUR CAR!

[A] Qualification

Previously, the Civil Procedure Law just stipulated that arbitrators shall be independent and impartial and perform their duties in good faith. However, due to systematic complaints regarding insufficient qualification and the work quality of arbitrators, the legislator amended the law. As a result, currently, in order to serve as an arbitrator, a person shall provide that she or he has an impeccable reputation, possesses a law degree, and has at least three years of practical experience (Article 14(2)). A person with criminal records or who has declared bankruptcy in the past five years cannot serve as an arbitrator (Article 15). Each arbitral institution shall submit documents to the Enterprise Register proving that arbitrators in its closed and mandatory lists (explained below) meet those requirements. However, in practice, it is a very formal review as, for example, it is not possible to verify on the basis of the submitted documents whether a lawyer has an impeccable reputation.

[B] Mandatory Lists of Arbitrators

The Arbitration Law also introduced a new and doubtful criterion that all arbitration institutions shall maintain a closed and mandatory list of arbitrators containing a minimum of ten arbitrators (Article 4(2)). A person may not be included in lists of more than three institutions (Article 14(4)). This new requirement not only limits the party autonomy because parties cannot agree or appoint an arbitrator out of this list but also may affect the independence and impartiality of arbitrators, i.e., particularly for this research, the authors went through all the lists of arbitrators and established that out of sixty-four arbitral institutions, thirty-five had a minimal number of arbitrators—ten and seventeen institutions had arbitrators up to fifteen. Arbitrators mentioned in those lists are predominantly Latvian lawyers, often family members or lawyers from one law firm. There is no diversity in terms of nationality, religion, etc. There could be situations when a three-member tribunal cannot be established because among ten arbitrators, there is none with particular expertise in specifics of a dispute or knowledge of a foreign language or because most of them have conflicts of interests.

42. Supreme Court, November 12, 2018, No. C29564416.

A very specific provision was also included in the Arbitration Law, i.e., a person who is or during the last five years has been on the list of arbitrators of the relevant arbitration institution may not represent a party in that arbitration institution, and he or she may not be invited to render legal assistance in proceedings conducted therein (Article 32). There was an attempt to challenge this provision before the Constitutional Court, arguing that an attorney at law had never been appointed as an arbitrator in the arbitration institution; however, she was denied the right to represent the client in this arbitration institution due to her presence on the list; thus her constitutional rights were violated. However, the Constitutional Court refused to initiate the case as it did not consider that there was a violation of constitutional rights.[43]

[C] Independence and Impartiality of Arbitrators

Article 22 of the Arbitration Law provides that an arbitrator shall perform his or her duties in good faith without being subject to any influence. An arbitrator shall be objective and independent in his or her operations and decision-making. Moreover, the Constitutional Court remarked that in accordance with the practice of ECHR, the lack of independence and impartiality can be observed not only in cases when it has been established but also in cases where doubt about the existence of independence and impartiality is well-grounded (*see*: *Delcourt v. Belgium* [1970]ECHR 1, paragraph 31; *Piersack v. Belgium* [1982] ECHR 6, paragraph 30). The structure of the arbitral institution, previous relations of the arbitrators with the parties as well as other factors may serve as the reason for such doubt.[44]

However, in practice, understanding of arbitrator's and arbitration institution's independence and impartiality differs.

The Arbitration Law contains, most likely, an exhaustive list of situations of conflicts of interests. Namely, an arbitrator is not entitled to act as arbitrator if he/she has been a representative of any of the parties, or an expert or witness in a matter *where the same parties have participated*; is in a relationship of kinship to the third degree, or relationship of affinity to the second degree, with any participant in the matter or representatives thereof; is in an employment relationship with any participant in the civil legal dispute or their representative, or if the arbitrator provides legal assistance to a or his or her spouse, or kin to the third degree, or business partner, or commercial company, which is a party to the civil legal dispute and whose participant, shareholder, member, or member of supervisory, control or executive body is this arbitrator or his or her kin to the third degree, has financial interest in the outcome of the civil legal dispute (Article 16(1)). Other possible situations are not directly considered conflicts.

43. The Constitutional Court, July 26, 2022, Application No. 118/2022.
44. On the Compliance of section 132 (Item 3 of the First Part) and section 223 (Item 6) of the Civil Procedure Law with Art. 92 of the Republic of Latvia Satversme (Constitution). Judgment in the case No. 2004-10-01, January 17, 2005, para. 10. Available in English at https://www.satv.tiesa.gov.lv/web/viewer.html?file=/wp-content/uploads/2004/05/2004-10-01_Spriedums_ENG.pdf#search=2004-10-01 (accessed April 11, 2023).

Moreover, even though the Arbitration Law states that a person who is asked to consent to their appointment as an arbitrator must disclose to the parties any circumstances, which may cause reasonable doubt as to the objectivity and independence of this person (Article 17(2)), there is no tradition in arbitrations of Latvia to fill out a written form of independence and impartiality.

The following practical examples demonstrate an awkward understanding of independence and impartiality. There are cases when a company or a bank includes the same arbitration clause in almost all commercial contracts, indicating that the dispute will be resolved by one particular arbitral institution. This institution may receive numerous cases from this claimant—a company or a bank per year, but if there are only ten arbitrators in the closed list, it means that one and the same arbitrator can be appointed many times in the disputes with the same claimant. This, definitely, is a fundamental derogation from international standards.[45] Furthermore, it is almost impossible to verify a conflict of interests of arbitrators because the arbitrators do not disclose such facts or other circumstances in writing.

Thus, the representatives of the parties shall be creative in this regard. For instance, Article 535 of the Civil Procedure Law includes a unique provision – a court may request a case or other information from an arbitration institution if it is necessary for taking the decision on issuing a writ for compulsory execution of the award. There have been instances when, at this stage of proceedings, the party asks the court to request information regarding the number of appointments of a specific arbitrator. But it must be admitted that courts do not understand all the nuances of conflicts of interests, for example, they do not see the problem of why one arbitrator cannot be appointed multiple times in a dispute with the same claimant.

In addition, it shall be added that this provision is very often used by the court *ex officio* – the courts request the case materials from arbitral institutions and review them before issuing a writ of execution. Usually, the file can show, for example, whether the parties have received correspondence from the arbitration, etc.

§18.05 EVIDENCE AND ABSENCE OF WITNESS TESTIMONIES IN ARBITRAL PROCEEDINGS: A MYSTERIOUS PATH?

Another anomaly of the Arbitration Law concerns witness testimonies. Article 41(3) of the Law states that "[e]vid곳tiary means in an arbitration court may consist of explanations of the parties, documentary evidence (written documents, audio recordings, video recordings, electronic data carriers, digital video discs, etc.), real evidence, and expert opinions." Thus, there are four types of evidence permissible in arbitration: "The Arbitration Law provides that admissible forms of evidence consist of: (1) statements of the parties; (2) written evidence; (3) physical evidence; and (4) expert

45. *See*: The IBA Guidelines on Conflicts of Interest in International Arbitration.

opinions."[46] Regarding this provision, it might be first asked whether the legislature really needs to make such a detailed enumeration of all evidentiary means. However, what is more important is the missing element. The list does not mention witness testimonies. And, indeed, "in principle oral witness testimony is not admissible in arbitral proceedings,"[47] and neither are testimonies of party-appointed experts.[48]

The Explanatory Report to the Arbitration Law explained that one of the main benefits of the arbitration proceedings was its speed; inadmissibility of testimonies ensured better speed.[49] The exclusion of testimonies—pursuant to the authors of the law—freed the tribunal from "unnecessary extensions of the process," e.g., from the need to deal with the situation where a witness does not attend the hearing.[50] Scholars also mention other justifications for this anomaly. Some consider that "[witness] testimony is not admissible since it is deemed that there is insufficient control over this type of evidence, especially as it cannot later be reviewed by a court when enforcing an arbitral award."[51] This statement seems rather ambivalent. It may be asked why and how courts could review other types of evidence when the Arbitration Law does not allow substantive review of an award.

Still, other authors consider that the inadmissibility can be justified by the impossibility of warning witnesses about criminal liability for a false testimony.[52] In fact, pursuant to the Explanatory Report, a party to the process could submit witness statements that are confirmed by notaries.[53] During this confirmation, the notary must warn the person about criminal liability in case of false testimony.[54] This fact gives credibility to the idea that the absence of the warning could have been the reason (or at least one of the reasons) for the absence of witness testimonies in arbitral proceedings.

Scholars have implicitly demonstrated how inadequate the Arbitration Law is. It is observed that "[i]n practice, parties often overcome this prohibition by presenting

46. Ģirts Lejiņš & Eva Kalnina, *National Report for Latvia (2018 through 2023)*, in ICCA International Handbook on Commercial Arbitration, 1-43, 21 (Lise Bosman ed., Kluwer Law International 2021).
47. *Ibid.*, 22.
48. *Ibid.*
49. *The Draft 2015 Arbitration Law, Preliminary impact assessment report (Explanatory report)*, https://titania.saeima.lv/LIVS11/SaeimaLIVS11.nsf/0/A182DD228B4DAF6CC2257C4E003D7B1B?OpenDocument#b (accessed April 23, 2023).
50. *Ibid.*
51. Ģirts Lejiņš & Eva Kalnina, *National Report for Latvia (2018 through 2023)*, in ICCA International Handbook on Commercial Arbitration, 1-43, 22 (Lise Bosman ed., Kluwer Law International 2021).
52. Kalvis Torgāns, *521.pants* [Art. 521], in Civilprocesa Likuma Komentāri: III daļa (61.-86.nodaļas) [Commentary to Civil Procedure Law: Part III (Sections 61-86), 120-122, 120 (Kalvis Torgāns ed., Tiesu Namu Aģentūra, 2014).
53. *The Draft 2015 Arbitration Law, Preliminary impact assessment report (Explanatory report)*, https://titania.saeima.lv/LIVS11/SaeimaLIVS11.nsf/0/A182DD228B4DAF6CC2257C4E003D7B1B?OpenDocument#b (accessed April 23, 2023).
54. Article 139[5] (2) of the Notariate Law states: "The sworn notary shall warn the participants of the notarial deed of the criminal liability in respect of the giving of knowingly false submissions, notifications (declarations) and testimonies to the sworn notary. It shall also be indicated in the notarial deed." Notariate Law (1.09.1993), Latvijas Vēstnesis, 48, July 9, 1993.

witnesses and also party-appointed experts as party representatives who would be allowed to appear in the hearing and to give "testimony" in the form of a statement by the party."[55] The need for parties to invent such a detour serves as a colorful illustration of the fact that the Arbitration Law often complicates life for those involved in arbitration and suppresses their actual needs. Truly, the Latvian legislature works in mysterious ways.

On a more theoretical level, the exclusion of witness testimonies demonstrates a crucial misunderstanding of the Latvian legislature of the arbitration process and its core principles. It is for the parties and the tribunal to decide which evidence is admissible. In fact, the great advantage of the arbitration process is not so much that it is fast as that it is flexible. For example, parties that otherwise would be subject to traditional continental evidence rules can model arbitration procedures that mimic evidentiary rules found in common law. This option may be particularly attractive in international arbitration. Recognizing that, in principle, parties have significant control over the arbitration procedure, one Latvian practitioner states that the parties could further limit the list of admissible evidence, agreeing that "no evidence can be submitted, no expertise can be made, only written evidence can be submitted or that the process will take place without party participation, on the basis of submitted documents."[56] However, while the parties can further reduce the scope of admissible evidence, the Arbitration Law does not seem to permit its extension to cover witness and party-appointed expert testimonies.

Unfortunately, the legislature seems to be plagued by a very narrow and parochial view of arbitration. For the Latvian legislator, it is quite possible that witness testimony is valuable only if accompanied by a warning of criminal liability. Seasoned parties and arbitrators might be willing to test testimonies via direct examination and cross-examination. But arbitration in Latvia is no place for creativity. If you want to employ witnesses and party-appointed experts, then you want to arbitrate outside Latvia. At least until the Arbitration Law is thoroughly reformed.

§18.06 SETTING ASIDE: THE MISSING WHEEL OF LATVIAN ARBITRATION?

By this moment, the reader should understand that the Arbitration Law can be characterized as a "legislative freak," containing several peculiar, incomplete and incomprehensive rules. However, it also lacks certain crucial rules that are generally considered standard for arbitration; it lacks the setting aside procedure. Of course, this does not mean that there is no recourse against an arbitration agreement and an arbitration award. There are these two forms of recourse. But they are unable to fully substitute the absence of the setting aside procedure.

55. Ģirts Lejiņš & Eva Kalnina, *National Report for Latvia (2018 through 2023)*, in ICCA International Handbook on Commercial Arbitration, 1-43, 22 (Lise Bosman ed., Kluwer Law International 2021).
56. Jurijs Ņikuļcovs, *Šķīrējtiesvedības principi* [Principles of Arbitral Adjudication], 9(1275) Jurista Vārds (2023).

It was already highlighted that parties always have recourse against the arbitration agreement. A person can at any time challenge the validity[57] of an arbitration agreement,[58] even if the tribunal has already rendered an award. Oddly enough, in such a case, a court decision rendering the arbitration agreement invalid does not retroactively invalidate the award; however, such an award can no more benefit from the writ of execution. Moreover, the award made on the basis of an invalidated arbitration agreement cannot be used as proof in future court proceedings.[59] In other words, the Latvian law completely disregards any negative effects of *competence-competence* principle.

Challenging the validity of an arbitration agreement is not an adequate substitute for a setting aside procedure. The challenge concerns only the legal basis of arbitration—the validity of the arbitration agreement—and cannot be aimed at irregularities of the arbitration procedure that have affected the arbitration award.

So, could a losing party challenge the award itself? Yes and no. For the institutional award to be enforced, the award creditor needs to receive a writ of execution from the national court. At this stage, the award debtor can challenge the issuance of the writ.

The grounds for the refusal of the writ are similar to those that are traditionally associated with the setting aside procedure. Let us just mention a few out of the seven grounds for refusal pursuant to Article 536(1) of the Civil Procedure Law: (1) the dispute is within the exclusive competence of courts; (2) the arbitration agreement has been revoked or declared null and void; (3) an arbitrator or an arbitration institution were not conforming to the legal requirements or the procedure was inappropriate; (4) tribunal went beyond the scope of the arbitration agreement, etc. Obviously, under no circumstances can the court review the award on merits.[60] More curiously, the list of the grounds for the refusal does not include the infringement of the public policy.[61] In theory, this means that courts have absolutely no control over the substance of the award. However, as we will show below, this statement is correct only in theory.

The refusal of the writ is not the same as a setting aside procedure. First of all, it is relevant only for institutional awards since *ad hoc* awards are not enforceable in Latvia. Second, it is relevant only for institutional awards that actually need enforcement. On the contrary, "[i]f an arbitral tribunal has issued a declaratory award or an

57. Invalidity, in this context, covers both original invalidity (null and void) and later annulment. Thus, for instance, also cases when the parties have concluded a termination agreement that has terminated the arbitration agreement. Se: Inga Kačevska & Kalvis Torgāns, *536.pants* [Art. 536], in Civilprocesa Likuma Komentāri: III daļa (61.-86.nodaļas) [Commentary to Civil Procedure Law: Part III (Sections 61-86), 151-163, 158 (Kalvis Torgāns ed., Tiesu Namu Aģentūra, 2014).
58. *See* above.
59. The Constitutional Court, February 23, 2023, No. 2022-03-01, para. 11.2.
60. Jurijs Ņikuļcovs, *Šķīrējtiesvedības principi* [Principles of Arbitral Adjudication], 9(1275) Jurista Vārds (2023); Inga Kačevska & Kalvis Torgāns, 536.pants [Art. 536], in Civilprocesa Likuma Komentāri: III daļa (61.-86.nodaļas) [Commentary to Civil Procedure Law: Part III (Sections 61-86), 151-163, 154 (Kalvis Torgāns ed., Tiesu Namu Aģentūra, 2014).
61. Cf., Inga Kačevska & Kalvis Torgāns, *536.pants* [Art. 536], in Civilprocesa Likuma Komentāri: III daļa (61.-86.nodaļas) [Commentary to Civil Procedure Law: Part III (Sections 61-86), 151-163, 155 (Kalvis Torgāns ed., Tiesu Namu Aģentūra, 2014).

award dismissing all claims, no enforcement is required and the affected party is left with no effective remedy to challenge the possibly defective arbitral award."[62] Third, it is relevant only for institutional awards that need enforcement in Latvia. For instance, if the award debtor is facing multiple enforcement actions in different countries outside Latvia, then the refusal of the writ is not helpful to establish that the award was set aside at the seat with the view to substantiate the refusal of enforcement abroad (Article V(1)(e) of the New York Convention).

The absence of the setting aside procedure is difficult to explain. Seemingly, the Latvian legislature has considered that the primary goal of the arbitration is to reduce court workload while the setting aside procedure would—in its logic—increase the workload.[63] The logic has been extremely flawed since the purpose of arbitration is an all-around qualitative dispute resolution mechanism that benefits parties. It cannot be reduced to speed for speed's sake.

Scholars have likewise insisted for years that "[regarding] total exclusion of setting-aside proceedings, the hypothesis is rather straightforward—a legislative approach failing to provide for the annulment mechanism arguably violates arbitrating parties' right of access to a court under Article 6(1) of the ECHR."[64] The Constitutional Court has consistently underlined the problem and every time doing it with more force. In 2005, the Court expressed doubts whether a system without a setting aside mechanism was optimal but concluded that the state could compensate for the absence of such a mechanism by exercising control over the awards during enforcement proceedings.[65] However, the Latvian legislature remained deaf to the Court's doubts. In 2014, the Constitutional Court rendered another judgment with another *obiter dictum* urging the introduction of the setting aside procedure.[66] As if in an act of spite, in 2015, the new Arbitration Law was adopted without the setting aside procedure.

2023 is expected to be the year of the revision. In February 2023, the Constitutional Court moved from *obiter dicta* to action. It finally ruled that the absence of the

62. Toms Krūmiņš, Arbitration in Latvia: A Cautionary Tale?, 34 J. Int. Arbitr. 303, 329 (2017) DOI: 10.54648/joia2017016. *See also* Inga Kačevska & Kalvis Torgāns, *537.pants* [Art. 537], in Civilprocesa Likuma Komentāri: III daļa (61.-86.nodaļas) [Commentary to Civil Procedure Law: Part III (Sections 61-86), 163-165, 164 (Kalvis Torgāns ed., Tiesu Namu Aģentūra, 2014).
63. Cf., Toms Krūmiņš, *Arbitration and Human Rights*, 330 (Springer, 2020).
64. Toms Krūmiņš, *Arbitration and Human Rights*, 316 (Springer, 2020). Other Latvia arbitration practitioners and academic also voiced criticism over the absence of the setting aside mechanism. *See* Inga Kačevska, *Ir normāla situācija, un ir Latvijas situācija* [*There Is a Normal Situation, and There Is a Latvian Situation*], 22(824) Jurista Vārds (2014), Maija Tipaine, *Šķīrējtiesu reputāciju rauj neitralitātes trūkums* [*The Reputation of Arbitration Courts Is Undermined by Lack of Neutrality*], 22(824) Jurista Vārds (2014); Ziedonis Ūdris, *Uzticību šķīrējtiesām var nodrošināt ar tiesas kontroli pār to nolēmumiem* [*Trust in Arbitration Courts May Be Achieved with Court Control over Arbitral Awards*], 22(824) Jurista Vārds (2014).
65. Constitutional Court of Latvia Case No. 2004-10-01 'On the Compliance of Section 132 (Item 3 of the First Part) and Section 223 (Item 6) of the Civil Procedure Law with Art. 92 of the Republic of Latvia Satversme (Constitution)', para. 91. Available also in English on www.satv.tiesa.gov. *See also* Toms Krūmiņš, *Arbitration and Human Rights*, 227-228 (Springer, 2020).
66. On Compliance of section 495(1) of the Civil Procedure Law with the first sentence in Art. 92 of the Satversme of the Republic of Latvia, Case No. 2014-09-01, November 28, 2014. Available in English at https://www.satv.tiesa.gov.lv/web/viewer.html?file=/wp-content/uploads/2014/03/2014-09-01_Spriedums_ENG.pdf#search=2014-09-01 (accessed April 11, 2023).

setting aside procedure was unconstitutional and requested that the legislator create that procedure.[67] However, even in the 2023 decision, the Constitutional Court found that the absence of setting aside procedure is incompatible with the Latvian Constitution only in three instances: (1) when the interested party (award creditor) does not request the writ of execution for a long time; (2) when the award is to be enforced abroad; (3) when the enforcement does not require the writ of execution. With the exception of the third criterion that covers declaratory awards, the other criteria are almost impossible to codify. For instance, when is it possible to say that the award creditor has not requested the writ of execution for a long time? How long is too long? And what is the point of postponing the setting aside procedure? Likewise, it is hard to codify the difference between awards that are to be enforced abroad and those to be enforced domestically. When the award is rendered, it might be unknown whether the award debtor has any foreign assets.

However, the decision of the Constitutional Court lays out only the dire circumstances when the setting aside procedure must be in place. In no way does it prohibit the legislator from once in a while choosing a path of wisdom and introducing a setting aside mechanism similar to that found in the Model Law. It remains to be seen which path the legislator will favor.

In regard to the review of arbitration awards, as it stands today, a few additional remarks deserve a brief discussion. First, at least in theory, the setting aside procedure must be available in Latvia for arbitration awards that fall within the scope of the European Convention on International Commercial Arbitration (Article IX).[68] However, the Civil Procedure Law does not contain a procedure for that.[69] This can be an obstacle to an actual exercise of the setting aside procedure, even in those few cases when it is mandated by international law.

Second, even though the Arbitration Law does not authorize courts to review arbitration awards on merits and even lacks the public policy clause, in practice, courts perform such review.[70] But it is done in disguise under a transparent veil of other grounds that justify the refusal of the writ of execution.

For example, in 2013, the Supreme Court decided that the court, when asked to issue a writ of execution, could refuse to do that because the tribunal had decided that the losing party was obliged to pay an unreasonably high contractual penalty.[71] The Supreme Court decision does not contain any clear justification for courts' competence to review an award on merits.

67. The Constitutional Court, February 23, 2023, No. 2022-03-01, conclusion.
68. Inga Kačevska & Kalvis Torgāns, *537.pants* [Art. 537], in Civilprocesa Likuma Komentāri: III daļa (61.-86.nodaļas) [Commentary to Civil Procedure Law: Part III (sections 61-86), 163-165, 165 (Kalvis Torgāns ed., Tiesu Namu Aģentūra, 2014).
69. *Ibid.*
70. In fact, this has been even encouraged by scholars. *See* Inga Kačevska & Kalvis Torgāns, *536.pants* [Art. 536], in Civilprocesa Likuma Komentāri: III daļa (61.-86.nodaļas) [Commentary to Civil Procedure Law: Part III (sections 61-86), 151-163, 154 (Kalvis Torgāns ed., Tiesu Namu Aģentūra, 2014). In that commentary, Prof. K. Torgāns noted that a judge is no robot that could turn a blind eye to doubts over the substantive legality of the arbitration award.
71. Supreme Court's Senate, April 18, 2013, No. SPC-14/2013.

A similar decision was rendered in 2017.[72] The Supreme Court found that the guarantor had an obligation to guarantee a debt of EUR 5,400, but the award imposed an obligation on the guarantor to pay EUR 16,594,35. The Supreme Court considered that the arbitration tribunal had failed to properly motivate (reason) its award. Hence, it could not benefit from the writ of execution.

In this decision, the Supreme Court put more effort into justifying its competence. The Arbitration Law requires that tribunals provide reasons for their award unless parties have agreed otherwise (Article 54(4)(5)). The Supreme Court used this purely procedural requirement as a gateway into substantive review of the award, stating that the tribunal has failed to provide reasons for its conclusion on the guarantor's obligations. Interestingly, if this decision is taken for its face value, there would have been no reason to refuse the writ had the parties agreed that the tribunal could adopt an award without reasons.

It is easy to see that under this very thin procedural disguise hides a simple desire to review arbitration awards, which sometimes can be understood based on their quality. The need for these detours could have been reduced while the transparency of judicial control increased, had the Civil Procedure Law allowed to refuse to issue the writ on the basis of manifest violation of public policy. The introduction of the public policy ground would have allowed courts to create transparent and honest practices for restricted substantive review of awards, i.e., when they are actually manifestly incompatible with the Latvian legal order. The absence of motivation does not reflect the gravity of the substantive error present in the award and does not allow to differentiate between those errors that prevent the issuance of the writ and those that do not.

In 2022, the Supreme Court[73] sneaked the substantive review under a different disguise. The arbitral tribunal ruled that the losing party had an obligation to provide the earnest money to the creditor. The Supreme Court considered that under the Latvian substantive law, the transfer of the earnest money could not be claimed because the agreement on the earnest money entered into force only after the actual delivery of the earnest money had been effected. Based on this consideration, the Supreme Court stated that the arbitral tribunal had decided a case that was not arbitrable—since the creditor had no right to request the earnest money under the substantive law, there simply was no infringed right and no dispute.

The latter decision is particularly appalling. Under the very thin, transparent veil of procedural justifications, the Supreme Court simply reviewed the award on substance and decided that it misapplied substantive law. The court fused together the existence of a dispute, the rights of a party to bring an action before an adjudicator and a substantive claim (right). The said award might have misapplied Latvian contract law by conferring a claim to request earnest money to a person who lacked it. However, this has absolutely nothing to do with the existence of a dispute or a right to initiate litigation. If extended *ad absurdum*, such an action could likewise be outside the

72. Supreme Court's Senate, September 15, 2017, No. SPC-20/2017.
73. Supreme Court's Senate, 20 December 2022, No. SPC-23/2022.

competence of courts due to the absence of a dispute. In practice, of course, a Latvian court would have heard such an action and, after applying Latvian substantive law to the facts of the case, decided whether the claim was to be satisfied.

These examples illustrate the inadequacy of the Latvian legal framework. The legislature has a twofold mission that it has failed to perform. On the one hand, to ensure that arbitration tribunals are not biased and plagued by conflicts of interests. On the other hand, to provide for a public policy clause that allows for substantive control in those cases where even unbiased tribunals produce unacceptable awards. Failure to perform the first task means that courts face the need to exercise excessive substantive control over awards. Failure to perform the second task means that they hide that control under other ill-fitted instruments.

§18.07 CONCLUSIONS: HOW TO TURN THE PUMPKIN INTO CARRIAGE?

2023 is expected to be the year of the revision. Currently, the legislature is planning to supplement the Arbitration Law and finally introduce the setting aside procedure. At the end of October 2023 the Working Group at the Ministry of Justice finalized amendments to the Arbitration Law and draft will be submitted to the Parliament for three readings in the nearest future. However, the big problem remains—arbitration in Latvia has a devastating reputation. The setting aside procedure is no fairy instantly turning Cinderella into a princess or a pumpkin into a carriage. The ugliness of Latvian arbitration is here to stay without fundamental and holistic reforms of the regulatory framework. And unfortunately, it will not be attractive for international cases and arbitrators in the nearest future.

Hopefully, the legislator will also take into account other more specific amendments and, it is possible to list the principal ones. First and self-evidently, Latvia should join the concert of Western countries and ensure domestic enforceability of *ad hoc* awards. Moreover, *ad hoc* and institutional arbitration should be treated in the same manner regarding the possibility for the parties to request provisional protection (measures) before a national court. To further improve the functionality of the *ad hoc* arbitration, the Arbitration Law should contain a mechanism that allows a party to seek assistance from a national court if its counterparty creates obstacles to the appointment of the tribunal.

Second, the legislator shall delete the requirement of the mandatory arbitrators' list and allow parties to freely choose arbitrators.

Third, the Arbitration Law should provide true freedom of evidence in arbitration proceedings. There is no need for the law to list all types of evidence that the parties can use in arbitration proceedings. And most importantly, there should be nothing in the law that prevents parties from relying on testimonies by witnesses and party-appointed experts. The law should either be that the tribunal is authorized to warn witnesses and party-appointed experts about criminal liability for false testimony or, alternatively, simply leave it to the tribunal to decide how to verify these testimonies.

Fourth, it is absolutely necessary to introduce the setting aside procedure. While this development now seems inevitable as it is mandated by the Constitutional Court, we consider that the mechanism should go beyond those circumstances mentioned in the court ruling. The setting aside procedure should not be limited to those awards that due to their nature cannot be enforced, where the award creditor seeks enforcement abroad, or where the award creditor delays domestic execution. No, the Arbitration Law reform should introduce a standard setting aside mechanism extending it to all arbitration awards.

Finally, it is also crucial to include all the standard grounds for the setting aside procedure found in the Model Law, most notably, the public policy exemption. Moreover, the manifest violation of public policy should be introduced not only as a ground for the setting aside of the award but also as a ground for refusal to issue a writ of execution of an award. In both procedures, this would allow courts to exercise very limited, yet occasionally inevitable, control over the substance of arbitration awards. And do it both openly and be subject to strict and, in fact, restrictive limits of this control that are imposed by the very concept of public policy.

STOCKHOLM ARBITRATION YEARBOOK

1. Axel Calissendorff & Patrik Schöldström (eds), *Stockholm Arbitration Yearbook 2019*, 2019 (ISBN 978-94-035-0692-0).
2. Axel Calissendorff & Patrik Schöldström (eds), *Stockholm Arbitration Yearbook 2020*, 2020 (ISBN 978-94-035-2410-8).
3. Axel Calissendorff & Patrik Schöldström (eds), *Stockholm Arbitration Yearbook 2021*, 2021 (ISBN 978-94-035-3524-1).
4. Axel Calissendorff & Patrik Schöldström (eds), *Stockholm Arbitration Yearbook 2022*, 2022 (ISBN 978-94-035-1876-3).
5. Christer Danielsson & Patrik Schöldström (eds), *Stockholm Arbitration Yearbook 2023*, 2023 (ISBN 978-94-035-0358-5).

www.ingramcontent.com/pod-product-compliance
Lightning Source LLC
LaVergne TN
LVHW020001031026
849161LV00023B/809